W9-AQO-072

WITHDRAWN

RUSSIAN FASCISM

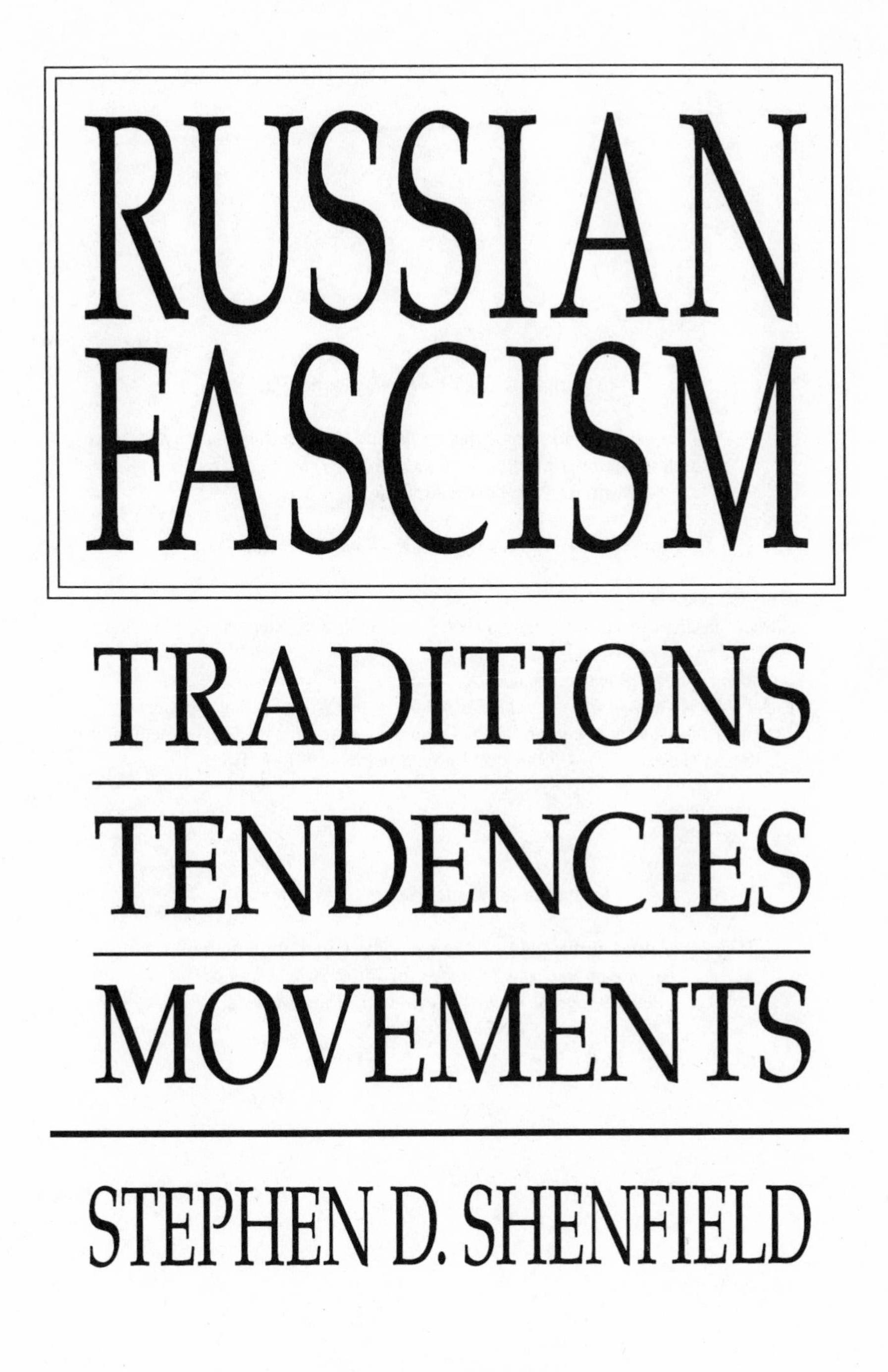

RUSSIAN FASCISM

TRADITIONS TENDENCIES MOVEMENTS

STEPHEN D. SHENFIELD

M.E. Sharpe
Armonk, New York
London, England

140316

Copyright © 2001 by M. E. Sharpe, Inc.

All rights reserved. No part of this book may be reproduced in any form
without written permission from the publisher, M. E. Sharpe, Inc.,
80 Business Park Drive, Armonk, New York 10504.

Library of Congress Cataloging-in-Publication Data

Shenfield, Stephen D.
Russian fascism : traditions, tendencies, movements / by Stephen D. Shenfield.
p. cm.
Includes bibliographical references and index.
ISBN 0-7656-0634-8 (alk. paper) ISBN 0-7656-0635-6 (pbk. : alk. paper)
1. Fascism—Russia (Federation) 2. Right-wing extremists—Russia (Federation)
3. Russia (Federation)—Politics and government—1991- I. Title.

JC481 .S478 2000
320.53′3′0947—dc21 00-059536

Printed in the United States of America

The paper used in this publication meets the minimum requirements of
American National Standard for Information Sciences
Permanence of Paper for Printed Library Materials,
ANSI Z 39.48-1984.

∞

BM (c) 10 9 8 7 6 5 4 3 2 1
BM (c) 10 9 8 7 6 5 4 3 2 1

Contents

Acknowledgments

I would like to thank the following people for helping me on this book in various ways, such as by sharing with me their insights, knowledge and experience, unpublished papers, literature collections, and audiotapes, by sending me research materials, by providing me with references, tips, advice, suggestions, and feedback on drafts, and/or by arguing with me, encouraging me, and nagging me to get on with it: Zoya Anaiban (Institute of Ethnology and Anthropology of the Russian Academy of Sciences), Marina Aptekman, Douglas Blum, Nickolai Butkevich (Union of Councils for Soviet Jews), Linda Cook, John Dunlop, Abbott Gleason, Lina Glebova-Goldman, Roger Griffin, Stephen Hanson, Terry Hopmann, Alan Ingram, Nikita Khrushchev, Jr. (*Moscow News*), Sergei Khrushchev, Jacob Kipp, Alexei Kozlov and Alexei Lychev (Voronezh Anti-Fascist Center), Jeffrey Kopstein, Irina Levinskaya (*Bar'er* magazine, St. Petersburg), Anna Levitskaya (Vladimir State University), Vyacheslav Likhachev and Alexander Verkhovsky (Panorama Group, Moscow), Matthew Morris, Cas Mudde, Hilary Pilkington, Yevgeny Proshechkin (Moscow Anti-Fascist Center), Stella Rock, Mark Sedgwick, Dmitri Shlapentokh, Vladimir Shlapentokh, Victor Shnirelman, Andreas Umland, and Ruben Verheul.

Bob Otto comes into a special category. He has helped me, consistently and over a long period, with sources, references, information, feedback on drafts, ideas, criticism, and encouragement. It is no exaggeration to say that this is his book too.

There are several other people who have helped me, but whose names I have not yet managed to recall. I would like to thank them too, and apologize for not remembering their names. Remembering names was never a strong point of mine.

I would like also to thank Patricia Kolb and Elizabeth Granda at M.E. Sharpe for their helpfulness and flexibility.

Finally, I would like to thank my wife, Hoa, who made it possible for me to get this book finished.

Introduction

It has become commonplace to draw an analogy between post-Soviet Russia and Weimar Germany. The idea is most succinctly expressed in the title that the well-known commentator on Russian politics, Alexander Yanov, gave to one of his books: *Weimar Russia* (Ianov 1995). Implicit in the analogy is the warning that conditions in Russia today, like conditions in Germany between the world wars, are conducive to the rise of fascism.

The parallels are indeed striking. An imperial power defeated in (cold) war and shorn of a large part of its territory. Millions of fellow countrymen stranded in new states where they are not welcome. From the status of a great power, and an object of universal fear and respect, to abject dependence on the former adversary. The heavy burden of foreign debt. The attempt to establish a democratic order under adverse conditions. Bouts of hyperinflation that wipe out people's savings. Deep and prolonged economic depression. Mass unemployment. Hunger. Homelessness. The spread of tuberculosis, the classical disease of poverty. Expanding prostitution. The explosion of venereal disease. Heightened mortality, a depressed birth rate, and the fear of national extinction. Rampant crime and corruption. Islands of luxury in an ocean of misery. Popular hatred of rapacious financial speculators. Anti-Semitism exacerbated by the belief (false or true) that the financial speculators are Jews.[1] Cultural disorientation and a growing nostalgia for the relative security and prosperity of the "good old days."

A list of the important differences between post-Soviet Russia and Weimar Germany would be no less long, though it might perhaps make a less vivid impression on the reader's imagination. The two countries have rather different cultural and political traditions. Much of the historical experience of contemporary Russians does not correspond at all closely to that of interwar Germans. It surely matters whether "the good old days" were lived under the Wilhelmine monarchy or inside the Soviet system. And does defeat in a cold war have the same kind of impact on a nation as defeat in a real "hot" war?

Nor is the way in which the political system operates the same in each case. Weimar Germany had a relatively centralized government based on the interaction of several well-developed national political parties. Political parties in post-Soviet Russia are weak and marginal to the exercise of power, which is effectively concentrated in the hands of provincial elites. Such a setup impedes the progress of a fascist party, as of any other ideological movement, to national power.[2] Finally, one may ask whether, despite the passage of time and the succession of generations, Russians have yet completely forgotten that they lost 20 million lives in a war against fascism?[3]

Various lines of inquiry, rooted in sociology, political economy, cultural studies, comparative history, and other disciplines, may fruitfully be brought to bear upon the problem of assessing the possible threat of fascism in contemporary Russia. However, one clear prerequisite to any serious analysis of the problem is an assessment of the current strength of fascist tendencies and movements in Russian society. After all, almost a whole decade has already passed since the final dissolution of the Soviet order in late 1991 and early 1992.[4] If the "Weimar Russia" analogy possessed a sufficiently high degree of validity, then we would expect by now to see a fairly large, united, and powerful fascist movement on the march in Russia. How does that theoretical expectation compare with the actual situation? How strong are the most important of the fascist organizations active in Russia, and what are their likely prospects? Besides unequivocally fascist organizations, how significant are fascist tendencies within other parts of Russian society, such as the Communist Party of the Russian Federation, the Russian Orthodox Church, the Cossack revival movement, and youth subcultures of different kinds? It is questions such as these that I seek to address in this book.[5]

Structure of the Book

The discussion of issues having to do with "fascism" is usually plagued by confusion and misunderstanding concerning the divergent meanings with which different people use the word. Therefore, I considered it well worthwhile to start in chapter 1 with a conceptual clarification of the various meanings that the word "fascism" can have, and of the way in which I myself shall be using the term.

Chapter 2 provides essential historical background. I survey the history of Russian political thought, including Russian émigré thought, in the nineteenth and twentieth centuries up to 1991, with a view to answering a question of crucial importance to our problem—namely: Does Russia have a fascist tradition upon which contemporary Russians can draw?

Chapter 3 tackles two tasks. The first is that of placing Russian fascism within the political and ideological spectrum of post-Soviet Russia by locating it in the broader context of Russian nationalism as a whole. Then I proceed to assess the significance of fascist tendencies within two very important—and in some respects not so dissimilar—social institutions of present-day Russia, the Communist Party of the Russian Federation (with a brief look at the smaller communist parties to its left) and the Russian Orthodox Church (with a brief look at the neo-pagan movement).

I continue my assessment of fascist tendencies in Russian society in chapter 4, focusing on the Cossack revival movement and on youth subcultures. I pay special attention to Russia's skinheads, and broach the little studied subject of soccer fan subcultures in Russia.

In chapter 5 my focus shifts from fascist tendencies in the broader Russian society to specific political organizations that may be regarded either as partly or wholly fascist or as close to fascism. Thus, chapter 5 is devoted to Vladimir Zhirinovsky's Liberal-Democratic Party of Russia, chapter 6 to the Russian National Unity of Alexander Barkashov, which was until its recent split the largest wholly fascist organization in Russia, and chapter 7 to another large fascist organization, Eduard Limonov's National-Bolshevik Party. Chapter 8 discusses six smaller fascist and near-fascist organizations, selected with a view to illustrating the variety that exists within the phenomenon of Russian fascism. Chapter 9 offers a comparative overview of the most significant characteristics of the organizations described in chapters 5 through 8.

Insofar as my sources permit, I try to present a rounded picture of each of the organizations with which I deal. I pay close attention to its leader, who is always an extremely important factor in this part of the political spectrum.[6] I also aim where possible to examine the ideology or worldview of each organization, its program, its symbols, its internal structure, its activities and mode of operation, and its strategy, and to assess its size and strength, its social base (to whom it appeals and why), and its likely prospects. I give most extended treatment to the Russian National Unity, the functioning of which I examine not only at the national level but also, through a series of local case studies, at the crucial regional or provincial level.

The main results of the investigation are summarized in the conclusion. Also, in September 2000, while this book was already in production, the Russian National Unity underwent a split. This important new development is discussed in an Afterword.

Stephen D. Shenfield
November 2000

List of Abbreviations

Comintern	Communist International
CPRF	Communist Party of the Russian Federation
CPSU	Communist Party of the Soviet Union
CPU	Christian-Patriotic Union
Komsomol	Communist Youth League
DOSAAF	Voluntary Society to Assist the Army, Aviation, and Fleet
FSS	Federal Security Service
IMF	International Monetary Fund
KGB	Committee for State Security
KRO	Congress of Russian Communities
LDPR	Liberal-Democratic Party of Russia
MIA	Ministry of Internal Affairs
NBP	National-Bolshevik Party
NRPR—Lysenko	National Republican Party of Russia (Lysenko)
NRPR—Belyaev	National Republican Party of Russia (Belyaev)
NSF	National Salvation Front
NSDAP	National Socialist German Workers' Party
NEP	New Economic Policy
NKVD	People's Commissariat of Internal Affairs
Patsomol	Patriotic Union of Kuban Youth
PNF	Party "National Front"
PNP	People's National Party
RCWP	Russian Communist Workers' Party
RNL	Russian National Legion
RNS	Russian National Union
RNSP	Russian National-Socialist Party
RNU	Russian National Unity

ROC	Russian Orthodox Church
ROS	Russian All-People's Union
UCR	Union "Christian Rebirth"
UNA-UNSO	Ukrainian National Assembly
UOB	Union of Orthodox Brotherhoods
URP	Union of the Russian People

RUSSIAN FASCISM

1
Defining "Fascism"

The multiplicity of meanings and connotations with which the word "fascism" is used remains a fertile source of confusion and misunderstanding. The clearest and least controversial usage is as a referent to what we may call "classical fascism"—that is, the movement in interwar Italy led by Benito Mussolini, who was the first to coin the term "fascism," and by extension the movements in other countries that closely modeled themselves on the Italian prototype. By the standards of customary political discourse, however, this usage is an extremely narrow one, not even encompassing German national-socialism, which never referred to itself as fascist.[1] It is, in any case, patently inadequate to an investigation of a society so far removed in space and time from interwar Italy as post-Soviet Russia. We therefore need a more broadly applicable definition of generic fascism.

My main purpose in this chapter is to explain how I shall be using the word "fascism," and to make clear why I have chosen to use the word in one way rather than another. To set my interpretation in the context of the continuing scholarly debate over the essence of fascism, I approach this task by means of a critical survey of the views of other writers on fascism. In the course of the survey, I shall point out not only the crucial distinctions that mark fascism off from other more or less closely related ideologies and movements, but also important divisions existing within fascism itself. As the primary focus of most analyses of fascism is the experience of non-Soviet Europe in the period 1918 to 1945, I shall pay special attention to the specific problems that arise in applying the concept to Russia in general and to post-Soviet Russia in particular.

In general political discourse, the meaning attributed to "fascism" is heavily dependent on the ideological commitments of the speaker. There is a tendency to attach the fascist label not only to movements with a genuinely strong resemblance to classical interwar fascism, but to all authoritarian regimes of the right (if the speaker belongs to the left) or to all authoritarian regimes of the left (if the speaker belongs to the right). "Fascism" easily comes to signify the reign of unconstrained violence and oppression, whoever may perpetrate it and for whatever purpose. Although scholars can hardly be satisfied by such a vague usage, this is roughly what most people mean by "fascism." The memory of World War II and the Nazi atrocities, kept alive with the help of magazines and movies, loosely associates the word in the popular imagination with the thirst for power and foreign conquest, racial hatred and genocide, cruelty, sadism, and human evil in general.

In the academic literature, two main approaches to the definition of "fascism" are found. One large group of authors construct descriptive definitions, primarily on the basis of a study of European (especially Italian and German) interwar experience, that in their view capture the most important and significant aspects of the phenomenon under study. The resulting definitions, although illuminating, are usually long and unwieldy, often inconsistent with one another, and sometimes even internally inconsistent. In reaction to these deficiencies, some influential scholars, most notably Ernst Nolte and Roger Griffin, have proposed "fascist minima"—that is, succinct and coherent definitions, to be understood as Weberian "ideal types," that highlight one or a few core features considered essential to fascism. All other characteristics that have been used to define "fascism" are regarded as either derivative from the fascist minimum or inessential.

Criteria for a Definition

Before proceeding further with issues of substance, it is worth pausing to consider a crucial methodological question that is rarely explicitly addressed. In formulating a definition of a political concept like fascism, our choice is inevitably guided by one or more criteria. Different criteria will yield different definitions. What criteria should we use?

What matters for the authors of descriptive definitions is evidently an accurate correspondence between the way "fascism" is defined and the reality of European fascism in the era that began in 1918 and ended in 1945. This is a criterion to which exception can hardly be taken, but exclusive reliance on it tends to generate inflexible definitions that have no wide application outside the context of Europe between those years. A definition should allow scope for fascism to develop over time and adapt itself to the conditions of different countries, provided that the changes occur without radical discontinuity. Thus, it seems reasonable to regard those thinkers of the West European "New Right" (such as the French writer Alain de Benoist), who have consciously striven to revise the ideology of pre-1945 fascism to take account of new realities while preserving core values, as fascist revisionists

(Griffin 2000), in the same way that the "Eurocommunists" who have pursued an analogous project within a different tradition are regarded as communist revisionists. The underlying continuity between interwar fascism and the postwar New Right is all the more worthy of recognition in light of the role played by key figures who span the two epochs—for instance, the Italian philosopher Julius Evola.

At the same time, the common tendency to extend the usage of "fascism" into areas already covered by other well-established semantic fields, such as communism or conservative authoritarianism, must be resisted if we are to keep the specific character of fascism in clear focus. This does not preclude the existence of borderline cases—such as Franco's Spain in the wake of the civil war, the last years of Stalin's rule in the USSR, or Ceausescu's Romania—in which a basically non-fascist communist or conservative regime exhibits definite tendencies pointing in the direction of fascism.

Having set inner and outer bounds for our definition, let us now turn to the problem of deciding between the descriptive and the "minimal" approaches. "Minimal" definitions, the most influential of which are those of Ernst Nolte and Roger Griffin, are justified on the grounds that they are "heuristically useful" as ideal types (Griffin 1998, p. 13)—that is, they generate productive and fruitful research programs. It may be added that minimal definitions are precise and elegant; they are free of ambiguities and superfluities. For all of these reasons, they have a natural appeal to the social scientist.

Considerations of this kind are not to be dismissed out of hand, but neither should they be granted a monopoly, at the expense of all other criteria. We should define our terms with a view to effective communication, not only within a narrow circle of scholars, but also with a broader public who are interested in politics but unfamiliar with the specialized debates of political scientists. Communicability requires that we take *some* account even of the popular associations of words like "fascism." Moreover, the assumption that everything really important about fascism as a real-life phenomenon can be captured by, or derived from, a single core concept is open to dispute. "It is doubtful," as Stanley Payne has argued, "that there is any unique hidden meaning in, cryptic explanation of, or special 'key' to fascism" (Griffin 1998, p. 227). Complexity in a definition need not be taken as evidence of analytical failure, but may be accepted as a reflection of the varied and multifaceted reality of fascism. Nor need we be unduly perturbed or surprised at our inability to eliminate completely internal inconsistencies from an ideology that eschews rationality in principle. Exclusive reliance on one core concept can in fact lead to rather arbitrary judgments. Thus, Griffin is forced to exclude from his definition of fascism, which focuses on a core fascist myth of national rebirth (palingenesis), the regimes of the Croatian

Ustasha and of Father Tiso in Slovakia, despite all that they had in common with fascist regimes elsewhere in Nazi-occupied Europe, because they were engaged in forging new nations rather than rejuvenating old ones and therefore lacked palingenetic myths (Griffin 1995, p. 10).

I conclude that choice of a definition of "fascism" should ideally be guided by a number of criteria: a sharp focus, the necessary degree of flexibility, descriptive accuracy, heuristic usefulness, and broad communicability. In practice, the requirements of different criteria are bound to contradict one another, and all one can hope to do is to work out what seems a reasonable compromise. It may also be helpful to supplement a general definition of fascism with specialized definitions that more consistently meet one or another criterion—for example, definitions of "fascism in the classical sense," "fascism in the palingenetic sense," or "fascism in the popular sense." Let us return to this point after discussing the substantive issues and formulating a general definition of fascism.

Working Out a Definition

I started work on a general definition of fascism by examining the way in which twenty-eight different authors about politics explicitly or implicitly define "fascism."[2] I identified the five problems that are most often discussed at length by the writers; these I took to be the main problems involved in understanding fascism. I then compared and critically assessed the different approaches taken by the authors to each of these problems. This helped me to clarify my views and to formulate the components of my own definition.

As regards my choice of writers to survey, I do not claim to have selected a fully representative sample, and I attached no special significance to the exact number of investigators who took one or another view. The authors surveyed do, however, represent a fairly wide range of theoretical approaches and political orientations.[3] Most of them focus solely on fascism; a few discuss fascism in the context of a broader analysis of nationalism. Although most of the writers are Western scholars, a few of the more interesting Russian scholars have been included, as have a few nonacademic authors, such as the English political novelist George Orwell.

As it would be repetitive and confusing to present and assess the frequently overlapping definitions of all the writers, I restrict myself to a survey of their views concerning each of the five main problems. Appendix 1 to this chapter presents the definitions of fascism offered by ten of the writers; Appendix 2 lists all the authors surveyed, together with the sources used.

The main problems that recur in the writers' discussions of fascism are the following:

1. What is the historico-philosophical outlook of fascism on the past, present, and future of humanity? How, in particular, does fascism relate to the process of modernization?
2. What general philosophy of life, including epistemology, aesthetics, and morality, is characteristic of fascism?
3. What position does fascism occupy in the contest between capitalism and socialism?
4. What kinds of human community serve as foci for fascists' loyalty and identity? Is fascism a special kind of nationalism?
5. What are the crucial structural characteristics of fascism as a movement seeking to win and keep power?

Let us consider these problems in turn.

The Fascist Outlook on History and Modernization

What role does fascism play in the historical development of human society? Are the goals it pursues progressive, conservative, or reactionary? Does it look forward into the future or backward into the past—or both at once? Is it partially or wholly hostile to the process of modernization, or does it advocate its own model of modernization? The orientation of fascism in the stream of human and national history is crucial to its identity as an ideology and movement. Many of the writers surveyed consider the problem at length; it is the focus of the "fascist minima" of Nolte and Griffin; and it lies at the center of concern of fascist ideologists themselves.

Unfortunately there is no generally accepted definition of "modernity" or of "modernization." Disagreements concerning what exactly these words mean are a fertile source of confusion and misunderstanding. For many people, the modernity of a society depends simply on how advanced are the technologies that it uses. For social scientists who take their ideas on the subject from Max Weber, a modern society is one whose major institutions operate in accordance with an impersonal rule-governed logic. In my view, these are both secondary and in some contexts misleading criteria. For me, the essence of modernity lies in a particular cast of mind that has its origins in the European Renaissance and Enlightenment but that did not become clearly predominant in society until after World War I. Central to the modern cast of mind is the willingness to rely on the empirical or scientific method of inquiry. Modernity is also closely associated with the moral stance known as *humanitarianism*—that is, the attitude that human suffering is an evil, that efforts to reduce it are praiseworthy, and that its deliberate infliction is reprehensible unless shown to be a necessary means to a greater humanitarian end. For example, the modern sensibility regards war as an evil, though (except for pacifists) one that may be justified under some circumstances. In both these respects, fascism is an antimodern movement, whereas communism is, at least in principle and to some degree, a part of modernity despite all its failures and barbarities.

The writers in my sample can be divided, in accordance with their views on this problem, into three broad groups.

Some writers regard fascism unequivocally as a socially conservative and/or reactionary movement, an "anti-modernist utopia" (Turner), the goal of which is to preserve and restore, by revolutionary means, traditional values that modern society has undermined or destroyed (De Felice, Moore, Verkhovsky and Pribylovsky). Thus, attention is drawn to the school of fascist philosophers who spoke of the "Conservative Revolution"—a term usually associated with the German cultural historian Arthur Moeller van den Bruck, although it seems to have actually been first used by the nineteenth-century Russian populist Yuri Samarin (as will be discussed further in chapter 2). Similarly, according to Nolte, fascism is to be understood as "resistance to transcendence"—that is, to the universalistic theoretical mode of reasoning that is the essence of modern scientific thought (Turner 1975, pp. 2–25, 39).

At the opposite extreme, some writers see fascism as a modernizing movement that, especially in Italy itself, served developmental functions—the acceleration of industrial development, the inculcation of discipline ("making the trains run on time"), and the strengthening of social cohesion in the face of deep class and regional divisions (Gregor).

Lastly, a large group of authors hold that fascism is, in different ways, both progressive and reactionary, both modern and archaic—even "the synthesis of all values" (Eatwell). It is, for example, "industrially modernizing but socially reactionary" (Wilkinson). It is typically argued that fascism rejects only some aspects of modernity—in particular, democratization, secularization, and international integration—or only a particular model of modernity, that is, "the rationalist, progressive, Enlightenment model" (Gentile), but not modernity as such. Alternative non-Enlightenment models of modernity have emerged, including models based on various kinds of religious fundamentalism as well as fascism.

Within this group of writers, we can identify a subgroup (Griffin, Payne, Galkin) who belong to the school that understands fascism as a movement inspired by a core myth of national renewal, rejuvenation or rebirth (palingenesis). Rebelling against the decadent present, fascists look simultaneously back in time to a past golden age of national greatness and forward to a new era of resurgence.

In general, it is the third group of writers who come the closest to grasping the complex character of fascism. It is necessary to distinguish clearly between fascism and those purely reactionary movements that seek literally to return to the past, as well as between fascism and those movements that seek to overcome and forget the past. The palingenetic paradigm is especially illuminating and productive. Its applicability to post-Soviet Russia is as evident as is its relevance to interwar Europe. "Ahead lies the Era of Russia," proclaims Alexander Barkashov, leader of the Russian National Unity, "and it has already begun!" (Barkashov 1994, p. 25).

At the same time, we must take care to strike the right balance between the forward-looking and the backward-looking components in the fascist worldview. It is, in my opinion, a mistake to portray fascism, as Griffin tends to do, as inspired by the past but primarily oriented toward the future. A deep attachment to the essential values of premodern eras (or what are perceived as such) is perhaps the most important of the characteristics that mark fascism off from its main ideological rivals on both the left and the right, and that make fascism so difficult for the modern mentality to understand.

Different tendencies within fascism attribute the crucial role in undermining true values to different historical developments. For many, it is above all the Enlightenment that must be undone. Thus, in 1934 the German SA leader Ernst Roehm proclaimed that "the national-socialist revolution has made a complete break with the philosophy that inspired the Great French Revolution of 1789."[4] For others, it is necessary to go back another couple of centuries. "We wish to put an end to the 400-year individualistic revolution of the West," explained the non-Nazi German fascist publicist Edgar Jung (Griffin 1995, p. 108). A primary emphasis on the Reformation is, naturally, characteristic of those fascists oriented toward Catholicism, such as Curzio Malaparte, who speaks of "our historical Catholic mission of implacable and sustained resistance to the modern spirit born of the Reformation" (Griffin 1995, p. 49).

Of course, the ultimate origin of the modern ideal of rational inquiry can be traced even further back, all the way to the natural philosophers and political thinkers of ancient Greece. Julius Evola accordingly dates the beginning of "the decline of virile and sacral ideals" to the seventh century B.C.E., and seeks the true "Tradition" in an even older heroic age of legend and myth, in "the world of Odysseus" (Evola 1995, p. 261).[5]

Evola's invocation of "virility" draws our attention to the important point that fascists are attached not to any and all premodern values, but only to premodern values of a specific kind. Ancient legend is indeed a magic trove in which lie buried more than one kind of treasure—not only the "virile and sacral ideals" of kingly dominion and warlike prowess, but also, for instance, the no less sacral but more peaceable and egalitarian "female" ideals of the earth and moon goddesses worshipped by some radical feminists and "deep" ecologists. It is not immediately clear where exactly one should draw the line between those premodern values that fascists do, and those that they do not, typically seek to revive. Medieval and feudal values are particularly highly valued by most fascists; the feudal aspects of Nazi ideology influenced the institutional structure of the Third Reich (Koehl 1972). The example of Evola, however, shows that fascists may draw upon traditions much more ancient than feudalism. As a rough approximation, we may say that fascists seek to restore the values of premodern class societies, whether feudal-aristocratic, slave or Oriental-despotic, while leftist utopians draw inspiration from an idealized image of primitive tribal communism. In any case, it needs to be kept in mind that fascism is not the only antimodernist utopia of the modern age.

Whenever the long process of the desacralization of life—what Max Weber called "the disenchantment of the world"—may have begun, it did not reach its culmination until the rise of industrial capitalism. As Marx and Engels observed in *The Communist Manifesto*:

> [The bourgeoisie] has drowned the most heavenly ecstasies of religious fervor . . . in the icy water of egotistical calculation. . . . [It] has stripped of its halo every occupation hitherto honored and looked up to with reverent awe. . . . All that is holy is profaned. . . . (*Karl Marx* 1968, p. 38)

The Marxists, nevertheless, mourn a little and move on—but the fascists call for "the return of the angels, the rise of the heroes from the dead, and the rebellion of the heart against the dictatorship of reason" (Dugin 1997b, p. 26).

The Industrial Revolution marked the culmination of the process, but not its completion. Life in times of peace had become profane, but a "virile and sacral" mystique continued to surround war. It was still held to be *dulce et decorum pro patria mori* [sweet and fitting to die for one's country]. That is why a conservative writer like Dostoevsky yearned for war, and why the Futurist Manifesto of 1909 acclaimed war as "sole hygiene of the world" (Griffin 1995, p. 45). It was the slaughter in the trenches of World War I that finally demystified war and made a negative attitude toward war part of the modern consciousness. Henceforth, war was to be regarded as an evil, though it might still be justified in certain circumstances as a necessary evil. But again, not everyone accepted the demystification of war, and a return to its glorification was an important part of the fascist program.[6]

The premodern vantage point of fascism is revealed, *inter alia*, by its penchant for interpreting the processes of modernization that it so detests as the deliberate destructive work of conspiratorial racial and religious sects. The idea of a world Judeo-Masonic conspiracy to destroy the nations (Cohn 1967) remains the most widespread, but other variants exist—for example, the Orthodox Christian idea of a grand conspiracy directed by Satan (within which the Judeo-Masonic conspiracy is likely to be subsumed), or the view of history, held by contemporary Russian Eurasianists, as a millennia-long struggle between secret orders of "Eurasianists" and "Atlanticists." It is not just that fascists do not like modernity: they find it very difficult to make sense of modernity in its own terms, and attempt to explain modernity by resorting to premodern modes of thought. Hence, also, their persistent fascination with magic and the occult (Goodrick-Clarke 1992), as well as with other medieval "sciences" such as astrology, alchemy, and sacral geography (the geography of sacred places and forces) (Dugin 1996a).

The premodern orientation of fascism is not, however, restricted to the sphere of ideal values and modes of thought. It readily reveals itself also at the programmatic level. The corporate state advocated by classical Italian fascism, for example, in which the citizenry are organized and represented through occupational, professional, and institutional "corporations," is clearly an attempted adaptation to modern conditions of the old system of feudal estates. Some contemporary Russian fascists similarly aspire to revive in a new form the old estates-based Assembly of the Lands [*Zemskii Sobor*].

What, then, of "the paradox of reactionary modernism," the claim that fascism represents not a rejection of modernity as such, but an alternative non-Enlightenment model of it? The real argument here has less to do with the nature of fascism than with the nature of modernity. If modernity is understood merely in terms of industrial and technological development, then non-Enlightenment models of modernity may be conceivable. However, if modernity is defined by reference to intellectual and moral ideals that largely originate in the Enlightenment, then "non-Enlightenment modernity" is a contradiction in terms. Even if we accept the former point of view, the long-term viability of the postulated "non-Enlightenment models of modernity" remains to be proven. For example, a great deal is made of the positive fascist attitude toward modern technology. Not only did the fascists in both Italy and Germany accept technology and harness it to their own economic, political, and military purposes, but following the lead of the futurists they made it the object of a veritable cult, celebrating its beauty, dynamism, and power (Herf 1984). True enough, but what of it? It is very significant that the fascist worship of technology did not extend to science itself. Yes, the practical products of science were welcomed, but the scientific mode of thought—rational, critical, and empirical—that had yielded those products was rejected in no uncertain terms. Moreover, the mystique with which the fascists surrounded the technological fruits of science is quite foreign to the spirit of scientific thought. The reign of fascist ideology over the long term would therefore inevitably lead to technological as well as social and cultural regression. The significance of technology in and of itself should not be exaggerated: it is a surface manifestation of modernity, not its essence.

Thus, fascism combines orientations toward modernity and the future and toward the premodern past in a peculiar fashion. Unlike reactionaries, fascists understand that the past cannot be restored in its original form, and that something new must be created.[7] Nevertheless, their minds, hearts, and spirits hark back to the past: the future for them is no more than the past revived in a new form. The past is ultimately more central to fascism than the future. On the continuum that has archaism at one pole and genuine futurism at the other, fascism occupies a segment in the middle, but closer to the archaist pole than to the futurist one.

Two further points of clarification are needed.

First, if we are to conceive of fascism as a movement arising in the modern era but oriented toward premodern values and ways of thought, then precision requires that we specify the boundary between the modern and the premodern. But where should the line be drawn? Modernization being a nonlinear and very long-drawn-out process, it is inevitable that any line should be to some extent an arbitrary one. Moreover, as different countries have passed through comparable phases of modernization at different times, the line separating the modern from the premodern should be drawn at a different point in the history of each. A movement may seek to conserve and restore traditional values but not qualify as fascist (even if fascist according to other criteria) if *either* the traditions in question are not premodern but belong to an earlier phase of modernity *or* the movement itself arises before the onset of modernity.

If, for instance, we date the transition to modernity in Russia as having occurred in February 1917, arbitrarily overlooking the modernization that occurred in Tsarist Russia since the time of Peter the Great as well as premodern elements that survived in Soviet (and even post-Soviet) Russia, then a contemporary traditionalist movement that draws its values purely from the Soviet, and not from the tsarist, period cannot be regarded as fascist (but might instead be classified as communist). Likewise, a movement that arose before 1917, such as the Black Hundreds, to be discussed in chapter 2, cannot be considered fascist, but only proto-fascist.

Second, if fascism is to be defined as a reaction to modernity, then modernity must be understood as encompassing both its liberal and its communist form. Fascism is not always a reaction to liberalism. In those countries that have experienced communism, such as Russia, fascism may equally well be a reaction to communism. The Program of the interwar émigré All-Russian Fascist Party made the point that "the main difference between Russian fascism and other fascist movements is that Russian fascism must take the place of communism, while fascism in Italy and Germany took the place of the liberal-democratic state and the capitalist system" (Prussakov and Shiropaev 1993, p. 7). Under the conditions of today's Russia, fascism is most likely to be a reaction simultaneously to communism and to liberalism (in its distorted post-communist manifestation).

The Fascist Philosophy of Life

Several writers emphasize the distinct characteristics that fascism displays in the sphere of cognitive, moral, and aesthetic philosophy. Thus, fascism is against the principles of materialism, empiricism, and reason; conversely, it highly values faith, myth, mystique, and ritual. It rejects the moral condemnation of violence and makes it the object of an aesthetic cult. Some writers go so far as to see the cult of death as an important part of the fascist outlook (Mosse, Neocleous).

These and other "barbaric" qualities are best regarded not as independent variables, but rather as derivative from the attachment of fascism to premodern values and ways of thinking. The cult of youth that many have noted in fascism may seem anomalous from this point of view, given the respect shown in past ages for elders, but it may be understood as a transitional phenomenon. The older generations who matured under conditions of "decadence" are rejected, and hope is placed in the "healthy instincts" of youth, who have yet to be corrupted, but once victory is consolidated the need for a cult of youth may be expected to fall away.

We have seen that fascism draws on premodern values of a specifically patriarchal kind. Several authors stress that a cult of virility or maleness plays a crucial role in fascism (Payne, Theweleit). On the basis of his study of the autobiographical writings of members of the *Freikorps*, paramilitary organizations active in Germany in the years after 1918 that many regard as precursors of Nazism, Klaus Theweleit attributes the obsession of the *Freikorps* fighters with maleness to fear of being engulfed by chaotic and formless forces associated with the female (Theweleit 1987, 1989). These same forces were also associated with Jews (Ostow 1996, pp. 155–70). A similar pattern of associations is readily observed in writing by contemporary Russian fascists —on the one side, manliness, Russianness, order, spirit, purity; on the other, effeminacy, Jewishness, Caucasianness, chaos, materialism, animality.[8]

Fascism, Capitalism, and Socialism

Several different points of view exist among the writers examined concerning where fascism fits on the conventional left–right continuum. Forman and Neocleous defend the standard left-wing interpretation of fascism as a right-wing movement in disguise, implementing a preemptive "revolution against the revolution" to save capitalism from the socialist threat. Other writers take the anticapitalist pretensions of fascism seriously: Sternhell, for instance, regards fascism as an anti-Marxist form of socialism. Orwell, his own left-wing views notwithstanding, also recognizes fascism as a form of collectivism. For yet others, the corporate state of fascism represents a "third way" between capitalism and socialism (Mosse, O'Sullivan), while Lipset sees fascism as an "extremism of the center."

On the one hand, there is no doubt that, in principle, the interwar fascists saw themselves as a force of neither "left" nor "right," but rather as representatives of a third, national alternative to existing forms of international capitalism and international socialism. On the other hand, the usual left-wing view of fascism as a right-wing and pro-capitalist movement is understandable enough. In practice, the fascist regimes were able to take power only with the tacit support of traditional conservative forces: non-fascist nationalist parties close to big business, the military command, and (in Italy) the monarchy and the Catholic Church. In contrast to the immediate ruthless suppression of all social democratic, communist, and trade union opposition, the prerogatives of the capitalists were only gradually reduced—for example, by the creation of a parastatal industrial sector under party control (De Grand 1995, pp. 82–86). There did exist, however, a left-wing tendency in the Nazi movement, associated above all with the Strasser brothers, which took its socialism no less seriously than it took its nationalism.[9] Although the Strasserites were crushed soon after the Nazis came to power, the survival of strains of anticapitalist sentiment was demonstrated by the wartime speeches of Leon Degrelle, leader of the Belgian fascist movement Rex and commander of the SS Walloon Legion.[10] "The radicals of the younger generation hoped that a renewed fascist revolution would commence with victory in the Second World War" (De Grand 1995, p. 84). As the fascist powers lost the war, the question of what kind of postwar economic system a victorious Axis would have established remained an open one.

Tensions between left-wing and right-wing tendencies can be found also in contemporary fascist and near-fascist movements. Pruss (1997) has surveyed the widely divergent economic views prevailing among radical nationalists in Russia, ranging all the way from the consistent national capitalism of some groups to the aspiration of the National-Bolshevik Party to restore the Soviet planning system.

The problem might best be approached by examining the general fascist outlook on history. To the extent that fascists are actuated by premodern values, it is difficult for them to decide where they stand in the contest between capitalism and socialism, as both sides belong to the modern "materialistic" world that they reject. If it were practicable, they would prefer to be against both capitalism and socialism. One way out of the dilemma is to reject not capitalism as a whole, but only those aspects of it that are worst from their point of view—that is, to oppose financial and international capital in the name of productive national capital. Another solution is to envision a new kind of "spiritual" socialism. Hence, the tendency for fascism to split into "national-capitalist" and "national-socialist" variants.

For all these reasons, concepts pertaining to socialism and capitalism should be excluded from the definition of fascism.

Fascism and Nationalism

There appears to be a near-consensus to the effect that fascism is to be considered an especially extreme or intense kind of nationalism ("ultranationalism" or "hypernationalism"). Thus, Hans Kohn calls fascism a "totalitarian nationalism in which humanity and the individual disappear and nothing remains but the nation." Fascism is also regarded by many investigators as a variety of "integral" or "organic" nationalism, in which the nation is envisaged not as a mere collection or association of separate individuals, but as a living being with its own body and spirit. Other characteristics often attributed to nationalism of the fascist type are that it is exclusive, xenophobic, and "tribal," based on racially defined ethnicity rather than culture or civic identity, and that it is supremacist, messianic, militaristic, expansionist, and imperialistic—even, according to one author (O'Sullivan), bent on world conquest.

The nationalist character of fascism is not, however, as unproblematic as most authors assume. True, fascism rejects as reference points both the individual and humanity, and this is one of the main features setting it apart from doctrines that claim to be based on universal human values, such as liberalism, socialism, and anarchism. The ethnic nation is by no means, however, the *only* group entity intermediate between the individual and humanity to which fascists have felt a sense of loyalty. Thus, for classical Italian fascism, the state was arguably an object of worship in itself. For the Nazis, the Nordic or Aryan race mattered at least as much as the German nation. For yet other fascist movements, religion—in most cases, Catholic or Orthodox

Christianity—has been a vital source of identity, alongside and closely linked to the nation, but not identical with it. A good example is Corneliu Codreanu's League of the Archangel Michael, founded in Romania in 1927.[11] A proto-fascist organization of almost the same name[12] had appeared in Russia, another country of Orthodox culture, in 1908. Nazi sympathizers in India developed a Brahmin-Hindu variant of fascist ideology (Goodrick-Clarke 1998). Fascists may, finally, attribute meaning to cultural or "civilizational" constructs of continentwide scope, such as "Europe" or "Eurasia." The relative importance attached to nation, state, race, faith, and civilization is a useful criterion for distinguishing one kind of fascism from another.

Alone among the writers surveyed, Gregor argues that fascism should not be defined in terms of nationalism at all, pointing out that the racism of the Nazis in fact took precedence over nationalism, which Hitler rejected as "a snare and a delusion." Whether such a sharp separation between Nazism and German nationalism was ever established is open to dispute, but we may at least conclude that it is misleading and one-sided to define fascism primarily in terms of nationalism.

The question of the relation of fascism to nationalism hinges, of course, on how "nationalism" itself is defined. Provided that "nationalism" is sufficiently broadly understood, fascism may be regarded as a kind of nationalism. The problem is that it has become common scholarly practice to define nationalism in the terms first suggested by Ernest Gellner—that is, as "a principle which holds that the political and the national unit should be congruent" (Gellner 1983, p. 1). In fact, fascism has never been committed in principle to the nation-state. Its ideal has been rather that of the multiethnic empire, within which to be sure one particular nation was to occupy the dominant position. The Italian fascists, dreaming of "the glory that was Rome," sought a Mediterranean empire, the German Nazis a continental empire in Europe (though both entertained colonial ambitions in Africa too). The West European New Right talks about a new European federal empire, within which each nation will enjoy cultural but not political autonomy (Griffin 2000), while Alexander Dugin, the foremost ideologue of the Russian New Right, offers a similar model for a future continental Eurasian empire built around Russia (Dugin 1997a). One can get around this problem by calling those who think like Dugin "nationalists of a non-existent Eurasian nation" (Verkhovskii and Pribylovskii 1996, p. 93), but in so doing one stretches the meaning of "nation" far beyond its usual contours.

In the Russian context it is particularly inexpedient to tie the concept of fascism too closely to that of ethnicity. Even today the traditional image of Russia as a multiethnic Eurasian empire rather than a nation-state of the ethnic Russians has broad appeal to the Russians. In her classification of radical Russian nationalist ideologies, Pruss (1997) distinguishes two broad camps: the ethno-nationalist and the imperial. There is no reason to expect that fascist movements (as defined in accordance with other criteria) can arise only from the former and not the latter.

All considered, it may be best, if only to avoid confusion, not to define fascism as a subcategory of nationalism. What we can say with confidence is that fascists place overriding value not in the individual and not in humanity as a whole, but in various kinds of delimited community that they envisage (with whatever degree of validity) as being socially integrated, based on tradition, and "natural" or "organic."

Fascism As a Movement

Fascist movements and regimes, most of the writers surveyed agree, have a highly authoritarian and elitist internal structure, in which a dictatorial leader stands at the top of a strict hierarchy of command. At the same time, fascist movements, in contrast to traditional conservative autocracies and dictatorships, are populist in character: they appeal to and mobilize the masses, with whose support they capture and maintain themselves in power.

This seemingly paradoxical phenomenon of authoritarian (that is, antidemocratic) populism may be taken as characteristic of fascism. It is not, however, unique to fascism, but is shared by modern totalitarianism in general, the other main historical embodiment of which has been Leninist (Bolshevik) communism. Authoritarian populism may therefore serve as a component of a definition of fascism, but should remain subordinate to other concepts that are more specific to fascism.

My Definition

The foregoing discussion suggests a composite definition of "fascism" along the following lines:

> Fascism is an authoritarian populist movement that seeks to preserve and restore premodern patriarchal values within a new order based on communities of nation, race, or faith.

As Griffin's definition of fascism is both influential and illuminating, it may be helpful to compare my definition with his. Griffin has defined "fascism" as follows:

> Fascism is a genus of modern, revolutionary, "mass" politics which . . .

> draws its internal cohesion and driving force from a core myth that a period of perceived national decline and decadence is giving way to one of rebirth and renewal in a post-liberal new order.

Or, more succinctly:

> Fascism is a genus of political ideology whose mythic core . . . is a palingenetic form of populist ultra-nationalism.[13]

Griffin's definition and the definition that I suggest differ in four important ways.

First, I specify that fascism is authoritarian as well as populist in character. Griffin leaves open the possibility of a "democratic" (though not "liberal") fascism, but I do not. Allowing for a fascism that is democratic in some genuine sense contradicts both a central characteristic of classical interwar fascism (the criterion of descriptive accuracy) and almost everybody's understanding of what fascism means (the criterion of broad communicability). In defining fascism as nondemocratic and antidemocratic, we recognize that former fascists who manifest a sincere commitment to democracy should no longer be considered fascists, even if their thinking continues to bear resemblances to fascism in other respects.

Second, as already explained, in my definition the new order that fascism introduces is not specified as being "post-liberal," as it may equally well be post-communist.

Third, my definition does not, as Griffin's does, tightly link fascism to ethnic nationalism, thereby allowing for the possibility of fascism existing in cultural contexts where ethnic nationalism is not deeply rooted, as among the Russians.

And lastly, my definition replaces Griffin's palingenetic paradigm by an emphasis on the attachment of fascism to premodern patriarchal values. In practice, a very wide overlap exists between the two concepts. However, my definition, unlike Griffin's, does allow new nationalisms, such as Croatian and Slovak nationalism in Nazi-occupied Europe, to qualify as fascist, provided of course that other criteria of fascism are met. Conversely, I do not recognize as fascist a movement actuated by a palingenetic myth if that movement draws its values and inspiration wholly from an earlier phase of modernity—in the case of post-Soviet Russia, for instance, wholly from the Soviet period.

Whichever academic definition of fascism one may prefer, one should not denigrate or leave out of account the popular understanding of fascism as a concentrated embodiment of racial or ethnic hatred, violence, and aggressive war. Scholarship that ignores popular meanings will itself be ignored by ordinary people. To those who use "fascism" in the popular sense and "know" from experience what it is, academic debate about the definition of fascism may seem tiresome and irrelevant. Thus, the former Soviet party official Alexander Yakovlev, learning that a presidential decree on the struggle against fascism had been held up by the inability of the Russian Academy of Sciences to agree on a definition of fascism, expressed his irritation in the following terms:

> What kind of definition do you need? There is, after all, historical experience. Fascism means inciting ethnic hatred. It is propaganda about the superiority of one people over another. Propaganda of war and violence is also fascism. (Iakovlev 1998)

In the wide gap that divides the various academic definitions of fascism from its popular meaning there lies a great potential for misunderstanding. For example, is Vladimir Zhirinovsky a fascist? As we shall see in chapter 5, there is room for argument concerning whether he can be considered a fascist in the sense of being attached to premodern values or in the sense of believing in a myth of national or imperial rebirth. However, his advocacy in the book *Final Spurt to the South* of a military campaign to conquer the lands separating Russia from the Indian Ocean suffices to make him a fascist as most people understand the word.[14] For that reason alone, it would be strange for a book on the threat of fascism in Russia to ignore altogether the question of his political prospects. (Logical consistency requires that the ideologies that justified the European conquest and settlement of the Americas, Australasia, and Africa also be considered fascist in the popular sense, although they were not fascist in an academic sense.[15]) Conversely, it is in principle possible for an ideology to qualify "technically" as fascism in accordance with one or another academic definition, even though it lacks the characteristics popularly associated with fascism.

Different readers of this book will prefer to use the word "fascism" in different senses. Each reader will naturally be concerned above all to assess the threat of "fascism" in Russia in the sense in which he or she uses the word. In the hope, therefore, of communicating effectively with a broad range of readers, I intend to use four definitions of "fascism" in parallel, taking due care to indicate which definition I have in mind at any point. Thus, "fascism in the classical sense" will refer to the original fascism of interwar Italy, or to any movement that is closely modeled on it. "Fascism in the palingenetic sense" will refer to an ideology built around a core myth of the rebirth of a decadent national, racial, imperial, or religious community (corresponding approximately, but not necessarily precisely, to Roger Griffin's definition of fascism). "Fascism in the popular sense" will refer to movements, ideologies, and regimes that possess the characteristics most closely associated with the word "fascism" in the popular imagination. And finally, "fascism" *tout court* will refer to fascism as I have defined it above.

Appendix 1
Selected Definitions of "Fascism"

A. Descriptive Definitions

A1. Renzo De Felice (1977)

The combination of conservative or reactionary socioeconomic and cultural goals with mass totalitarian mobilization. Europe's moral disease.

A2. James D. Forman (1974, p. 17)

Reactionary revolution. Intense nationalism, anticommunism, militarism, and imperialism.

A3. George L. Mosse

Ritualistic, mystical, idealist (antimaterialist), organic nationalism. Mass-mobilizing. Exalts struggle, war, and death.

A4. Mark Neocleous (1997)

Chapter 1. Replacement of Marxist materialism and determinism by voluntarism and vitalism. Eradication of the Enlightenment, the destruction of reason. Biological mysticism. The will to perpetual war.
Chapter 2. Messianic racial nationalism.
Chapter 3. The conservative revolution: preemptive revolution in defense of capitalism.
Chapter 4. Reactionary modernism: technological advance plus restoration of tradition.
Chapter 5. The worship of nature. The return to barbarism. The obsession with death.

A5. Noel O'Sullivan (1983, p. 131)

1. The corporate state as a third way between capitalism and socialism.
2. Rejection of reason and stability in favor of myth and dynamism, culminating in the ideal of permanent revolution.
3. The leadership principle.
4. The messianic concept of a redemptive mission.
5. Creation of an autarkic state through world conquest.

A6. Stanley G. Payne

A form of revolutionary ultranationalism for national rebirth that is based on a primarily vitalist philosophy, is structured on extreme elitism, mass mobilization, and the *Führerprinzip*, positively values violence as end as well as means, and tends to normatize war and/or the military virtues.

A7. Zeev Sternhell

A synthesis of exclusive, tribal, biologically based (integral, organic) nationalism with anti-Marxist socialism: anti-individualistic, antiliberal, antidemocratic, and antimaterialist (vitalist). An anti-intellectual reaction in favor of irrationality and instinct.

A8. Paul Wilkinson

Supremacist, messianic, militaristic, and expansionist ultranationalism. Elitist and dictatorial ("the absolute state"), but mass-mobilizing. Industrially modernizing, but socially reactionary.

B. "Fascist Minima"

B1. Ernst Nolte

Resistance to transcendence. Revolt against certain aspects of modernization—specifically: secularization, democratization, and international integration.

B2. Roger Griffin

A genus of political ideology whose mythic core . . . is a palingenetic form of populist ultranationalism. (Griffin 1991, p. 2; Cronin 1996, p. 143)
A genus of modern, revolutionary, "mass" politics which . . . draws its inter-

nal cohesion and driving force from a core myth that a period of perceived national decline and decadence is giving way to one of rebirth and renewal in a post-liberal new order.

Source: (unless otherwise indicated) Griffin 1998. Where quotation marks are not shown, my own summary.

Appendix 2
List of Writers on Fascism Surveyed

Walker Connor	Hutchinson and Smith (1994, p. 41)
Renzo De Felice	De Felice (1977); Griffin (1995, pp. 300–301)
Roger Eatwell	Griffin (1995, pp. 306–7)
James D. Forman	Forman (1974, p. 17)
Aleksandr Galkin	*Nuzhen* (1996, p. 95)
Emilio Gentile	Griffin (1995, pp. 295–96)
Leonid Gordon	*Nuzhen* (1996, p. 138)
A. James Gregor	Griffin (1995, pp. 298–99); Gregor (1997)
Roger Griffin	Griffin (1991, pp. 26–38; 1995, pp. 2–8; 1998, pp. 35–39); Cronin (1996, p. 143)
Hans Kohn	Hutchinson and Smith (1994, p. 163)
Juan B. Linz	Griffin (1995, pp. 299–300)
Seymour M. Lipset	Griffin (1995, pp. 285–86)
Michael Mann	Periwal (1995, p. 59)
Sergei Markov	*Nuzhen* (1996, pp. 123–34, 128)
Barrington Moore	Griffin (1995, pp. 293–94)
George L. Mosse	Griffin (1995, pp. 303–4; 1998, pp. 137–47)
Mark Neocleous	Neocleous (1997)
Ernst Nolte	Turner (1975, pp. 26–42); Griffin (1995, pp. 297–98; 1998, pp. 106–12)
George Orwell	Griffin (1995, pp. 269–70)
Noel O'Sullivan	O'Sullivan (1983, p. 131)
Stanley Payne	Payne (1980, p. 211); Griffin (1995, pp. 304–5; 1998, pp. 147–55)
Wilhelm Reich	Reich (1970)
Anthony D. Smith	Smith (1979, pp. 53–54)

Zeev Sternhell	Laqueur (1976, p. 349); Griffin (1995, pp. 305–6; 1998, pp. 30–35)
Klaus Theweleit	Griffin (1995, pp. 292–93)
Henry A. Turner	Turner (1975, pp. 117–40); Griffin (1995, pp. 294–95)
Aleksandr Verkhovsky and Vladimir Pribylovsky	Verkhovskii and Pribylovskii (1996, p. 92)
Paul Wilkinson	Griffin (1998, pp. 27–30)

2
Does Russia Have a Fascist Tradition?

Do fascist tendencies exist in the history of Russian and Soviet political thought and practice prior to the collapse of the USSR in 1991? If so, how significant are they? What influence do they exert on Russians living today? In other words, to what extent may post-Soviet Russia be said to possess a living fascist tradition? Answers to these questions will provide a useful historical background to the study of fascist tendencies in contemporary Russia.

First I consider some tendencies in nineteenth-century Russian political thought that arguably point in the direction of fascism, and the character of the largest and most famous of the early twentieth-century Russian political movements that have been called fascist or proto-fascist—that is, the Union of the Russian People, or "Black Hundreds." Then I turn to examine fascist and semifascist movements and writers among the White Russian émigrés. Next I discuss the question of the existence of fascist groups and tendencies in Soviet Russia, at the official, semiofficial, and dissident levels. Finally, I consider how strong an influence fascist tendencies from earlier historical periods have on the minds of Russians living today.

Nineteenth-Century Precursors

Yuri Samarin

In 1875, there appeared in Berlin a short book by two Russian writers of Slavophile orientation, Yuri Samarin and Fyodor Dmitriev; the book was titled *Revolutionary Conservatism*. Coming across this book shortly after I had clarified my concept of fascism, I was intrigued. Could a philosophy of revolutionary conservatism really have existed at such an early date in Russia?

As it turned out, there was less to the book than met the eye. First of all, Samarin and Dmitriev were by no means advocating "revolutionary conservatism." This was rather their label for the views of "a small party, group or school" of landowners resident in St. Petersburg, the most prominent being apparently General Rostislav Fadiev,[1] who in the late 1850s had begun to express opposition to the land reform of Tsar Alexander II that was in the process of emancipating the serfs. Not that Fadiev and his friends considered themselves revolutionary conservatives either. Their intentions were conservative, explain the authors, and they were not consciously aiming at revolution, but given Russian realities their methods of public agitation inevitably led toward "the forceful rupture of what exists" (Samarin and Dmitriev 1875, pp. 1–3, 139).

Samarin himself was to be led by his conservative convictions into conflict with the reforming tsar. Although he supported the land reform, and as a government official actively took part in its implementation, he was against the reform of local government that created the elective bodies known as the *zemstva*, and opposed all constitutional demands, believing that Russia needed an unlimited monarchy. The censor's office prevented the publication of Samarin's views, and a book that he circulated privately in the early 1860s led to his arrest and a rebuke from the tsar, mainly on account of his hostility to the ethnic Germans in the government (Nolde 1978, pp. 172–79).[2]

In different ways, therefore, both Fadiev and Samarin exemplify the paradoxical phenomenon of conservative opposition to a reforming autocrat. On the one hand, they did not lay claim to any right to oppose the sovereign and sincerely wanted to be loyal to him. Such loyalty was indeed an essential part of their conservatism. On the other hand, their attachment to aspects of the existing order that the tsar sought to change tempted them into opposition—opposition that could only be revolutionary in character, as no "loyal opposition" was recognized. Once they realized the nature of the dilemma they faced, however, their loyalty to the tsar had to take precedence over their misgivings about his reforms. As long as the ultimate state authority retained its traditional legitimacy, conservative critics could not really turn into "conservative revolutionaries." Such a transformation was to become possible only after the overthrow of the old order. Nevertheless, the *idea* of revolutionary conservatism, as a conceivable attitude directed against the early phases of state-sponsored modernization, had been formulated, in itself a highly significant development. In this sense, Samarin may well have made an inadvertent contribution to the emergence of a proto-fascist, and eventually a fascist, tendency in Russia.

Nikolai Danilevsky

Another, more prominent writer, the neo-Slavophile Nikolai Danilevsky (1822–1885), merits our attention. In his book on Danilevsky, Robert MacMaster argues that he is "a Russian totalitarian philosopher" and forerunner of modern totalitarianism, though closer in spirit to bolshevism than to fascism (MacMaster 1967, p. 300). What grounds are there for linking Danilevsky either with totalitarianism in general or with fascism in particular?

Danilevsky certainly possessed some of the traits that characterize fascism, especially fascism in the popular sense. He was an ultranationalist, a militarist, and an imperialist. His ultranationalism found clearest expression in the view, taken in defiance of mainstream Slavophile as well as westernizer thinking, that "humanity" is a meaningless concept, and that there are no universal human values, universal human culture, or universal human history.[3] According to Danilevsky, there are only specific "historico-cultural types," incommensurable with one another and developing in parallel along separate paths (Danilevskii 1889, p. 121; MacMaster 1967, p. 203; Walicki 1975, p. 505; Avdeeva 1992, p. 81). Concerning Danilevsky's militarism and imperialism, suffice it to say that he believed that a great war between Russia's Slavic civilization and the Romano-German civilization of Western Europe was inevitable, and he dreamt of the restoration of a pan-Slav, neo-Byzantine empire stretching from the Arctic Ocean to the Mediterranean Sea (Ianov 1995, p. 141).

However, the picture of Danilevsky as either a totalitarian or a fascist (in any sense) breaks down when account is taken of his stance in domestic affairs. As Alexander Yanov points out, Danilevsky was no supporter of autocracy; constitutional development was integral to his notion of social progress. Yanov even goes so far as to call Danilevsky "an imperial liberal of the purest dye" (Ianov 1995, p. 141).

How can one and the same writer be perceived as a totalitarian by one critic and as a liberal by another? What makes Danilevsky suspect in the eyes of a modern Western scholar, especially one trained in the Anglo-Saxon empiricist tradition, is his belief in a divine plan for human history, which it is the philosopher's task to make clear (MacMaster 1967, pp. 123–25). But this speculative teleological approach to history was by no means peculiar to Danilevsky: it was commonplace in nineteenth-century Russian and German philosophy. Russian philosophers such as Danilevsky and Vladimir Solovyov borrowed it from the Prussian idealist school of Ranke, Fichte, and Hegel, for whom "world history was moving toward a higher, divinely sanctioned, and harmonious order" (Berghahn 1994, p. 177).[4] The deeper origins of the outlook undoubtedly lie in the conception of the progressive revelation or unfolding of God's will through human history that Judaism bequeathed to its daughter faiths. Sir Karl Popper, in his book *The Open Society and Its Enemies* (1966), found in Hegel's teleology the root cause of twentieth-century totalitarianism, and MacMaster makes the same case, this time with reference to Danilevsky. It is not my intention here to argue that it is a case completely devoid of merit. What bears emphasizing, however, is that none of the writers in question ever actually advocated the creation of a totalitarian society: their ideas may have had totalitarian implications, but they were not themselves totalitarians. For this and other reasons, their heritage is at most of limited and indirect value to any contemporary politician with totalitarian ambitions.

Whatever may be his relation to ultranationalism or to totalitarianism in general, Danilevsky was far removed from fascism in any scholarly sense of the word. He was not moved by a palingenetic myth, and he wholeheartedly embraced the Enlightenment ideals of science, reason, and progress, the full potential of which—he believed—was to be realized not by the West, but by Russia (MacMaster 1967, pp. 295–96). It is important in this respect to take full cognizance of the fact that, besides his philosophical writings, Danilevsky was active as a geographer, statistician, and naturalist, with special interests in the study of climate, fish, and the plant world (MacMaster 1967, pp. 101–10).

Danilevsky's most original contribution to social thought was his concept of Russia as "Eurasia," a geographical and cultural world distinct from those of both Europe and Asia. He was to be a seminal influence on the émigré movement of the 1920s and 1930s known as the Eurasianists (Hauner 1990, pp. 23–24; Bassin 1991).

Konstantin Leontiev

A far more promising candidate for the role of intellectual precursor of fascism is Konstantin Leontiev (1831–1891). Like Danilevsky, Leontiev was an imperialist who looked forward to the conquest of Constantinople and the creation of a great neo-Byzantine empire, although he adhered to a pan-Orthodox rather than a pan-Slavic concept of imperial identity.[5] Leontiev's ideals, however, were unambiguously reactionary in character. Central to his whole outlook was an aristocratic esthetics of beauty, excellence, strength, and heroism (Lukashevich 1967, pp. 117–20; Dolgov 1997). He rejected "progress" as the triumph of bourgeois boredom and mediocrity, and he "saw that excellence was on the side of the Church, the monarchy, the military, the gentry, and inequality" (Korol'kov 1991, p. 58).[6]

Nevertheless, Leontiev was not simply a conservative or a reactionary. What makes him of special interest to our study is that he prophesied the renewed triumph of traditional values in what he thought of as a new order. Just as Leontiev's namesake, the Roman Emperor Constantine, had adopted Christianity and made it into the state religion, so would a future Russian tsar "take into his hands the leadership of the Socialist movement and, with the blessings of the Church, introduce a Socialist form of life which would replace the bourgeois-liberal form of life." This "socialism," while collectivistic, would be based not on equality, but on the deep inequality of castes, a "new feudalism" (Korol′kov 1991, p. 52), "a new and stern, triple slavery—a submission to communities, Church, and Tsar" (Lukashevich 1967, p. 162).

This is as yet, of course, far from a fully fascist vision. Although in Leontiev's time the old tsarist order was already in the process of being undermined in the socioeconomic realm by the growing new "bourgeois-liberal way of life," its political pillars still stood firm. The "new order" to which he looked forward was hardly distinct from the old order, revived in a new, "socialist" form. Above all, Leontiev was not a fascist because he was not a populist. Rather than try to build a mass movement from below to achieve his goal, he loyally awaited an initiative from above.

The Black Hundreds

The first attempts to create a mass movement in Russia oriented in a conservative or reactionary direction were made in the opening years of the twentieth century. The Russian Assembly [*Russkoe sobranie*] was formed in 1900, and it served as the precursor to the Russian Monarchist Party, founded in 1905, but these organizations were restricted to the nobility. Three leagues, collectively known as the "Black Hundreds" [*chernosotentsy*], were open to broader strata of Russian society: the Union of Russian People [*Soiuz russkikh liudei*], founded in April 1905; the Union of the Russian People [*Soiuz russkogo naroda*], by far the largest of the three, founded in October 1905; and finally the Russian People's Union named after the Archangel Michael (the Union of the Archangel Michael), founded in 1908.[7]

The creation of these organizations, which not by chance roughly coincided with the proto-Soviet uprising of 1905, marked a radically new departure for Russian conservatives who had previously shunned mass politics as a disreputable and subversive activity, but who had come to see the need for a grassroots counterweight to the liberal and socialist left. The initiative, assisted by one part of tsarist officialdom but opposed by another,[8] might be regarded as at least modestly successful. The Union of the Russian People (URP) had at its height about 350,000 members,[9] and garnered between 5 percent and 10 percent of the vote in elections to the prerevolutionary Duma (parliament) (Sakharov 1999).

An overview of the ideas and goals of the URP is given in its program, adopted in 1906 (*Programmy* 1995, pp. 440–44). The first point affirms the loyalty of the URP to the throne, insisting that the tsar's Manifesto of October 17, 1905, and the subsequent establishment of the Duma did not abolish the autocracy, or limit in any way its prerogatives. The second point affirms loyalty to the Russian Orthodox Church, and proclaims Russia's Christian mission to inaugurate the Kingdom of God on Earth, which is the kingdom of faith, love, good, and justice. The sixth point reflects the ideal of the people's monarchy: "the system of officials has hidden the bright face of the Tsar from the people, and must be basically changed" by reconvening the Assembly of the Land. Much attention is devoted to the "Jewish question": the fourteenth point advocates that it be solved humanely by expelling the Jews to Palestine, where they are to create a Jewish state with Russian aid. Unofficially, the Black Hundreds encouraged Jews to emigrate by instigating pogroms, to the accompaniment of the famous slogan *Bei zhidov, spasai Rossiiu!* [Beat the Yids, save Russia!].

Two tendencies could be distinguished within the URP: a reactionary tendency that aimed to restore a vanished past, and a conservative tendency that strove merely to preserve what could still be saved. In either case, members strove to achieve their goals not directly, through their own action, but indirectly, through the influence they might exert on the tsar. They hoped to encourage the tsar to stand firm by conveying to him the message that "the true Russian people" remained loyal, at the same time as they made known to him the people's needs. They found themselves in the paradoxical situation of taking independent public action in order to place autocratic power in the ruler's hands (Rawson 1995, pp. 225–29).

In light of the rise of fascism in Italy in the early 1920s, a Soviet historian was to characterize Vladimir Purishkevich, the leader of the URP, as the first fascist (Liubosh 1925). The best-known contemporary writer on the Black Hundreds, Hans Rogger, argues that while the members of the URP were reactionary populists who prefigured many of the themes and contradictions of fascism, they cannot be considered fascists, because fascism is defined as a reaction against modern society, which had not yet been established in Russia (Rogger 1986, pp. 228–32). The same view is taken by Rawson, who puts somewhat more emphasis, however, on the similarities and continuities between the pre-fascism or proto-fascism of the Black Hundreds and fascism proper (Rawson 1995, pp. 229–30).

I too do not consider the Black Hundreds to have been fascist—and not only because they did not live in a modern society. If we compare Leontiev with the Black Hundreds, we see that by one criterion the Black Hundreds were closer to fascism, insofar as they were, however reluctantly, populists. According to another criterion, however, it was Leontiev who was closer to fascism, for he had a vision of the restoration of old values in a new order. It was above all the lack of any such vision that made the Black Hundreds conservatives or reactionaries rather than fascists. The revolutionary tendencies that their critics on the right, following in the footsteps of Yuri Samarin, claimed to detect in the Black Hundreds—tendencies noted also by some modern scholars: one calls them "revolutionaries inside-out" (Stepanov 1993, p. 154)—were to remain incipient.

Fascist Tendencies in the Russian Emigration

After the Bolshevik Revolution of 1917 and the ensuing civil war, millions of Russians found themselves in exile, mainly in Europe, China, and Manchuria, though also in the Americas and other places. Most of the Russian émigrés did not integrate themselves into their new countries of residence, but maintained a vigorous political and intellectual life focused on Russia, to which they hoped eventually to return.[10] Émigré political thought, the broader import of which may at the time have seemed marginal, now acquires a new significance as a result of the growing interest in it in post-Soviet Russia.

A large majority of the Russian émigrés—Nazarov (1993) estimates the proportion at 80 percent—were "Whites" who had been supporters of the tsarist regime. Some of them had taken part in the Black Hundreds. Many White émigrés[11] remained monarchists of a traditional kind, dreaming of the restoration of the old order. As the years passed, however, increasing numbers of émigré political activists began to reconsider their views in the light of new conditions. Among these, four tendencies can be distinguished:

> (1) *The Outright Fascists.* The rise of fascism in Europe in the 1920s and 1930s inspired some émigrés to develop specifically Russian variants of fascism and to found Russian fascist parties. The largest and best organized of these was the All-Russian Fascist Party of Konstantin Rodzayevsky in Manchuria. In Germany there was the Russian National Socialist Movement, and in the United States the All-Russian Fascist Organization of Anastasy Vonsyatsky.[12] Mention should also be made of Ivan Solonevich, editor of the journal *Golos Rossii* [Voice of Russia] and an influential intellectual figure in the Russian fascist movement, whose works have recently been republished in Russia (Solonevich 1997). Some émigrés joined foreign fascist movements, including the German national-socialists.
>
> (2) *The Fellow Travelers.* Besides the outright fascists, there was a large section of émigré opinion that, viewing fascism from the vantage point of traditional monarchism, sympathized with it to some degree, but also entertained serious misgivings about it and maintained a certain distance from it. It is in this category of fellow

travelers of fascism that the influential philosopher Ivan Ilyin, whose works have also been republished in post-Soviet Russia (Il′in 1993, 1997), is best placed.

(3) *The National-Bolsheviks.* This is the term commonly attached to the group led by Nikolai Ustryalov, originally known as the "sign-post-changers" [*smenavekhovtsy*], after their manifesto "Changing of Signposts" [*Smena vekh*]. They reconciled themselves to the Bolshevik regime, recognizing it as the historically legitimate successor to Tsarist Russia (Hardeman 1994; Shlapentokh 1997a).

(4) *The Eurasianists.* Yet another group created a new totalitarian ideology and movement known as Eurasianism. The works of one of the central figures among the Eurasianists, Pyotr Savitsky, have also been republished in Russia (Savitskii 1997).

Let us consider the ideologies of these groups, and in particular the relation that each of them bore to fascism, in more detail.

The Outright Fascists

Analysis of the program of Konstantin Rodzayevsky's All-Russian Fascist Party (ARFP) shows that the core of its ideology was an adaptation of classical Italian fascism to contemporary Russian conditions. Communism was to be replaced by a "national-labor state" built on corporativist principles, with the population organized in national unions of workers, peasants, and the professions (Prussakov and Shiropaev 1993, pp. 4–19). The new order would draw its inspiration from the tradition of the Assembly of the Land.

As mentioned in chapter 1, Russian fascism was viewed as being different from Italian and German fascism inasmuch as it was to follow communism rather than liberal-democratic capitalism. In Russia, therefore, it was the task of fascism not to constrain but to expand human rights: private property was to be recognized, as were "the freedoms of labor, religious belief, scientific creativity, and even within certain limits freedom of the press and speech." The state would guarantee the basic welfare of the population, outlaw speculation, prevent the degeneration of "creative entrepreneurial capital" into the "anonymous capital" of trusts and syndicates, and block the penetration of international capital, maintaining for that purpose a monopoly of foreign trade.

The ARFP extended its relatively liberal approach to civil rights to all but one of the non-Russian ethnic minorities. All peoples of Russia who had participated in the national revolution were to be granted cultural autonomy, and the possibility of a federal state structure was not excluded. The sole exception was to be the Jews, who would be tolerated only as undesirable aliens, for they were "the main culprits in the destruction of the Russian nation." The party emblem showed a worker gripping the snake of "Judeo-Communism" in his fist and poised to finish it off with a hammer.[13]

In the introduction to their commentary on the program of the ARFP, Prussakov and Shiropaev (1993) stress another distinction between Russian émigré fascism and Nazism: the Russian fascists rejected "biological racism of the Rosenberg type," basing their beliefs instead on Orthodox Christianity (p. 3). A religious orientation is also reflected in the motto: "God, Nation, Labor" (Stephan 1978, p. 337). The anti-Semitism of the ARFP was directed against the Jews not as a race, but as a religious community. In this respect they remained within the Black Hundreds tradition.

Ivan Solonevich needs to some extent to be considered separately. On the one hand, he allied himself with Rodzayevsky's party, and he did not conceal his sympathy with Hitler, expressing regret that Russia had not protected itself against the Jews as Germany had done.[14] On the other hand, while calling for "a synthesis of the national with the contemporary," he was uncertain whether post-communist Russia should be a monarchy or a republic, although in either case it would have to use dictatorial methods (Solonevich 1997, pp. 70–71, 311). Solonevich had yet to complete the transition from traditional monarchism to fascism.

The Fellow Travelers of Fascism

In an article in the Russian "patriotic" journal *Nash sovremennik* on the relationship between the Russian emigration and fascism, Mikhail Nazarov offered an apologetic interpretation of the pro-fascist mood among the White émigrés. Like many other right-wing Europeans at the time, he explained, the émigrés saw in fascism above all an ally in the struggle against communism, overlooking the contradiction between their own Christian outlook and the racist paganism of the Nazis. However, as the Nazis' real nature became more evident, especially in the wake of German aggression in World War II, émigré organizations increasingly grasped the necessity of clearly separating themselves from Nazism (Nazarov 1993, pp. 124–25).[15]

The philosopher Ivan Ilyin was the most prominent representative of this fellow-traveling tendency, marked by critical sympathy for fascism. Ilyin himself remained a monarchist, although he saw the need for a transitional "national dictator" after the collapse of communism, one who would stop the chaos, restore order, defend Russia from enemies and embezzlers, and initiate the spiritual reeducation of the people (Il′in 1993, pp. 139, 151).

Ilyin described fascism as "a complex and multi-sided phenomenon [that] arose as a healthy and necessary reaction to bolshevism, as a concentration of state-preserving forces on the right." Other praiseworthy features of fascism were its patriotic feeling and its search for just social reforms. However, fascism was marred by six "deep and serious errors"—namely hostility to Christianity and to religion in general; totalitarianism; one-party monopoly, leading to corruption and demoralization; nationalist extremism, belligerent chauvinism, and a mania for national grandeur; a tendency toward state socialism; and "idolatrous caesarism, with its demagogy, slavishness, and despotism" (Il′in 1993, pp. 67–70).

The first of Ilyin's objections does not serve to separate him from fascism in the generic sense, which, as was demonstrated in the last chapter, is compatible with a variety of religious orientations. Nevertheless, a person who rejects totalitarianism, chauvinism, and caesarism can hardly be considered a fascist. We might also note his reference to the traditionalist conservative regimes of Franco in Spain and Salazar in Portugal as positive alternatives to "fascism" (Il′in 1993, p. 70). Ilyin sensed that he shared many of his premodern values with the fascists—hence his perception of them as basically well-intentioned people who had made unfortunate "errors"—but he could not bring himself to accept the new order. Of course, the fascists, like their totalitarian cousins on the left, did not welcome criticism, however "sympathetic" it might be, making the position of their fellow travelers rather an awkward one.

The National-Bolsheviks

"National-bolshevism" as an explicit ideology was mainly the invention of Nikolai Ustryalov (1890–1938), an émigré living in Manchuria. Although he had been the director of the press agency of the White Admiral Kolchak, he had also been active in the Constitutional Democratic (Kadet) Party, and so should not perhaps be counted as a "White" émigré.

It is necessary to make a clear distinction between the early and the later phases of Ustryalov's movement. In the beginning, national-bolshevism meant recognition of the positive national role that the Bolsheviks had played, irrespective of their ultimate antinational aspirations, in preserving and restoring the Russian state. At the same time, the hope was entertained—as it was by many Western liberals—that the Bolsheviks would gradually shed their antinational Marxist-Leninist doctrine and evolve into subjective as well as objective Russian nationalists. The adoption of the New Economic Policy in 1921 was seen as a sign that things were moving in the right direction.

The Soviet regime, however, did not change either as rapidly or as radically as the national-bolsheviks had anticipated. As I shall show below, Soviet ideology stabilized as an amalgam of internationalist Marxism-Leninism and Russian nationalism. Had he remained true to his original nationalist rationale, Ustryalov would have distanced himself from the Bolsheviks. Instead, he did the opposite. The mountain had not come to Muhammad, so Muhammad went to the mountain! By the mid-1930s, Ustryalov was praising the USSR not as an embodiment of Russian statehood, but as a prototype of a future united humanity. And it was from this internationalist point of view that he rejected fascism (Hardeman 1994, pp. 54, 223). The label of national-bolshevism was retained out of inertia, but it was no longer accurate as a characterization of the ideology of Ustryalov and his circle.

The Eurasianists

The Eurasianists constituted another movement within the Russian emigration. Their leading figures were Pyotr Savitsky and Prince Nikolai Trubetskoi. The focus of their ideology was the idea of Russia not as part of Europe or Asia, but as a distinct "cultural-historical world," which they called "Russia-Eurasia" or "continent Eurasia"—an idea that they took from Danilevsky and developed further.[16]

The Eurasianists rejected Russian nationalism in the ethnic sense. Russia-Eurasia was to be understood as "a special kind of symphonic personality" to which all its peoples had contributed (Savitskii 1997, p. 99). The Eurasia of the future would be not just for Russians, but for all Eurasian peoples, "an assembly [*sobor*] of peoples" in which every people would be "assigned a place corresponding to its cultural capacity" (Savitskii 1931, p. 42). Even the Jews might find a place in the Eurasian Symphony (Shnirel′man 1996).

The Eurasianists occupied in some respects an ideological space in between the national-bolsheviks on one side and the monarchists and fascists on the other. Like the national-bolsheviks, they saw in the Bolshevik Revolution a positive as well as a negative significance for Russia. For the Eurasianists, however, its positive significance resided not only in the restoration of Russian statehood, but also in the separation of Russia from Europe. Savitsky proposed to retain the basic political structure of the Soviet regime, comprising a one-party system, the ideocratic selection of rulers, and a reformed system of Soviets as a non-Western form of popular representation. Marxism-Leninism would be replaced by an "Orthodox Eurasian-Russian" ideology (Savitskii 1931, p. 42; 1997, pp. 58–59). He also advocated a system of socialism based on Orthodox religious precepts and the concept of "stewardship" [*khoziainoderzhavie*] instead of property, although these ideas aroused controversy among the Eurasianists themselves (Savitskii 1997, pp. 217–53).

Eurasianism was clearly a totalitarian movement. Savitsky himself set out the areas of similarity that existed between Eurasianism and Italian fascism and between Eurasianism and bolshevism. The Eurasianists regarded their ideology as a "third maximalism" alongside bolshevism and fascism. Bolshevism was perhaps the more important of the two as a source of inspiration: Alexander Dugin reports a participant in the Eurasianist movement as telling him that Savitsky dreamt of being like Lenin, "a leader and prophet of the masses" (Savitskii 1997, p. 437).

What most of all distinguishes Eurasianism from fascism, as it has been conceptualized in the last chapter, is the absence of a sense of the present as a period of decadence. The Eurasianists were attached to tradition—Savitsky called it "the spiritual backbone" of Eurasia (Savitskii 1997, p. 99)—but they did not believe that modernity in general or the Bolshevik Revolution in particular had disrupted it in any serious way.[17]

In 1945, Savitsky was arrested in Prague by the Soviet army, and sentenced to ten years in a labor camp for anti-Soviet activity. He was released and rehabilitated in 1956, and returned to Prague, where he died in 1968 (Savitskii 1997, pp. 438–39). While imprisoned he happened to meet the young historian Lev Gumilyov, son of the famous poets Nikolai Gumilyov and Anna Akhmatova, who became his pupil. Later Gumilyov, after his release and rehabilitation, transmitted the Eurasianist doctrine within the Soviet elite, and by the 1980s it had its adherents in the Central Committee, the General Staff, and the Foreign Ministry (Yasmann 1993, pp. 24–25).[18] In this way, one school at least of Russian émigré thought was to have an unanticipated impact on Soviet society.

It is striking that, of the four émigré groups that we have examined, three were attracted to one of the two powerful totalitarian ideologies of the time—that is, either to fascism or to bolshevism—and the fourth constructed a new totalitarian ideology of its own. Perhaps there were some among the White émigrés who developed in a democratic direction, but I am not aware of their writings.

Soviet Russia: Was Stalin a Fascist?

In 1945, Rodzayevsky, the leader of the Russian émigré fascists, wrote a letter to Stalin, confessing his guilt and begging for forgiveness. His greatest mistake, he explained, had been his failure to realize that the USSR was evolving naturally toward fascism (Stephan 1978, pp. 337–40). Perhaps Rodzayevsky was moved by a genuine insight, and not just by the forlorn hope of saving his own skin as the Red Army swept through Manchuria? He was not, after all, the first to make this particular discovery. For example, Sergei Dmitrievsky, a defector from Stalinist Russia, had already proclaimed Stalin a great fascist in the 1930s, promoting his own fusion of fascism and Stalinism (Shlapentokh 1997a, p. 25).

To assess the extent to which fascist tendencies may have been present in official Soviet ideology at different periods, we must first determine the nature of that ideology. It is generally agreed that from a fairly early stage, and certainly from the late 1920s onward, Soviet ideology consisted of a mixture of dogmatic Marxism-Leninism and imperial Russian nationalism. What has always been a matter of dispute is the underlying significance of the mixture. For some, Marxism-Leninism was the permanent driving force of the Soviet system, and Russian nationalism merely a manipulative facade.[19] For others, especially those inclined to interpret world politics exclusively in terms of Realpolitik, it was the other way around: Russian nationalism was the driving force, and Marxism-Leninism the facade.

Less arbitrary and therefore more convincing are those interpretations that view Soviet ideology as an amalgam within which the two components were equally genuine or equally fraudulent (if one so prefers), each fulfilling essential functions of its own. Marxism-Leninism provided the founding myth of the USSR as a *Soviet* state, as well as an effective framework for the regulation of interethnic relations. At the same time, what the political scientist Dmitry Furman calls "the logic of the imperial space" imposed a Russian imperial character upon the bolshevik state, which soon came to see itself as the successor to the Russian empire of the tsars. "As a result, there arose a monstrous eclectic compromise, with Stalin tracing his origins simultaneously from Ivan the Terrible and Peter the Great and from Marx and Engels" (Furman 1997, p. 8).

The two components of Soviet ideology were to some extent represented by different individuals and groupings within the Soviet political system. Mikhail Agursky identifies the two tendencies as Marxist-Leninists and national-bolsheviks. "National-bolshevism is the ideology of a political current that legitimizes the existing system from a Russian national point of view. It expresses the vital interests of a certain segment of the Soviet elite." However, strict constraints were placed on conflict between the tendencies by the top leadership, which ensured the continued integration of the amalgam. Thus, the national-bolsheviks inside the Soviet elite never directly challenged communist ideology, but only strove "to minimize its importance to the level necessary for political continuity" (Agursky 1986, pp. 87–88).[20] In this respect, intraregime national-bolshevism differed from émigré national-bolshevism, which in its early phase did aspire to the de-communization of Soviet ideology.[21]

While neither component of Soviet ideology ever disappeared completely, the balance between the two components did fluctuate over time. The early years of revolution and civil war (1917–1921) were the heyday of Marxism-Leninism, although national-bolshevism was already present and serving important functions—for example, attracting former tsarist officers into the Red Army to fight as Russian patriots against foreign intervention. The national-bolshevik tendency was greatly strengthened by Stalin, who introduced the doctrine of "building socialism in one country." In the 1930s, Stalin rehabilitated certain tsarist traditions in fields ranging from historiography and military regulations to educational practice and family life. During what is significantly remembered as the Great Patriotic War, further concessions were made to traditional Russian nationalism, including the resurrection of the Orthodox Church and the dissolution of the Communist International (Comintern). The process reached its apogee in the immediate postwar period, when the "anti-cosmopolitan campaign" targeted foreign influences, as well as the "rootless" and "cosmopolitan" Jews as the presumed carriers of such influences.

There is ample reason to consider Stalin a fascist in the popular sense of the word. Besides his totalitarianism, imperialism, and xenophobia, and the state slavery of the Gulag, we may adduce as evidence his wartime deportation of several ethnic groups in their entirety; and his plan to deport the Jews was disrupted only by his death (Vaksberg 1995, pp. 238–80). Rodzayevsky's confession was not devoid of insight. Nevertheless, Stalin was not a fascist in the academic sense. His revival of tsarist tradition was very partial and selective in scope, even by comparison with post-Soviet Russia: today's vast Cossack revival was scarcely conceivable in Stalin's day, let alone the apotheosis of the last tsar. A fascist transformation of the Stalinist regime would have required the open repudiation of that regime's Leninist origins and Soviet structure—in other words, an ideological and constitutional revolution. In fact, a cardinal rule of Stalinist ideological control to the very end was that "Soviet" and "Russian" values never be counterposed.[22] No one knows what Stalin would have done had he lived on a few more years, but there is no indication that he was contemplating such a leap.[23]

But even if Stalin was not quite a fascist, his legacy remains highly pertinent to the potential for fascism in Russia today. Indeed, Alexander Barkashov, leader of the fascist movement known as the Russian National Unity (RNU), claims that he owes his worldview to a grandfather who was a Central Committee official and "one of the organizers of the struggle with the cosmopolitan Yids in the late 1940s" (Allenworth 1998, p. 228). True, no such grandfather existed (see chapter 6), but it is significant all the same that Barkashov should have invented him.

Fascist Tendencies in the Post-Stalin Period

The process of de-Stalinization undertaken by Nikita Khrushchev led to a return to something approximating the balance between the two components of official Soviet ideology that had preceded Stalin's rise to power. Official Soviet ideology shifted away from fascism. Another consequence of de-Stalinization, however, was the emergence of underground opposition groups of various political orientations, and among these there were some groups of fascist youth. According to some writers, the activity of the participants was "playful" or "romantic" in character. The political scientists Alexander Galkin and Yuri Krasin attribute this phenomenon to the influence of the popular television serial *Seventeen Moments of Spring*, which romanticized the leaders of the Third Reich. According to former party official Alexander Yakovlev, the Central Committee received information in the late 1950s about fascist youth groups being formed throughout the country, but the leadership did not regard these groups as a threat and ignored them, preferring that rebellious young people be against the "Judeo-Masons" rather than against the government.[24] Another source does, however, refer to three tiny fascist parties that were active in Moscow at this period and were repressed (Verkhovskii and Pribylovskii 1996, p. 5). Presumably fascists were tolerated only provided that their propaganda did not directly attack the regime.

In the 1960s, a small fascist underground existed in Leningrad. One group, led by Alexander Fetisov, espoused a fusion of fascism and Stalinism, while another group, led by Nikolai Braun, combined fascism with monarchism (Verkhovskii and Pribylovskii 1996, p. 6).

Of much greater significance for the future was the appearance, following the fall of Khrushchev, of fascist tendencies in certain official and semi-official circles. In the late 1960s, the officially recognized All-Russian Society for the Preservation of Monuments of History and Culture, informally known as "the Russian Club," took on the role of a gathering place for both moderate and extreme "patriots."

Most disturbing was the *Code of Morals* that Moscow University philosophy student Valery Skurlatov prepared in 1965 at the behest of Valery Trushin, Secretary of the Moscow city committee of the Communist Youth League (Verkhovskii and Pribylovskii 1996, pp. 6–7). This document, while not explicitly rejecting communist doctrine, pointed clearly in the direction of fascism. Skurlatov called, *inter alia*, for "the resurrection of the cult of the soldier" (for "there is no baser calling than to be a thinker"), "the militarization of youth from primary school onwards," "the corporal punishment, branding, and sterilization of women who give themselves to foreigners," "the revival of ancient peasant customs," and "various forms of stratification of a caste type" (Yanov 1978, pp. 170–72).

The early Brezhnev period was marked by a relatively open struggle between different tendencies in the Soviet political and intellectual elite. In 1972, the national-bolsheviks were able to consolidate their position with the defeat of Yakovlev, the main representative of the internationalists in the Central Committee apparatus, who was "exiled" as ambassador to Canada (Yanov 1978, pp. 57–60). Between 1971 and 1974, a journal of "the loyal patriotic opposition" titled *Veche*, edited by Vladimir Osipov, was permitted to appear (Yanov 1978, pp. 62–84; Verkhovskii and Pribylovskii 1996, pp. 8–10; see also chapter 8). Besides Osipov and his friends, there gathered in Moscow from the 1960s a small closed circle of "New Right" intellectuals, interested in mysticism, metaphysics, and other esoteric subjects ("Ia liubliu" 1993, pp. 50–51; see chapter 7).

Finally, in 1978, three clubs joined together to form the *Pamyat* [Memory] society, soon to become the main organizational vehicle for the Russian nationalists. *Pamyat* functioned at first under the patronage of the Ministry of Aviation Industry, then from the end of 1982 under that of the Administration of the Moscow Metro. In 1984, the artist and photographer Dmitry Vasilyev joined the society, becoming its secretary in late 1985. Vasilyev, whom Alexander Yakovlev (among others) regards as an agent of the KGB, for the first time made the theme of the Jewish world conspiracy, until then promoted only in private, part of the public repertoire of *Pamyat* (Iakovlev 1998; Verkhovskii and Pribylovskii 1996, pp. 10–13). *Pamyat* was to serve as the seedbed out of which numerous Russian nationalist groups of either a reactionary or a fascist type were to emerge in the late 1980s and the 1990s.

The "patriotic" groupings of the late Soviet period took diverse attitudes toward the ruling regime. At one extreme was the loyalist "Russian-Soviet" or national-bolshevik tendency. These people were close to, and protected by, the official establishment—for instance, the group around *Veche*—or even, like the Moscow Komsomol officials, inside the establishment. At the other extreme were openly anti-Soviet dissident Russian nationalists of various kinds, such as the All-Russian Social-Christian Union for the Liberation of the People (Yanov 1978, pp. 21–38). In between were figures like Alexander Solzhenitsyn (before he broke decisively with the regime) and the artist Ilya Glazunov, whose relationship to the regime was characterized by a measure of ambiguity (Wimbush 1978; Spechler 1990).

Thus, there existed in Soviet Russian society three main tendencies on "the national question": the internationalist "Soviet" tendency, national-bolshevism, and (openly or latently) anti-Soviet Russian nationalism. The regime was divided between the first and the second of these tendencies, the "patriotic" movement between the second and the third.

The impact that the three tendencies had on the general public was explored by Vladislav Krasnov (Krasnov 1986). His method was an ingenious one: he analyzed over two thousand comments left by visitors in the guest books of exhibitions of the art of Ilya Glazunov, held in Moscow in 1978 and in Leningrad in 1979. Glazunov's work is permeated by a strongly Russian nationalist spirit. Most of the comments (77 percent) were positive in tone, but some positive comments identified Glazunov with both Russian and Soviet patriotism (the national-bolshevik position), while others identified him with Russian as opposed to Soviet patriotism (the anti-Soviet nationalists). Of the minority (20 percent) who reacted negatively to Glazunov's art, over half (54 percent) gave esthetic reasons, but others criticized him for lack of Soviet patriotism (the Soviet internationalist position).

Among those Russian nationalists who were opposed to the Soviet regime, different ideological tendencies were detectable, and with the decline and collapse of the regime these differences naturally came to the forefront. The two major tendencies, both claiming allegiance to Christian Orthodoxy, were relatively moderate nationalists influenced by the Slavophile tradition, on the one hand, and more extreme nationalists, to whom the epithet "Black Hundreds" was commonly attached, on the other (Barghoorn 1980). In addition to the major Orthodox tendencies, there were on the margins a number of minor tendencies of a non-Orthodox character (pagan, Nazi, classical fascist, New Right, etc.).[25]

Thus, within that part of the Russian nationalist spectrum that might be considered fascist or fairly close to fascism, the Black Hundreds tendency, typified by *Pamyat*, was at this stage by far the most important. The term "Black Hundreds" is not used merely by way of analogy or metaphor. Although the inside story of how it came to pass has yet to be told, there are many indications that the Russian "patriots" of the late Soviet period had access to the literature of the Union of the Russian People (URP), and used it extensively in their own propaganda. A number of researchers have demonstrated cases in which they copied URP texts, making revisions that amount only to minor paraphrases. For example, a text included in the bulletin of the Soviet Embassy in Paris in 1972 was almost identical to a 1906 article on "the Jewish question" by Rossov, a member of the URP.[26] Also indicative of the significance attached to the legacy of the Black Hundreds was a pamphlet, published in 1991 by the Military Publishing House with a print run of one million, that purported to "tell the truth, for the first time in the Soviet period, about the Union of the Russian People" (Ostretsov 1991).[27] Indeed, a couple of the groups formed in the early 1990s claimed the title of direct successors to the Black Hundreds.[28]

Central to the ideology of both the old and the new Black Hundreds was the revelation of an age-old Jewish (or in more recent times, a Judeo-Masonic) conspiracy to dominate the world and destroy its nations. This message was disseminated by "patriotic" publicists throughout the late Soviet period, in books, in the press, and in lectures, on a semiofficial level but on a very large scale. It should be noted that the world Jewish conspiracy, presumably for the purpose of camouflage, was referred to as "Zionism," so that this word—and, correspondingly, "anti-Zionism"—acquired in Soviet and post-Soviet Russia a dual usage: on the one hand, it had the generally accepted meaning of the movement to build a Jewish state in Palestine, and on the other, it had the special meaning of the supposed conspiracy to establish Jewish world dominion.[29]

Lev Gumilyov

We have already encountered Lev Gumilyov as a pupil of Pyotr Savitsky. He is best known, however, for his writings on the life cycle of the "ethnos" or ethnic group, which were widely publicized and highly praised by the "patriotic" part of the Soviet establishment in the 1980s. His most important book was even brought out by Progress Publishers in English (Gumilev 1990). As Gumilyov remains after his death an influential ideologist of Russian nationalism, and the only one whose ideas are to any great extent original, and as his thought has been characterized by some critics as fascist (Ianov 1995, pp. 201–14; Raskin 1996), we should consider him as a possible source of a fascist tradition in post-Soviet Russia.[30]

For Gumilyov, the ethnos is a bio-cosmic entity: a living being that passes through a natural cycle of birth, maturation, aging and death, and that receives its life-energy in "passionary" bursts from sources in outer space. It is these bursts that bring about the birth of an ethnos, its conquests of territory and statehood, and its scientific, technological, and cultural progress. A number of compatible "ethnoses" may fuse into a super-ethnos. Some ethnoses, like the Jews, and some "chimera" states, like the United States, are dangerous and parasitic on healthy ethnoses and states.

Gumilyov therefore certainly espoused an extreme form of organic nationalism that can easily be used to justify military aggression, racism, ethnic cleansing, and perhaps even genocide. He can be considered a fascist in the popular sense. He is not, however, a fascist in the sense in which I have defined it, lacking as he does any sense of a historical watershed between premodernity and modernity. Nor does there seem to be room for a myth of palingenesis in Gumilyov's ethnology. An ethnos cannot be reborn after its death, and there is no point in resisting the natural and inevitable decadence or decay of old age. Fortunately, the problem of decadence is no concern of the contemporary Russian ethnos, which is only 500 years old—according to Gumilyov's reckoning—and still bursting with youthful vigor.

Contemporary Impact

Does Russia have a living fascist tradition?

So far as the intellectual side of the matter is concerned, we cannot but conclude from this survey that Russia's fascist tradition, to the extent that it can be said to exist, is—by comparison with the fascist traditions of Italy, Germany, or even France—a very weak and fragmented one. Of the galaxy of prerevolutionary Russian philosophers, only one, Konstantin Leontiev, may reasonably be regarded as a precursor of fascism. Among the authors of the White emigration, only the publicist Ivan Solonevich comes really close to fascism, and even he did not complete the transition. Neither does Lev Gumilyov, the only original Russian nationalist thinker produced by the Soviet era, qualify, for all his racism, as a full-fledged fascist.

We must also take into account the limited direct impact of these writers on the Russian public. Studies of Leontiev cannot be read by many outside the narrow circles of literary and historical scholars.[31] The collected works of Solonevich (as also those of Savitsky) were produced with a print run of only 5,000.

The public impact of Lev Gumilyov has been rather greater. His ideas have been publicized quite widely; the print runs of his books have averaged 50,000. Moreover, an image has been created of Gumilyov as a great man, criticism of whom is sacrilege. Following the publication of a critique of Gumilyov by Alexander Yanov in the journal *Free Thought* [*Svobodnaia mysl'*], Yanov was excoriated on television by a group of "patriotic" intellectuals for insulting a sacred national figure. He searched in vain for Russian colleagues willing to take part in a public dialogue about Gumilyov; many of those he approached frankly admitted that they were frightened to do so (Ianov 1995, pp. 26–27).

Of course, the indirect impact of all these authors must also be taken into account. To what extent do contemporary Russian nationalist publicists read prerevolutionary and émigré "classics" and then, through the medium of their own writing, pass key ideas on to a wider readership?

In an attempt to answer this question, I examined the collection of fifty programmatic documents of twenty-seven Russian nationalist organizations published by the Panorama group (Verkhovskii and Pribylovskii 1996, pp. 105–83). Only two of the fifty documents make any reference to prerevolutionary authors (Speransky, Gogol, Dostoevsky, Pobedonostsev,

Khomyakov), and only one to émigré authors (Berdyaev, Ilyin).[32] This result suggests that contemporary Russian nationalists are not very interested in demonstrating their adherence to an intellectual tradition.[33]

Another interesting case study is provided by the Manifesto for the Rebirth of Russia, composed on behalf of the moderate nationalist Union for the Rebirth of Russia,[34] the precursor of the Congress of Russian Communities (see chapter 3). In their preface, the authors of the manifesto state that they have used the ideas of eight named Russian philosophers (*Manifest* 1996, p. 168). Four of these are writers whom we have analyzed in this chapter: the liberal imperialist Danilevsky, the reactionary proto-fascist Leontiev, and the monarchist (and more or less fascist) émigrés Solonevich and Ilyin. Another is Konstantin Pobedonostsev, head of the Holy Synod under Alexander III, the very symbol of tsarist official reaction. Finally, the authors include some well-known religious philosophers of the late Tsarist period—Vladimir Solovyov, Sergei Bulgakov, and Nikolai Berdyaev, all three of them (though especially Berdyaev) of a rather liberal disposition in both theology and politics. Thus, the authors of the manifesto claim to have been influenced by writers of diverse, often opposing, views: by imperialists (Leontiev, Danilevsky) as by anti-imperialists (e.g., Solovyov),[35] by anti-Semites (Solonevich) as by opponents of anti-Semitism (Berdyaev),[36] and so on. Judging by the contents of the manifesto, its authors seem to have been influenced the most by Solovyov—that is, the document is in fact permeated by a spirit a good deal less reactionary than the list of the eight philosophers would suggest.

A perusal of other literature associated with contemporary Russian nationalism reveals similarly scattered evidence of the direct influence of prerevolutionary and émigré writers. For example, one may note how the prolific nationalist ideologist Igor Shafarevich derives his ideas on "people's monarchy" from Ivan Solonevich (Znamenski 1996, p. 45). Eurasianist ideas have been aired quite widely, especially as a result of the literary activity of Alexander Prokhanov, a publicist and author of a series of novels and editor of the major nationalist journal *Zavtra* (formerly *Den*), which has a print run of about 100,000. The publications of Alexander Podberyozkin's "Spiritual Heritage" Foundation, which exerted a formative influence on Gennady Zyuganov's amalgam of Russian imperial nationalism and communism, pay homage to Danilevsky and Leontiev as well as to Gumilyov and the Eurasianists.[37] Nevertheless, from a reading of contemporary Russian nationalist literature one does not get the impression that the impact of the ideas of prerevolutionary and émigré writers has been very strong or very deep.

To put this point in a broader context, it may be noted that a failure effectively to revive pre-Soviet traditions of political thought is characteristic not only of Russian nationalists. Seventy years of totalitarian rule have broken the continuity of intellectual effort across the whole of the political spectrum. Thus, the eminent historian Roy Medvedev regretfully notes that "today the names and legacy of the ideologists of [prerevolutionary] Russian liberalism—Struve, Chicherin, Novgorodtsev, Kavelin, Druzhinin—have been forgotten" (Medvedev 1998, p. 62).

The main intellectual tradition available to today's Russian nationalists is that of the Slavophiles. From the point of view of the more extreme nationalists, and especially for those inclined in the direction of fascism, Slavophilism is a mixed blessing. While valued as a nativist and traditionalist alternative to the westernizing tradition, Slavophile thought abounds in vague and sentimental speculation about "the Russian soul" that some extreme nationalists find irritating, useless, or even harmful. The contemporary Russian fascist writer Eduard Limonov, leader of the National-Bolshevik Party (see chapter 7), exclaims in exasperation:

> That fucking Russian Soul! The fact of having it should be considered high treason, punishable by death, by strangulation perhaps. (Limonov 1998f)[38]

A crucial case in point is the Slavophile idea of the "all-worldness" or the "pan-humanity" [*vsemirnost', vsechelovechnost'*] of the Russian spirit, the expression of which Dostoevsky[39] perceived in Pushkin:

> Russia's all-worldness, its responsiveness, and the real and deep kinship of its genius with the genius of all times and peoples of the world. . . . To all these peoples [Pushkin] declared that the Russian genius knows them, has understood them, has touched them as kin, that it may be fully re-embodied in them, that to the Russian spirit alone is given the future mission of uniting the whole gamut of nationalities and overcoming all their contradictions. (Dostoevskii 1877)

Imperial arrogance and self-delusion, no doubt, but hardly the stuff out of which fascism is made.

Whether Russia has a fascist tradition in the specifically political sphere depends, as always, on what we mean by fascism. Russia certainly has a tradition of autocracy, imperialism, militarism, and genocide. Both Ivan the Terrible and Stalin belong to this tradition, not to mention such lesser luminaries as Danilevsky and Gumilyov. So in the popular sense Russia does have a fascist tradition. And ever since the modern age first made a significant impact on Russia at the time of Peter the Great, Russia has had a reactionary tradition, with a long line of authors and statesmen wishing for nothing better than to restore a fading past. The Black Hundreds at the beginning of the twentieth century lay firmly in the reactionary tradition and, as we have seen, the Black Hundreds are alive and well as the twenty-first century commences.

And yet reaction and fascism (in the scholarly sense) are not one and the same. Only in emigration did Russians ever create a sizable fascist movement. Apart from the small National Front and Front for National-Revolutionary Action,[40] today's Russian nationalists do not seem particularly interested in paying homage to the memory of émigré fascism or in reviving its tradition. There are many reasons why there may be a threat of fascism in contemporary post-Soviet Russia, but the existence of a strong historical tradition of fascism is not among them.

3
Nationalists, Communists, Orthodox Christians, and Neo-Pagans

In this chapter I try to situate the issue of fascism in the context of four ideological movements that occupy a more or less important place in the society of post-Soviet Russia: Russian nationalism in a broad sense, communism, Orthodox Christianity, and neo-paganism.

Of these four movements, Russian nationalism occupies the central place, inasmuch as it widely overlaps each of the others. There is no need to prove here that fascist tendencies exist within contemporary Russian nationalism, as several of the specific organizations embodying such tendencies are to be examined in chapters 5 through 8. But if we are to view Russian fascism in proper perspective, we need to map the ideological structure of Russian nationalism and show the relationship between fascism and the other types of nationalism within this structure.

In considering the communist, Orthodox Christian, and neo-pagan movements, we shall seek to answer the following questions: Do these movements contain tendencies that can be regarded as actually or potentially fascist? If so, how significant are such tendencies in determining the overall character of the movements in question? How are they likely to develop in the future?

Russian Nationalism and Fascism

Russian nationalism is an extremely complex and multifaceted phenomenon. For the purposes of this study, it is not necessary to analyze and classify all its varieties. It will suffice to consider the "moderate–extreme" dimension within Russian nationalism, which is recognized in one way or another by most Western and Russian observers, and then to locate Russian fascism within the most extreme of the categories identified.

It is useful to distinguish first between a vague "centrist" Russian nationalism on the one hand and stronger and more doctrinally determinate versions of Russian nationalism on the other. Centrist nationalism is the kind that one finds in the mainstream of Russian politics: it is represented by such well-known figures as former prime minister Viktor Chernomyrdin, General Alexander Lebed, Moscow mayor Yuri Luzhkov, and the current president Vladimir Putin, and appeals to a large though not overwhelming proportion of the Russian population. The stronger versions of nationalism are espoused by the various organizations that make up Russia's self-styled "patriotic movement"; they have more limited public appeal.[1] The "patriotic" organizations may in turn be divided into those that stand for a relatively moderate kind of Russian nationalism, such as Dmitry Rogozin's Congress of Russian Communities and Sergei Baburin's Russian All-People's Union, and those that advocate Russian nationalism of a more extreme nature. Some, but not all, of the more extreme "patriotic" organizations can be characterized as fascist. A similar distinction can be drawn in Russian cultural life between the representatives of "enlightened patriotism"—for example, the late historian of culture, Academician Dmitry Likhachev, the writer Sergei Zalygin (also recently deceased), who was editor of the liberal literary journal *Novyi mir* in the late 1980s, and Alexander Solzhenitsyn—and the more extreme nationalist men of letters such as Yuri Vlasov, Eduard Limonov, and the philosopher Alexander Dugin (see chapter 7).

What specific criteria might be used in assessing the degree of "moderation" or "extremism" of a given variant of Russian nationalism? Different authors prefer to use different criteria, and thereby obtain somewhat different results, because an organization that is moderate according to one criterion may be more extreme according to another. For example, the Russian All-People's Union may be considered fairly extreme in terms of its territorial aspirations, aiming as it does at forming a "Russian Union" [*rossiiskii soiuz*] within the borders of the former Soviet Union. It may, however, be considered moderate in the sense that its conception of "Russianness" is primarily civic [*rossiiskii*] rather than ethnic [*russkii*] in character. The Congress of Russian Communities entertains more moderate territorial aspirations, but is more extreme in the stress it places on the ethnic aspect of national identity (Ingram 1999). Moreover, the best criteria for distinguishing between centrist nationalism and the nationalism of the "patriotic movement" are not necessarily the best for distinguishing between more moderate and more extreme "patriotic" organizations.

Two criteria distinguish fairly well between centrist nationalism and other varieties. One such criterion pertains to the idea, generally taken for granted in the "patriotic movement" but not salient in the discourse of centrist nationalism, that Russia is destined to follow a special historical path of her own. Another criterion is the attitude taken toward the existing institutional and territorial form of Russian statehood—that is, the Russian Federation. Centrist politicians may wax eloquent about restoring Russia's status as a great power,[2] but they are sufficiently realistic to acknowledge at least the formal independence of the other post-Soviet states. On the whole, they are even prepared to recognize existing post-Soviet borders, although Yuri Luzhkov's campaign to reclaim Sevastopol, Russia's "city of glory," from Ukraine was an exception.[3] By contrast, no self-respecting "patriot" is willing to accept the Russian Federation—"RF-land" [*erefiia*], as some of them contemptuously call it—as the final and legitimate embodiment of Russian statehood.[4]

It is more difficult to find criteria that distinguish sharply between the relatively moderate and the more extreme wings of the "patriotic movement." One possible criterion has been suggested by Alan Ingram: extreme nationalists blame the sorry plight of Russia and the Russians on a powerful conspiracy of geopolitical or ethnic enemies, whereas moderate nationalists are prepared to consider whether the Russians might themselves have been at fault (Ingram 1999).[5] As the enemy conspiracy is often, though not always, perceived as being Jewish or Judeo-Masonic in character, militant anti-Semitism may serve as an alternative criterion of extremism. The absence of anti-Semitism—or at least of anti-Semitism in a crude and open form—is commonly regarded in Russian society as the mark of a civilized or enlightened patriot. (Some other ethnic minorities are not so fortunate in this regard: for instance, Vladimir Putin's reputation as a moderate or centrist is not blemished by his anti-Chechenism.) Another criterion that may serve to distinguish between moderate and extreme "patriots" is the attitude taken toward democracy. Moderates typically strive to combine their "patriotism" with an attachment to democracy, ideally democracy of a specifically "Russian" kind[6]; extremists tend to be either indifferent to democracy or hostile to it as an alien philosophy.

Extreme Russian nationalism comes in a great variety of forms, but two main branches can be identified. One branch is the backward-looking Orthodox monarchism that draws inspiration from the Black Hundreds tradition, as exemplified above all in *Pamyat.* The other branch is fascism. We can therefore locate fascism as one of the branches of the extreme type of Russian nationalism. As is the case with any other nationalism, there is no justification for branding Russian nationalism as a whole as actually or incipiently fascist, nor is there any justification for denying the link between Russian nationalism and fascism.

The Communist Party of the Russian Federation

Many observers, both in Russia and in the West, argue that it is not from the relatively small and marginal extreme nationalist organizations to which the later chapters of this book are devoted that the most serious threat of Russian fascism comes. The most serious threat, they declare, derives from the much larger and more influential communist movement, above all from the Communist Party of the Russian Federation (CPRF), because the ideology dominant within what still goes under the name of the communist movement is no longer communist, but fascist or close to fascist.

The most unequivocal of these observers go so far as to claim that "the CPRF is in effect a fascist party, both at the top and at the provincial grassroots" (Radzikhovskii 2000), or that "the CPRF has for a long time been following the ideas not of communism and socialism, but of national-socialism" (Proshechkin 1999). Others make more nuanced judgments. An open letter circulated by the anti-fascist magazine *Tum-balalaika* calls the CPRF "an ultra-conservative party approaching fascism," while Gorbachev Foundation analyst Dmitry Furman writes:

> In the ideology of our largest party, the CPRF, fascistoid features are so salient that one has to be blind and deaf not to notice them.

Thus, according to Furman the ideology of the CPRF is not fully fascist, but merely has certain features that resemble fascist ones.

The task of assessing these claims with respect to the CPRF requires us to tackle two questions. First, to what extent does the "ideology of state patriotism"[7] expounded in several books and numerous articles by the leader of the CPRF, Gennady Zyuganov, qualify as a fascist ideology? Second, to what extent is Zyuganov's ideology dominant within the CPRF? It will also be pertinent to consider future prospects: Is Zyuganovism likely to become more or less dominant within the CPRF?

Zyuganovism and Fascism

Gennady Zyuganov's nationalism is a state nationalism that seeks to restore the might of Russia as a great power. To this end, it is in his opinion necessary to reassert "the continuity of the history of the Fatherland and of our national self-consciousness" by means of a "Russian idea" that will integrate into a new synthesis the heritage of the "White" Russia of the tsars and that of the "Red" Russia of the communist regime:

> Having reunited the "red" ideal of social justice . . . and the "white" ideal of statehood infused with national significance, . . . Russia will at last acquire . . . social harmony and great-power might. (Ziuganov 1996, pp. 220–21)

The ideological allegiances of the past that the labels "red" and "white" represent are to be superseded by a new patriotic consensus. "Today," we are assured by the compilers of a pamphlet distributed in support of Zyuganov's 1996 presidential election campaign, "people are divided not by the color of their party tickets, but by their attitude to Russia and its people. . . . If Zyuganov wins, all patriots—communists and non-party people, Orthodox Christians and Moslems, entrepreneurs and workers—will be able to come to agreement with one another. For they have a common language, the language of compassion for people and love for the Fatherland" (Il′ina 1996, pp. 3–4). Thus Zyuganov delegitimizes the quintessential Marxian cause of the workers' class struggle, at least insofar as "patriotic" employers are concerned, and he reduces political categories to moral ones: on one side are the good people who love Russia, on the other the evil people who hate her.

For Zyuganov, Russia is one of those "territorial, economic, cultural, and religious communities" known as civilizations, and "the historical process is to a great extent the process of the interrelation, competition, and alternation of civilizations on the Earth" (Ziuganov 1995a, p. 10). In developing his conception of the confrontation of civilizations and of the "Russian idea," Zyuganov acknowledges his debt to a long line of Russian thinkers, including Danilevsky, Leontiev, Solovyov, Berdyaev, and Gumilyov and the Eurasianists, as well as to Spengler, Toynbee, and Francis Fukuyama (Ziuganov 1995b, pp. 16–17). Zyuganov is also strongly influenced by the classical geopolitical ideas of Sir Halford Mackinder, who viewed history in terms of a recurrent struggle between oceanic and continental powers (Parker 1985; Razuvaev 1998). Class struggle does not disappear from the picture completely, but is relegated to the background as one of the intrasystemic factors operating within individual states in specific contexts such as employment and production. At the global level, the most serious fault-lines are said to be geopolitical (Atlanticism versus Eurasia), socioeconomic (rich North versus poor South), interracial, interethnic, and interconfessional.

Zyuganov's views on foreign policy correspond to his Eurasianist geopolitics. Russia should promote the emergence of a "Eurasian continental bloc" capable of thwarting the efforts of the foremost "oceanic power," the United States, to unify and homogenize the world under its hegemony in a "new world order." The goal of this strategy is to establish a balanced multipolar system of fruitful interaction among heterogeneous and self-sufficient civilizations (Ziuganov 1995b, pp. 20, 71, 92).

I find myself in full agreement with Professor Vladimir Zaharescu, who argues that with Zyuganov one is no longer dealing merely with a "national communism," in the sense of a communism that has been adapted to national specificities and has incorporated elements of nationalism, but rather with a "communist nationalism": nationalism is explicitly elevated to the status of the goal, while communism is demoted to a means that may serve this goal (Zaharescu 1998). Zyuganovism should certainly be classified as a variant of Russian nationalism, and a fairly extreme one at that (Karatnycky 1996). Of course, this does not suffice to make Zyuganov a fascist in the sense defined in chapter 1, any more than Danilevsky and the Eurasianists, from whom Zyuganov borrows his main concepts, were fascists.

The aspect of Zyuganov's ideology that commentators most usually have in mind when speaking of "fascistoid" or "fascist" features is his anti-Semitism. Anti-Semitism is not an overt part of Zyuganov's discourse, but unmistakable hints are dropped frequently enough. For example, Jewish names are prominent among those decried as haters of Russia,[8] but they never figure among those praised as lovers of Russia. Zyuganov tries to avoid making any direct public statements on the Jewish question, considering that it is the sort of issue best dealt with discreetly by state leaders, as it was in Soviet times. When forced to react to scandals raised by the more overt anti-Semites in the CPRF, he expresses sympathy for the way they feel about Jews, but urges them to behave with more restraint and decorum (Ziuganov 1998).

It is not, however, simply a matter of Zyuganov harboring a personal dislike for Jews. There are signs that he believes in the existence of a world Jewish conspiracy. He refers quite often to an "international financial oligarchy" or a "cosmopolitan elite of international capital" that controls the Western world from behind the scenes—expressions that are generally understood as euphemisms for the Jewish world conspiracy. The word "Zionism" is likewise used with the same connotation (Zaharescu 1998; Proshechkin 1999). Zyuganov, however, inherits this idea not from Nazism, but from the semi-official anti-Semitism of the late Soviet period, and indirectly from the Black Hundreds (see chapter 2). This too does not count as evidence of fascism as such, although the question does arise of the potential of Zyuganovism to develop in the direction of fascism.

It is pertinent that Zyuganov is a great admirer of Stalin's "new course" of 1944–1953, which sought to make the Soviet regime more "Russian" and included a strong anti-Semitic component. Zyuganov has speculated that if only Stalin had lived five to seven years longer, he would have been able to complete his ideological perestroika and make it irreversible, and within ten to fifteen years the USSR would have "completely overcome the negative spiritual consequences of the revolution." De-Stalinization was, from this point of view, a terrible historical setback for Russia (Ianov 1996). We may infer that Zyuganov sees himself as finishing the job that Stalin left unfinished at his death. Just as we cannot exclude the possibility that Stalin might have moved in the direction of fascism had he lived longer, so we cannot exclude a similar evolution in the event that Zyuganov comes to power. But the likelihood does not seem very great: Zyuganov's ideas may possess some fascist potential, but the coherence and "revolutionary" élan necessary to realize this potential fully are lacking.

Zyuganov and Intraparty Pluralism

Although the CPRF is far from democratic in its internal workings, it is not a monolithic structure tightly controlled by a single man or a small oligarchic group. It operates according to the principle of "democratic centralism," which is supposed to combine diversity of opinion and free discussion with unity and discipline in the implementation of decisions once reached.[9] Groups of like-minded members are not allowed to constitute themselves formally as factions, but they are nonetheless part of the informal reality of party life, as are divergent social and institutional interests and cliques based on personal connections.

Many members and informal party groups have been and are ambivalent or hostile to the incorporation into party doctrine of Zyuganov's ideology. As these people have been able to exert some influence over the wording of the party program and other party documents, Zyuganov's personal views cannot automatically be equated with the official position of the party that he heads. This means that conclusions about the ideological character of the CPRF cannot be directly drawn from an analysis of Zyuganov's ideology. It is also necessary to delve into the internal politics of the CPRF.

A distinction needs to be made between the pattern of ideological tendencies existing within the CPRF, which has been fairly stable over time, and the shifting configuration of informal groups, especially those within the party bureaucracy and the CPRF fraction of Duma deputies. These groups are based in part on ideological sympathies, but they also often reflect such factors as disagreement over electoral tactics, institutional divisions of interest (for instance, Duma deputies versus regional leaders), and—always an important consideration in Russia—personal connections. For this reason, and also because intraparty politics is semiclandestine, it is difficult to assign clear and reliable ideological labels to some of the groups.

The CPRF's Ideological Field

Let us start by mapping the field of ideological tendencies within the CPRF. For our purpose it will suffice to envisage the ideological positions of CPRF members as points in a two-dimensional field, with one axis corresponding to a conventional left–right continuum on economic issues and the other axis indicating attitudes with respect to nationalism (from extreme Russian nationalism to extreme internationalism).

Along the left–right axis, the following four positions can be identified:

A. *extreme left*: in favor of return to a fully state-owned economy;
B. *left*: in favor of return to a predominantly state-owned economy, but with provision for a small private sector;
C. *center*: in favor of a mixed economy with the "commanding heights" remaining in state hands, as at the time of the New Economic Policy (NEP) in the 1920s—sometimes called "neo-nepism"; and
D. *right*: in favor of a mixed economy of an indeterminate nature—in effect, an orientation toward the Keynesian management of the existing post-Soviet economy, without drastic changes in its ownership structure.[10]

It is also useful to identify four positions along the nationalist–internationalist axis:

1. *ultranationalist*: Russian nationalists even more extreme than Zyuganov;
2. *nationalist*: Zyuganovite Russian nationalists;
3. *moderate-nationalist*: those who wish to moderate or reduce the salience of Zyuganovism in the party's ideology, but not to eliminate it altogether; and
4. *internationalist*: uncompromising opponents of Russian nationalism.

By combining letter with number codes, we can specify up to sixteen distinct positions in the two-dimensional field, from extreme left ultranationalists (A1) to right internationalists (D4). It should be noted that the two dimensions are independent of one another. Russian nationalists may be left-wing on economic issues, or they may be (by communist standards) right-wing. The same applies to internationalists. Similarly, advocates of a given economic program often part ways when it comes to issues relating to nationalism.

Groups Within the CPRF

What are the main groups among CPRF activists, officials, and Duma deputies, and where can they be situated on the ideological field that we have mapped?

The schema most popular among Western scholars of the CPRF identifies three groups—namely:

- "orthodox Marxist-Leninists," who occupy the left-internationalist corner of our ideological field (A4 and B4);
- "Marxist reformers," who are relatively right-wing on economic issues and moderately nationalist (C3 and D3); and
- Zyuganovite "nationalists," who are also right-wing on economic issues (C2 and D2).[11]

The leading figure among the "Marxist reformers" is the CPRF's deputy chairman Valentin Kuptsov, to whom many of the party's regional leaders (provincial committee secretaries) owe allegiance.[12] The "orthodox Marxist-Leninists" have no single leader; the individual most often mentioned as their representative is Richard Kosolapov, who in the late Soviet period was a prominent theorist and editor of *Kommunist*, the theoretical journal of the Communist Party of the Soviet Union. They are not in fact a single group, but a number of groups that have emerged at various times. All are relatively "orthodox" by comparison with other tendencies in the CPRF, but some, like Boris Kurashvili's "new socialists," are prepared to revise or modernize orthodox doctrine in significant respects.

However, a number of well-informed Russian observers propose alternative schemas for internal CPRF politics.[13] The author of one monograph presents intraparty politics essentially as a two-sided struggle between orthodox Marxist-Leninists and a "reformist current" that includes both Zyuganov's nationalists and the followers of Kuptsov (Kholmskaia 1998). Analysts at the Russian Academy of State Service perceive three groups, but not the same three as those mentioned by Western scholars: Zyuganov and Kuptsov are again lumped together in an "intraparty-centrist" group, while a distinct "radical state-patriotic" group led by Oleg Shenin makes its appearance (*Tekhnologiia* 1995, p. 74).

Most sophisticated and well-supported is the schema provided by experts of the information and research agency "Panorama" in a wide-ranging and in-depth study of Russia's left (Tarasov, Cherkasov, and Shavshukova 1997, p. 169). These researchers identify five groups:

- Zyuganov's personal "inner cabinet," all the members of which are fully committed to his ideology and leadership;
- a group of "pragmatist" central and regional party officials with good connections inside commercial structures and the state apparatus, headed by the CPRF's "main apparatchik and organizer" Valentin Kuptsov;

- a group of Duma deputies, comprising about half of the CPRF Duma fraction, who by and large support Zyuganov but want the party to take a stronger line against the executive branch[14];
- a group of radical Russian nationalists, such as General Albert Makashov and the secretary of the Leningrad party organization Yuri Belov; and
- a group of relatively orthodox Marxist-Leninists openly opposed to Zyuganov, leading figures of which are Teimuraz Avaliani, Tatyana Astrakhankina, and Richard Kosolapov.[15]

Taking these alternative schemas into account, I conclude that certain adjustments to the schema used by Western scholars are in order.

First, a fourth group of some significance has emerged besides the three customarily identified—namely a group of ultranationalists who are dissatisfied with Zyuganov because his anti-Semitism is not more militant and overt. Their positions may be placed at B1 and C1 on our map. The emergence of the ultranationalists allows Zyuganov to present himself as a centrist on the national question, embodying the golden mean between ultranationalism and internationalism.

Second, although there do exist distinct groups associated with Zyuganov and with Kuptsov, respectively, fuller cognizance needs to be taken of the close partnership that has existed between these two leading figures ever since the founding congress of the CPRF in February 1993.[16] Differences of ideological emphasis have not prevented Zyuganov and Kuptsov from working well together over a period of several years. On the key economic issues they see eye to eye: both have sought to edge the CPRF rightward against resistance from below, and to form an alliance with "national" entrepreneurs whose interests the party will represent in exchange for financial support. From this point of view, Zyuganov's ideology has served the purposes of Kuptsov and his party and business allies (in many cases one and the same) well enough, even if it is not really to their personal taste. Zyuganovism blurs and diverts attention away from divisive economic questions, and it made it possible to mobilize popular discontent against the Yeltsin regime on a "patriotic" rather than a leftist basis.[17] It is doubtful whether the Zyuganov–Kuptsov leadership could have pushed their economic agenda through without some such smokescreen.

Third, any realistic schema of intra-CPRF politics must take account of the huge power differential that separates the allied ruling groups of Zyuganov and Kuptsov, who between them control most of the party's organizational and financial resources, from all rival groups. The "orthodox Marxist-Leninists" may once indeed have been a mighty force, but today they occupy a peripheral position in the party's structure:

> The orthodox communist tendency is the largest numerically, but it is weak organizationally, and is hardly represented at all in the CPRF leadership. Its main base of support is rank-and-file members educated in Marxism-Leninism, leaders of some regional organizations, and a narrow circle of scholars, former higher education teachers of Marxism who belong to the organization "Russian Scholars of Socialist Orientation." (Buzgalin 1997)

It is true that verbal concessions have been made to orthodox rank-and-file communists critical of Zyuganovism. Thus, many changes were incorporated into the new party program adopted at the CPRF's Third Congress in January 1995, increasing the stress placed on "socialism" and generating an "intellectually incoherent synthesis of Marxism and the national idea" (Sakwa 1998, p. 141).[18] The political line of the CPRF was further modified, with a view to pleasing all tendencies, at the Fourth Congress in April 1997. However, when we shift our attention from the wording of documents to the composition of leading party bodies, we see that the new Central Committee elected at the Fourth Congress was dominated by the Zyuganovites to an even greater extent than its predecessor. In particular, the informal leader of the orthodox communists, Richard Kosolapov, was no longer a member of the Central Committee (Kholmskaia 1998, p. 73).

Prospects for Change

One Russian analyst has suggested that the dominant position of Zyuganovism within the party may be further consolidated when discontented orthodox communists, increasingly marginalized within the CPRF's organizational structure, give up all hope of changing the party from within and depart from its ranks en masse.[19] In this event, there would no longer be any need to mix Zyuganovism with leftist phraseology, and the CPRF might then abandon completely its identity as a left-wing movement and "become a state-patriotic organization pure and simple" (Kholmskaia 1998, pp. 72–73). However, such a drastic shift, presumably requiring a change in the party's name, might be opposed by moderate nationalists in the CPRF, who are reluctant to forgo the benefits of historical continuity. It is, moreover, unlikely that internationalists will disappear altogether from the CPRF. The place of the orthodox communists of the older generation will be taken by the many young communists who are less orthodox but no less internationalist. It is worthy of note that in some cities the communist youth organizations have participated in campaigns against the Russian National Unity ("Novye komsomol′tsy" 1999).

Another Russian analyst takes a less jaundiced view of the CPRF. Accusing those who equate the CPRF as a whole with Zyuganov and the ultranationalists of "anticommunist hysteria" and "ideological racism," he sees Russia's salvation from the threat of fascism in the emergence of a strong centrist bloc, an essential component of which has to be the "civilized segment" of the CPRF (Kostikov 1998). This presupposes either that the "civilized" communists, presumably Kuptsov and his group, somehow gain the upper hand in the party and marginalize the Zyuganovites or (more likely) a split of the CPRF into two parties.

The advent of Yevgeny Primakov's government in the wake of the August 1998 financial crash led some observers to hope for the imminent creation of such a strong centrist bloc on the basis of a deal between Primakov and Kuptsov over Zyuganov's head.[20] Was it not, after all, a member of Kuptsov's group, former head of the State Planning Agency (Gosplan) Yuri Maslyukov, who had been appointed first deputy prime minister in the Primakov government? However, no deal was to be struck, then or later, between Primakov and his centrist allies and Kuptsov and his group. Those who awaited such a deal underestimated the strength of intraparty discipline within the CPRF. For Kuptsov, the organization man par excellence, it was a deeply ingrained habit to preserve party unity at any cost. He is not easily to be tempted by the prospect of an alternative alignment with forces outside his party.

The CPRF: Summing Up

For all its internal tensions, the CPRF has shown itself to be quite a stable organism, possessing enormous inertia. Dramatic changes in any direction do not seem to be in the cards. It is very unlikely that Zyuganov's nationalist ideology will either wither away or become completely dominant in the CPRF in the near future. While rejecting formulations that exaggerate either the closeness of Zyuganovism to fascism or its preponderance in the CPRF, one cannot deny the element of truth in charges that the CPRF under Zyuganov's leadership has played a part in making conditions in Russia more conducive to the rise of fascism.

Left Communists Outside the CPRF

To the left of the CPRF, several other communist parties and organizations are active in Russia today. While all of them are small by comparison with the CPRF, some of them are fairly large in absolute terms. The most successful of the left-communist blocs that took part in the Duma elections of December 1999, Viktor Tyulkin's Communists and Working People of Russia for the Soviet Union, won 2.3 percent of the votes—and over 3 percent in the Far East—despite very limited financial resources (Pravosudov 1999b). The possibility cannot be excluded that a left-communist bloc may in a future election manage to surmount the 5 percent barrier and enter the Duma.[21]

One of the main lines of division among left communists outside the CPRF, as among communists within the CPRF, is that between Russian nationalists and orthodox "Soviet" internationalists. Within the largest of the left-communist parties, the Russian Communist Workers' Party (RCWP), this line of division was for a long time one factor in the rivalry between the two leading figures: Viktor Tyulkin, an orthodox internationalist communist, and Viktor Anpilov, a great-power nationalist and anti-Semite. The rivalry culminated in the expulsion of Anpilov from the RCWP in September 1996, since which time the RCWP has adopted a more consistent internationalist line.[22] Anpilov went on to become the leader of a new Stalinist bloc (Ofitova 1999). Also nationalist and Stalinist in orientation is the All-Union Communist Party (of Bolsheviks) of Nina Andreyeva.[23] There are, finally, a number of small left-communist organizations that profess allegiance to internationalism and democracy and advocate views reminiscent of those of the New Left: the Russian Party of Communists of Anatoly Kryuchkov, the Union of Communists of Alexei Prigarin, and the Union of Communists of Sergei Stepanov.[24]

The Russian Orthodox Church

Besides the Communist Party of the Russian Federation (CPRF), there is another very large organization in Russia that many consider to be a bastion of fascist tendencies—the Russian Orthodox Church (ROC).[25] The worldview of the fundamentalist wing of the ROC has in fact been characterized as "Orthodox fascism" (Steeves 1994).

Any fascist tendencies within the ROC are a matter of special concern for a number of reasons. First, between one-half and three-quarters of Russia's population—different surveys give estimates ranging from 51 to 75 percent (Krotov 1994; Bacon 1997)—now identify themselves as Orthodox believers. It is true that relatively few self-identified believers are deeply religious, and that most call themselves Orthodox because Orthodoxy has become socially respectable and fashionable,[26] but even nominal believers are presumably influenced by trends within the ROC to some degree. Second, the ROC enjoys considerable respect and moral authority in Russian society.[27] Intrachurch developments are, finally, of some political significance in light of the increasingly close relationship between the ROC and the state. Hierarchs of the ROC participate in official state ceremonies,[28] and in the armed forces Orthodox priests serve as chaplains and bless submarines, armaments, and boundary posts (Golts 1999). Faculties of Orthodox theology are opened in state institutions of higher education; a fifteen-minute Orthodox sermon completes each day's transmission on the educational channel of state television; and the ROC and the Ministry of Internal Affairs cooperate in persecuting religious minorities (Dennen 1997). The process of interpenetration of church and state has already gone so far that Russia as it enters the twenty-first century can no longer be considered a secular state.

As in the case of the CPRF, an assessment of fascist tendencies in the ROC requires us to consider first how close to fascism are those tendencies within the organization that some consider fascist, and then the strength and future prospects of the tendencies concerned. However, before I embark upon this assessment I would like to set the context with some general remarks about the nature of Orthodox religiosity in present-day Russia, the organizational structure of the ROC, and the phenomenon of intrachurch pluralism.

Orthodox Religiosity in Russia Today

At the Raifa Monastery

In June 1999, my colleague Terry Hopmann and I visited Kazan, the capital of the Republic of Tatarstan in the Volga region. Our kind host, Nail Mukhariamov, took us out into the countryside to see the old Raifa Monastery. A monk named Father Mark showed us around and recounted the history of the monastery. After the Bolshevik Revolution the buildings had been used as a prison: Father Mark pointed out the place where the prisoners were tortured, and described the tortures for us. He told us about the various icons that belonged to the monastery, and the miracles that were associated with each.

The monks had converted part of the monastery into a boarding school for abandoned children. There was a dormitory and a schoolroom for about twenty boys. Each boy, Father Mark assured us, was free to choose for himself whether or not he wanted to become a monk. On one table in the schoolroom stood four brand-new computers, donated by Boris Berezovsky following a visit he had made to the monastery. They were not plugged in. I strongly suspected that they had never been used: it was highly doubtful whether the monk-teachers knew how to use them. I found the school library on a little wooden shelf—a dozen or so children's books, old and dog-eared.

Our tour ended on the shore of the beautiful lake close to which the monastery was built. This, explained Father Mark, was formerly a sacred grove of a neighboring pagan people, the Mari, who burned down the first wooden church built here by Russian settlers. Then he revealed to us a truly remarkable miracle. The frogs that live around this lake do not croak! Never!

"Perhaps," I suggested tentatively, "they are not really frogs, but some other species that looks like a frog except that it can't croak, the poor thing. . . ."

"No, no. You take it and drop it in a different lake, and you'll hear how it croaks! But in this holy place it stays silent."

"But how do we know why it is silent, Father Mark? Perhaps in honor of the Mari gods?"

An Archaic Faith

Western Protestants may think that the age of miracles is past, but a belief in present-day miracles remains well within the mainstream of Russian Orthodoxy. So does a belief in demons. Russian folk belief envisaged hordes of invisible demons hovering all about (Ivanits 1989, ch. 3). Christianity preserved this vision, conceiving of demons as fallen spirits in thrall to Satan and offering new magical means of protection against them. A pamphlet issued by the Moscow Patriarchate of the ROC reminds the believer of an old saying: "In the house where there are no icons in the rooms, there live demons" (*Kak* 1998, p. 59). Another pamphlet on sale at church bookstalls warns of the dangers that the spiritually inexperienced face when they explore changed states of consciousness by indulging in meditation as taught by Oriental religions. As the defenseless soul ventures into the unseen world, it is set upon and led astray by beings who do not identify themselves, beings that are in fact demons (Rodion 1991; Eliseev 1995). The obsessive fear of demons is criticized by some Orthodox priests—for instance, Georgy Chistyakov, who complains of a religious treatise that it "says almost nothing about God but sees Satan everywhere, his actions and machinations and his innumerable servants" (Chistiakov 1996).

Not only demons but also live human beings number among the servants of Satan. In Russia as in the United States, there are many who believe that society is threatened by a secret, well-organized, and widely ramified Satanist movement.[29] Orthodox publishers distribute works with such titles as *People of Perdition. Satanism in Russia: Attempt at an Analysis* (*Liudi* 1994). Police chiefs are not immune: in opening remarks at a meeting of representatives of the Ministry of Internal Affairs and the ROC in January 1997, the then minister of internal affairs Colonel-General of Militia Vladimir Kolesnikov stated that it was "necessary to intensify the interaction between law enforcement agencies and the ROC in the struggle against the offensive of satanism" (Kolesnikov 1997). Not all government ministries, however, are doing as much as they should to fight satanism, and it appears that some may even have been infiltrated by satanists. Thus, on March 9, 2000, the Holy Synod of the ROC issued a statement accusing the Ministry of Taxes and Duties of using satanic symbols in some tax documents. The vigilant hierarchs had discovered bar codes containing the image of the apocalyptic number 666 ("Sataninskie" 2000).

There is, in general, a medieval quality in much of the religiosity of contemporary Russian Orthodoxy. Particularly alarming is the revival of the medieval belief that Jews commit ritual murders. In the most common version of this ancient myth, Jews kidnap a Christian child and use his or her blood to make unleavened bread (matzos) for the Passover. Another version arose in certain White émigré circles, who believed that the shooting of the last tsar and his family by the Bolsheviks in 1918 had been a Jewish ritual murder. (Some of those who took part in the shooting were of Jewish origin.) The ritual murder myth was widely current in tsarist Russia up to the beginning of the twentieth century, but was weakened by the Beilis trial of 1907, in which a Jew accused of ritual murder was successfully defended and found not guilty. In post-Soviet Russia (and also in Belarus) the myth has been revived. It is propagated, for instance, in a new novel by Alexander Prokhanov (Prokhanov 1999). There are even press reports of police arresting individuals on charges of ritual murder. Not only Jews but also non-Jews suspected of being "satanists" have been charged with ritual murder.[30]

While the belief in ritual murder is more characteristic of the fundamentalist wing of the ROC, my observation concerning the medieval quality of Orthodox religiosity applies to a significant degree even to the mainstream of the ROC. Even the most cautious attempts to adapt ritual or doctrine to present-day needs are denounced as "modernism." For example, Father Georgy Kochetkov was defrocked by Patriarch Alexy because he read the Gospel in his Moscow church not in Old Church Slavonic alone, which is the accepted practice, but first in Old Church Slavonic and then in contemporary Russian (Krotov 1994; Platonov 1998).

The archaic nature of Russian Orthodoxy reflects the destructive impact of the Soviet regime. The years immediately preceding 1917 were a time of cultural and intellectual ferment in the ROC as in Russian society as a whole. This "Silver Age" witnessed the public activity of a new generation of creative Orthodox theologians such as Nikolai Berdyaev, Sergei Bulgakov, and Semyon Frank, who saw themselves as independent philosophers rather than functionaries of church and state (Zernov 1963, pp. 155–58).[31] Had the Silver Age not been cut short by the Bolshevik dictatorship, it might have led to a modernized Orthodoxy. In the early Soviet period religion was completely suppressed; from 1944 onward, the ROC was again allowed to exist, but was kept under tight control. One of the purposes of Soviet state policy regarding religion seems to have been precisely that of preserving the church in an archaic condition and preventing its renewal or modernization. As Metropolitan Kirill among others has observed, the ROC was deprived of all opportunity to engage in intellectual or educational activity, and was allowed only to perform its "cult"—that is, rituals (Kyrlezhev 1995, p. 289; Ellis 1996, p. 101). An archaic church would be ill-equipped to appeal to the younger and more educated strata of society, or to provide a haven for intellectual and political dissent.

As a result, the Russian Orthodox Church has undergone no reformation since tsarist times comparable either to the original Protestant Reformation in the West or even to the more limited renewal of the Roman Catholic Church associated with the Vatican Council. The potential of the ROC for intellectual development remains very low on account of other legacies of the Soviet era—a weak system of theological education and a poorly educated priesthood.[32]

Organizational Structure and Intrachurch Pluralism

The ROC, like the CPRF, is a strictly hierarchical organization with some elements of collective leadership. The patriarch, currently Alexy II (Ridiger), has supreme authority and is greatly revered by believers. Below him come the ecclesiastical ranks of Metropolitan, Archbishop, Bishop, and Hegumen. The most important body of collective decision making—the ROC's Politburo, so to speak—is the Holy Synod, which meets every few weeks and consists of the patriarch, five or six permanent members—primarily metropolitans occupying key posts in the apparatus of the Moscow Patriarchate—and five rotating members. Broader gatherings are convened at irregular intervals: Bishops' Councils (in principle at least every two years) and Church Councils (less frequently).[33]

The ROC resembles the CPRF in another respect. Organized factions are not considered legitimate. One of the accusations that church liberals and church fundamentalists most commonly make against one another is that of creating a "subchurch" or "church within the church" (Alferov 1996). At the same time, an informal pluralism of religious and political opinion exists de facto. The main division is that between a liberal or modernizing wing that draws inspiration from the philosopher-theologians of the Silver Age and a fundamentalist or reactionary wing that looks back to a golden age of true Orthodoxy under the tsars. In political terms, the liberals tend toward Christian democracy—entailing, *inter alia*, the separation of church from state (Pashkov 1999)—and the fundamentalists toward extreme Russian nationalism. Between the two wings there lies a broad center that is theologically conservative and politically loyal to the government of the day. The center is represented at the top by Patriarch Alexy himself, although some of the other senior hierarchs are associated with either the liberal or the fundamentalist wing.

Although the two wings of the ROC are not organized as openly declared factions, they do not lack organization altogether. Certain institutions within the ROC are generally regarded as strongholds of the liberals—for example, the Bible-Theological Institute; others are known to all as strongholds of the fundamentalists—for example, the Cloister (or Monastery) of the Holy Trinity at Sergiev Posad (Steeves 1994). The two wings have their own journals—for example, the liberal *Russkaia mysl'* [Russian Thought] and the conservative *Pravoslavnaia beseda* [Orthodox Conversation]. There are also on each wing voluntary associations of Orthodox believers, such as the fundamentalist Orthodox Brotherhoods (Pospielovsky 1995).[34] Patriarch Alexy, however, has intervened to prevent the self-organization of the two wings from developing beyond a certain point, or from assuming too openly political a form. The action that he took in the mid-1990s to rein in and depoliticize the Union of Orthodox Brotherhoods is a case in point (Verkhovskii, Papp, and Pribylovskii 1996, pp. 46–47). He fears that the process would inevitably culminate in a split of the church—an eventuality that it is his overriding priority to avert (Liubin 1998).

The bipolar schema of intrachurch pluralism has been elaborated in an illuminating way by Alexander Kyrlezhev and Konstantin Troitsky, who are scholars at the Center for the Study of Religions and graduates of the Moscow Spiritual Seminary (Kyrlezhev and Troitskii 1993; Kyrlezhev 1995). These authors identify eight categories of Orthodox believer:

- "politicians" of a "patriotic" (that is, extreme Russian nationalist) orientation;
- "politicians" of a Christian democratic (that is, liberal) orientation;
- "ascetics" who cultivate their own spirituality, understood in terms of personal asceticism;
- "spiritual liberals" who seek enlightenment by means of an independent intellectual and spiritual quest;
- "ritualists" who are content simply to observe the prescribed rituals;
- "professional clerics" who understand their duty in terms of meeting the needs of the ritualists;
- "esthetes" who value religion primarily as a source of cultural and artistic values; and
- "centrists" who seek a "balanced and constructive" middle path between dogmatic adherence to tradition and radical change.[35]

Despite the large number of categories identified, the schema is basically bipolar, because the two types of "politicians" constitute the most dynamic forces in the ROC around and between which the other categories tend to cluster. Thus, the "ascetics" ally themselves with the "patriots," while the "spiritual liberals" join forces with the Christian democrats. The "centrists"—the category to which the authors count themselves as belonging—have some sympathy for the "spiritual liberals," but they also respect tradition and seek to occupy the middle ground. The mainly elderly or poorly educated "ritualists" and the "professional clerics" who cater to them, and also the intellectual "esthetes," lack a clear political stance: they follow the prevailing trend, although they are inclined more to the fundamentalist than to the liberal wing.

Metropolitan Yoann

By far the most influential single figure on the fundamentalist wing of the ROC has been the late Metropolitan Yoann of St. Petersburg and Ladoga.[36] Besides rising to occupy the second highest ranking position in the ROC after the patriarch himself, Yoann was a permanent member of the Holy Synod. He set out his views in several books as well as in numerous articles and interviews in the "patriotic" (including Zyuganovite) press.[37]

Yoann owed his considerable erudition wholly to the church. Born Ivan Snychev in 1927 to a peasant family, he became an Orthodox monk in 1946 at the age of nineteen. He was educated at the recently reopened seminary in Saratov, then at the ecclesiastical academy in Leningrad, where he specialized as a historian. In 1965 Yoann was appointed Bishop of Syzran. The next year he defended a master's dissertation at the Moscow Ecclesiastical Academy on dissent within the church in the aftermath of the declaration of loyalty to the Soviet regime made by Metropolitan Sergius Stragorodsky in 1927—a topic suggestive of his own hostility toward the Soviet regime, which distrusted him in turn. In 1990, when the then Metropolitan of Leningrad, Alexy Ridiger, was elected patriarch, Yoann was transferred from Kuibyshev to take his place (Steeves 1994).

Yoann's Teaching

At the roots of Metropolitan Yoann's worldview lies the assumption of "the eternal struggle of Satan against the human race" (Ioann 1995a, p. 17). Satan seeks above all to destroy the Russian Orthodox Church and its protector, the Russian state, because it is to the Russian people that God has entrusted the mission of preserving Christianity in its pure and undistorted form, thereby giving all other peoples the chance to turn to the true faith and save themselves right up to the last moments of history, which is to end with the Second Coming of Christ and Judgment Day (p. 18).

In pursuing his evil purpose, Satan relies on the Jews. The Jews believe that they are a people chosen by God for world dominion, but their real master is Satan, and it was at his bidding that they rejected Christ and declared war on the Christian church. However, Christianity spread. The Jews were no longer strong enough to fight it openly, so they invented a new weapon—the secret society. Among the secret societies used by the Jews have been "heretical medieval sects, pseudo-monastic orders at the time of the crusades, philosophical circles at the time of the Enlightenment, [and in our own era] scholarly associations, masonic lodges, . . . innumerable international banks, foundations, committees, conferences, and organizations" (Ioann 1995a, pp. 21–23) and—last but certainly not least!—the World Council of Churches.[38] By means of war, upheaval, and revolution, the Jews seek to crush Christianity, destroy national states, and unite the world under a single government with the Antichrist as dictator (p. 21):

> Over the ruins of once Christian states . . . is raised the perverse Tower of Babel of the "new world order." (p. 22)

For a long time Russia remained a mighty obstacle in the Jews' path, guaranteeing that their "terrible aims" could not be achieved, but by the nineteenth century the secret forces had grown so strong that they dared put the destruction of Russia on their agenda. The upheaval of 1917 was their "attempt to destroy Russia as God's Throne and the Russian people as the god-bearing people" (pp. 23–24). The same purpose was served by Gorbachev's perestroika (p. 17).

Yoann freely acknowledged the debt that his conception of the world Jewish conspiracy owed to *The Protocols of the Elders of Zion*. He admitted the possibility that *The Protocols* might be a forgery, but he insisted that in any case events have borne out the essential truth of their contents (Steeves 1994).

What kind of social order did Yoann wish to see in Russia? Not democracy, for he believed that democracy is impossible in principle:

> "People's power" . . . is a trick of corrupt politicians. . . . The people have never held power.
>
> In Russia the church has always had an interest in a strong, healthy, and responsible authority . . . to prevent civil conflicts, to bring up worthy citizens, . . . and to teach people to find the meaning of life in saving the soul, and not in the chase after money and glory. (Ioann 1995a, p. 37)

Yoann wished rather to restore the ideal of "the symphony of the secular and the spiritual authorities"—that is, the close cooperation and mutual support of church and state, with neither subordinated to the other but each fully responsible in its own sphere. The church "makes no claim to independent political leadership," but it takes "solicitous fatherly care . . . of the moral and spiritual aspects of political and social life" (pp. 37–38). Ultimately, however, primacy belongs to the spiritual sphere, for "the state is not an end in itself, but a means of preserving the faith." The secular ruler "disposes of power given him by God, and is responsible before God" (p. 35). This ideal of the equal "symphonic" partnership of church and state has its origin in pre-Petrine Muscovy, although even at that period it did not correspond at all closely to reality.[39] Yoann rejected the model of church-state relations that held sway between 1700 and 1917, when the church was formally subordinated to the state and functioned in effect as a government department (Warhola 1993).

Yoann's views concerning monarchism are set out in his address to the 1994 All-Russian Monarchist Convention. He described monarchy as the optimal, most harmonious, just, natural, and historically tested form of Russian statehood (Ioann 1995a, p. 339). "The supreme power of the Orthodox sovereign secures social stability and guards Russia from party divisions" (p. 340). However, the restoration of the monarchy must be preceded and accompanied by the spiritual rebirth and enlightenment of the Russian people (p. 339). It may be accomplished by convening an Assembly of the Lands [*zemskii sobor*], like the one that put an end to a similar time of confusion [*smuta*] in 1613. But this step should be taken only when the Russians are spiritually ready for it, because the Assembly of the Lands is no ordinary political gathering:

> The Assembly of the Lands is not a congress of people's representatives, but a symbolic spiritual and religious act that restores to the people, the state, and the church the unity that they lost in the time of confusion, that after repentance reconciles them with one another and with God, and that affirms God's Law as the renewed basis of Russian statehood. (p. 39)

Orthodox Fascism?

Is the teaching of the late Metropolitan Yoann Orthodox fascism?

If we are to rely on the definition of fascism developed in chapter 1, then the answer must be no. Yoann's teaching is a clear example of a purely reactionary ideology, resembling that of the Black Hundreds, which seeks to reanimate a lost premodern golden age. Unlike the fascists, Metropolitan

Yoann takes no account of the experience of modernity, and does not attempt to envisage a new revolutionary order within which traditional values are to be revived.[40] This is not, of course, in the least surprising, considering that Yoann led the whole of his life as a monk–scholar sequestered inside an archaic institution and that from the age of nineteen he had no further exposure to modern secular knowledge.

My general conclusion is that Yoann, and the great majority of the Orthodox fundamentalists whom he influenced and represented, should not be referred to as fascists. At the same time, I would like to qualify this statement with three provisos.

First, there are individual believers and priests who do cooperate with, or even actively support, fascist organizations, especially the Russian National Unity (RNU) (Clark 1997).[41] However, full-blown fascist convictions are not typical of the laity or priesthood of the ROC, even in its fundamentalist wing.

Second, I do not mean to deny the common ground that Orthodox fundamentalists share with fascists. Both reject the Enlightenment and democracy; both believe in a world Jewish conspiracy.

Finally, some of the activities of the Orthodox fundamentalists cannot but bring back to mind the experience of European fascism. One associates fascism, for instance, with the spectacle of the Nazis burning books on the public squares of German cities. The Nazis began burning books after they came to power. The Orthodox fundamentalists have not yet come to power in Russia, but they have already started burning books. Several public book-burnings by Orthodox believers have been reported in the Russian press in recent years. Thus, on May 2, 2000, "anti-Orthodox literature and [literature] not in accordance with the spirit and mentality of the Russian nation" was set aflame in the town of Nizhnevartovsk in the Khanty-Mansy Autonomous Province of northern Russia.[42] Another book-burning is reported to have occurred in the Urals city of Yekaterinburg in June 1998 on the orders of Bishop Nikon. The latter report is more specific concerning the kind of "anti-Orthodox literature" that was burned. The reader might suppose that it was antireligious propaganda left over from Soviet times or something of that sort. In fact, it was books by Orthodox theologians of liberal views that the bishop ordered to be burned (Platonov 1998).[43]

How Strong Is the Fundamentalist Wing?

Widely divergent views of the strength of the fundamentalist wing within the ROC have been expressed by different observers.

In March 1998, Professor Dmitry Pospielovsky of the University of West

Ontario, the leading historian of Russian Orthodoxy, sent a letter to Patriarch Alexy in which he conveyed his impression of the situation in the ROC, gained from his extensive travel in Russia:

> The overwhelming majority of the clergy are theologically illiterate and ignorant, . . . are engaged in terrorizing their flocks with all sorts of myths about the hostile world and the Judeo-Masonic conspiracy. . . . The obscurantist priests are prospering in their churches, and *The Protocols of the Elders of Zion* are being distributed.[44] (Platonov 1998)

A somewhat less alarming picture is drawn by the liberal hierarch Hegumen Innokenty. In his view, Orthodox fundamentalism is not in reality a very substantial force. He admits that the fundamentalists' "vigorous rejection of westernization" has a certain appeal, conditions in Russia being indeed comparable with those in Iran in the years preceding Ayatollah Khomeini's revolution against the Shah. However, the fundamentalists lack charismatic leaders, and they are unable to attract students and other educated people. They are active but socially marginal. Nonetheless, the fundamentalists do endanger the inner life and mission of the ROC, for they alienate "normal people" from the church and upset newcomers.[45] Moreover, the leaders of the ROC, who are not in close touch with "the real life of church people," perceive the fundamentalists as a more significant force than they really are, and for this reason make unnecessary concessions that serve to strengthen them (Innokentii 1996).

Hegumen Innokenty's last argument is a plausible one. Except for a brief period in the mid-1990s, when Patriarch Alexy was prepared to voice public criticism of Metropolitan Yoann, the Union of Orthodox Brotherhoods, and other fundamentalists,[46] the patriarch has avoided open confrontation with the fundamentalist wing of the ROC. For example, he has refused to accede to numerous requests that he speak out against the myth of Jewish ritual murder. In fact, the Holy Synod even gave a certain credence to the myth by requesting that the government commission appointed to investigate the circumstances of the murder of Tsar Nicholas II and his family by the bolsheviks in 1918 include on its agenda the question of whether it was a Jewish ritual murder, on the grounds that this was a matter of concern to many believers (Reznik 1998).[47] The patriarch, when asked at a press conference a question about his attitude toward the cooperation of some priests with the Russian National Unity, replied evasively:

> I am not personally aware of such facts, but the church distances itself in principle from all political organizations, and especially from those that

> preach fascist views. At the same time, the church does not have the right to refuse succor to Orthodox believers who belong to extremist groups. (Shevchenko 1997)

Why is the patriarch so reluctant to take a strong stand against fundamentalism, anti-Semitism, or even fascism in the ROC? His overriding priority, as already mentioned, is to avert the danger of splits within the church.[48] His anxiety on this score is exploited to the hilt by the fundamentalists, whole parishes of whom have threatened to leave the ROC and join its rival based in the Russian emigration, the Russian Orthodox Church Abroad (Komarov 1998).[49] I suspect, however, that this is not the only factor involved. Alexy and other "centrist" hierarchs may not personally share such fundamentalist beliefs as those in the Jewish world conspiracy and Jewish ritual murder, but as deeply conservative men they may well find the views of the fundamentalists *less* alien and disconcerting than those of the Western-oriented modernizing reformers in their church. Both the fundamentalists and Alexy himself believe that the West is trying to undermine and destroy Russia.[50] Or to take another example: the obsessive fear of demons that is part and parcel of mainstream Orthodox religiosity leads very easily to anti-Semitism. If one believes that demons live in a house that has no icons, and if one also knows that the Jews have no icons, then is it not logical to make the deduction—as did the medieval Orthodox writer Yoann Zlatoust[51]—that demons live in the houses and synagogues of the Jews?

So how strong is Orthodox fundamentalism? I find myself once again in agreement with the "Panorama" experts, who argue that fundamentalism is not currently very strong as an organized force, but that its potential strength is very great. Patriarch Alexy has at least done something to hold the fundamentalists in check; there is no guarantee that his successor will do likewise. "The political expression of fundamentalism may reappear if the situation in the ROC changes, . . . [depending] on who is patriarch and the political situation in the country" (Verkhovskii, Papp, and Pribylovskii 1996, p. 47).

Whither the ROC?

From their analysis of intrachurch dynamics, Kyrlezhev and Troitsky conclude that the ROC may be expected to drift gradually rightward, stabilizing on the basis of a ritualistic and fairly monolithic Orthodox state nationalism. At the same time, it is likely that "spiritual liberals" will in increasing numbers drift away from the church. As a result, the ROC will become less and less relevant to contemporary life (Kyrlezhev and Troitskii 1993, pp. 259–60). This prognosis is in accordance with sociological findings suggesting that the shift away from atheism and toward religion that took place in Russian society in the late 1980s was followed by a shift of people's religious allegiance "away from Orthodoxy, and especially away from the ROC as an institution, and toward 'Christianity in general' and a vague 'New Age' spirituality" (Filatov and Furman 1992). However, the decline in public support for the ROC is not precipitous or dramatic in character, and is more than compensated for by its steady consolidation as a quasi-state institution.

The liberal Orthodox journalist Yakov Krotov is similarly pessimistic about the future of the ROC, at least so far as the near and medium term are concerned. His prediction is based on expected generational change in the church leadership. The rising generation of bishops who will start to take up leading positions in the first decade of the twenty-first century will be less open-minded, more stubborn and rigid than the men they replace, many of whom traveled abroad in the 1960s and 1970s and "understand that things can be different." True, the new hierarchs will be men who never collaborated with the KGB,[52] but that will make them much worse, much more dangerous. The present church leaders are aware that they have sinned, and this gives them a certain tolerance for human frailty, but their successors will believe that their conscience is pure, and their fanaticism, typical of neophytes, will know no bounds. Krotov places his hopes on the generation who will follow the fanatics—the young laypeople now just entering the church, animated by a fresh and living faith (Krotov 1994).

Neo-Paganism

In Russia today one finds a widespread interest in ancient pagan myths and beliefs. This interest is manifested in the popular literature that is produced on the subject (for instance, Voloshina and Astapov 1996), as well as in such phenomena as newspaper advertisements for the services of wizards and magicians and the employment of astrologers and clairvoyants as forecasters in government departments.[53] In certain respects neo-paganism and Orthodox fundamentalism bear a close resemblance to one another: in particular, the demonic threat to humanity is a common theme in both kinds of fantasy (Klimentovich 1998).[54]

Most of the public interest in things pagan is neither fascist nor even political in nature. The study of paganism is rather one form of escapist entertainment that is available to people. It may be motivated by harmless curiosity or by a genuine personal search for spiritual values. Many small societies and communities have arisen that propagate, and to varying extents try to live by, pagan beliefs: their members generally view paganism as a religious, and not as a political, choice. Nevertheless, this broader nonpolitical paganist social movement does also provide a pool of potential recruits to pagan fascist organizations, just as the broader movement of nonpolitical Christian revivalism gives scope to the activity of fascist organizations of a Christian orientation. Of course, the prospects of pagan fascist organizations are limited by the fact that even many people who like to read about paganism do not really take it seriously, and by paganism's continuing lack of prestige and public legitimacy.

4
Cossacks, Skinheads, and Soccer Fans

The Cossack Revival Movement

One of the most remarkable phenomena of recent years in Russia has been the apparent revival of the Cossacks.[1] In this section I explain who the original Cossacks were and how the Cossack revival movement arose and developed in the late 1980s and early 1990s, and then consider the nature of the revival movement and the extent to which it may contain fascist tendencies.

The Original Cossacks

The original Cossacks were mainly Russian peasants who from the sixteenth century onward ran away from serfdom to live as free men in the borderlands of the southern steppes, beyond the control of the Russian state.[2] Here in the "wild field" [*dikoe pole*] they survived as fishermen and warriors, and later as farmers—for at first they refused to till the land, associating agriculture with serfdom. They were joined over the years by wanderers of diverse ethnic background, including destitute Jewish vagrants (Borovoi 1997).

In relation to the tsarist state, the Cossacks played an ambiguous role. On the one hand, they constituted an advance guard of Russian colonization, facilitating Russia's expansion into new lands. On the other hand, as fugitives from serfdom they were enemies of the ruling order, who took part in all the great peasant uprisings. In 1773, following the suppression of Pugachev's Cossack-peasant rebellion, the tsar crushed the Cossacks as an independent force. Those Cossacks who survived were "invited" to enter the imperial service as a special estate. Thenceforth the Cossacks would serve the tsar as soldiers and gendarmes, and in return be granted various privileges: above all, they would not be re-enserfed but would continue to live as free farmers. The Cossacks' commanders, the *atamans*, would no longer be elected leaders, but officers appointed by and answerable to the government. The Cossacks had been "harnessed" by the state.

A new myth of the special personal relationship between the Cossacks and the tsar was cultivated to take the place of the old myth of "the free Cossack" (McNeal 1987, ch. 1). Among the victims and opponents of tsarism, the word "Cossack" came to evoke the image of the cruel horseman, whip in hand, trampling demonstrators underfoot or terrorizing Jewish townlets. However, the old myth of the Cossack as free rebel was never completely extinguished. Even in the late nineteenth century the Cossacks continued to resent their enforced subservience to the Russian state, a feeling that they expressed in the rhymed couplet: "Cossack glory is a dog's life" [*Slava kazach"ia da zhizn' sobach"ia*] (McNeal 1987, p. 154).

The survival of the old myth helps to explain the variety of Cossack responses to the collapse of tsarism in 1917. Many Cossacks did fight with the Whites to restore the old regime, but there were also liberal Cossack "autonomists" who tried in the summer of 1917 to create a Cossack Republic federated with democratic Russia (Derluguian and Cipko 1997). Cossacks even proved responsive to anarchist propaganda on those occasions when they were exposed to it. Nestor Makhno, the anarchist leader of the armed "Green" peasant rebellion against both Whites and Reds that took place in southern Ukraine during the civil war, recalls how Maria Nikiforova, an anarchist orator from Alexandrovsk, upbraided a crowd of thousands of Cossacks:

> Until now you have been tormentors of the working people of Russia. Is that what you will remain, or do you acknowledge the vile role you have played and join the family of the working people, . . . whom you have crucified alive for the sake of the tsar's ruble and a glass of wine?

In unison, the crowd of Cossacks removed their tall fur hats and hung their heads on their chests. Many wept like children (Makhno 1991, pp. 134–36).

The open expression of Cossack identity was suppressed in the 1920s. The Cossacks were in fact the first ethnic or quasi-ethnic group to be subjected to systematic repression by the Soviet regime. All that seemed to remain were a few Cossack dance troupes, preserved as a tourist attraction. However, some memory of Cossack traditions must have been passed down through the generations, because as soon as Mikhail Gorbachev relaxed the constraints on public life in the late 1980s a Cossack revival rapidly took shape.

Rise and Evolution of the Cossack Revival Movement

The Cossack revival movement has passed through several distinct stages. The following account pertains to the Krasnodar Territory, a part of southern Russia abutting on the northern Caucasus and also known as the Kuban. It is here that the Cossack revival emerged earliest and took its strongest form. Developments elsewhere have been basically similar, though with significant local variations.[3]

At first Cossackry seemed just a harmless hobby or craze of enthusiasts interested in local history and folklore. The political potential of the movement became evident only in January 1990, when a call-up of reservists bound for Azerbaijan, where Moscow was at that time trying to suppress the Azerbaijan Popular Front, sparked massive popular protest in the city of Krasnodar. At the protest rallies Cossack folk songs were sung, and orators addressed the crowd as "people of the Kuban" [*kubantsy*]. The Soviet authorities feared that Cossack revivalism was crystallizing as yet another of the anticenter regional separatist movements that were hastening the disintegration of the USSR. Their response was to co-opt the Cossack cause. The revival movement now received an infusion of official support of all kinds—political, organizational, and financial. Fancy Cossack uniforms and other paraphernalia were made available in state stores at subsidized prices, attracting large numbers of people, far from all of them hereditary Cossacks. At the same time, the authorities took control of the political orientation of the movement. Organized in the Union of Cossack Troops, the Cossacks were repackaged as "Red" or pro-Soviet Russian nationalists, ready to be mobilized against the anti-Soviet nationalism of the non-Russian peoples of the Caucasus. Other possible interpretations of Cossack identity were, for the time being, marginalized.

The situation changed dramatically in August 1991, when the failure of the attempted putsch by the Soviet hard-liners effectively brought Boris Yeltsin to power in Moscow.[4] Kuban governor Nikolai Kondratenko, who had been the key figure behind the official co-optation of the Cossack movement, was removed from office and briefly jailed by Yeltsin, and a new governor was installed—Vasily Diakonov, the manager of a plumbing supply company. Diakonov embarked upon a second reconfiguration of the Cossack movement. He created the Kuban Cossack Army, which laid claim to a "White" or "democratic," but in any case anticommunist, identity. However, Diakonov's local power base was weak, and within a year he had been ousted. Kondratenko was reelected governor in December 1996.

The political upheavals of the post-Soviet transition gave rise to considerable pluralism within the Cossack revival. By 1993 there were several competing interpretations of Cossack identity. There were "Red" Cossacks, "White" Cossacks, and "Green" (anarchist) Cossacks. There were Russian nationalist Cossacks, who considered themselves Russians, only better; Ukrainian nationalist Cossacks, who considered themselves Ukrainians; and autonomist Cossacks, who considered themselves neither Russians nor Ukrainians but members of a separate Cossack people.[5] Most Cossacks could agree in counting themselves Orthodox Christians, although there was also a circle of neo-pagan Cossacks and even a few Jewish Cossacks.

Under Kondratenko the Cossack movement has been reintegrated into the official structures of regional government. Cossacks enforce order, patrol the streets, and teach horsemanship and Orthodox patriotic morality in the schools. In some localities, the old system of "ataman administration" [*atamanskoe pravlenie*] has been reintroduced,[6] while Cossack custom—including the public whipping of wrongdoers—supplants the law code of the Russian Federation. A charter has been adopted that declares Krasnodar "the homeland of the ethnic Russian people" and "the historical territory of the Kuban Cossacks," thereby legitimizing unequal rights for ethnic minorities and even (to a lesser extent) for non-Cossack Russians.[7]

Similar measures to assign state functions to Cossacks have been taken in some other parts of Russia, even in places far from the traditional areas of Cossack settlement. In St. Petersburg, for instance, General Viktor Vlasov, himself of Cossack descent, introduced armed Cossack patrols on intercity trains in 1993, when he was head of the North-West Transportation Police. In June 1998, Vlasov was appointed police chief of St. Petersburg, and proceeded to organize mounted Cossack patrols in the city (Badkhen 1998).[8]

Repeated efforts have also been made to integrate the Cossacks into governmental structures at the national level, and in particular to give them a special position in the police and military. An Administration of the President for Cossack Affairs has been established, and presidential decrees have been issued on such subjects as Cossack land use, Cossack self-government, and the creation of Cossack units in the army and internal troops. In this way it is hoped to neutralize the problem for state security presented by uncontrolled and politicized armed formations.[9] There are, of course, practical limits on the extent to which the Cossacks can nowadays be harnessed to the state: after all, the cavalry is a rather outdated arm of service. Cossack units are, however, used to maintain order in the "liberated" areas of Chechnya (Minasian 1992; Deinekin 1999).

Estimates of the total number of Cossacks vary widely, depending on what definition of "Cossack" is used. Millions of people might claim some kind of connection, hereditary or spiritual, with the Cossack tradition, but the number of active politicized Cossacks is much smaller. One expert estimate suggests about 20,000 active Cossacks in the three provinces of southern Russia where the revival movement is strongest—the Krasnodar and Stavropol Territories and Rostov Province (Laba 1996, p. 389).

The Cossack Revival and Fascism

Clearly the Cossack revival movement is extremely heterogeneous in character. For some, dressing up in Cossack gear and strutting around in it is a satisfying pastime. For others, Cossack activism is a serious attempt to bring an almost lost ancestral identity back to life. For yet others, being a Cossack provides a valued opportunity and excuse for drunken escapades, ethnic pogroms, banditry, extortion, and other forms of criminality (Gamaiunov 1993; Laba 1996, p. 391). For some, the Cossacks are the elite and avant-garde of the Russian (or possibly Ukrainian) patriotic cause; for others, they are an unjustly repressed people fighting for their God-given right to national self-determination.

What, if anything, has the Cossack revival movement to do with fascism?

First, a large part of the Cossack movement does adhere to extreme variants of Russian ethnic and imperial nationalism. It is not therefore in the least surprising that many Cossacks are susceptible to the appeal of fascist movements. The Russian National Unity in particular is strongly entrenched in the areas where the Cossack movement is also most active—that is, in the Krasnodar and Stavropol Territories.

Second, the Cossack revival movement as a whole shares some common ground with fascism by virtue of its orientation toward an archaic premodern past. Valery Tishkov, director of the Institute of Ethnology and Anthropology of the Russian Academy of Sciences, has argued that the Cossack movement constitutes one part of a broader "neo-totalitarian" and "anti-modernist" revolution in the northern Caucasus that also comprises such phenomena as reactionary Islamism among the Chechens (Tishkov 1998). The belief in the Jewish world conspiracy is widely held among the Cossacks. In this sense, the Cossacks bear a relation to fascism similar to that of the fundamentalist wing of the Russian Orthodox Church.[10]

Nevertheless, the ambiguity at the root of the Cossack tradition, as well as the heterogeneity of the contemporary revival movement, should give us pause before making sweeping and categorical judgments. Many Cossacks, it is true, have allied themselves with the Russian National Unity, but many others have steadfastly refused to do so. The Don Cossacks, declared their ataman Nikolai Kozitsyn, "will never stand together with those who wear the black uniform of the chastizers" (Bondarenko 1998). Moreover, when one examines closely the attitude of the "patriots" toward the Cossacks, one finds a corresponding ambivalence. On the one hand, the Cossacks are praised to the skies as the very epitome of Russia's rebirth. On the other hand, Russian nationalist analysts see in Cossack autonomy a factor of Russia's disintegration (Tabolina 1994), and Russian nationalist propagandists severely warn the Cossacks to guard against any tendency to see themselves as somehow separate from Russia (RNU Website). One "patriotic" commentator criticizes the Cossack revival as weak, superficial, and lacking in authenticity: the movement, he complains, has been joined by profit-seeking opportunists and even—horror of horrors!—by Jews (Samokhin 1997).[11]

So an element of uncertainty surrounds the question of the part to be played by the Cossacks in shaping Russia's future. That is because flight from bondage and rebellion against oppression were the earliest Cossack traditions, and not all Cossacks have completely forgotten it.

Youth Subcultures

Several distinct youth subcultures arose in Russia during the late Soviet period. In the course of the 1990s, youth subcultures have multiplied, and the pattern of their interaction has become more complex (Pilkington 1994). One of these subcultures, that of the skinheads [*skinkhedy*, *britogolovye*], is clearly fascist in character, and fascist tendencies also exist in some of the other youth subcultures. In this section I focus first on two opposed streams of youth culture, the *gopniki* and the "informals," and I consider the extent to which fascist tendencies have emerged in each stream. I then give an account of the skinhead phenomenon, and finally offer a few remarks concerning fascist tendencies among some groups of soccer fans.[12]

Gopniki and Informals

The terms *gopnik* and "informal" [*neformal*] came into use to refer to the two most visible streams of Russian youth culture in the second half of the 1980s, although the subcultures themselves have earlier origins in the hidden unofficial realm of Soviet reality before perestroika. By the late 1990s these two streams were losing their coherence as distinctive entities, dissolving into a more differentiated, shifting, and inchoate pattern of youth subcultures. It needs to be emphasized that while the *gopniki* and the "informals" have been the most salient cultural groupings among Russian youth, at no time have the majority of young Russians belonged to either grouping.

The "informals" were young people who identified themselves with various parts of the youth counterculture that was penetrating Russia from the West. They included hippies, punks, and the creators and consumers of heavy metal and rock music. The followers of each style in a given city would gather in a specific public place, often a café or a central square, that was known as a *tusovka.* Under Gorbachev such young people were permitted to form their own "informal organizations": hence the term "informals." (At an earlier period such youngsters were referred to as *stilyagi.*)

Gopniki is a term that was invented by "informals" to refer to other youngsters who "made their lives on the street difficult" (Pilkington 1999). Like much of youth slang, the word is thought to derive from criminal argot, in which "gop-stop" means "pick-pocketing." The *gopniki* were young men who cultivated a tough "Russian" style and—by definition—hated the un-Russian "informals." They typically lived in working class towns or suburbs, belonged to territorially based youth gangs, and took an interest in body-building and combat sports. Particular notoriety was gained in the late 1980s by the *gopniki* of Lyubertsy, a satellite town to the southeast of Moscow; the *gopniki* undertook periodic expeditions into the capital to hunt down and beat up young men with long hair.

One might expect that fascist tendencies would find a natural home among the *gopniki*, and that they would not be detectable in "informal" circles. To a certain extent this would be a valid generalization. The Russian National Unity (RNU) in particular has created or taken over many body-building and combat sports clubs with a view to attracting *gopnik* youth into their ranks, and Lyubertsy and the other satellite towns to Moscow's east and southeast have become an RNU stronghold.

Many *gopniki*, however, have nothing to do with fascism. It may be significant that when in December 1998 the RNU seemed set to defy a ban imposed by Moscow's mayor, Yuri Luzhkov, on holding a congress in the capital, the All-Russian Karate Federation issued a statement offering the services of their members to prevent the congress from taking place (Arshanskii 1999; Karachinskii 1999). Another example is provided by the "baldies" [*lysie*], whose "hard look"—their knuckles-to-the-ground walk, sports gear, and army-style haircut—identifies them unequivocally as *gopniki*, but who are quite distinct from skinheads and have no particular ideology. Conversely, far from all skinheads are *gopniki*. Many of them, in fact, come from quite well-off backgrounds, and some are former rockers and other "informals."[13] As one veteran skinhead explained disdainfully to a press interviewer, a real skinhead is not "a street *gopnik*" who simply wants to swill vodka and kick someone, but "a patriot of the white nation" (Slivko and Babich 1998).

The evolution of rock music in Russia illustrates the way in which fascist tendencies have made their way into "informal" milieus. A rock underground first emerged in the Soviet Union in the first half of the 1970s. At that time rock was inseparable from the hippie movement, and it suffered the same political persecution as the latter. In the 1980s rock began to attract a much wider and more heterogeneous clientele, weakening its earlier connection with the hippies. By the 1990s rock had undergone intensive commercialization and had lost its dissident associations altogether (Kozlov 1998, pp. 161, 171, 181–91). From 1993 onward there began to emerge the trend that came to be known as "national rock" or "Russian rock," prompting "patriotic" publicists to reconsider their previous hostility toward rock music as an art form. (They had been accustomed to associate rock and heavy metal not only with their political enemies but also with a more potent foe, Satan.[14]) Several, though not all, of the musical performers associated with "national rock" have views that are clearly fascist.[15]

The Skinheads

Skinheads in the West

The skinheads are an international politico-cultural youth movement with a crude white racist and Nazi ideology. They are recognizable by their shaven heads, steel-toed boots, and tattoos, and they listen to what they call "Oi" music (from the Cockney greeting).[16] They hate nonwhites, Jews, homosexuals, and also—to varying degrees—white foreigners, and they frequently give violent vent to their hatred.

The skinheads originated in Britain in the early 1970s. They were transformed into an organized force by Ian Stuart Donaldson, whose memory is still revered by his followers. In 1977 Donaldson created a rock group called *Skrewdriver*, who performed their songs in celebration of Viking and Nazi myth in several countries. In 1979 Donaldson set up a political action group by the name of White Noise, which allied itself to the neo-fascist British National Front. In 1985 a skinhead periodical was launched, its title taken from an SS motto: *Blood and Honor*. The same name was given to a loose skinhead organization that Donaldson founded in 1987.

Donaldson died in a car crash in 1993. After his death, Blood and Honor came under the influence of the non-skinhead neo-Nazi organization Combat-18.[17] It also has close ties with the American neo-Nazi Gary Lauck of Lincoln, Nebraska. Blood and Honor remains the largest skinhead organization today (*The Skinhead International* 1995, pp. 5–7; Lööw 1998, pp. 1157–59).[18]

Skinheads in Russia

Skinheads made their appearance in Russia some time in the early 1990s, and they have grown quite numerous. By 1997, according to various estimates, there were over 10,000 of them in Russia as a whole (Rstaki 1998a). In 1998 it was estimated that there were 3,000 to 4,000 skinheads in Moscow alone; by the spring of 2000 the figure had probably reached 5,000 to 6,000.[19] Besides Moscow, skinheads have been reported in St. Petersburg, Lipetsk, Belgorod, and Voronezh (Fishkin 1999), in Ivanovo (Sirotin 1998), in Volgograd (Barkov 2000a, 2000b), and in Krasnoyarsk, Tomsk, Irkutsk, and Vladivostok (Rstaki 1998a).[20] If we assume that the number of skinheads in the whole of Russia has grown at the same rate as the number in Moscow, we get a rough estimate of 15,000 for the total number of skinheads in Russia at the present time.

The ideology of the Russian skinheads is a nonspecific white or "Aryan" Nazi racism, copied straight from the Western skinhead movement, rather than any kind of specifically Russian nationalism. Nor does there seem to be anything specifically Russian about the dress, music, or behavior of Russian skinheads. Armed with knives, chains, and brass knuckles, gangs of skinheads—sometimes as few as five, sometimes as many as seventy—attack African and Asian students studying in Russia, as well as Armenians, Azeris, Uzbeks, and other people from the Caucasus and Central Asia, usually inflicting serious injuries and sometimes killing their victims (Cherkasov 1999).[21] In May 1998, an Afro-American marine, a guard at the American Embassy, was badly beaten by five skinheads in Filevsky Park, a customary meeting place for skinheads. This was one of the relatively few cases in which the police, presumably under pressure from Embassy officials, took some action against skinhead assailants (Banerjee 1998).[22]

The typical skinhead is, of course, a male, but there are also girls in the movement. Female skinheads fall into two distinct categories: "skingirls," who take full part in the violence, and "girls of skins," who share the views of their skinhead boyfriends but do not take part in the violence themselves. Male skinheads do not consider fighting obligatory for girls; many prefer their girls not to fight, feeling that it does not accord with the proper female role (Zav'ialova 2000).

Many Russian skinheads, perhaps a majority, do not belong to any formal organization. A certain proportion belong to fascist organizations under non-skinhead leadership. Some fascist organizations, such as Konstantin Kasimovsky's Russian National Union (see chapter 8), have made a special effort to recruit skinheads.[23] In between the two extremes of unorganized and fully politicized skinheads, there are many who prefer to form their own purely skinhead organizations. Examples are the Moscow Skin Legion [*Moskovskii Skinlegion*], with several hundred members, Russian Goal [*Russkaia tsel'*],[24] another Moscow group called The White Hunters [*Belye okhotniki*], and the Volga National Front in Volgograd. Finally, the international skinhead organization Blood and Honor has a branch in Moscow with several hundred members (Rstaki 1998a).

Volgograd merits some attention as a rare, perhaps a unique, case of a city that has taken serious action against skinhead violence. Following repeated skinhead attacks on foreign students studying at Volgograd's medical academy and other institutions of higher education, the foreign students organized a protest movement to demand police protection. The protest was supported by the rectors of the institutions concerned, who successfully brought pressure to bear upon the governor of Volgograd Province, Nikolai Maksyuta, to force the city's reluctant police department to take the necessary measures. As a result, fourteen cases of assault were brought before the courts.[25] It was discovered that the attacks were the work of the Volga National Front, a Nazi skinhead organization of about eighty members,[26] mainly boys aged between fourteen and seventeen. The youngsters whom the police detained had an emblem with the name of their organization sewn on their shirtsleeves, wore a swastika on their chest, and greeted one another with the Heil Hitler salute. At interrogation they defended themselves by pointing out that they did not beat Russians, their task being that of "cleansing Russia of blacks" (Barkov 2000a, 2000b).[27]

Soccer Fans

The skinheads overlap with another category of young Russians who are often violent and sometimes inclined toward fascist ideas—namely soccer fans. Needless to say, there are also very many Russian soccer fans of all ages who are completely nonviolent and have no inclination toward fascist ideas.

The websites maintained by the fan clubs of the various Moscow soccer teams provide us with a window on this particular youth subculture. It needs to be explained that there are four popular soccer teams in Moscow: Spartak, Torpedo,[28] Dinamo, and the Central Army Sports Club (CASC).[29] These teams have been sponsored since the Soviet period by different institutions—Spartak and Torpedo by the trade unions, Dinamo by the Ministry of Internal Affairs and the KGB and its successors, and the CASC—as might be expected—by the Army. The four teams have long traditions behind them, in the case of the CASC going back to before World War II, and they enjoy the enthusiastic support of loyal followings.

Let us explore the site of the fan club of the CASC. We find blow-by-blow accounts, composed in the style and language of military communiqués, of battles waged against "the enemy"—that is, against the fans of rival teams.[30] As if to disabuse us of any facile assumption that soccer violence is hooliganism devoid of higher meaning, a long essay is posted by one Kiryan

Matroskin, entitled "Yet Again on Institutional Solidarity," in which he expounds the inherent moral and ideological superiority of Dinamo, and especially of CASC, fans over Spartak fans. He contrasts the populist, egalitarian, and cosmopolitan ideology of Spartak, "a hangover from the gray communist past," with "the harsh but grandiose idea of the restoration of a strong, united, and indestructible Russian empire." How, he asks rhetorically, can a team like Spartak, named in honor of Spartacus, leader of a slave rebellion against another great empire, that of the ancient Romans, serve as a symbol of the great Russian empire? Appended to the essay is a commentary from the Ideological Department of the CASC fan club:

> Never mind that Spartak is more popular than us. . . . A minority can be superior to a majority. . . . We must continue to create a real combat structure. We are not so numerous, but we are a strong elite, infused with an aristocratic spirit.

Do these sentiments not epitomize the spirit of fascism as we have defined it?

5
Zhirinovsky and the Liberal-Democratic Party of Russia

Western opinion is accustomed to associate the threat of fascism in Russia primarily with the name of Vladimir Zhirinovsky. Until recently, indeed, Zhirinovsky was generally regarded as the sole significant Russian fascist politician. The attention devoted to him reached a peak in the aftermath of his dramatic success in the Duma elections of December 1993, when his Liberal-Democratic Party of Russia (LDPR) came in first, with about a quarter of the votes cast. Only toward the end of the 1990s did Zhirinovsky recede somewhat from center stage as his electoral performance sharply declined and other fascist figures and organizations, notably Alexander Barkashov and his Russian National Unity (RNU), started to attract coverage in the Western press.

Zhirinovsky's high profile on the world scene reflected not only the real support he enjoyed in Russian society, but also his outstanding performance as a showman, feeding the media an unending stream of new sensations. In part, he owes his continuing fame to inertia, as he and his party have now been in existence for over a decade. The Liberal-Democratic Party of the Soviet Union (LDPSU)—as it was originally called—was the first political party to offer itself as an alternative to the Communist Party of the Soviet Union (CPSU). It was created in December 1989, and held its founding congress at the end of March 1990, the very month that Article 6 of the Soviet Constitution, which had enshrined the legal monopoly of the CPSU, was repealed.[1] Zhirinovsky first displayed his electoral appeal in June 1991, when he garnered over 6 million votes (about 8 percent) in the election of the first president of Russia, taking third place after Boris Yeltsin and former Soviet prime minister Nikolai Ryzhkov.

Zhirinovsky and the LDPR have never been able to repeat, let alone surpass, their triumph of December 1993 at the national level. Zhirinovsky won

5.7 percent in the presidential election of 1996, and only 2.3 percent in the presidential election of March 2000, although his bloc still obtained 6.0 percent in the Duma elections of December 1999.[2] The LDPR retains fairly strong positions in some regions, such as the Far East and Pskov Province in northwestern Russia, where the party's candidate Yevgeny Mikhailov won the governorship in November 1996.[3] The LDPR remains, after the Communist Party of the Russian Federation (CPRF), the political party with the second largest membership, numbering in the tens of thousands,[4] and the second most extensive network of local branches. The LDPR still exerts a significant influence in Russian society.

Nevertheless, the LDPR is a force in rapid decline. The party's further decline seems a much more likely prospect than does any revival in its fortunes.

Why then study the LDPR?

Above all, because we need to gauge the impact that the vast propaganda of the LDPR has already had on Russian society over the decade in which the party has been active. An understanding of the nature of the LDPR will also help us foresee where its numerous local activists and sympathizers are likely to find their new political homes if it does contract sharply or even disappear altogether—that is, which political forces stand to gain the most from the decline and possible fall of the LDPR.

As a man and as a politician, Vladimir Zhirinovsky is unusually difficult to fathom. His long rambling speeches and prolific writings are marked by numerous contradictions. Many have questioned his sanity.[5] There are three main ways in which Zhirinovsky's politics have been interpreted by observers, analysts, and other politicians. First, there are those who basically accept Zhirinovsky's "official" self-portrayal as a "liberal democrat"—or, to be more precise, as a "national liberal" or "imperial liberal." Second, there are those for whom Zhirinovsky is a fascist who hypocritically employs "liberalism" as a superficial camouflage. Lastly, there are those who consider Zhirinovsky merely an unprincipled opportunist and populist, without real convictions of any kind.

In the first section of this chapter, I clarify these three interpretations, and offer my own view of Zhirinovsky's ideological position on the basis of a study of his published writings and speeches and of recent programmatic literature of the LDPR.[6]

In the second section, I broaden the focus of attention from Zhirinovsky to the LDPR as a collective body. I examine the internal regime of the party, demonstrating that an extreme concentration of power in Zhirinovsky's hands is accompanied by a certain measure of tolerated ideological diversity. I proceed to consider the main ideological tendencies within the party and how the party ideology has changed over time. I also discuss other criteria of the character of the LDPR—namely, the nature of its activity, and its links with other political organizations at home and abroad—and suggest an interpretation of the LDPR that seems to best fit available evidence.

In the final section, I return to the assessment of the LDPR's electoral performance and prospects. I approach the problem first by examining those two cases in which LDPR candidates have won election to major office at the regional level, and I then comment briefly on the condition in which the LDPR finds itself in the wake of the Duma and presidential elections of December 1999 and March 2000. In conclusion, I discuss the significance of Zhirinovsky and his party for the development of politics in post-Soviet Russia.

Zhirinovsky: National Liberal, Fascist, or Opportunist?

Three Interpretations

Zhirinovsky as National Liberal

Both the programmatic literature of the LDPR and Zhirinovsky personally have repeatedly proclaimed such liberal principles as the rule of law, constitutionalism, individual freedom, private initiative, social justice, the "social market economy," reason, progress, republicanism, secularism, and multiparty democracy (*Programma* 1998, pp. 7–9; Zhirinovskii 1997b). The only widely accepted liberal principle that is rejected is "the rights of minorities (ethnic, sexual, etc.) that stand against the majority of the people."[7] At the same time, a sharp distinction is drawn between the "patriotic" liberalism of the LDPR and the "cosmopolitan" liberalism of the "radical democrats," who are accused of "servility toward the West" and "antipathy to a mighty state and its power structures" (*Programma* 1998, pp. 8–9). Thus, the LDPR presents itself as a liberal party of a special kind—one that passionately defends the ethnic interests of Russians and the national interests of Russia at home and abroad. It is convenient to refer to this combination of liberalism and patriotism, as summed up in the Party motto "Freedom, law, Russia," as national liberalism—or as imperial liberalism, for the LDPR belongs to that broad sector of Russian opinion that holds that Russia is inevitably an imperial state.[8]

Besides Zhirinovsky and his party colleagues themselves, the "national liberal" interpretation of the LDPR is accepted by a number of political commentators. One such is Vladimir Kartsev (1995), the author of a rather apologetic biography of Zhirinovsky, whom he knew from his time as director of the Mir Publishing House, where Zhirinovsky was employed as a legal specialist in the 1980s. Another sympathetic biographer, Sergei Plekhanov,[9] portrays Zhirinovsky as a politician sincerely committed to electoral democracy (Plekhanov 1994, p. 127). And Andrei Andreev (1997, pp. 32–44), a sharp analyst whose personal allegiance lies with the "patriotic" camp, in his work on Russia's political spectrum places the LDPR in the chapter devoted to liberalism, and not in the chapter on nationalist and imperialist movements, where one might expect to find it. More surprisingly, Alexander Yanov (1995, pp. 114–51)—a writer whom nobody could suspect of sympathizing with Zhirinovsky's outlook—draws attention to certain parallels between Zhirinovsky and Hitler, but eventually locates Zhirinovsky within the tradition of Russian imperial liberalism that goes back to Nikolai Danilevsky (Ianov 1995, pp. 114–51).[10]

Zhirinovsky as Fascist

For the great majority of liberal observers, however, whether in Russia or the West, Zhirinovsky is a fascist, a Russian Hitler in the making. This, for instance, is the assumption that pervades the biography written by the émigré writers Vladimir Solovyov and Elena Klepikova (1995, p. 119), for whom all Zhirinovsky's talk of liberalism and democracy is a mere "figleaf."

Rarely is a systematic argument advanced to justify considering Zhirinovsky a fascist: it is regarded as a self-evident fact. Reference is commonly made to Zhirinovsky's xenophobia, especially his hostility to Jews and people from the Caucasus, to his harsh invective against the West, which he accuses of deliberate genocide of the Russian people (Zhirinovskii and Davidenko 1997), and to his expansionist foreign policy ambitions, as proclaimed in his notorious book *Final Spurt to the South* (1993). These features may indeed suffice to label Zhirinovsky a fascist, but only in what I have called in chapter 1 the popular sense of the word. There is no necessary inconsistency between being a fascist in this popular sense and being a national or imperial liberal: at most, it is a matter of a difference in emphasis.

Zhirinovsky as Opportunist

Zhirinovsky is frequently called an opportunist and populist, but this can mean different things. It may mean simply that he is unscrupulous in the methods he uses to win votes, raise funds, and acquire influence, without any implication that he lacks a definite ideological orientation. There are those, however, who consider Zhirinovsky an opportunist in the sense that he has no fixed convictions whatsoever. In this case, the struggle to find a coherent logic in his speeches and writings can be abandoned, as the desire to appeal simultaneously to different audiences is assumed to account for all apparent contradictions.

Some of those who believe in such a "non-ideological" interpretation of Zhirinovsky see in him a would-be dictator, bent upon power for its own sake; others believe that he no longer really seeks power—if indeed he ever did—but is now content to play his role within the existing political establishment, which has successfully co-opted him (Tishkov 1999). There is, finally, the view that Zhirinovsky is simply out to enrich himself (Solovyov and Klepikova 1995, p. 102).

Assessing the Interpretations

National Liberalism

The speeches and books of Zhirinovsky, as well as the periodicals and pamphlets issued under the LDPR imprint, dwell at great length on such classically liberal themes as the advantages of free individual initiative, the rule of law, and multiparty competition. Even if, for the sake of argument, we suppose that all this talk is intended merely as camouflage for Zhirinovsky's real intentions, it does at least generate a pervasive "noise" that blocks the elaboration and propagation of any coherent antiliberal ideology, fascist or otherwise. For example, while Zhirinovsky has often mentioned the need for a temporary dictatorship to restore order in the country, and while it is true that few things turn out in practice to last as long as "temporary" dictatorships, the formal adherence of the LDPR to liberal ideology makes it difficult for Zhirinovsky to make a virtue out of the supposed necessity. A world of difference exists between the familiar call for a spell of dictatorship as an extreme remedy, heard in many countries suffering from all-pervasive chaos, crime, and corruption, and the explicit contempt for democracy that marks full-blown fascism, in Russia as elsewhere.[11]

It is, however, far from self-evident that Zhirinovsky's professed liberalism is nothing but camouflage. Completely absent from Zhirinovsky's discourse is any sign that he feels nostalgia for—or indeed has an understanding of—the premodern values that partisans of fascism (as I have defined it in chapter 1) strive to revive in a new post-liberal order. Thus, among the points listed in the LDPR Program as "setting us apart from extreme right parties and movements (fascists, nationalists, monarchists)" are adherence to a republican and secular state order, refusal to idealize prerevolutionary Russia, and "an orientation not to the past, but to the future, to the third millenium" (*Programma* 1998, p. 9). In his writing on the late tsarist period, Zhirinovsky (1997b, pp. 36–39) praises not the Black Hundreds but such liberal thinkers as Milyutin, Milyukov, and Struve, and the reformist Constitutional-Democratic Party and Party of Legal Order. Thus, it does appear to be the case that "the LDPR considers itself the successor to . . . the spirit of the 'great reforms' of Alexander II, the *zemstvo* movement,[12] and the constitutionalism of the beginning of the twentieth century" (Andreev 1997, p. 32).

While standing in principle for a secular state, the LDPR recognizes a special role for Orthodoxy in Russian society as the country's "main religion" (*Programma* 1998, p. 11)—an ambivalent stance similar to that of the Yeltsin regime. Zhirinovsky tries to present himself as a loyal son of the Russian Orthodox Church, supporting, for instance, the Church's campaign against foreign religious sects.[13] At the same time, little attention is devoted by the LDPR to questions of religion or "spirituality," and the general outlook on life that Zhirinovsky expresses in his speeches is a thoroughly materialistic and hedonistic one. In contrast to the puritanism and asceticism typical of religious "patriots," Zhirinovsky takes a highly permissive approach to sex, his somewhat idiosyncratic ideas concerning which constitute a not unimportant part of his popular appeal. The section of the party program on "the LDPR and women" is likewise composed in a contemporary spirit, with reference to issues of practical concern to women, including sexual harrassment at work and the need to reduce the number of abortions by promoting modern means of contraception (*Programma* 1998, pp. 50–54).

Care is needed in assessing Zhirinovsky's stance in relation to the West. Although Zhirinovsky condemns "the West" in no uncertain terms—one of his pamphlets is entitled *Spit on the West*! (Zhirinovskii 1995)—the West upon which he pours his vitriol is the grouping of Western powers that stand opposed to Russia's national and imperial interests. He is not hostile to the West as a civilization, and he has no problem in acknowledging that the liberal principles to which his party adheres originally came to Russia from the West (Zhirinovskii 1997b, p. 35). The ideal way of life that he promises to deliver to his electors is readily recognizable as the secure, comfortable, and well-ordered existence of the Western middle class—the same existence that the "patriots" profess to scorn as philistine and soulless. Even Zhirinovsky's imperial dream of Russia's last drive south to the Indian Ocean and the Mediterranean Sea seems inspired less by a thirst for glory than by his wish to secure for his fellow Russians the quintessentially petty bourgeois boon of "peace and quiet"—and the additional resorts that they need for their summer holidays (Zhirinovskii 1993, p. 73). His grievance against the West is that the West, acting in collaboration with Russia's parasitic and treacherous ruling elite, plots to reduce Russia to the status of its dependent "raw-material appendage" and destroy the technological potential that could be harnessed to bring Russians the comforts of a Western lifestyle. Zhirinovsky, like Peter the Great and Lenin, is a Westernizer against the West.

But what of Zhirinovsky's imperialism, his bellicose foreign policy, his rabid hatred of various ethnic groups, especially Turkic and Caucasian peoples and Jews? Are these not inconsistent with liberalism? They are indeed, if by "liberalism" is meant what tends to go by that name in the contemporary West—and especially in the United States, where "liberalism" is commonly used to refer to attitudes that in Western Europe are called "social democracy." Zhirinovsky's liberalism, however, is of a distinctly old-fashioned kind, disinterred from an age before the idea of universal "human rights" became conventional wisdom. In Gladstone's Britain or in Teddy Roosevelt's America, respectable opinion found no difficulty in reconciling adherence to "liberal" principles of politics and economics with unabashed racism and imperialism. The same applies *a forteriori* to Zhirinovsky's predecessors among prerevolutionary Russian liberals. Yanov draws an analogy between the imperial liberalism of Zhirinovsky and that of Danilevsky, which I discussed in chapter 2 (Ianov 1995, pp. 142–45). The analogy is recognized as valid by Yevgeny Mikhailov, one of the LDPR's most coherent ideologists as well as its sole provincial governor, who lays claim on behalf of his party to Danilevsky's heritage:

> A reactionary and chauvinist for radical-democrats and Bolsheviks, for us [Danilevsky] will always be the ideologist of Russian national-liberalism, the one who first formulated its credo. (Mikhailov 1995, p. 95)

Turning to the specific question of racism, it should be noted that Zhirinovsky's derogatory comments on various ethnic groups, however insulting they may be, are not based on racial categories. Zhirinovsky has often stated that, in contrast to the "ultra-rights," the LDPR asks no questions about an individual's ancestry, accepting as a Russian anyone who so considers himself or herself (Zhirinovskii 1997c, pp. 100–101). In the controversy over removing the entry for ethnic origin from citizens' internal passports, the LDPR was among those in favor of the change. Zhirinovsky's own half-Jewish origin, of course, has a bearing on his party's stance on this issue. Similarly, the LDPR advocates abolition of the federal system inherited by Russia from the Soviet Union, with its ethno-territorial republics that embody the autonomy of various titular minorities, and a return to the purely territorial provinces [*gubernii*] of Tsarist Russia—certainly a highly contentious policy, the attempted implementation of which would probably provoke widespread interethnic conflict, but one fully in accord with liberal ideas of civic nationalism and the separation of ethnicity and the state.[14] In general, the patriotism of Zhirinovsky and the LDPR is primarily a *state*, and only secondarily an ethnic, patriotism. Russia is defined as "the country of the [multiethnic] Russian [*rossiiskaia*][15] nation, the backbone of which is the Russian [*russkii*] people" (Zhirinovskii 1997d, p. 28).

Whether liberalism, nationalism, and imperialism can again be successfully combined in practice under contemporary conditions is admittedly quite another question. It is indeed open to serious doubt whether the combination of liberalism at home with imperialism abroad was ever a practical option for Russia, which unlike the Western powers is separated by no oceans from the lands it traditionally covets as colonies. Certainly today Russia's prospects of consolidating any kind of liberal democracy would be fatally undermined by large-scale imperial adventures even within the limits of the former Soviet Union, let alone over the broader expanses of Eurasia. Nevertheless, the example of the LDPR shows that at the level of ideology "imperial liberalism" can and does exist in post-Soviet Russia.

Besides its nationalism and imperialism, Zhirinovsky's liberalism is also distinctive in another respect. The economic part of the LDPR program envisages a much stronger role for the state in the economy than one would expect a West European liberal democrat to espouse, including a strong state sector, a state investment program, protectionism, and agricultural supports (*Programma* 1998, pp. 33–42). Zhirinovsky advocates for Russia a third way between socialism and capitalism, although this third way—in contrast to that of more traditionalist "patriots"—is not specifically Russian in character: Russia must become "a social state of liberal democracy [that is] not socialist and not capitalist" (Zhirinovskii 1997b, p. 93). Both the economic policies and their theoretical formulation might be understood as adaptations of liberalism to the conditions prevailing in Russia after the collapse of communism—in particular, the weakness and corruption of the state and the continuing aversion of much of the public to the word "capitalism." They also bring Zhirinovsky close in this field to West European social democracy, so that one might equally well call him an "imperial liberal" or an "imperial social democrat." That the distinction between "liberal democracy" and "social democracy" was from the outset an inessential one for Zhirinovsky is suggested by a telling detail in the story of the party's creation: the first party program, drafted by Zhirinovsky in May 1988, was called a "Program for a Social-Democratic Party," and it was this draft that in the spring of 1989 served as the basis for the work of the initiative group on the first program of what became the LDPSU and then the LDPR (Ushakova 1998, p. 5).

But an Infected Liberalism

The old-fashioned imperial character of Zhirinovsky's liberalism and the stress he places on the role of the state in the economy do not, however, fully account for the discrepancy between his worldview and what is nowadays generally understood as liberalism in the West. Especially in his discussions of geopolitics and "the Russian question," one notices the penetration of concepts that definitely come from outside the liberal tradition, "imperial" or otherwise. Now and then, for instance, Zhirinovsky alludes to "Russia's historical mission to save human civilization" (Zhirinovskii 1993, p. 123; 1997c, p. 81). Of particular significance are his references to "the international Zionist financial-industrial oligarchy" that controls Russia's "mafia dictatorship" (Zhirinovskii 1997b, p. 69) or to the "hidden functioning structures [of Judaic civilization] in many countries of the world" (Zhirinovskii 1998b). Although he more often identifies Russia's main enemy simply as "the West"[16] and seems never to express the idea of a Jewish conspiracy to dominate the world in its full-blown form, his occasional statements on the subject do bring him close to the fascist position. Yet other examples of this same phenomenon are Zhirinovsky's occasional use of such expressions as "the dark forces of Europe and America" (Zhirinovskii 1997b, p. 118) or of the term "chimera"—presumably taken by him from Gumilyov (see chapter 2), for whom it meant a state, like the United States, that lacks adequate ethnic foundations (Zhirinovskii 1997c, p. 4).

There is also a certain overlap between Zhirinovsky's worldview and that of classical fascism in the sphere of geopolitics. Geopolitics occupies a very prominent position in the ideology of the LDPR. It is a subject of abiding fascination to Zhirinovsky, who spends long periods alone with his maps, pondering how to reorder the territorial division of the world. At such times he is not to be disturbed!

Zhirinovsky's basic geopolitical concept is that each great power of the Northern Hemisphere should possess an exclusive sphere of influence in adjacent areas, primarily in those lying to its south. As he put it in his report to the Fifth LDPR Congress in April 1994:

> Let us divide up spheres of influence once and forever: in North America and South America, that is all one continent, and let the Organization of American States act there; let Europe continue to dominate the African continent—they love one another very much, but that is none of our business; let Japan and China fish in the region of the Philippines, Indonesia, Australia, South-Eastern Asia, but *not* in the Sea of Okhotsk—that will be Russia's inland sea. . . . And Russia, as always, takes least of all for itself: . . . we are interested only in the South, to our North there is peace and quiet, to our West we shall have, in the main, friends, . . . we shall never again allow a clash with the West. To our East we have the Pacific Ocean. Our problem is in the South. That is why we want our children once more

> to sing the song: "Wide is my native land, it has many forests, fields, and rivers." [Applause] So that there should be peace and quiet from the northern borderlands to the southern seas. [Applause] (Zhirinovskii 1997b, p. 82)[17]

Zhirinovsky does not disclose the source of his geopolitical ideas, but they bear a suspiciously close resemblance to those of the geopolitical school established in Munich in the years after World War I by Professor Karl Haushofer. There is clearly a close correspondence between Zhirinovsky's ideas and Haushofer's concept of the "Large Space" [*Grossraum*] that defines the geopolitical identity of a great power, and Haushofer, like Zhirinovsky, advocated the division of the world into longitudinal zones controlled by different northern powers.[18] While relations between Haushofer and the national socialist regime were not always smooth and there were contradictions between his geopolitics and Nazi racial doctrine, there is no doubt that Hitler was greatly influenced in his foreign-policy thinking by Haushofer. The neo-fascist publicist Alexander Dugin has done much to make Haushofer's ideas more widely known in post-Soviet Russia.[19] Haushofer is an especially appealing figure to Russian fascists as a consistent advocate of the German–Soviet alliance, never having reconciled himself to Hitler's invasion of the USSR. Haushofer is the key link that connects Hitler's "drive to the East" to Zhirinovsky's "spurt to the South."

While bearing in mind those specific elements of Zhirinovsky's worldview that reflect a fascist influence, we should also remember that Zhirinovsky has repeatedly made an effort to distinguish the ideology of the LDPR clearly from fascism. In his speeches and writings, he condemns German national-socialism and takes pride in the role that Russia played in saving the world from Nazism (Zhirinovskii 1997b, pp. 104–5; 1997d, p. 7).

An Anti-Semitic Jew

Zhirinovsky claims that his mother was Russian, but that he does not know the ethnic origin of his father. Hence his statement, which immediately acquired the status of a joke: "My mother was Russian; my father was a lawyer." But there seems to be sufficient evidence to the effect that Zhirinovsky's father was a Jew by the name of Edelshtein, and that Zhirinovsky took his surname from his mother's former husband.[20] Zhirinovsky himself once came close to admitting the fact when he said to insistent journalists: "Well, let us suppose that he even was a Jew. So what? What does that change?" (Plekhanov 1994, p. 26). And it does seem somewhat perverse to consider Zhirinovsky a Jew—not so much because Jewish religious law determines who is a Jew according to the female line, a point made by Zhirinovsky himself, but because Edelshtein had no opportunity to influence his son's upbringing, having died about the time of Zhirinovsky's birth.

In making sense of Zhirinovsky as a politician, however, the questions that matter are whether Zhirinovsky is regarded by others as being Jewish, and whether he so regards himself. There is some reason to believe that the answer to both questions is yes. If Eduard Limonov, who has no qualms in calling himself a fascist, sees Zhirinovsky as a Jew, and presents his own break with him as the indignant reaction of a "real" Russian to the audacity of a Jew "pretending" to be a Russian nationalist ("A Jew masquerading as a Russian nationalist is a sickness")—well, that is only to be expected (Limonov 1994a). But then we discover that the commentator Leonid Radzikhovsky, himself a Russian Jew, agrees with Limonov in characterizing Zhirinovsky as a specifically Jewish type of madman (he uses the Yiddish word *meshugene*) (Radzikhovskii 1996). The Russian writer Andrei Sinyavsky, a former Soviet dissident, also perceived Zhirinovsky as a Jew—a circumstance that he found reassuring:

> If such a large percentage of the Russian people could vote for . . . a man who looks so obviously Jewish, that means that my great people is not so terribly anti-Semitic. (Sinyavsky 1997, p. 13)

Zhirinovsky himself, while explicitly denying knowing that his father was a Jew, has been reported as saying: "For me, fascism is a most repulsive thing. Almost the whole of my father's family were shot by the fascists" (Solovyov and Klepikova 1995, p. 27)—implying both that his father was indeed a Jew and that for this very reason he (Zhirinovsky) cannot possibly be a fascist.[21] Moreover, in the late 1980s, in the period directly preceding his creation of the LDPSU, Zhirinovsky passed through a phase during which he openly professed a Jewish identity, involving himself in the affairs of the Jewish cultural society *Shalom* and even taking initial steps toward emigrating to Israel (Solovyov and Klepikova 1995, pp. 35–36). Even if he no longer mentions it, the memory of this phase in his life can hardly have disappeared from his consciousness.

What then of Zhirinovsky's notorious anti-Semitism? Zhirinovsky's anti-Semitic utterances are in fact relatively mild and restrained, whether by comparison with the extreme anti-Semitism to be found in many "patriotic" circles or by comparison with the abuse that he heaps on the heads of Caucasian and Turkic peoples. The LDPR program itself states that the party rejects the "pathological anti-Semitism" of the extreme right movements (*Programma* 1998, p. 9). "Healthy anti-Semitism," by implication, is not rejected. It is by no means unusual for Russians, Jews as well as non-Jews, to be mildly anti-Semitic, and Zhirinovsky may be one of them.[22] This fact would not in itself make him a fascist, and any attraction to fascism that Zhirinovsky might feel as an anti-Semite could well be counterbalanced by an equally genuine repulsion arising from awareness of his partly Jewish origins. Alternatively, Zhirinovsky may be cynically exploiting the political potential of anti-Semitism, at the same time trying to keep it within limits and under control.

An Opportunist?

Few would seek seriously to dispute that Zhirinovsky is a consummate opportunist and populist insofar as his choice of methods is concerned. He routinely says different things to please different audiences. He makes attractive promises to the Russian people, never bothering to substantiate their feasibility in any but the vaguest and most cursory way. He assures them that he will restore Russia's economy in three years (*Programma* 1998, pp. 35–36), return all the savings that the population has lost as a result of hyperinflation and bank fraud (*Programma* 1998, p. 41), suppress crime in two weeks (Solovyov and Klepikova 1995, p. 125), and even provide husbands to lonesome women. It has been plausibly suggested that he consciously plays the role of the eccentric clown [*iurodivy*] of Russian folklore (Lee 1997, p. 323).

In and out of the Duma, the LDPR maneuvered skillfully between the Yeltsin camp and the communist opposition, making deals now with one side and now with the other. While presenting a united front with the communists on many issues, the LDPR repeatedly lent its support to Yeltsin at critical junctures. Zhirinovsky strongly supported Yeltsin's decision to intervene militarily in Chechnya in December 1994, thereby winning the praise of Minister of Defense Pavel Grachev (Lee 1997, p. 328). In 1997 there was much speculation concerning the imminent formation of an alliance between the LDPR and the Communist Party of the Russian Federation (CPRF) (Zhirnov 1997), but in early 1998 the LDPR Duma deputies swung the vote in favor of the confirmation of Sergei Kirienko as prime minister, earning a congratulatory missive from Yeltsin to the LDPR congress held shortly thereafter (Martin 1998). Not surprisingly, Gennady Zyuganov regards the LDPR as an unreliable alliance partner.

There is also much evidence to the effect that the LDPR sells its political support to business lobbyists. It is this that particularly upset Eduard Limonov, who headed the LDPR's intelligence department from June to November 1992 before breaking with Zhirinovsky to form his own National-Radical Party and later the National-Bolshevik Party:

> At a rally in a Cossack community club, [Zhirinovsky] loudly promised the Cossacks that he would rid them of the Armenian mafia. Then, on the next day, in my presence, he swore to a representative of the Armenian mafia to protect Armenian interests in exchange for financial transactions favorable to the party. After hundreds of such incidents, I understood that Zhirinovsky is an opportunist. (Limonov as quoted in Solovyov and Klepikova 1995, p. 102)

Another high-level LDPR defector, Alexander Vengerovsky, has revealed that the party's Duma seats are also up for sale—for amounts of up to a million dollars apiece (*FBIS Daily Report* FBIS-SOV-96–096).

So Zhirinovsky is an opportunist. It is not very plausible, however, to claim that he is nothing but an opportunist. For one thing, there are limits on what he is prepared to say for the sake of popularity. When General Alexander Lebed further enhanced his own popularity by signing an agreement to bring the Chechen war to an end, Zhirinovsky denounced it as a shameful and dangerous capitulation (Zhirinovskii 1997c, p. 7)—hardly the stance of a man out for popularity at any price. The commercialization of politics is also not unique to Zhirinovsky, though he is among the frontrunners in this process. In post-Soviet Russia as in the United States, a politician unwilling to advance the interests of financial backers cannot hope to raise the huge sums required for successful campaigning. The favors that Zhirinovsky owes to various vested interests reduce, but by no means eliminate, his ability to pursue ideological goals. Moreover, the LDPR has obtained most of its funding not from the "Armenian mafia" but from groups whose interests it can advance in full accordance with its ideology, such as military industry, "national" entrepreneurs,[23] and the regimes of former Soviet allies like Iraq, Libya, and North Korea, with which Zhirinovsky would like Russia to restore broken ties (Zainashev 1998).

In the absence of reliable information on the way the LDPR uses its funds, it is difficult to assess the specific accusation, made by Limonov and others, that Zhirinovsky is in politics for the purpose of enriching himself. Even if there is some truth to the claim, it does not explain very much. Why should he choose this particular way of making money? This interpretation of Zhirinovsky does not fit what we know about his personality. I suspect that it is a product mainly of anti-Semitic prejudice.

Besides ideology, a thirst for power, or a desire to get rich, there may be another motive that is important in Zhirinovsky's psychology. It seems that his emotionally deprived childhood and youth, which he describes so graphically in the autobiographical passages of *Final Spurt to the South*, have left him with an insatiable psychological craving for the attention, praise, and adoration of others—though above all for attention. Zhirinovsky is a political exhibitionist. This does not exclude the probable presence of other motives, including ideological ones.

When assessing Zhirinovsky's opportunism and populism, we would do well to beware of double standards. What American politician never says different things to different audiences, or never rewards a campaign contributor with political support? In fact, Zhirinovsky has a strong claim to being post-Soviet Russia's first real politician in the Western sense of the word—and this goes a long way to explain why he so shocks many of his rivals and compatriots.

Summing Up

Let us sum up the results of the argument so far. I have argued that Zhirinovsky is a highly opportunistic populist politician, but one with a definite, albeit less than fully coherent, ideological orientation. The basic structure of his ideology is liberal, tending in some respects in the direction of what in the West would be called "social democracy." However, not only is this liberalism of an old-fashioned national and imperial kind, but it is severely infected in certain areas with ideas originating in a fascist or semi-fascist milieu. The result is a nationalist and imperialist ideology of a composite liberal-fascist character.[24]

The LDPR as a Collective Body

Ideological Diversity and Change

The LDPR's Internal Regime

Up to this point, my analysis has focused on a single man, Vladimir Zhirinovsky. But is it correct to identify a large party like the LDPR with the lone figure of its leader?

There is much to be said in favor of making such an identification, at least as a first approximation. Zhirinovsky created the LDPR and drafted its first program. Except for a brief period in the summer of 1990, when a group of liberal founding members around Vladimir Bogachev[25] made an unsuccessful attempt to oust him, Zhirinovsky has always been in firm control of the party. Until 1993, certain democratic formalities were observed. As had been the practice in the CPSU, members of the party's leading bodies—the Central Committee, the Supreme Council or Coordinating Council, and the Central Revision Commission—were elected by, and in principle responsible to, the party congress. Besides these elected leading bodies, there was from June 1992 onward a "shadow cabinet," a consultative body comprised of "ministers" appointed by Zhirinovsky. However, starting with the Fifth Congress of February 1994, there have been no more intraparty elections. Since this date, all central functionaries, Duma deputies, and local coordinators of the LDPR have been appointed by Zhirinovsky, and they are responsible to him alone. The same congress confirmed Zhirinovsky's prerogatives as chairman, and extended them by ten years up to the year 2004. The reorganization of the central apparatus of the party in July 1996[26] and the reconstruction of the Supreme Council and Central Committee in November 1996 completed the transition from formal Soviet-style "democratic centralism" to the open (albeit still formally elective) dictatorship of Zhirinovsky. The change was justified on the grounds that it would "bring order into the work of party structures," facilitate more timely decision making, impede splits, especially on the part of the LDPR's Duma deputies, and thwart the efforts of enemies to undermine the party (Ushakova 1998, pp. 40–41, 73–75; Zhirinovskii 1997c; 1998b, p. 72).[27]

Likewise more suggestive of fascism than of liberal democracy is the cult surrounding the personality of Zhirinovsky. Even such an otherwise sober activist as Yevgeny Mikhailov (1995, p. 38) writes in awe of "the faith-inspiring voice of Zhirinovsky, [in whose form] are concentrated and embodied the millennial forces of the mighty vital streams of the Russian nation." One of the party publications bears the title "Zhirinovsky's Truth" [*Pravda Zhirinovskogo*], while the members of the LDPR youth organization are "Zhirinovsky's falcons" [*sokoly Zhirinovskogo*]. Admittedly, the cult of Zhirinovsky lacks the ecstatic intensity reached by the cults of Hitler, Mussolini, and Stalin at their height, but the family resemblance is unmistakable.

Nevertheless, even in a political party with a dictatorial internal regime, the personality of the supreme leader is not the only factor of significance. Many other figures have played significant roles in the development of the LDPR. Presumably some of them have influenced Zhirinovsky as well as being influenced by him, and presumably also one of them will eventually inherit from him the party leadership. Before proceeding further in our assessment of the LDPR, we should accordingly consider the ideological orientations of a few of the more prominent of Zhirinovsky's past and present party colleagues.[28]

When I set out to explore the available sources pertaining to other political figures who are or have been active in the LDPR, I was surprised to discover quite a few ideological differences of some importance, both among these personages and between each of them and Zhirinovsky. Given the organizational structure of the party, it is clear that this limited ideological heterogeneity does not reflect any lack of control on Zhirinovsky's part, let alone genuine intraparty democracy. Rather, it is Zhirinovsky himself who chooses not to impose on the LDPR any detailed and rigid ideological doctrine, but to allow party members a certain amount of freedom in this sphere. Similarly, Zhirinovsky allows LDPR deputies considerable freedom in deciding how to vote in the Duma, with the result that the LDPR Duma fraction demonstrates a degree of internal variation in voting behavior about average for Duma party fractions—somewhat less than in the CPRF fraction, somewhat more than in the pro-governmental fractions (Sergeev et al. 1999). But when Zhirinovsky considers it necessary for all party members to toe a single line, he has the means to make them do so.

What does this tell us about the LDPR's internal regime? Yevgeny Mikhailov, the LDPR governor of Pskov Province, prefaces his exposition of national-liberal thought with the following explanation:

> The book [The Burden of an Imperial Nation] is written from the positions of the theory of Russian national-liberalism. . . . *National-liberalism is not the official theory of the LDPR* [underlined in the original—S.D.S.], but inasmuch as the party in its charter and the general instructions of its leader professes freedom of conviction, giving everyone equal opportunity for creative exploration, this presupposes the presence in its theoretical arsenal of various models of action (and even of worldview), which depending on concrete conditions will permit the use of one or another kind of ideological armament, one of which is Russian national-liberalism. (Mikhailov 1995, p. 3)

In other words, Zhirinovsky wishes to preserve for himself a range of options, giving him scope for ideological maneuver, and to that end deliberately maintains a system of limited intra-party pluralism, within which he himself plays a unifying and balancing role.[29] Such an intra-party regime, which closely—and no doubt not coincidentally—resembles the intra-party regime of the CPSU under Brezhnev, has other advantages for the leader: it enables him to build a larger party membership and mobilize broader support in society, and impedes the formation of intra-party coalitions directed against himself.

Ideological Tendencies in the LDPR

The information available on the ideological positions of LDPR figures is far from complete, but the general character of the intra-party ideological spectrum is clear enough. At one end of a continuum, we find groups and individuals with unmistakably fascist views and connections, who strive to turn the LDPR into a more consistently fascist organization. At the other end of the continuum, there are groups and individuals whose views fully correspond to the doctrine of "national liberalism." In the middle are individuals who, like Zhirinovsky himself, expound a mixture of national-liberal and fascist ideas.

Let us review briefly some of those individuals and groups at or near the fascist end of the continuum who have played a significant role in the LDPR.[30]

Viktor Yakushev, who was formerly active in Alexander Barkashov's Russian National Unity (RNU: see chapter 6), ran the LDPR's Youth Department from early 1991 until early 1992, with the assistance of his friend, Igor Vagin, who had left the RNU together with him. After leaving the LDPR, Yakushev was to found his own national-socialist organization, the National-Social Union.

More significant was the role played after the departure of Yakushev's group by the trio made up of the writer Eduard Limonov and the musicians Andrei Arkhipov and Sergei Zharikov, who occupied important positions in the LDPR leadership between June and November 1992, when they left the party together in disillusionment at Zhirinovsky's "opportunism." Limonov headed the LDPR "secret police" or Intelligence Department,[31] while Arkhipov served as Zhirinovsky's press secretary and as "minister of culture and youth affairs" in Zhirinovsky's shadow cabinet, enabling him to turn the party's youth publication into a vehicle for explicitly Nazi ideas (Solovyov and Klepikova 1995, pp. 100–101). Limonov, Arkhipov, and Zharikov were united not only by friendship and by fascist convictions, but also by shared artistic and esthetic concerns. Arkhipov and Zharikov, who led the punk-rock group *DK*, were well known in Moscow as "rock Nazis" for their invention of the musical school called "national rock." On leaving the LDPR, the trio also created their own fascist organization: the Right-Radical Party, and later the National-Bolshevik Party, led by Limonov, which I discuss in chapter 7.

Another fascist faction was the semi-clandestine and rather mysterious "St. Petersburg group," which took shape about 1993 and attempted to infuse the LDPR with its peculiar brand of fascist systems theory. It does not seem to have had a great impact.

A number of other individuals on the fascist wing of the LDPR deserve brief mention. Alexei Vedenkin, an adventurist and "financier" boasting connections with both the state security agencies and the business world, was aide to Alexander Vengerovsky, the LDPR deputy chairman of the Duma in 1994–95; at the same period, he headed the economic department of the Russian National Unity (Pribylovskii 1995, p. 38). Major General Viktor Filatov, who in the late 1980s as editor of the *Military-Historical Journal*, organ of the Institute for Military History of the Ministry of Defense, created a scandal by publishing Hitler's *Mein Kampf*, became head of the LDPR Propaganda Department in 1995 (Cherniak 1995). Another military man, active in the St. Petersburg LDPR and other extreme nationalist groups in the early 1990s, was Captain Mikhail Ivanov, who had neo-pagan inclinations and called himself a *volkhv* [magician]; he was appointed "first deputy prime minister" in Zhirinovsky's shadow cabinet in 1992. Also a member of the LDPR is the publicist Valentin Prussakov, a U.S. resident who has striven in his writings to rehabilitate the German Nazi regime.

At the liberal end of the party spectrum, mention should first be made of Leonid Alimov and Akhmet Khalitov, who were elected deputy chairmen at the founding congress of the LDPSU. Both these individuals had been liberal dissidents under Brezhnev. Alimov was an electrical engineer; Khalitov was a collective farm chairman and prominent agronomist, expelled from the CPSU in 1981 for his numerous appeals to leading bodies for the reform of agricultural policy. Now in his old age, he operates a water tower on a state farm near Moscow. In the LDPR he headed the Central Revision Commission, was elected as the member of the Supreme Council responsible for organizational work, and edited the early issues of the party journal *Liberal*. Khalitov, who is an ethnic Tatar, used his influence to counteract the fascist figures active in Zhirinovsky's entourage at the time, especially Eduard Limonov and his friends. Thus, in the fall of 1992 there appeared two rival versions of the fourth issue of the LDPR youth periodical—a fascist version produced by Arkhipov and Zharikov, and a liberal-populist version produced by Khalitov (Umland 1997, p. 503). At the party's Fourth Congress in April 1993, however, Khalitov was removed from his leading positions.[32] At the end of 1993, Alimov also left the party leadership.

Mention has already been made of Yevgeny Mikhailov, the LDPR's foremost theorist of "national liberalism"—indeed, one of its few real theorists of any kind. Mikhailov developed his views as a "Russian national democrat and national liberal" while a student activist at Moscow State University in the late 1980s. During 1990–91 he served as a deputy to the Moscow Soviet. Together with a group of fellow students, he joined the LDPR in April 1992 after a long talk with Zhirinovsky (Mikhailov 1995, pp. 27–41). Returning to his native Pskov, he built up the provincial LDPR organization there, and was elected as the party's first provincial governor in November 1996 (Vaguine 1997).

The most influential of the "national liberals" were the group of "technocrats" who entered Zhirinovsky's inner counsels in 1993, in the wake of the departure of the fascist Limonov–Arkhipov–Zharikov trio. The "technocrats" were oriented mainly toward economic issues, and they enjoyed close ties to "national" entrepreneurs and to high-technology—primarily military—industry. Three names in particular should be mentioned: Mikhail Bocharov, Alexander Vengerovsky, and Viktor Lymar. Bocharov was a reform economist under Gorbachev, and in 1991–92 he was active in Arkady Volsky's centrist Industrial Union. A co-founder and president of the prestigious International Russian Club, he joined the LDPR and became an adviser to Zhirinovsky, in whom he saw a future temporary dictator who would create the political conditions needed for thoroughgoing liberal economic reform (Umland 1997, p. 496). Vengerovsky was in turn a radio engineer, a military cosmonaut, and a computer technologist, rising to head a main administration of the State Committee for Computer Technology and Informatics, where he was responsible for the organization of all computer programming work in the USSR. On joining the LDPR, he became "deputy prime minister" in Zhirinovsky's shadow cabinet as well as head of the LDPR intelligence service, and from December 1993 a deputy chairman of the LDPR Duma fraction (Lanting 1996). Lymar was a physicist in a military research institute, specializing in the gyroscopes used in missile guidance. He became "minister of science and technology" in the LDPR shadow cabinet and a member of the party's Supreme Council.

A number of prominent LDPR figures cannot be placed unequivocally either in the "fascist" or in the "national liberal" camp. One such is Stanislav Zhebrovsky, a physicist by profession and Zhirinovsky's oldest and most constant party colleague—indeed, the only founding member of the LDPSU, apart from Zhirinovsky himself, who still belongs to the party leadership. Zhebrovsky first met Zhirinovsky in 1983, when they were working together in the Mir publishing house. In addition to being a deputy chairman of the LDPR, Zhebrovsky was appointed in 1996 head of the Department of Ideological Work in the party's central apparatus. He has edited several of the LDPR's periodicals.

Alexei Mitrofanov, until recently the party's "minister of foreign affairs" and chairman of the State Duma's Committee for Geopolitical Questions,[33] is likewise difficult to place ideologically. In his works on geopolitics, Mitrofanov expounds an unashamedly ruthless and imperialist power politics of "Russian national egoism" (Mitrofanov 1997; 199[–]). He is a great admirer of Stalin's statesmanship. His geopolitics is combined in a curious fashion with economic liberalism, Eurasianism, a concern with astrological trends,[34] and other arcane elements. Mitrofanov once worked for the Soviet Ministry of Foreign Affairs, which he represented at the International Atomic Energy Agency in Vienna. He is rumored to be the grandson of former Soviet foreign minister Andrei Gromyko.

Another idiosyncratic LDPR figure was the renowned television hypnotist Anatoly Kashpirovsky, who was associated with the party between 1992 and 1995.

A Changing Ideology?

Andreas Umland (1997, pp. 372–78) has carried out a detailed analysis of the contents of the LDPR's official publication *Liberal* over the period 1990 to 1993. He traces a sequential shift in the ideological character of the journal from "contaminated [national] liberalism" in 1990 through a mixture of liberalism and "authoritarian restorationist ultra-nationalism" in 1992 to outright fascism in early 1993, characterized by such features as leader-worship and the explicit rejection of democracy. In the spring or early summer of 1993, however, a new issue of *Liberal* appeared that signaled a sudden return to national liberalism.

These changes in the content of the party periodical can be closely correlated with concurrent changes in the composition of Zhirinovsky's entourage. The people with whom he founded the party, for the most part genuine liberal democrats, quickly became alienated and—after an unsuccessful attempt to expel Zhirinovsky himself—left the LDPR. We may presume that it was under the influence of Yakushev and his associates in 1991, and especially of the Limonov—Arkhipov—Zharikov group in 1992, that the party drifted rapidly in a fascist direction, and that the abrupt return to liberalism in 1993 was connected with the arrival of the "technocrats."[35]

Unfortunately, no content analysis comparable with that conducted by Umland for the years 1990 to 1993 is available for later years. However, on the basis of a careful study of nine pamphlets published by the LDPR in 1997 and 1998, including six of a programmatic character, I would characterize the party ideology in the most recent period as one of national-imperial liberalism, severely contaminated, but not overwhelmed, by fascist elements. In other words, a certain balance between liberalism and fascism has been maintained, and while there have clearly been significant fluctuations in party ideology over time it is doubtful whether there has been any clear long-term trend.

Other Criteria

In assessing the character of any organization, account should be taken not only of the ideology that it espouses, but also of other criteria. What principles are embedded in the internal structure of the organization? To what extent are the activities of the organization consistent with a commitment to seek power only by electoral means? What links does the organization maintain with other political forces at home and abroad?

In terms of its internal structure, as we have seen, the LDPR is far from being either a liberal or a democratic organization. However, party documents and other evidence make it clear that the LDPR does have a strong orientation toward electoral activity, in sharp contrast to militarized movements like Barkashov's Russian National Unity (RNU). The contrast, however, is not an absolute one. The LDPR, like the RNU, runs youth clubs at which teenage boys not only play soccer and undergo political indoctrination, but also receive military training. Thus, the party has strong youth clubs in Pskov Province, where an LDPR governor holds office. (Moiseenko and Iurenkov 1999). In the military townships near Pskov, nearly all the boys and many of the girls join the LDPR youth organization. A group of twenty-three parents of pupils at a school in the town of Ostrov submitted a petition to the local authorities, complaining that the LDPR recruits children as young as seven without their parents' permission, and that the "young falcons" start fights, extort money, and beat up people of non-Slav origin. Violence and intimidation as well as electoral campaigning have a place in the LDPR's strategy.

The LDPR does not maintain direct top-level links with unambiguously fascist organizations like the Russian National Unity, and indeed the latter are occasionally criticized (in rather mild terms) in the party's publications. At the local level, however, some links do exist, as in Pskov, where Mikhailov enjoys the backing of the Russian Party. It is part of the LDPR's strategy to establish regional alliances with other "patriotic" organizations (Zhirinovskii 1998b, p. 43). If the LDPR does tend to find itself isolated from the broader "patriotic" milieu, that is not necessarily by its own choice: most fascists despise Zhirinovsky as an imposter, for the simple reason that he is a "Jew." Indirect links between the LDPR and the fascist organizations are nevertheless fostered by a constant two-way flow of members, at the grassroots as well as at higher levels. As we have seen, quite a few prominent fascist figures have passed through the LDPR at one time or another; Alexei Vedenkin even worked for the LDPR and for the RNU simultaneously. A new example is the Duma deputy for Novosibirsk, Vladimir Davydenko, who in early 1999 left the party to form his own movement *Spas* (Salvation) as an electoral cover for the RNU. The LDPR coordinator for Novosibirsk, Yevgeny Loginov, was quoted as saying that he saw nothing tragic in the exchange of personnel between the LDPR and the RNU; he did not consider Davydenko a traitor or Barkashov an enemy (Albaut 1999).

The foreign links of the LDPR are likewise suggestive of a close connection with fascism. There have been friendly contacts between Zhirinovsky and leaders of West European semi-fascist parties, such as Jean-Marie Le Pen, of France's

National Front. The LDPR's closest external ties have been with Gerhard Frey and his German People's Union (GPU). Frey, a wealthy publisher, has helped finance Zhirinovsky's campaigns; Zhirinovsky has spoken at conventions of the GPU; and in August 1994 the two parties concluded a friendship accord (Ebata 1997, p. 225; Lee 1997, pp. 325–26; Parfenov and Sergeeva 1998).

At the same time, it should be noted that Zhirinovsky has also sought links with West European liberal democratic parties. At first, his overtures to them were not rebuffed. In October 1990, Zhirinovsky attended the Forty-third Congress of the Liberal International in Espu, Finland. (It was while Zhirinovsky was away in Finland that the liberal group around Vladimir Bogachev tried to oust him.) Subsequently, the LDPSU adopted the programmatic documents of the Liberal International (Ushakova 1998, p. 50). Following their initial hesitation, Western liberals refused to have anything further to do with the LDPR. Nevertheless, it appears that Zhirinovsky would like, if he could, to straddle the two horses of right-wing radicalism and establishment liberalism.

Zhirinovsky and the LDPR: An Interpretation

It is reasonable to suppose that Vladimir Zhirinovsky deliberately "plays" along a continuum that stretches from national liberalism at one end to outright fascism at the other, viewing the LDPR as a flexible alliance of national liberals and fascists that may be allowed to develop in one direction or the other depending on circumstances.

But what of Zhirinovsky's real views and goals? The question reminds me of a comedy sketch in which a number of look-alikes unpredictably swap places; one is never sure who is the imposter. Will the real Zhirinovsky please stand up?

Not having access to Zhirinovsky's innermost thoughts, all the analyst can do is weigh up the relative plausibility of alternative conjectures in the light of the evidence available. And so—is Zhirinovsky a closet fascist, biding his time until conditions are ripe for him to declare his true colors? Or is he a closet liberal, playing a subtle game with fascism that only he fully understands? Or does he himself not know whither he is bound?

The view of Zhirinovsky as a camouflaged fascist cannot be disproven, but the evidence suggests on balance that this is not the most plausible view. There are crucial elements of the fascist worldview that simply cannot be detected in the opinions and attitudes expressed by Zhirinovsky. Zhirinovsky's links with the neo-fascist right in Western Europe seem to point to a different conclusion, but he has attempted to establish links with West European liberal democratic parties also—without success, to be sure, as in the eyes of the Western establishment Zhirinovsky falls outside the pale of respectability. It is only in the amorphous world of post-Soviet Russian politics that one can play Zhirinovsky's liberal-fascist double act; in the West this is not a feasible option.

The opposite interpretation, that of Zhirinovsky as a closet liberal, has certain attractions. It is the interpretation most consistent with Zhirinovsky's apparently sincere (given his awareness of his partly Jewish origins) condemnation of German Nazism. Perhaps Zhirinovsky hopes to make good use of the energy of those fascists willing to join his party, but does so with the firm intention of keeping them on a tight rein and discarding them at a later date. In considering this question, I have been struck by a possible parallel between the LDPR and the British Labour Party. The Labour Party accepts Trotskyists and other radical leftists as members, and such people provide a disproportionately large share of its local activists. The radicals enter the party in the hope of bringing about its leftward evolution—a strategy called "entryism" that was originally advocated by Lenin—but never have any sustained success in this endeavor. Might Zhirinovsky not have a similar attitude toward his own fascist entryists? Or is this wishful thinking?

I find it most plausible to assume that Zhirinovsky is neither a convinced liberal nor a convinced fascist, but that—as Yevgeny Mikhailov hints—he strives to keep his options open. This, however, is far from asserting that Zhirinovsky is a pure opportunist, totally lacking in convictions. We should not forget that there is a powerful common denominator that unites all ideological tendencies within the LDPR—namely, Russian imperial nationalism. All members of the party share a commitment to restore Russia to the status of a strong and independent world power. It is undoubtedly Zhirinovsky's dream too that Russia's national revival will come to pass—and that it will be he who leads Russia to this revival. It may well seem to him that ideological distinctions within this broadly conceived Russian nationalism, though not without importance, are nonetheless secondary to the main goal. In that case, he is not necessarily being "opportunistic" if he leaves his ideological options open for the time being.

Who, then, is the real Vladimir Zhirinovsky? If there is a revival in Zhirinovsky's fortunes, time will probably provide us with a clearer answer. But if Zhirinovsky slowly fades from the political scene without ever fully defining himself, we may never know.

Electoral Performance and Prospects

Regional Case Studies: Pskov and Kyzyl

An illuminating approach to assessing the electoral performance and prospects of the LDPR is to focus on the only two cases so far in which LDPR candidates have won election to major political offices at the regional level—namely, the election of Yevgeny Mikhailov as governor of Pskov Province in 1996, and the election the following year of Alexander Kashin as mayor of Kyzyl, capital of the Republic of Tuva, in southern Siberia. In both these cases, the LDPR candidate won by a fairly narrow margin: Mikhailov garnered 56 percent of the vote, while Kashin scraped in with a bare 52 percent. Nevertheless, the LDPR did achieve the coveted breakthrough to majority support in Pskov and Kyzyl. An examination of how the LDPR won in these places may help us assess the likelihood of its ever achieving the same result at the national level.

It is widely held that Russian nationalists enjoy the strongest public support in border regions where Russia faces challenges to its territorial integrity (whether in the form of border disputes with neighboring states or in that of secessionist movements) and/or where there is acute tension between Russians and other ethnic groups. The situation in Russia's southern region, plagued by the dangerous border with breakaway Chechnya and by tension between Caucasian ethnic communities and the Russian population, is clearly consistent with this generalization. So is the situation in the Russian Far East, with its locally contentious border with China[36] and widespread fear of massive Chinese immigration. At first glance, the LDPR victories in Pskov and Kyzyl would appear to fit the same pattern. Pskov lies close to Russia's borders with the Baltic states and Belarus, and the territorial dispute between Russia and Latvia concerns areas that are currently part of Pskov Province. In Tuva there is persistent tension between Russians and the indigenous Tuvin population, tension that manifests itself in a considerable amount of low-level violence (such as ethnically motivated murders) as well as in non-violent political forms such as demonstrations. In 1991 there were open interethnic clashes. Tuva, which became part of the USSR as late as 1944, is situated on Russia's border with Mongolia, and the Tuvins are culturally and ethnically closely related to the Mongols. Outside of the Caucasus and with the possible exception of the isolated exclave of Kaliningrad Province, there is no other territory that Russia is more likely eventually to lose.

So far so good. However, a closer examination of the circumstances of the LDPR victories in Pskov and Kyzyl reveals that in fact these two cases by no means correspond to the standard pattern of borderland Russian nationalism.

In Pskov Province, Yevgeny Mikhailov actually won a higher proportion of the vote in those districts furthest from the Russian–Baltic border than he did in the disputed border areas themselves. This differential may be connected to the benefits derived by the residents of the border districts from trade with their Baltic neighbors (Alexseev and Vagin 1999a, 1999b). Russian nationalist issues played a lesser part in Mikhailov's electoral victory than did his success in presenting himself as an honest and competent administrator capable of reviving the province's economy. Another factor that almost certainly helped secure Mikhailov's victory was the intensive campaigning in the province by Zhirinovsky himself in the period immediately preceding the second round. (In the first round, Mikhailov came in second, with only 23 percent of the vote.) In a whirlwind tour, Zhirinovsky—accompanied by Mikhailov, who apparently hardly managed to get a word in—held public meetings in numerous villages in which the inhabitants had never before in their lives set eyes upon a famous national politician, and many of them clearly felt flattered (Vaguine 1997).

The case of the LDPR victory in Kyzyl is in its way even more remarkable, above all because a little over half the population of the city consists of ethnic Tuvins, a considerable number of whom must therefore have voted for the LDPR mayoral candidate. Alexander Kashin's Tuvin supporters were primarily politically unsophisticated new arrivals from the countryside—the very same marginal stratum from which Tuvin nationalists draw their most active support. Many of these bewildered people naively believed Kashin's promises to solve their housing and other social problems. Kashin also won popularity across ethnic lines through his opposition to the local establishment represented by the republic's president, Sherig-Ool Oorzhak; Kashin claimed that he was fighting only against the Tuvin leaders, in defense of the interests of ordinary people of all ethnic backgrounds.[37]

Of course, neither Mikhailov nor Kashin has solved any of the social and economic problems of their constituents, and this is the main reason why they have both lost much of their support since they were elected. Under the LDPR regime in Pskov Province, unemployment has continued to rise, the provincial government budget adopted in mid-1999 has a deficit in excess of 70 percent, and the payment of teachers' salaries is six months in arrears (Moiseenko and Iurenkov 1999). Some former LDPR supporters have reportedly been alienated by the entry into the provincial party organization of members of the fascist neo-pagan Union of Veneds. People have been bringing their LDPR party cards to the editorial office of the sole opposition newspaper *Novosti Pskova* [Pskov News], just as at the beginning of the 1990s many of them had brought to the same office their CPSU party cards. At the end of March 1999, the head of the provincial organization of the LDPR, Vyacheslav Sukmanov, abandoned his post. According to a poll of the Institute of Applied Social Research in the spring of 1999, a mere 7 percent of Pskov Province voters said they intended to vote for Zhirinovsky in the forthcoming national presidential elections. Zhirinovsky actually fared even worse, winning a mere 2.7 percent of the vote.[38] Even Governor

Mikhailov himself was preparing to abandon the sinking ship of the Pskov LDPR by establishing ties with the *Otechestvo* [Fatherland] movement of Yuri Luzhkov, Moscow's mayor. In June 2000, he switched allegiance to Putin.

As for Kashin, he lost his initial Tuvin supporters not only because he failed to fulfill his promises to them, but also because the ethnopolitical motif became more salient in local politics. Two months after he was elected mayor, he began to demand that the city of Kyzyl be detached from the Republic of Tuva and incorporated into the neighboring Krasnoyarsk Territory, thereby provoking a sharp confrontation between himself and President Oorzhak, who proceeded very effectively to play the "anti-Russian card" against him. Street protests of ethnic Tuvins against Kashin were orchestrated from behind the scenes by the Oorzhak administration. These protests carried anti-Russian overtones, the slogan "Kashin get out of Tuva!" being felt by local Russians to imply "Russians get out of Tuva!" In response, Russian inhabitants of Kyzyl staged counterprotests, and a renewal of interethnic clashes seems likely.[39]

Both in Pskov and in Kyzyl, the LDPR has resoundingly failed the test of regional power. In May 1999, the party made an attempt to capture yet another borderland when Zhirinovsky himself stood for election as governor of Belgorod Province, situated on Russia's border with northeastern Ukraine. In an election marked by an unusually high voter turnout of 71 percent, Zhirinovsky came in last of three candidates, with 18 percent of the vote (*Russian Regional Report* of the Institute for EastWest Studies 4, no. 21, June 3, 1999).

On the basis of the LDPR's experience at the regional level, it may be surmised that while the party's nationalist rhetoric may tap strong support from certain social groups, especially the military and those linked with them, the crucial breakthrough to majority support is achieved only when an LDPR politician convinces people that he will be able to solve their socioeconomic problems. The party's poor performance in this sphere in the regions where it has already held power undermines its capacity both to persuade people to re-elect its candidates in those regions and to persuade people to vote for it in other regions. On an optimistic reading, the gradually maturing political judgment of the Russian public may also be a factor in the LDPR's continuing electoral decline.

After the Duma and Presidential Elections

The LDPR has been further weakened by its poor performance in the Duma elections of December 1999, which reduced the size of the party's Duma fraction by one-half, and in the presidential elections of March 2000. At a meeting between Zhirinovsky and regional LDPR leaders held on April 25, 2000, Zhirinovsky announced that, in view of the party's difficult financial situation, its offices in the regions where it had fared the worst would be closed and the property sold. The regional leaders complained—in itself a sign of failing intra-party discipline—that Zhirinovsky's erratic behavior had discredited the LDPR. Zhirinovsky, however, had a better explanation for the disappointing election results: the regional leaders were drunks and thieves.[40]

Zhirinovsky and his colleagues in the LDPR leadership believe that the advent of a more nationalist president undermines the distinctiveness of their party in the public mind. So as "not to end up in the bog," they intend to move somewhat to the right, and to adopt "the defense of ethnic Russians" as their main slogan. Zhirinovsky denied that the contemplated rightward shift would entail the adoption of fascist ideology.[41]

Conclusion

What future lies in store for the LDPR? It is indeed very hard to envisage a dramatic and sustained reversal in the party's fortunes. Even Irina Ushakova, the LDPR's official historian, virtually admits as much:

> Even if the LDPR does not win in future elections, it is sufficiently strong and well-organized to exert a substantial influence on the actions of the state authorities and on the alignment of political forces. (Ushakova 1998, p. 45)

It is more difficult at this stage to be sure whether the decline of the LDPR will be slow and extended over a long period of time or even—as Irina Ushakova presumably expects—level off in the near future, or whether the decline will be precipitous and lead to the party's early demise. The latter possibility certainly cannot be excluded. In any case, Zhirinovsky must eventually leave Russia's political scene, and in light of the complete dependence of all other party members on his leadership, that is bound to lead to the breakup and disappearance of the LDPR, at least in anything like its present form.

What will be the likely impact of the decline of the LDPR on Russian politics? And how might future historians judge the significance that Zhirinovsky and his party will have had for Russia?

However and whenever the LDPR falls apart, its experienced local activists will constitute a large reservoir upon which a new and possibly more clearly fascist Russian nationalist movement will be able to draw. Locked into the party's rigid structure, the activists belonging to the fascist wing of the LDPR are rendered relatively harmless: the political impact they can have while remaining in the ranks of the party is limited, whereas if they leave they find themselves isolated from their former comrades and deprived of the use of the LDPR's massive material resources.[42] However, once the LDPR implodes, this stored-up fascist potential is bound to be released into the "open space" of Russian society. Similar considerations apply with regard to the loyal core of the LDPR's mass electorate.

As concerns the historical significance of the LDPR, I would like to recall some perceptive remarks that the chairman of the Moscow Anti-Fascist Center, Yevgeny Proshechkin, made when I interviewed him in October 1992. One of my questions concerned the political characterization and prospects of Zhirinovsky. He replied that Zhirinovsky was not fully a fascist, and also that he did not believe Zhirinovsky would ever come to power, in part because he was half-Jewish in origin. However, he continued, that did not mean that Zhirinovsky presented no danger. Zhirinovsky fulfilled the function of a battering-ram. He had destroyed taboos that previously protected Russian society from fascism, such as the taboo on the open public expression of ethnic hatred. Thus, Zhirinovsky had prepared the way for a new charismatic nationalist politician who would come after him. This successor would be a "pure-blooded" Russian, and he would be fully fascist.

In all fairness, Zhirinovsky is not the only Russian politician who bears responsibility for "breaking the taboos." But his role has been a very substantial one. Although the LDPR is not a fascist party, it does contain strong fascist tendencies. It is therefore largely, though not wholly, as a result of the rise of the LDPR that fascism is no longer clearly on the periphery of Russian politics. The massive propaganda of the LDPR has not embodied a coherent fascist ideology, but it has helped to familiarize the Russian public with certain ideas characteristic of fascism. One reassuring circumstance is that the new charismatic leader, fully Russian and fully fascist, whom Proshechkin expected to succeed Zhirinovsky has yet to make his appearance.

6
Barkashov and the Russian National Unity

In the literature and on the website of the organization that called itself the Russian National Unity (RNU; in Russian, *Russkoe natsional'noe edinstvo* or RNE), one could in January 1999 read the following announcement:

> For those wishing to join the Moscow Regional Organization of the RNU:
> *Meeting places*
> Metro Station "Novogireyevo"—by the last carriage from the center, Saturdays and Sundays 12.30.
> Metro Station "Kuntsevskaya"—by the first carriage from the center, Saturdays 12.30 and Tuesdays 17.30.
> Metro Station "Semenovskaya"—in the middle of the hall, Saturdays 12.30.
> Metro Station "Avtozavodskaya"—in the middle of the hall, Saturdays and Sundays 12.30, Tuesdays 17.30.
> Metro Station "Ryazansky prospekt"—in the middle of the hall, Saturdays and Sundays 12.30, Tuesdays 17.30.
> Bring your passport with you.[1]

And so Russian investigative journalist Oleg Pavlovsky turned up one sunny Sunday afternoon in the summer of 1998 at the Novogireyevo Metro. He recounts what happened:

> Four fellows in black uniform awaited us. They were talking among themselves, ignoring the gathering crowd.
> Twenty minutes later, our ragged procession set off at a rapid pace along the street and into the park by the Terletsky Ponds. An atmosphere of leisure reigned around us: couples strolled, children ran, someone was sunbathing. It distracted my attention from fascism.

Here we were. A little house lost in the woods, surrounded by a metal grid, like a bunker. A guard casually looked us over as we passed through the gates. We were shown into a small dark room with a single window, chairs, and a table on which lay a pile of freshly printed copies of the latest issue of [the RNU newspaper] *Russkii poryadok* [Russian Order]. . . . The twenty or so of us had difficulty fitting ourselves in. . . . The room sank into silence.

Around me were mainly lads 15–17 years old, many with crewcuts, a couple in khaki uniform. There were three older men: one, with glasses, looked like an intellectual; another seemed to be a tramp. . . .

At last, the sound of firm footsteps. Before us appeared a man of about forty-five, wearing army boots and khaki pants, a Russian commando. Before he even reached the table, he took the situation under control. In a tone that brooked no objection, he asked us not to interrupt him with comments and to keep our questions until later.

His harangue was severe and energetic, accompanied at times by blows of his fist against his palm or the table. He bitterly attacked the numerous adversaries of the organization: the West, the Jews, the communists, the democrats, aliens on Russian soil, even Patriarch Alexy II. The audience reacted sincerely, but with reticence: the barracks atmosphere was oppressive. . . .

The speaker explained to us the meaning of the Russian Nazi symbolism, and began to sketch the ideology of the movement. . . .

He had been speaking already for fifty minutes. I felt fatigued. I watched a roach crawling over the pile of newspapers on the table, but the insect soon disappeared from sight, forcing me again to focus on the RNU. Most of the others remained in rapt attention, all the more so as the speaker was turning to the practical side of the matter.

Straight away we were given to understand that here questions were not appreciated and innovators not needed. In this militarily precise hierarchy, the function of thinking belonged exclusively to the top leadership. . . .

Before joining, we had to pass through a "natural selection." You could not be a patriot if you were undergoing psychiatric treatment, if you were a homosexual, a pervert, a drug addict, an alcoholic, or a tramp. Or if you had a serious criminal charge on your record, or more than two minor ones. . . .[2]

They did not intend to stand on ceremony with us. "You need us, we do not need you."

The organization was a way of life. Strict discipline, use of specified symbols only (Third Reich symbols unofficially permitted), compulsory instruction twice a week. First of all, sports and street fighting. The orator lunged at an imaginary enemy with his fist: the blow was right on target! Excited, the audience applauded, and proceeded to listen to information about learning to shoot.

There would in addition be compulsory theoretical sessions, followed by an examination.

Applicants for membership were obliged to undergo a check of their ancestry. You were required to indicate the full names of your ancestors for as many generations back as possible. It was desirable to include also maiden names on the female side. These data would then be carefully verified "through our own channels." If you tried to lie, you would be "convinced" that it is not good to lie. . . .

The meeting was over. Those wishing to join were requested to complete questionnaires. Everyone except me crowded round the table. I left alone. My curiosity had been fully satisfied.

Coming out through the gates, I saw that people were still strolling in the park. Happy and carefree. (Pavlovskii 1998)

Overview

The harsh world that so aroused the curiosity of this intrepid explorer originated as one of many small offshoots of Dmitry Vasilyev's *Pamyat*, and from this modest beginning grew to become the largest of the unequivocally fascist organizations in Russia.

The RNU was founded, and until its recent split was led, by a former electrician named Alexander Petrovich Barkashov. I begin with an account of Barkashov's personal background and character, and tell the story of how he came to create the RNU. I make some remarks about the style and symbolism of the RNU before proceeding to its worldview, its program, and the sources from which its ideas were taken. Having thereby established the fascist character of the RNU's ideology, I examine the way in which the RNU was organized and operated: its organizational structure, internal divisions, whom it recruited and how, membership turnover, the range of activities in which the movement engaged, and the RNU's general mode of operation.

To give a fuller and more vivid picture of the way the RNU operated, and of how it interacted with Russian society, I next present three pairs of local case studies. I describe first the position of the RNU in the two regions of Russia where it was strongest: the Stavropol and Krasnodar territories of the Northern Caucasus in southern Russia, and the provinces of Oryol and Voronezh in central-western Russia. Then I recount what happened in two medium-sized towns where attempts by the RNU to establish itself failed—Borovichi, Novgorod Province (in northwestern Russia), and Zlatoust, Chelyabinsk Province (in the Urals).

Following the case studies, I assess the size and strength of the RNU prior to its split: the number of members, their geographical distribution, the extent and nature of the public support that the movement enjoyed, its material assets and military potential, and the degree to which it penetrated the structures of central and regional government. A balance sheet is set out of the RNU's strengths and weaknesses.

Next I analyze the place that the RNU occupied in the politics of post-Soviet Russia in the 1990s, and discuss the political strategy of the movement. I describe the campaign that was waged against the RNU in 1998–99 by the presidential administration and Moscow's mayor, Yuri Luzhkov, and finally consider the RNU's prospects as they appeared before the split.

Alexander Barkashov and the RNU

Almost all the accounts of Alexander Barkashov's life that have been published, in Russian or English, are based on the biography disseminated by the RNU itself. This biography contains a number of striking points, such as the influence exerted on young Alexander by his grandfather, allegedly a highly placed party official who had been an organizer of Stalin's "anti-cosmopolitan" campaign, Barkashov's black belt in karate, and his army service as a member of a special Soviet commando unit in Egypt. In February 1999, however, there appeared in a popular Moscow newspaper an article by an investigative journalist who had gone to the trouble of tracking down and interviewing people who had known Barkashov at school, in the army, and at work, only to discover that all these colorful "facts" were myths that had been fabricated to enhance Barkashov's image as a hero and a committed enemy of the Jews (Sukhoverkhov 1999). The truth was more prosaic.

Although he was born in Moscow, on October 6, 1953, Barkashov has purely peasant roots. His parents and grandparents all came from the village of Sennitsa in Moscow Province.[3] His father was an electrician, his mother a nurse. His schoolmates remember him as an indifferent scholar with a penchant for football and fighting, on account of which he was not admitted to the Komsomol (Communist Youth League). In 1971, he left school and entered the military. He passed his military service in an ordinary army unit in Belarus. He did, it is true, volunteer to go to Egypt, but there was no possibility of his doing so, because it was at this time that President Anwar Sadat threw the Soviet military out of his country. Barkashov was not even promoted, and left the army still a private, unlike the Barkashov of RNU legend, who—like Hitler—was promoted to corporal.

Returning to Moscow after his discharge, Barkashov found employment in the enterprise closest to his family's apartment—one of the underground thermal energy stations that control the city's residential heating. He worked there for fourteen years, until 1987, learning to monitor the heating equipment and qualifying (like his father) as an electrician-fitter. But Barkashov was not very interested in his work. Three passions animated him. One was reading books about the great conquerors of history, Alexander the Great and Genghis Khan being his favorites. Another was karate. He attended a well-known karate club and although he won no belts—it was actually his brother Vladimir who won the black belt—he learned to stand up for himself in the beer hall, and set up his own karate club at the heating station to train the local lads. His third passion was cold steel. He learned to make bows and daggers with his own hands.

In 1985 Barkashov joined *Pamyat* (see chapter 2). He rose rapidly within its ranks. Within a year he was elected to the Central Council. By 1989, he was second only to Vasilyev, in effective control of crucial aspects of the organization's activity: security, combat training, and ideological and sports work with youth.

The RNU Emerges

By March 1990, a conflict was developing between Vasilyev and Barkashov. Barkashov accused Vasilyev of preferring fancy-dress drama to serious politics, and also of pocketing the proceeds of *Pamyat*'s cooperative farm "Teremok," where members were put to work gardening, tending vines, and making toys, supposedly to earn money for the organization. Vasilyev accused Barkashov in turn of trying to undermine *Pamyat* on behalf of the KGB. On June 14, Barkashov demonstratively asserted his independence by organizing, behind Vasilyev's back, a march of about sixty blackshirted "fighters" along the Arbat, a fashionable Moscow street (Likhachev and Pribylovskii 1997, p. 7).

The parting of the ways came in August 1990. According to Barkashov, he "led the most disciplined and active members, dissatisfied with empty talk and theatrical stunts, out of *Pamyat*" with a view to forming a more effective vehicle for serious work. Vasilyev claims that it was he who expelled Barkashov, for Nazi propaganda and as a KGB agent.[4] Of no less significance may be the motives of the young men who chose to follow Barkashov rather than remain in *Pamyat*: they resented the labor Vasilyev made them do at "Teremok," the bans he imposed on smoking, on public display of the Nazi swastika, and on the raised-arm "Roman salute"—and the obligation he placed on them to learn prayers by heart (Likhachev and Pribylovskii 1997, p. 8).

Initially, Barkashov and his friends looked around the "patriotic" camp for a new home. Then they decided, while drinking at a café in the GUM shopping center, to create their own organization. On October 16, 1990, a few dozen of Barkashov's followers gathered in an old house on Moscow's Dubinin Street, which was to become the RNU's first headquarters, to establish a new organization. The new movement was initially called "the National Unity for a Free Strong Just Russia."[5] This unwieldy title soon gave way to "the Russian National Unity," which the *Barkashovtsy* informally reduced to the even more compact "the Unity" [*Edinstvo*]. The RNU had been born.[6]

Barkashov as Hero

Barkashov's image-makers continued to spin a heroic legend around his name. An important part of the legend concerned Barkashov's leadership of the RNU fighters who took part in the defense of the White House, the building of the Supreme Soviet, against Boris Yeltsin's forces in October 1993. Thus, the picture was drawn of Barkashov leaning out of a window machine-gunning the troops who were storming the building. It seems very doubtful whether Barkashov really performed any such feat: eyewitnesses report that he is "not at all courageous or cool under fire" (Sukhoverkhov 1999).

In the wake of the defeat of the opposition, Barkashov and some of his close comrades managed to get out of Moscow, thereby escaping arrest. They made their way to Brest, whence his comrades clandestinely crossed the border into Poland. Barkashov lacked the nerve to make the border crossing himself. Instead, he took refuge in a dacha (villa) near Moscow belonging to friends. In the course of a stormy argument at the dacha, a comrade shot him in the hip. Barkashov was taken to a hospital, where he was recognized by a nurse and imprisoned on charges of organizing and inciting mass disorder and illegally bearing arms. The RNU rank-and-file were told that Barkashov had been injured and captured in an enemy assault.

Like the other politicians who had been imprisoned for fighting on the side of the Supreme Soviet, Barkashov was given amnesty in early 1994 by the newly elected Duma. The period following his release was marked by a shift in his spiritual outlook. Under the influence of a guru by the name of Igor Antonov, who combined Orthodoxy with Buddhism and astrology, Barkashov pored over astrological charts in an attempt to determine the date on which he would come to power, and attached an "antenna" to the back of his head to facilitate his communication with the cosmos. By mid-1994 the RNU was seriously weakened and disorganized, and took some time to reconstitute itself (Chelnokov 1999).

Barkashov is no hero, nor is he impressive as a Führer in other respects.

He is not an eloquent orator, and the articles that appear under his name are ghostwritten. Observers describe him as short and pale, though he prefers to describe himself as of medium height (Sukhoverkhov 1999).

The RNU's Style

The most cursory comparison of the literature of *Pamyat* with that of the RNU, or of the websites of the two organizations, reveals how sharply the style of the RNU diverged from that of its parent movement. *Pamyat*, with its intense Orthodox piety and yearning for a restored tsarist autocracy, clearly strives to re-create the style and atmosphere as well as the ideological substance of the Black Hundreds. The rhetoric is long-winded and declamatory, the language often obscure in its archaisms to the uninitiated modern reader. Even the prerevolutionary Cyrillic orthography has been lovingly revived.[7] The style of the RNU's discourse was one that generations coming to maturity in the 1980s and 1990s must have found much more familiar. Homage was still paid to Orthodoxy, and occasional reference was made to a "higher mystical reality"; sacred imagery was invoked in the poems; and there was even an RNU hymn, sung to a tune more than faintly reminiscent of *The Internationale*. But religion no longer occupied the central place. One can hardly imagine Barkashov boasting, as does Vasilyev, that "all his activity he carries out only with the blessing of the hierarchs of the Russian Orthodox Church"! Most of the time, the RNU spoke in a straightforward and forceful everyday contemporary idiom, sometimes with a mildly bureaucratic flavor rather reminiscent of late Soviet officialese. In short, the contrasting styles of the two organizations highlight the fact that *Pamyat* is merely reactionary, whereas the RNU had made the transition to fascism proper.

The RNU's Symbols

The symbols adopted by the RNU reflected an attempt at compromise between the evident preference of some members for openly Nazi symbols and the unacceptability of such symbols to a broader public. In general, Nazi symbols were slightly modified and reinterpreted in terms of Russian tradition. Thus, the emblem that appeared on the RNU flag and on the sleeve of the RNU uniform was indeed constructed around a swastika—not, however, the right-handed swastika [*svastika*] that the Germans used, but the left-handed swastika or *kolovrat* which (so it was pointed out) is an ancient *Russian* symbol, appearing on weapons and clothing from the time of Prince Svyatoslav and signifying the presence of God in Russia and His protection in the struggle against Russia's enemies.[8] This swastika was embedded in the eight-pointed star of the Mother of God [*bogoroditsa*], another traditional Russian symbol that counterposed the "Judeo-Masonic" five-pointed star of the Bolsheviks.

The RNU emblem was held to possess mystical power. By arousing ancient archetypes deeply embedded in the racial memory, the sight of the *kolovrat* on the fighter's sleeve acted upon his subconscious to strengthen his inner powers, as it acted upon the subconscious of his occult enemy to paralyze, weaken, and demoralize him (*Russkii stiag*, October 1995, p. 7). Barkashov believes that the contest of psyches, using occult means of influence against one another, is an important part of the political struggle,[9] and that symbols play a vital role in this contest.

When one member of the RNU greeted another, he would clasp his hand around the other's wrist, or raise his right arm forward with palm open and cry: *Slava Rossii!* [Glory to Russia!]. Lest this seem too close to the German *Heil*, it was explained that the salute signified the priority given to the spiritual over the material. As for the black shirts and quasi-military uniforms, which "stimulate the will of the people and demoralize the enemy," these were meant to recall to memory none other than the original "Black Hundreds"—that is, the black-clad warrior monks who led Russian troops into battle in times of old.[10]

The RNU's Worldview

Barkashov's followers were Russian nationalists, for whom the interests of the Russian nation were the supreme value.[11] Two features of their nationalism served to distinguish them from the general run of less extreme Russian nationalists or "patriots." First, as will already be clear from the prologue, who counted as "Russian" was determined primarily on the basis of racial descent, rather than on that of language, culture, self-ascription, or loyalty to the Russian state.[12] Second, a sharp distinction came to be drawn between "nationalism" and mere "patriotism."[13] While the "patriot" regarded Russia as a state as the highest value, and subordinated to it the interests of the Russian nation, for the true nationalist it was the interests of the Russian nation that were supreme, and Russia as a state was to be placed in the service of those interests by turning it into an ethnic-Russian "national state" (Barkashov 1994, pp. 72–80). Thus, the RNU defied the negative connotations that, since the Soviet period, have surrounded the word "nationalist." Moreover, the interests of the Russian nation were understood in a messianic rather than a purely utilitarian sense. Hence, the analyst Andrei Andreyev, who distinguishes among "statist," "nationalist," and "national-fundamentalist" varieties of Russian national-patriotism, assigns the RNU to the national-fundamentalists (Andreev 1997, pp. 94, 117).

As in the case of classical fascism, the basic schema in terms of which the RNU interpreted historical events was that of a remorseless struggle between the destructive conspiratorial forces of cosmopolitan Jewry, intent upon world domination and aided in recent times by Freemasonry, and the Gentile nations, striving—once they become aware of the peril facing them—to preserve or restore their own independent national states. Nazi Germany and fascist Italy were states that had broken free of the control of the international Jewish financial oligarchy, whereas the West, especially the United States, was in thrall to Jewish power.

What was the place of Russia in this schema? Russia's struggle against the Jews, it was said, dates from the formative period of its statehood, for "the first foreign enemy of the Russian Land" were the Khazars (Volgin 1997). (The Khazars were a semi-nomadic Turkic people who adopted Judaism and whose empire, based in the lower reaches of the Volga, lasted from the seventh century to the thirteenth century.[14]) The tsars had kept Russia more or less independent until the catastrophe of 1917, when the country fell under the yoke of the Jewish-dominated Bolshevik regime. Stalin led a counteroffensive against the Jews. The struggle continued under Stalin's successors, until the second catastrophe of 1991 restored the power of Jewry over Russia in a new "democratic" form. Now the Russian people faced the threat of chaos, enslavement, and genocide. But "the era of Russia approaches" (Barkashov 1994, pp. 5–25).

A special problem here for the RNU was the interpretation to be given to the "Great Patriotic War" of 1941–45. Barkashov has often expressed his admiration for Adolf Hitler (Simonsen 1996a, p. 38). In an interview for *Den,* Barkashov went so far as to declare that Hitler had in his own way been right to consider the Slavs cattle worthy of extermination, but the subsequent reaction demonstrated that such complete identification with the Nazis, logical as it might be within the terms of the schema, was likely to alienate even the "patriotic" Russian public (Peresvet 1995). A more palatable version presented the war as a tragic misunderstanding between two fraternal nations, caused by the provocation and manipulation of the Jews, although Barkashov granted that the older generation would find this hard to understand (Barkashov 1994, pp. 81–86). It seems, however, that the RNU later decided that it was necessary to take a clear anti-German stance with regard to the Great Patriotic War. Reports appeared of the RNU assisting in searches for the remains of Russian soldiers killed in the war,[15] and of RNU members marching to war memorials to lay flowers by the eternal torch "in memory of Russian warriors who perished in battle against German chauvinism" ("Far Eastern Nazis" 1998; "Tsvety vozlozhili" 1999). In invading the USSR, Hitler had presumably betrayed the true principles of national-socialism.

Another thorny problem for the RNU, as for all Christian anti-Semites, was that Christ had been a Jew. One possible solution was to reject Christianity as a Jewish religion and try to return to the pagan beliefs of pre-Christian Rus. This is in fact the solution favored by some neo-pagan fascist groups (see chapter 8). Although Barkashov's outlook does include pagan elements, such as a belief in astrology and the power of magic, he had always stopped short of any open repudiation of Christianity. When the RNU organization in Samara Province adopted its own neo-pagan variant of the RNU doctrine, it was expelled by the central leadership (Likhachev and Pribylovskii 1997, p. 55). The RNU preferred an alternative solution to the problem of Christ's relationship to the Jews: to deny that Christ had been a Jew. An RNU theorist explains that the Galileans, to whom both Jesus and all the apostles except Judas belonged, were racially distinct from the Jews, and suggests that they may have been of Aryan and Slavic origin (Rogozhin 1994). A former member of the RNU reports how this theme was elaborated at a political instruction session for new recruits:

> Jesus Christ was no Jew, as Zionist propaganda claims. He was a pure-blooded Slav from Novgorod,[16] who went to Palestine with the aim of impeding Jewish expansion in the Roman Empire. It was precisely for that that he was crucified. But his cause lives on. (Khudokormov 1994)

In some contexts, the simple basic schema based on the Jewish–Gentile polarity was recognized to be inadequate. Thus, in describing the contemporary world situation, Barkashov identifies not one but two separate centers of hostile power: the Western center, headed by the United States and dominated by the Jewish financial oligarchy, and the Eastern center, which includes China, India, and Japan. Both these centers seek to expand at Russia's expense, aiming at "a deliberate reduction in Russia's population in order to vacate territory and resources for other peoples," but while the West is concerned mainly to plunder Russia's raw materials with the assistance of a dependent regime, the East relieves its overpopulation by sending migrants to conquer Russian land (RNU Website). Here then we have a double polarity: Russians/Jews and Russians/Asiatics. In practical terms, the threat from the East was most immediately embodied in the Chinese and the Muslim peoples of the Caucasus and Central Asia.

A modified schema likewise emerges when Barkashov delves into the prehistoric origins of the Jewish–Gentile polarity. The Russians, we are told, belong to the white Aryan race, and are descended from the Etruscans. The Jews, in contrast, were created by the priests of ancient Egypt out of a Hamitic–

Semite (that is, Negro–Arab) mixture. Egypt, in its turn, was a post-Atlantean civilization, founded by descendants of refugees from submerging Atlantis. The Jews are therefore a relatively recent offshoot of Atlantis, the Aryans' ultimate enemy (Barkashov 1997a). Barkashov seems to have borrowed this account from the *Pamyat* theoretician Valery Yemelyanov (Shnirelman 1998, p. 2).

Yet another form is taken by the Jewish–Gentile polarity when viewed from the vantage point of the "higher mystical reality" that determines the world-historical mission of the Russian nation. Here we are back in the medieval world of Christian apocalyptic and millenarian prophecy portrayed by Norman Cohn (1957). The "soulless West" appears as the Kingdom of Antichrist, in thrall to the Devil, the Jews as Satan's servants, and national-socialism as God's Kingdom on Earth. As for the Russians, they have been chosen by God and Christ "to bring to God, and keep out of the Kingdom of Antichrist, both ourselves and any other peoples we can" (RNU Website; Barkashov 1997b). For Armageddon is approaching.

Involuntarily, Voltaire's maxim comes to mind: "Those who believe in absurdities will commit atrocities."

The RNU Program

The RNU program has many gaps. One learns hardly anything from it about the constitution or political system of the future "national state." Nor is much attention devoted to the way the economy of the new Russia is to function (with the exception of agriculture). However, the program does provide some insight into the thinking of the RNU concerning the policy it hoped to implement upon coming to power in such areas as interethnic relations, education, and defense. Moreover, to a certain extent gaps in the program can be filled by drawing upon other RNU sources, such as "The Principles of the RNU" (Barkashov 1994, pp. 26–50).[17]

The Political System of the "National State"

The RNU set its overall goal as "the restoration of Russia as a national state and the rebirth of the Russian Nation"—a formula corresponding closely to Griffin's concept of fascism as palingenesis. The new Russia envisaged by the RNU was accordingly to be a "national state" or a regime of "national power"—that is, a state in which the Russian nation reigns supreme and its interests have priority.

The program does not explain the mechanism by means of which the Russian nation was to exercise its supremacy, but the "Principles" mention a representative body to be called the "National Assembly" [*natsional'nyi sobor*].[18] The National Assembly is to secure just and balanced "vertical" representation of the nation's "estates" or social groups, of which six are listed, presumably in declining order of prestige: the clergy, the military, state employees, workers, peasants, and entrepreneurs. At the same time, it is to secure "horizontal" representation of Russia's regions. Each estate and each region will be responsible for its own specific contribution, to be determined as far as possible on the basis of tradition, toward the fulfillment of the tasks facing the national state. A state organized in this fashion is identified as a "national-labor state" (Barkashov 1994, pp. 27–28). This term, however, was not widely employed in RNU literature.

Nationalities Policy

For the RNU, as ethno-racial nationalists, a nationalities policy was naturally of central importance in ensuring the supremacy of the Russian nation, a category understood to include Ukrainians and Belarusians as well as Great Russians. The principle that Russians are once again to play their "natural" leading role in the state is to be implemented in educational and personnel policy. Russian young people, for instance, are to enjoy priority access to higher education.

Non-Slavic indigenous peoples for whom "Russia is the only homeland and the defense and building of Russia have become a historical tradition" will also have a place in the new Russia. They will be represented in state bodies and in social institutions such as the media in proportion to their share in the population, and will be granted a measure of cultural, but not political or territorial, autonomy. The RNU, like the LDPR, advocated restoration of the three-tier system of administrative-territorial subdivisions used in tsarist times (*guberniia*, *uezd*, *volost'*). At the same time, non-Slavic ethnic minorities will be expected to "respect Russians and the decisions taken by Russians" (Lunin 1996).

Which non-Russian peoples are considered to satisfy the conditions laid down for toleration is not specified in the open sources, nor is it explained what fate lies in store for those peoples who fail to do so.[19] Presumably they are to be deported or exterminated. Some reports in the Russian press have mentioned the existence of secret RNU documents that state that all Jews and Gypsies are to be killed.[20] The alternative of forcing all Jews to leave the country, still favored by some contributors to the RNU Forum website, is rejected by Barkashov on the grounds that it will only strengthen Jewry abroad, thereby increasing the external threat to Russia. Consistent with such reports are the lists of names, addresses, and telephone numbers of Jewish families found in police searches of the apartments of local RNU leaders in Oryol and other places (Dunlop 1996, p. 525; Union of Councils 1997, pp. 22, 71).

Economic and Social Policy

The RNU program envisages a mixed economy within which the state will exercise control over "vital branches" and hold land and natural resources as its inalienable property. Russian entrepreneurs are to be assisted and protected by the state. Wages are to be "sufficient for the dignified life of the worker and his family," so that women with children do not have to go out to work unless they wish to. The state will provide free education and health care, and will support the elderly and disabled.

Great importance is attached to "the rebirth of the Russian peasantry," for the peasantry is "the healthiest and genetically purest part of the Nation, the basis of the Nation's physical existence, and the link between the rest of the Nation and the Russian soil." Peasant families will be assigned land for permanent use, with the right to bequeath it to their descendants but not to sell it. They will be free to choose between individual and collective forms of farming. They will also receive grants and tax privileges, and interest-free state loans will be made available to them through a network of land banks.

The national regime will employ both moral and material incentives to strengthen the family and encourage a high birth rate among Russians, thereby ensuring that their demographic preponderance is strengthened, or at least not weakened. Special priority is assigned to "guarding the health and genetic purity of the Russian Nation": there will be a state program of eugenics, and interethnic sexual relations and mixed marriages will be strongly discouraged.[21]

Educational, Ideological, and Religious Policy

A new general educational program is to be developed in accordance with national principles, and the educational system will be purged of "anti-national" personnel. The intelligentsia inherited from the Soviet period is "an internationalist, anti-national stratum," and must therefore be completely replaced by "a new national intellectual elite."

The dissemination of "anti-Russian views" and the use of "anti-Russian symbols" are to be liable to criminal prosecution as serious state crimes. Also to be forbidden by law are "propaganda of mixed marriages" and "propaganda undermining the foundations of the family or the spiritual and physical health of Russian youth," such as pornography and the advocacy of free love, perversions, drugs, and drink. Religious freedom will be permitted only to the extent that it "strengthens Russians' spiritual forces," and any religious teaching that "weakens Russians' national self-consciousness, patriotism, unity, and spirit" will be suppressed.

Foreign and Defense Policy

In the sphere of foreign policy, the main priority of the RNU was clearly the consolidation of Russia's control over the post-Soviet region, leading to the establishment of a unitary Russian Empire within the boundaries of the former Soviet Union.[22] Should Russia fail to achieve this goal, "our place [in the newly independent states] will be occupied by the strategic adversaries of our survival on this planet." Russians living in the other post-Soviet states may advance tactical demands for cultural and territorial autonomy, but ultimately Russia will have to reannex these states, by military means if necessary ("Neizbyvnaia" 1998). The policy of the RNU with regard to the post-Soviet region was therefore similar to that of Zhirinovsky's LDPR.

The new Russian Empire is conceived as a closed autarkic economic system. Raw materials will not be sold abroad but preserved for the benefit of future generations of Russians. Russian entrepreneurs will be protected by the state and given priority over foreigners.

The RNU program states that "all unequal international agreements concluded by the anti-Russian rulers of Russia will be declared null and void. Persons directly or indirectly guilty of concluding such agreements will be liable to criminal punishment, wherever they may live." Which agreements are covered by this provision is not indicated.

As concerns defense policy, it is considered necessary for Russia to maintain parity in military capability with the United States. Military industry is to be reconstructed in order to provide the armed forces with the most powerful and up-to-date armaments. Both the pay and the prestige of the officer corps are to be enhanced, and it is to be purged of individuals holding democratic and internationalist views. There is to be a compulsory universal draft, but only for Russians, suggesting that it may be intended to staff the armed forces solely with Russians.

Little specific information is available concerning the RNU's longer-term global aspirations. Barkashov's eschatological vision implies that in the aftermath of the coming "final battle between Good and Evil" Russia will emerge as master of the world. Another RNU leader is quoted as declaring that "if 70 percent of Russia's national income were spent not on parasitic peoples, who in gratitude spit in Russians' faces and kill them, but on the armed forces, then they would impose order first on the country and then on the world" (Shatrov 1998b). And the RNU hymn culminates in the couplet:

> For in the world there must be one Order,
> And by rights it must be Russian.

The Sources of the RNU's Ideology

Four immediate sources of the RNU's ideology in twentieth-century political thought are identifiable: German Nazism, Italian fascism, Romanian fascism, and the Black Hundreds tradition of late tsarist Russia.[23]

By far the most important of these was undoubtedly Hitlerite national-socialism. Besides the close correspondence between the Nazi and the RNU worldview, the RNU program is similar at many points to the program of the National Socialist German Workers' Party (NSDAP). The resemblance is especially striking with respect to such themes as racial purity and agriculture, in which the motif of *Blut und Boden* [Blood and Soil] is salient. A more contemporary touch is added by references to genetics (as in "the genofund of the Russian Nation"). The borrowing from Nazism was undoubtedly deliberate, Barkashov's personal sympathy and self-identification with Hitler being well known. Of course, in borrowing from German Nazism, Barkashov introduced some necessary revisions—elevating the Slavs, for instance, from *Untermenschen* to a branch of the Aryan race.[24]

Next in importance was the influence of prerevolutionary Russian conservatism. The Orthodox and anti-Semitic elements of the Black Hundreds tradition were retained from *Pamyat*, although the central element of that tradition, devotion to autocracy, was abandoned. The links that remained to the Black Hundreds tradition served to soften and russify somewhat the harsh and alien racism of German Nazism by adding to it a "spiritual" and—above all—a native Russian dimension. Articles that have appeared in *Russkii poriadok* on the life and ideas of Corneliu Codreanu, founder of the interwar Romanian League of the Archangel Michael and of the Iron Guard, suggest that Romanian fascism was another source of Barkashov's "spiritual" mysticism (Dunlop 1996, p. 526).

Less essential was the contribution of classical Italian fascism. The idea of the "national-labor state" bears the clear imprint of Italian fascist corporatism, possibly mediated through Russian émigré fascism (although this link is not acknowledged in RNU sources), but as we have seen this idea was not given much prominence.

Ideas from these and other sources were not successfully synthesized into a coherent whole. The RNU's ideology remained somewhat of a mishmash.

The RNU's Organizational Structure

In principle, the RNU functioned as a strictly centralized, hierarchical, and disciplined organization, operating in accordance with the principle of authoritarian leadership. This does not mean that all significant decisions were taken at the top. On the contrary, each lower-level leader or "commander" was assigned undivided and broad responsibility within his[25] sphere of competence. Nor was provision lacking for consultation: each leader was assisted by an advisory council made up of his subordinates (RNU Website). But when a superordinate in the RNU hierarchy did give an order to his subordinate, implicit obedience was expected. This was one of the ways in which the RNU resembled a military structure. Clashes of personality and differences over ideology, strategy, and tactics could and did arise within the RNU, especially within the leadership stratum, and the passionate debate on a wide range of issues (albeit rarely if ever calling ideological fundamentals into question) to be found on the RNU's Internet forum showed that discussion did take place in and around the RNU milieu. However, the organizational structure provided very limited scope for the open expression of differences. Certainly, as Likhachev and Pribylovsky (1997, p. 41) argue, the RNU stood out as an effectively centralized organization by comparison with other large Russian political organizations—even by comparison with the LDPR, within which important ideological differences are tolerated (see chapter 5). At the same time, serious tensions were able to develop inside the RNU, culminating in an internal leadership coup.

The leading body of the RNU was the Central Council, the chairman of which was Barkashov. (During the months following October 1993, when the RNU was forced to operate underground, the Central Council was replaced by another body, the Council of Commanders, better adapted to running the organization under conditions of illegality.) Full information on the composition of the Central Council is not available, but it is known that its members fell into two main groups: Moscow-based individuals personally beholden to Barkashov, and leaders of the larger regional organizations from other cities, who had built local power bases of their own and were consequently a little less dependent on Barkashov. Barkashov was accused of packing the Central Council with his Moscow loyalists and including as few of the regional leaders as he could (Zverev et al. 1999). The very existence of the issue suggested that the Central Council, while hardly a body of genuine collective leadership, placed some limits on Barkashov's authority and might in certain circumstances constitute a threat to his position.

Thus, there is some uncertainty concerning the real role that Barkashov has played in the RNU in recent years. Despite his title of "chief comrade-in-arms" [*glavnyi soratnik*] and the display of his portrait in RNU offices, his position was not very secure. Given his personal inadequacies, he must have relied heavily on more competent colleagues in running the organization. For this reason and also in view of his lack of charisma, he did not enjoy the kind of unquestioned authority that his idol Adolf Hitler had in the NSDAP. Nor did Barkashov claim to be indispensable; on the contrary: he stated that he had created an organization of an original type, the vitality of which would not be affected by his own departure (Prokhanov 1998). A defector from one of the RNU intelligence agencies reports his chiefs telling him that "Barkashov is the leader of our fighters, but not the leader of the movement, not a fuhrer" (Khudokormov 1994), from which we may guess at least that Barkashov was not in full control of the RNU intelligence agencies.

Central Agencies

We do not have a complete organizational chart for the RNU, but some of its central agencies can be enumerated.

First, there was a press service and the editorial boards of the main newspaper *Russkii poriadok*, the less important *Russkii stiag* [Russian Banner],[26] and the new periodical *Znaki vremen* [Signs of the Times].

Second, there were the RNU intelligence agencies. There must have been several of them, for the pseudonymous author of what remains the most important single source on the RNU is a former agent of the RNU's "Counter-Intelligence B" (Khudokormov 1994). The first RNU security agency was created at the end of 1992 by a former secret agent of the Ministry of Internal Affairs (MIA), Alexander Denisov (Likhachev and Pribylovskii 1997, p. 17).

Third, there was a specialized organization called "Kolovrat" [Swastika], led by Konstantin Nikitenko, the RNU leader for Moscow and Moscow Province, which was created at the time of the first All-Russian RNU Congress in February 1997 in order to coordinate the organization's "military-patriotic work"—that is, the predraft military training of youth ("I Vserossiiskii" 1997).

Finally, RNU leaders mentioned that the organization was engaged in the "training of national cadres" to fill administrative positions under the future national regime, for which purpose a special department was created at Volgograd State University (RNU Website). Presumably, some specialized agency of the RNU controlled this work.

Territorial Structure

Turning to the RNU's territorial structure, the direct subordination of city and provincial organizations to the central leadership appeared to be giving way to a more complex system in which an intermediate layer of "supervisors"[27] controlled or "coordinated" all organizations within a broad region and reported directly to the top leadership. For instance, in September 1998 Barkashov issued a decree appointing Andrei Dudinov, until then leader of the RNU organization in the Stavropol Territory, supervisor for the whole of the South of Russia.[28] There was a supervisor for the Urals region, for the Far East, and so on (Kaminskii 1999).

Organizations in areas where the RNU was better established were also assigned the task of supervising and assisting weaker organizations in other areas—usually, but not always, neighboring areas. Thus, the strong Voronezh organization was made responsible for building up the RNU's position in St. Petersburg, where for various reasons—in particular, the strength of rival nationalist groups, especially Yuri Belyaev's National Republican Party of Russia (see chapter 8)—the RNU had great difficulty in establishing itself.[29] The organizations of the Voronezh and Rostov provinces, which both border eastern Ukraine, supervised the RNU organizations in Ukraine ("Neizbyvnaia" 1998).[30] Similarly, the strong Volgograd organization carried out propaganda in the neighboring Astrakhan and Saratov provinces and in Kalmykia, as well as in the neighboring "Russian" territories of Kazakhstan.[31]

Departmental Structure

In addition to the "vertical" geographical structure of the RNU, Barkashov has described a "horizontal" structure, based on the "three-in-one principle of Aryan statehood: Strength—Glory—Riches" (Barkashov 1994, pp. 48–49). In accordance with this principle, the RNU was supposed to be divided at all levels into three departments, dealing, respectively, with self-defense, ideology, and finances. To what extent this particular system was implemented in practice is unclear.

Levels of Membership

Another important triad—Barkashov evidently shares the belief that the number three brings good luck—pertains to the three levels at which an individual could participate in the RNU.[32]

The lowest level of participant was that of "supporter" [*storonnik*] or "sympathizer" [*sochuvstvuiushchii*]. Supporters were by far the largest of the three categories, and constituted the RNU's social base and reservoir of potential activists. Apart from compulsory attendance at a meeting once or twice a month, the supporter was free to decide what work he would do for the RNU in accordance with his personal circumstances. He would be asked to carry out certain tasks, but might decline if he so chose.

The middle level was that of "associate" or "candidate member" or (more literally) "fellow-builder" [*spodvizhnik*], and the top level was that of "comrade-in-arms" [*soratnik*] or "member." Barkashov himself bore the special title of "chief comrade-in-arms" [*glavnyi soratnik*]. The activism of associates and comrades-in-arms, unlike that of supporters, was compulsory. Comrades-in-arms were subject to strict military discipline. They were required to devote a major part of their time to the RNU, and be willing to subordinate their personal interests to the interests of the organization. It seems that "associate" was a temporary status: either the associate would, within a certain period, prove himself worthy of elevation to "comrade-in-arms," or he would revert to "supporter" or leave the movement altogether.

It should be noted that RNU terminology in this sphere did not correspond to that used by most ordinary political parties and movements (although there are evident parallels with the traditional practice of the Communist Party). The RNU counted only the comrades-in-arms as "members," but even the supporters were involved in its activity to no lesser extent than the passive majority of members are involved in the activity of most other political organizations.

Set apart from the three levels of supporters, associates, and comrades-in-arms, there was in fact a fourth type of participant in the RNU—the secret RNU collaborator who occupied a position in central, provincial, or local government, in the police, armed forces, or state security agencies, in a political party or trade union, in the media or the Russian Orthodox Church, in a bank or commercial structure, or even in a criminal gang. Secret collaborators might be referred to as "sympathizers," "allies" [*soiuzniki*], "friends," or simply as "our people." The collaborator maintained contact with the RNU solely through one of its intelligence agents: even Barkashov might not be aware of his identity. The defector from the RNU's "Counter-Intelligence-B," for example, maintained liaison with four RNU collaborators within the Federal Counter-Intelligence Service (Khudokormov 1994).

Internal Divisions

In principle, as we have shown, the RNU was a highly centralized organization. In practice, ideological, personal, and other differences could not be totally eliminated.

The most common type of internal conflict was the clash between rival claimants to the leadership of a regional organization. Where a single informal leader arose in a given city and was recognized by the RNU center, he could build an active and united branch. If, however, two informal leaders appeared, each with his own coterie of followers, then a debilitating struggle between them was likely to ensue. The struggle usually ended only when one of the rivals was forced out of the RNU, or possibly when the center imposed a new leader brought in from another city. An example is provided by a recent conflict between two informal leaders of the RNU organization in Yekaterinburg (the Urals city formerly known as Sverdlovsk), who "[pulled the organization] in opposite directions—one inclined to turn it into a kind of Masonic lodge, the other favoring more meetings and demonstrations" (Kaminskii 1999).

Occasionally, situations arose in which the leaders and members of a regional organization fell out for some reason with the central leadership. In a conflict of this type there was more likely to be an ideological element. We have already come across the case of the Samara neo-pagans. Another case was a protest made by the Sakhalin organization in the Far East at the military support that the RNU had rendered to the "Judeo–Communist" Supreme Soviet in October 1993.[33] No doubt Russia's vast expanse makes it difficult for the central leadership of any countrywide organization, even one as disciplined as the RNU, to maintain effective control over the periphery. However, significant disagreements between regionally based groups and the central leadership did not persist for long, being resolved either by the submission of the dissidents or by their departure from the RNU. The central leadership would face a more serious challenge to its authority only when a substantial number of discontented regional leaders formed a united front.

There also appears to have been a division between the visible public hierarchy and the chiefs of the RNU intelligence agencies. The intelligence specialists regarded themselves as the RNU's intellectuals, and despised the stupid but conceited "supermen" who headed the regional organizations and sat on the Central Council. They wanted to rationalize, deritualize, and modernize the RNU's ideology, moderating the "outdated" emphasis on anti-Semitism (Khudokormov 1994).

Recruitment and Turnover

From the prologue to this chapter the reader will already have gained some idea of the process of recruitment into the RNU. According to the standard procedure, the applicant attended a recruitment meeting at which he completed and handed in a questionnaire. There were variations on this procedure. In Moscow in the winter of 1998–99, for example, the publicity surrounding Mayor Yuri Luzhkov's ban on the RNU holding a congress in the capital triggered a sudden surge in applications, and it was necessary to speed up the recruitment procedure. Questionnaires were distributed in Terletsky Park; those wishing to join completed them and lined up before tables in outdoor pavilions for a preliminary interview with an RNU representative. It was also possible to apply for membership by turning up at an RNU office and asking to join, although one might have to convince the comrades on duty of one's sincerity before they would hand over the necessary questionnaires (Aksenov 1999).

Following verification of the information provided, especially regarding racial pedigree and criminal record, a decision was taken whether to admit the applicant into an induction program of combat training and political instruction. The program had two variants: one, the less demanding, for those content to enter the RNU as "supporters"; the other, called the "quarantine," for those recruits who wished to become "fellow-builders" without delay. The quarantine entailed intensive training in a group under the close observation of a leader, who decided which applicants would be admitted as associates and which only as supporters.

Political instruction was not limited to formal theory:

> To back up the theory, meetings are arranged with those who have allegedly suffered from Jewish genocide: embittered retired people, drunk actors, unrecognized poets, expelled students, hungry workers, prostituted intellectuals, . . . who have suddenly (not without payment) become ardent patriots. (Khudokormov 1994)

Upon being accepted for elevation to full membership, the new recruit "entered the ranks of comrades-in-arms of the RNU" by taking the Oath. He swore loyalty to Russia and the Russian nation, undertook to be guided by the orders of the Chief Comrade-in-Arms and his own "national consciousness" without regard to any other laws, and acknowledged that the rightful penalty for treason was death. At the same time, he became subject to the RNU Code of Honor. The Oath and Code of Honor were so important in defining the ethos of the RNU that I append full translations of them to this chapter (see page 187).

All observers are agreed that the main social base of recruitment to the RNU was urban youth, and especially unemployed and poorly educated adolescents and young men from a working-class background. This is consistent with sociological findings to the effect that Russian nationalist attitudes are concentrated most heavily in the youngest age groups.[34] At the same time, the role played in recruitment to the RNU by preexisting ideological orientation should not be exaggerated. Much evidence bears witness to the fact that the appeal of the RNU to deprived and neglected youth derived less from its ideology than from the material and psychological benefits it had to offer them. Inculcation of the RNU ideology came after recruitment, not before it.

The youngster who joined the RNU did not need to fear being left at a loose end, as did others of his generation after the demise of the Komsomol (Communist Youth League) and the curtailment of official youth activities such as the military games *Zarnitsa* [Summer Lightning].[35] The combat skills that he would learn free of charge, besides enhancing his self-respect as a "real man," would equip him to earn a livelihood—most likely in the burgeoning and prestigious private protection and debt collection business,[36] or possibly in an elite unit of the armed forces, a criminal gang, or (for the lucky few) as an RNU leader. The RNU would even arrange a job for him, as a guard or perhaps just a loader—and in exchange dock a hefty share of his pay, typically one-third (Karachinskii 1999; "Sponsory" 1999). In addition, there would be free food to eat, a free uniform to wear, and perhaps free travel around the country. And as a member of a "wolves' pack," he would have companionship, a sense of identity and superiority, an outlet for his understandable feelings of frustration and resentment, the security of being reliably protected in a dangerous environment by a powerful organization, the excitement attendant upon the anticipation of violence, and a purpose in life.[37]

An eloquent description of the social milieu from which the RNU drew its recruits is that of the journalist Anna Politkovskaya, who spent a Sunday morning in December 1998 talking with applicants standing in line outside the RNU pavilions in Moscow's Terletsky Park (Politkovskaia 1998). Her interlocutors, aged between fourteen and twenty and of both sexes, had come to the park in groups of friends from Moscow suburbs and satellite settlements, having heard about the RNU from leaflets or (via parents) from television. The journalist is struck by their "extremely primitive and ignorant minds," by their poor diction and limited vocabulary (except for *mat*, the traditional Russian screw-your-mother swearing), by the semi-illiteracy revealed in their questionnaires, by their boundless hatred for the authorities, the media, their teachers, and their parents, and by their "empty eyes," which she is inclined to attribute either to addiction to drugs[38] or bad alcohol or to the effects of prolonged malnutrition. Many had dropped out of school early, even though they had no jobs to go to. Why did they want to join the RNU? They denied having any ideological reasons:

> We need some kind of entertainment. In our neighborhood there's nothing at all to do, unless you're on drugs. Today the whole gang of us came down to join the RNU. If it's interesting, we'll stay. If not, we'll get out quick.

One girl admitted to an even more basic motive:

> "Will you put on a black uniform, if they give you one?"
> "Yes, I like black. And if they feed us at the sessions, then you won't be able to tear me away from there."

As Politkovskaya argues, the RNU's strength lay in the weakening or collapse of all components of the previous system of upbringing: the schools, the youth organizations, apprenticeship into secure employment, and the family. The resulting vacuum gave the RNU the opportunity to present itself to disoriented youth as an alternative provider of paternal care and authority. Politkovskaya compares fascism with drug addiction: it is a means by which "ignorant and bored youngsters needed by nobody drown their feelings of insignificance and fill their inner emptiness." To this it might be added that if for some young people the RNU served as an alternative to drugs, then for others it was an alternative to the world of organized crime (Tarasov 1996, p. 26). The RNU may be likened to a suction apparatus, ingeniously designed to draw in the members of Russia's abandoned post-Soviet generation and transform them into the foot soldiers of an unknown future war.

This is not to imply that the efficiency of the suction apparatus was very high. The turnover of the RNU's young recruits was enormous. Many left when they discovered that belonging to the RNU was much less "interesting" than they had hoped; others left out of disappointment that the material rewards offered were so meager, or because they felt stifled by the regimentation:

> Young lads think that in the RNU they'll be able to earn some money, but there are no decent wages there, and you get fed up with these stupid military games. (Former member, interviewed in Tokareva 1999)

> People are leaving the RNU. And when you shake all this off, a new life begins. At last I felt myself a personality, an independent living organism, and not part of a blind black mass, following an incomprehensible idea. Although what idea? There is none. (Sergei, twenty, interviewed in Kulakova 1999)

Yet others found that the climate of personal relations within the movement did not live up to their expectations of selfless companionship in a common cause. Thus, one investigator likens the Vladivostok RNU organization to "a big vipers' nest" in which the leaders embezzle funds and exploit the rank-and-file members for their private benefit, everyone spies and informs on everyone else, and deception and betrayal are the norm (Karachinskii 1999). But even in those places where the RNU leaders were not corrupt, the self-sacrifice and sheer hard work that were required of members sufficed to alienate all but the most dedicated.

Thus, while the number of youngsters who passed through the RNU was evidently very large, the inner core of those with a long-term commitment to the movement was much smaller. The pressures that impelled even many of these committed individuals eventually to leave are movingly portrayed by a former RNU member:

> Drinking is prohibited, but many smoke, out of nervousness. Every evening political instruction or combat training, every day distribution of leaflets and journals, some nights on duty at headquarters, and on days off, work expeditions to distant districts. Few can withstand the insane tempo. Many are those who leave, broken. . . . Or they leave under pressure from their wives, as a result of the stress it imposes on family life.. . .
>
> Youthful romanticism dissipates when you realize how much you are sacrificing. And if your parents are against [your involvement in the RNU], and the old women in the courtyard whisper that you're a fascist, and drunkards and wisecracks accost you in the street. . . . I left because my faith in victory was not strong enough. (Interview in Subbotin 1999)

Some of those who left the RNU remained sympathetic to the ideals, as opposed to the practice, of the movement. Others—the most deeply alienated—worked against the organization to which they used to belong, despite the great personal risk entailed by such "treason." Of particular interest is a group of former members who helped young people leaving the RNU to readjust to normal life and sought to provide more constructive outlets for the patriotic energies of Russian youth.

The RNU: A Military Machine

What requires emphasis is that the RNU was no ordinary political party. Although, like other political organizations, it made an effort to disseminate its ideas among the public and (on a quite limited scale) participated in electoral campaigns, public propaganda and electoral campaigning were much less central to its activity and strategy than they are to those of most of Russia's political parties. For the RNU, propaganda and electioneering were only parts—and by no means necessarily the most decisive parts—of a tightly interconnected network of activities, all directed toward the accumulation of military, financial, and political power.

First and foremost, the RNU was a *military machine*. Barkashov is dangerous, one disillusioned recruit is reported as saying, in a way that mere demagogues are not, however inflammatory their rhetoric, because Barkashov has an army (Womack 1998). And Barkashov himself declares: "We are not politicians—we are in spirit Warriors, Warriors of Rus" (Barkashov 1994, p. 87). It is as fighters [*boeviki*] or soldiers of the RNU army that the young recruits were trained. Admittedly, the youth auxiliaries of other political forces in Russia also possess some measure of military capability—the CPRF has its "Komsomol Operations Squads," the Congress of Russian Communities its "Slavic Knights," the LDPR "Zhirinovsky's Falcons"—but only the RNU (and other smaller groups of a similar kind) has devoted such a high proportion of its resources to building up its potential for directed violence.

Activities of the RNU

Predraft Military Training

"The Germans began with brawls in beer halls," observed one RNU fighter, "but we began with the military-patriotic training of youth" (Gritchin and Urigashvili 1997). There can be no doubt as to which of the two beginnings he thought the more promising. One of the first priorities of any new RNU regional organization was to establish a "military-patriotic club" in which teenage recruits could be prepared physically and psychologically for the rigors of army service. As military instructors for these clubs, the RNU hired former officers of the special forces, paratroops, internal troops, and military intelligence, many of whom had combat experience in Afghanistan and Chechnya.[39] At a minimum, the recruits learned shooting and hand-to-hand combat and received political instruction, while at some clubs they might be trained in survival techniques and night combat, learn special fighting skills (such as kick-boxing, SAMBO,[40] traditional Cossack martial arts, and, of course, karate), run obstacle courses and go on parachute jumps, and study reconnaissance, crowd control, military theory—and the history of Russia and of the Russian Orthodox Church. They were also taught the extremely useful skill of how to cope with the brutal hazing [*dedovshchina*] that conscripts face in the Russian army (Merkacheva 1999). Military instructors did not need themselves to belong to the RNU, although the club organizers and political instructors were RNU members.

The RNU's military-patriotic clubs worked with the support of, and in close cooperation with, the official military authorities at all levels. They worked most closely with the regional military commissariats, which are responsible for organizing the draft. The commissariats often promised that a lad who had successfully completed a training course at an RNU club would be called up to serve in an elite unit. Cooperation between the RNU and the Russian armed forces in this field was quite open, and was legitimized by reference to presidential decree 727, signed by Boris Yeltsin on May 16, 1996: "On Measures of State Support for Public Organizations Carrying Out Work for the Military-Patriotic Education of Youth"—although the RNU is not specifically mentioned in the decree (Shatrov 1998a).

With its network of military-patriotic clubs, the RNU grasped the opportunity to fill a gap in the system of military service that had arisen in the process of the breakdown of Soviet social structures. Formerly predraft training had been conducted within the framework of the educational system, with the assistance of the Soviet "public organization" known as the DOSAAF (Voluntary Society for Assistance to the Army, Air Force, and Fleet). In recent years, predraft training has been neglected,[41] with the result that, in the estimation of one senior paratroop commander, "about 70 percent of draftees are physically, morally, and psychologically unprepared for service in the armed forces" (Shpak 1998). The RNU stepped into the shoes of the defunct DOSAAF. As one RNU leader remarked, "We do useful work which nobody else will do" (Gritchin and Urigashvili 1997). Only recently has an official successor organization to the DOSAAF been set up in the form of the Russian Defense Sports-Technical Organization (Korbut 1999).

Predraft training was not the only way in which the RNU helped the military authorities to maintain the functioning of the crisis-ridden system of compulsory universal military service. The RNU also combatted Russia's antidraft movement. Thus, in Yekaterinburg RNU fighters physically attacked antidraft protestors from the Movement Against Coercion who were trying to stage a sit-in at the military commissariat, preventing all but a handful of the protestors from entering the building. Police officers present at the scene did not intervene (Dobrynina 1998).

It has been reported that in some places (for example, in Belgorod Province) the RNU has been able to take part in the training of conscripts, including political instruction, inside army units (Bal'burov 1997).

Volunteer Police Patrols

A second sphere in which the RNU strove to assume state functions was that of policing. As in its "military-patriotic" work, the RNU succeeded in developing close relations of cooperation with the relevant state agency—in this case, the Ministry of Internal Affairs (MIA). Here again its activity did not contravene the law, for the RNU was able to take advantage of the institution of volunteer police auxiliaries, the Voluntary People's Militia or Patrol [*narodnaia druzhina*], that Russia has inherited from the Soviet Union. This enabled the RNU, on the basis of agreements often willingly entered into by underfunded and overstretched city and provincial police departments, to patrol city streets and parks, railroad stations, and other public places. Together with the militia and with a view to catching illegal migrants or on some other pretext, RNU squads raided open-air markets and cafés, beating up and detaining "blacks" or "persons of Caucasian nationality" (Babich 1996).[42] They might also extort regular payments from non-Russian traders "for the right to breathe Russian air" (*Komsomol'skaia pravda*, October 14, 1997).

Let us take a few examples pertaining to past RNU patrolling in Moscow; similar examples could be mentioned for other cities in which the RNU established a substantial presence. Until the winter of 1998–99, RNU park patrols were a common phenomenon. Between 1995 and the end of 1998, by agreement with the park management and with the permission of the deputy head of the district administration, RNU blackshirts patrolled Terletsky Ponds, a woodlands park in Moscow's Eastern District. Here, as we recall, the Moscow City Organization of the RNU had its headquarters and held weekend recruitment meetings. The patrols were unarmed, but often accompanied by dogs. The RNU had, in effect, taken full control of the park, which it declared a "Jew-free zone" (Kozyreva 1996; Union of Councils 1997, p. 40). Anyone in the park whom the RNU patrolmen believed to be a non-Russian was at risk of being beaten up (Karamyan 1999a). "Near the park, guys with swastikas stop cars and demand to see drivers' licenses" (Babich 1996).

Besides Terletsky Ponds, RNU men also used to patrol the electric commuter trains on the lines that run east and southeast from the city, as well as the depots in Lyubertsy and Ramenskoe at the end-points of these lines. (As noted in chapter 4, the eastern and southeastern parts of Moscow Province were an RNU stronghold.) The RNU men doing this work were paid 600 rubles per month before the financial crash of August 1998, rising to 800 rubles (equivalent to $30) after the crash. A fixed proportion of their pay was retained by the RNU.[43]

At certain times the RNU has guarded local government buildings in some of Moscow's districts. For instance, in 1992–93 the RNU guarded the building of the Sverdlovsk District Council (Likhachev and Pribylovskii 1997, p. 50).

A number of the lifesaving stations at Sosnovoi Bor on the Moscow River, where people go to swim and sunbathe, were RNU bases. "Sometimes you can spot a lifeboat flying the RNU flag" (Shatrov 1998c).

Criminal Activity, Threats, and Violence

Despite the fact that the RNU untiringly presented itself as a bastion of law and order, numerous press reports attest to the involvement of many RNU members, including quite a few leaders of regional organizations, in criminal activity (for example: Filonenko 2000; Karachinskii 1999; Kurkin 2000; "Aktivistov" 2000). Some RNU members have been prosecuted for such crimes as theft, extortion, illegal trade in arms, the violent takeover of businesses, and murder. Murders were commonplace: they were committed to avenge personal grievances, as favors to friends inside or outside the RNU, and for money. Of about fifty RNU members in Oryol, no fewer than seven were found guilty of murder (Zhdakaev 2000). In 1999 the St. Petersburg police uncovered a plot by a group of terrorists, some of whom belonged to the RNU, to blow up schools until the authorities handed them a large sum of money (Tsyganov 1999).

It is difficult to tell whether many of these crimes were performed out of political or personal motives. When a squad of RNU members took over a commercial firm at gunpoint, as happened in 1999 in the Siberian city of Omsk, did they do it to fill the movement's coffers, or to fill their own pockets as well? Was the victim of one or another RNU murder killed as a political or racial enemy, or simply for money?

There are numerous reports of violent attacks by RNU fighters upon political opponents (including "traitors" who used to be in the RNU) and people belonging to ethnic and religious minorities. Non-white foreign students have often been attacked and severely beaten by RNU members, as well as by other fascists and by skinheads. Activists who were brave—or foolhardy—enough to hold an antifascist demonstration in Terletsky Ponds were beaten by about fifty blackshirts and had their banners torn to shreds (Union of Councils 1997, p. 40; Likhachev and Pribylovskii 1997, p. 35). Distributors of the left-radical and communist press were often assaulted too (Tarasov et al. 1997, p. 31). An RNU patrol in the country town of Saltykovka, near Moscow, on two separate occasions beat five Jewish youths (Maksimov 1998); the RNU website did not deny the incidents, but claimed that the victims had provoked the assault by insulting the "people's patrolmen."[44] In general, verbal "insults" against the RNU or its members were deemed sufficient justification for violent assault.[45] As already noted, people from the Caucasus were a constant target of RNU violence. The violence might not be explicitly ordered by RNU leaders, who were concerned to avoid legal liability, but there is ample indication that they implicitly encouraged it: certainly they never took action to stop it.

Occasionally the RNU even ventured to use more than mere words against a local government official who stood in its way. For example, an official in the Moscow Parks Department who tried to evict the RNU from Terletsky Ponds not only received no support from her colleagues, but had her house vandalized (Union of Councils 1997, p. 40). More commonly, especially where more highly placed adversaries were concerned, the RNU contented itself with verbal denunciation and a warning of the severe punishment awaiting the miscreant when the RNU came to power. Such denunciations and warnings, directed at named individuals, became a standard feature of the conference speeches and press releases of RNU leaders.[46] Indeed, detention centers were reportedly prepared to hold the RNU's future political prisoners—or those of them fortunate enough not to be liquidated out of hand (Khudokormov 1994).

Fund-Raising

Raising money was foremost among Barkashov's concerns from the start. The chief "financier" of the RNU in its early years was a former KGB agent and adventurer by the name of Alexei Vedenkin, who apparently still had influential friends in the special services. Vedenkin offered to help Barkashov obtain money, weapons, and uniforms. Strangely enough, Barkashov also approached the Chechen president, Jokhar Dudayev, for financial support, though without success (Sukhoverkhov 1999).

Certain sources of funding for the movement can be identified with confidence. The RNU received material support from state structures, in particular from sympathetic regional administrations and from the Ministry of Internal Affairs, in recognition of its "military-patriotic" and policing services (Borodenkov 1997; Likhachev and Pribylovskii 1997, p. 38). Another major source of funds was the private protection firms belonging to the RNU (Karachinskii 1999; Sukhoverkhov 1999).

There were also businessmen prepared to give money to the RNU (Oganian 1999). In Voronezh, for instance, it was rumored that the RNU's main sponsor was a local entrepreneur named Sergei Fedorov ("Sponsory" 1999). In Samara, the RNU formed a mutually advantageous partnership with a politically ambitious businessman named Oleg Kitter, owner of a protection firm, former first deputy mayor, and—despite being half-Estonian by origin—an extreme Russian nationalist (Akopov 1999a). Most sponsors, however, preferred to stay out of the limelight. Identifying and maintaining contact with such individuals was one of the main tasks of the RNU's intelligence agencies.

Other possible sources of funding are more difficult to verify. Persistent allegations have been made to the effect that the RNU was financed by ethnically Slav criminal gangs, such as Moscow's Solntsevo gang, who sympathized with its politics and conceivably hoped to make use of it in any showdowns they might have with "alien"—that is, non-Slav—gangs (Verkhovskii, Papp, and Pribylovskii 1996, p. 61; Buldakov and Selezneva 1999). Yuri Shutov, a recently arrested ace of organized crime in St. Petersburg, was known as an active supporter of the RNU (Tokareva 2000).

Finally, broad hints have been dropped in the press and elsewhere suggesting that prominent financial oligarchs—in particular, Boris Berezovsky and Vladimir Gusinsky—have given large amounts of money to the RNU (Rstaki 1998a; Kharatian 1999). Given the Jewish origin of the individuals concerned, this seems at first sight an astonishing accusation. The motive usually attributed to the oligarchs is the desire to cultivate a "devil in a sack" who will frighten the electorate into accepting them, and the regime associated with them, as a lesser evil. For this purpose, they were supposedly willing to fund the RNU, which they did not consider capable of posing a serious threat. One commentator reveals what purports to be a specific deal concluded between Vedenkin, acting on behalf of the RNU, and Berezovsky (Chelnokov 1999). In exchange for financial support, the RNU was to carry out a commercial operation that would create the impression of a connection between it and Berezovsky's business rivals, thereby discrediting the latter. The story is consistent with what we know generally of Berezovsky, being preoccupied more by his rivalries with the other oligarchs than with any grand political strategy.

Intelligence Work

Two important functions of the RNU's intelligence agencies have already been mentioned—namely, the recruitment and use of secret sympathizers inside state, social, and commercial structures, and fund-raising. Some RNU intelligence agents were infiltrated into other political organizations, the media, and commercial structures. Besides general information gathering, they compiled dossiers on a wide range of individuals, paying special attention to the acquisition of compromising material that could be used to blackmail anyone who might start to oppose or obstruct the RNU (Likhachev and Pribylovskii 1997, p. 17). Such people might be "neutralized, isolated, and discredited" by various other methods: in particular, pressure was exerted with a view to having them fired from their jobs. In some factories, educational institutions, and military units, where the management was "loyal" to the RNU, all active political opponents of the movement, whether democrats or communists, were fired, together with Jews and other non-Russians (Khudokormov 1994).

Work in the Trade Union Movement

In March 1994, the RNU attempted to penetrate the trade union movement by concluding an agreement with the Confederation of Free Trade Unions of Russia (CFTUR), which from radical democratic beginnings had begun in

1993 to evolve in a nationalist direction.[47] The practical effect of the alliance varied from place to place. The most promising results, from the RNU's point of view, were obtained—not without extensive resort to the intimidation of opponents—at the metallurgical combine "Severstal′" in Cherepovetsk, an industrial city in Russia's northwest. In the fall of 1994, however, the CFTUR decided to withdraw from its alliance with the RNU, which it decided had been a mistake, and to form its own National Labor Party.[48] Barkashov, complained his former trade-unionist partners, "has nothing interesting to offer in the social sphere" (Likhachev and Pribylovskii 1997, pp. 26–27). In other words, the RNU turned out to be, from their point of view, merely nationalists rather than genuine national-socialists. If, as Marakasov (1996) suggests, the episode was an experiment on the part of the RNU, then it was an unsuccessful one.[49]

Work in the Russian Orthodox Church

Another institution with which the RNU sought to associate itself was the Russian Orthodox Church. The main form taken by the Church activity of the Barkashovites appears to have been the "maintaining of order" at church services, processions, and other religious events. The RNU took on such tasks by agreement with sympathetic priests and local church officials. The contribution that the RNU made to church life was not universally appreciated, as we may infer from an account of the behavior of RNU men at the Holy Virgin monastery:

> The blackshirts tried to marshal the pilgrims inside the church into strict rows, taking no account of age or health or the spiritual mood of those who had come to this sacred place. (Borisov 1999)

Another area of cooperation between the Russian Orthodox Church and the RNU was the struggle against "foreign" religious confessions such as Seventh Day Adventists and Jehovah's Witnesses. For example, in January 1999 in the town of Kotelnich, Kirov Province, a group of RNU men accompanied a priest from the St. Nicholas Cathedral to break up an open-air missionary meeting being conducted by Seventh Day Adventists. An attempt was made to prosecute the culprits, but nothing came of it (Garin 1999).

The RNU also involved itself in intra-church disputes. Thus, the Tomsk organization of the RNU collected signatures for a petition on behalf of Bishop Arkady, who had been transferred from the local see, claiming that the bishop had been victimized by "priests with non-Russian surnames." The bishop denied that he had authorized the RNU to act in his support (Borisov 1999).

The RNU cultivated ties not only with the official Orthodox Church, but also with the sect known as Old Believers, who remain loyal to the form of Orthodoxy that prevailed prior to the Petrine reforms. At political instruction sessions, RNU members had explained to them the merits of the Old Belief, and many became Old Believers, although this was not required of them. In some places, such as Perm, the RNU organization emerged out of the local Old Believer community and was actively supported by the latter (Subbotin 1999).

Legal Activity

A considerable effort was devoted by the RNU to establishing, consolidating, and protecting the legal position of the organization, and to defensive and offensive action against its opponents in the courts. The highest priority was assigned to repeated attempts to obtain official registration as a public organization from the Ministry of Justice, both at the federal level (where the attempts failed) and at the provincial and city level (where in many places, though far from all, they succeeded). The emphasis on winning registration—and on thwarting possible moves to withdraw registrations already won—had a strong rationale, because official registration gives an organization many legal rights. For example, the fact that the Moscow city justice department registered the RNU in July 1993 put the RNU in a strong position to challenge the legality of the decision by Moscow's mayor, Yuri Luzhkov, to prohibit the RNU from holding its second all-Russian congress in Moscow in December 1998 (Babichenko 1998b; Miloslavskaia 1998).

The RNU frequently had to defend its members in court both against "political" charges, the usual one being that of inciting ethnic and religious hatred, and against ordinary criminal charges such as illegal possession of arms, assault, and murder. Such cases gave the RNU free publicity and provided an additional and very effective platform for propaganda. However, it was often the RNU that initiated court proceedings against its opponents—usually with a view to "defending [its] reputation" against those who called it "fascist" in the media or drew analogies between the RNU and Hitlerism (Graev 1998).[50]

Propaganda and Electoral Campaigning

While most of its activities sharply distinguished the RNU from ordinary political parties, it also engaged in public propaganda. Enormous amounts of RNU literature were distributed in public places. The print run of *Russkii poriadok* rose from 25,000 in 1992 to 500,000 in 1997 and 800,000 in 1998

(Belasheva 1999). It was claimed that over 2 million copies of a "mini-newspaper" containing an interview with Barkashov were distributed in 1998 (RNU Website). Open-air public meetings were held at weekends in the parks—for example, in St. Petersburg's Victory Park between eleven and one o'clock on Saturdays and Sundays. Sometimes free pancakes [*bliny*] were handed out at such meetings.

Observers tend to agree, however, that the RNU's propaganda was rather boring and stereotyped, and not very effective in appealing to a broad public. The decision to abandon the sale of literature and switch to its free distribution was presumably prompted in part by the fact that so few Russians were willing to spend any money on it.

Instances occurred of the RNU distributing "black propaganda"—that is, texts made to look as though they originated from its adversaries. In April 1999, for example, leaflets left in post boxes and spread around the pedagogical university in the Siberian city of Tomsk purported to come from Jewish organizations that did not in fact exist. The leaflets urged Jews to enslave and destroy the Russian people and harm them by other means.[51] Suspicion soon fell on the leader of the Tomsk RNU, engineer Pavel Rozhin. Witnesses were found; Rozhin was duly charged with inciting ethnic hatred, found guilty, given a suspended sentence, and then released under an amnesty (Kashcheev 2000).

Like other Russian political organizations, the RNU attracted young people by staging musical events. Some groups, in particular the folklore ensemble *Ristala*, were associated with the RNU (Likhachev and Pribylovskii 1997, p. 43). Another publicity stunt was the holding of soccer matches in RNU-controlled stadiums, in which RNU teams took on famous teams such as *Dinamo* as well as less well-known teams like *Moscow Veterans* (Bal'burov 1997; Likhachev and Pribylovskii 1997, p. 36).

Sporadically the RNU put up candidates in local elections.[52] In October 1994, for instance, the RNU waged a vigorous campaign in Moscow's Mytishchin District, where an election was scheduled to fill a vacant seat in the State Duma. The RNU candidate came in sixth out of twelve candidates, with 6 percent of the vote. The RNU officially ignored the Duma elections of December 1995, but RNU members stood as "independent" candidates in five electoral districts, two in Moscow and three in the provinces. The most successful of the five won 2.5 percent of the vote, the least successful a mere 0.6 percent. These were fairly typical results (Polivanov 1996; Likhachev and Pribylovskii 1997, pp. 27–28, 33–35). In the presidential election of 1996, Barkashov at first announced his candidacy, but later decided (for reasons that were not made clear) to withdraw, although he claimed that a sufficient number of signatures had been collected for him to stand. A number of RNU members and sympathizers stood as independents in the 1999 Duma elections. Barkashov promised to stand as a candidate for president in 2000, if necessary as an "independent," but was not permitted to do so.[53]

RNU's Mode of Operation

Surveying the whole range of the RNU's activities, one gains the impression of a complex, powerful, and synergistic mechanism for the accumulation of paramilitary potential, financial and material assets, and political influence. If one breaks down the overarching goal of the accumulation of coercive, economic, and political power into a series of subordinate objectives, then each of the activities that we have examined is seen to serve not one but several purposes.

The probable purposes of the RNU's main activities are shown in Table 6.1. Thus, "military-patriotic work" served to train and indoctrinate RNU fighters, helped the RNU to penetrate and influence the officer corps of the Russian army, and generated a positive attitude toward the RNU among the many parents who were grateful to anyone who kept their teenage sons out of trouble and prepared them for the looming ordeal of military service.[54] Similarly, participation in policing won the RNU friends within the Ministry of Internal Affairs, and accustomed the public to the officially approved presence in the streets, parks, and marketplaces of blackshirted young men with swastikas on their sleeves. The RNU's private protection agencies made money for the organization, gave its members employment, expanded its legal access to weapons, and by providing protection services to important people afforded the RNU another channel for penetrating influential circles.[55] And the work of the RNU's intelligence agencies, as we have demonstrated, might serve a host of purposes.

An important purpose of several of the RNU's activities was to secure access to weapons. That running military training camps provides such access is obvious. Volunteer patrolmen also have legal access to weapons, including firearms, as did RNU members working for private protection and debt-collection agencies. Presumably the RNU intelligence agencies played their part here too. The RNU also stocked up on more primitive weapons: Barkashov instructed his members to equip themselves with spades, allegedly for the purpose of planting trees to beautify the environment ("Barkashovtsy" 1998).

Regional Case Studies

The Stavropol and Krasnodar Territories

Background

The Stavropol and Krasnodar Territories are situated on the plains of the northern Caucasus, directly to the north of Chechnya, Abkhazia, and the

Table 6.1

Purposes of the Main Activities of the RNU

Purposes	Main activities				
	Predraft military training, sports clubs	Patrolling streets, parks, trains, etc.	Protection and debt-collection agencies	Intelli-gence work	Public meetings and propaganda
Build up paramilitary power					
Train fighters	X				
Secure access to arms	X	X	X	X	
Accumulate financial and material assets			X	X	
Build up political power					
Penetrate and secretly influence state and social institutions, block hostile action	X	X	X	X	
Accustom public to presence and activity of RNU	X	X			X
Spread RNU ideas	X			X	X

republics of the Russian Federation that belong to other Caucasian peoples (Dagestan, North Ossetia, Kabardino-Balkaria, and Karachaevo-Cherkessia). The Stavropol Territory is landlocked, midway between the Caspian Sea and the Black Sea, while the Krasnodar Territory, also known as the Kuban, borders it to the west and has a long coastline, with a string of popular tourist resorts, on the Black and Azov Seas. Both territories belong to the temperate and fertile black-earth zone, and about half of their combined population of about 8 million is rural—a high proportion by contemporary Russian standards. Besides agriculture and tourism, there is significant, mainly light, industry.

Politically, too, the Stavropol and Krasnodar Territories closely resemble one another. The strongest electoral force is the Communist Party of the Russian Federation (CPRF), to which belong their respective governors, Alexander Chernogorov and Nikolai Kondratenko. In this region especially, the CPRF may reasonably be considered part of the extreme Russian nationalist camp: Kondratenko in particular inveighs untiringly against the Jewish world conspiracy.[56] He has sponsored the formation of two quasi-official regional political organizations: his own "party of power" called *Otechestvo* [Fatherland], which since November 1998 has held forty-eight out of sixty-three seats in the legislature of the Krasnodar Territory,[57] and the Patriotic Union of Kuban Youth, or *Patsomol* for short (Khokhlov 1998; Serdiukov 1998). Other, noncommunist nationalist organizations, including the LDPR as well as the RNU, are also well entrenched. In addition, as noted in chapter 4, these territories are the cradle of the Cossack revival movement.

The inhabitants of the two territories are mainly ethnically Russian, but there is a substantial and heterogeneous minority population, most of which belongs to Caucasian ethnic groups. Parts of this population, in particular some of the Armenian communities, are long established in the area, but many are recent immigrants, attempting to flee destitution and violent conflict in their homelands. A very significant factor behind the strength of Russian nationalist feeling in the region is the high level of ethnic tension between the Russian majority and the Caucasian minorities (Kritskii and Savva 1998). Migrants undermine the standard of living of the local people (for example, by driving up the price of housing), and politicians are able to win popularity by calling for their exclusion and expulsion. Thus, in the eastern part of the Stavropol Territory, a recent influx of some 10,000 people from Dagestan is blamed for rising crime, and fights have broken out between Russian and Dagestani youngsters (Gritchin 1998).[58] Russian nationalist politicians link such "criminal migration" to a geopolitical threat to Russia. "The South," proclaims RNU Central Council member Alexander Rashitsky, "is Russia's front line in its struggle for territorial integrity" (Conference of RNU Organizations of the South of Russia, September 1998).

In the Krasnodar Territory, following Kondratenko's election as governor in December 1996, the territorial legislature introduced at his initiative a system of legalized discrimination and terror against ethnic minorities, based upon a charter that declares the Kuban "a homeland of the Russian people" (in the narrow ethnic sense). Worst treated of all are the Meskhetian Turk refugees stranded in the Krasnodar Territory, able to return neither to their former places of residence in Uzbekistan, whence they were evacuated in the wake of pogroms in 1989, nor to their original homeland in southern Georgia (Osipov and Cherepovaia 1996; "Meskhetian" 1998).[59]

Another factor to which some Russian social scientists attribute the receptivity to "patriotic" politics of the population of the Stavropol and Krasnodar Territories is their continuing closeness to traditional village culture. Here more than elsewhere in Russia, it is argued, old patriarchal and patriotic values have been preserved (Kolosov and Turovskii 1997, pp. 24–27; Davydova 1998).

The RNU in the Stavropol Territory

The RNU was registered in the Stavropol Territory in December 1994. At that time, the Territorial Organization of the RNU numbered only a few dozen members. By July 1997 it claimed about 2,000 members (Gritchin and Urigashvili 1997), and by September 1998 over 3,500 members, with primary organizations in the majority of counties, cells in numerous enterprises, offices, villages, and settlements, and no fewer than seven military-patriotic clubs at which about 2,000 youths have undergone training.[60] Such a dense RNU presence, covering rural areas and the smaller towns as well as the regional center, appears to have been unique to the Stavropol Territory.

The RNU was especially strong in those areas of the territory that are close to Chechnya. Until the recent war, the inhabitants of these areas were living in the constant fear of being robbed, killed, kidnapped, or enslaved by Chechen gangs from beyond the officially unrecognized and unprotected border. It was not uncommon for entire collective farms to join the RNU in the hope of some kind of protection (Leont′eva 1999).

The Stavropol RNU enjoyed good relations with Governor Chernogorov and his administration. Three secret supporters of the RNU sat on the territorial legislature, two elected as independents and one as a communist. "Our people are everywhere," boasted Stavropol RNU leader Andrei Dudinov, "—in the territorial administration, in the security service, in the Ministry of Internal Affairs, in the army" (Gritchin and Urigashvili 1997). Close ties were also maintained with the leaders of the Terek Cossacks.

Besides its usual predraft training and volunteer patrols, RNU activities in this region included raids against illegal tree-felling (carried out on behalf of the forestry enterprise in Mineralnye Vody), keeping order at church services, and the provision of instructors to higher educational institutions, secondary schools, and even kindergartens.[61] Stavropol's main RNU military-patriotic club, *Russkie Vitiazi* [Russian Knights], founded in 1995, had a network of county branches and played a central role in the whole system of RNU combat training, holding special courses to train instructors for other clubs (Shatrov 1998d).

In Stavropol the RNU also, to a greater extent than elsewhere, took over state functions in the military sphere. It took under its wing units of the 205th Army Motor-Rifle Brigade and of the 101st Brigade of Internal Troops (belonging to the Ministry of Internal Affairs), which had been hastily redeployed from Chechnya to the Stavropol Territory, "thrown by uncaring politicians in the midst of winter into tents on the open field."[62] The RNU publicized the plight of the servicemen and their families, encouraged the public to offer them aid, arranged accommodation for them in hotels and barracks,[63] supplied eight tons of food products, and even paid for a large quantity of military training literature (Gritchin and Urigashvili 1997; RNU Website). The influence of the RNU within the power structures of the territory grew to the point where the RNU flag was sometimes raised at police checkpoints and by army and internal troop units (Shatrov 1998c).

The extent of support for the RNU among the general public of the territory was probably somewhat smaller. Mikhail Burlakov, head of a department at the Ministry of Nationalities and Federal Relations in Moscow, standing as the RNU candidate in the Duma by-election held in the Georgievsk District in September 1997, came in sixth out of eight candidates, winning a mere 3.6 percent of the vote. In contrast, the leader of the Mineralnye Vody County Organization of the RNU reported in September 1998 that over 40 percent of respondents in a survey carried out by his organization had said that they support the RNU—a proportion that had allegedly been continually increasing (Conference of RNU Organizations of the South of Russia, September 1998). Although a survey carried out by the RNU itself can certainly not be regarded as an objective source of information concerning individuals' *private* views, it is of great political significance that so many people should have been prepared, for whatever motive, to take a *public* stance of support for the RNU. There are many reasons why such nominal RNU supporters might not actually vote for an RNU candidate in an election: they might be privately opposed to the RNU; they might sympathize with the RNU but not want to "waste their vote," or they might "support" the RNU in the limited sense that they approved of some or all of its activities without fully agreeing with its ideology.

Stavropol has attracted some publicity as the site of a landmark legal case concerning the RNU (Tuz 1997; Graev 1998; Meek 1998; Subbotich 1998). The case began following the appearance in *Stavropolskaia pravda* in April 1995 of an article by local journalist Galina Tuz, entitled "Do Russians Have Hatred for Fascism in Their Blood?" ("Russians have hatred for fascism in their blood" was a Soviet cliché.) The article did not make explicit reference to the RNU, but was clearly aimed against the organization. In May 1995, the Stavropol Territory Organization of the RNU petitioned a district court in Stavropol in defense of the business reputation of their organization, which Tuz had allegedly maligned by falsely implying that it was fascist.[64] The RNU won its case, the court ruling that it was "not a fascist organization guided by fascist ideology." The newspaper was forced to publish a repudiation of the analogy that Tuz had implicitly drawn between the RNU and Hitlerite fascism, and both she and the newspaper had to pay damages to the plaintiff.[65] The verdict was appealed, and finally in August 1998, in response to the protest of the procurator of the Stavropol Territory, the presidium of the Stavropol Territory Court voided the decision of the district court and sent the case to be heard a second time—in the same court as before, but with a new judge. Meanwhile, Tuz herself, disappointed that so few of the people around her were prepared to offer their support, had left the region.

The RNU in the Krasnodar Territory

The RNU formed an organization in the Krasnodar Territory in the summer of 1994. Its leader, Viktor Zelinsky, was a former police chief. According to Zelinsky, the RNU had in September 1998 more than thirty town and county branches spread throughout the territory. The Krasnodar RNU conducted pickets and "agitation raids," maintained good relations with the commanders of locally deployed army, internal troops, and border troop units; enjoyed the support of "nationally thinking [government] leaders and entrepreneurs," and received broad media coverage (Conference of RNU Organizations of the South of Russia, September 1998). The media coverage was of a favorable character, especially since the forced closure of the liberal antifascist newspaper *Kubanskii krai* following a lawsuit against it for alleged libel of its officially financed rival *Kubanskie novosti* (Gessen 1997). In short, the RNU operated under favorable conditions in the Krasnodar Territory and had a substantial presence there, although its position was not as strong as in the Stavropol Territory.

In Krasnodar as elsewhere, the RNU had close ties with some, though not all, Cossack leaders. Barkashov himself was named an honorary Cossack by the regional Cossack Council (Jackson 1999, p. 38). A signal example of joint Cossack–RNU action occurred in November 1995 when, following a quarrel among neighbors and in revenge for an alleged rape, some sixty Cossacks and RNU fighters carried out a pogrom against a Meskhetian Turk settlement in Krymsky County, beating and whipping men, women, and children (Osipov and Cherepovaia 1996; Likhachev and Pribylovskii 1997, pp. 48–49).

In December 1998, leaflets appealing for anti-Jewish pogroms were distributed through Krasnodar mail boxes:

> Help rid our dear Kuban of the damned Yids! Destroy their apartments, burn down their homes! They have no place here on Kuban soil. Let us help our beloved leader N.I. Kondratenko in this difficult struggle. . . . All who hide the damned Yids will be numbered among them and also destroyed. The Yids will be destroyed, victory will be ours! ("Krasnodarskie" 1998)

The leaflets were unsigned, but the RNU was a plausible suspect.

It should not be thought that the Krasnodar Territory lacks an antifascist movement. On April 22, 2000, the Moscow newspaper *Izvestiya* reported that a public foundation called "The School of Peace" was planning to hold an antifascist demonstration on May 1 in the Black Sea port of Novorossiisk. Alerted by the report, the Novorossiisk police raided the house where out-of-town activists intending to take part in the demonstration were staying, took them to the police station for interrogation and fingerprinting, then frog-marched them in a column to the railroad station, and told them to get out of town and not come back. The more persistent of them did return, and were again detained and interrogated. As a result, only ten people, instead of fifty as planned, demonstrated against fascism on May 1 in Novorossiisk. The city's chief of police denied receiving any specific instructions on the matter from the local authorities. He explained he had got wind of an unsanctioned meeting, and had acted to prevent it, that was all. Besides, there was no room in the Kuban for long-haired youths (Averbukh 2000).

Oryol and Voronezh Provinces

Background

Oryol and Voronezh Provinces, with populations of about 1 million and 2.5 million, respectively, are situated south of Moscow, in central-western Russia. About three-fifths of the population of each province is urban. Voronezh has a substantial defense industry along with other industries, and Oryol has mostly light industry (although it has significant untapped mineral resources). The city of Voronezh also has a considerable number of institutions of higher education: a state university, an agricultural university, and various academies and colleges. Much of the agricultural soil of both provinces is black-earth.

Both provinces are dominated electorally by the Communist Party of the Russian Federation. Voronezh's governor, Ivan Shabanov, belonged until recently to the CPRF—in the spring of 2000 he broke with the communists and offered his support to Vladimir Putin—although he also had close ties to Moscow's mayor, Yuri Luzhkov (*Russian Regional Report*, September 23 and December 22, 1998, April 12, 2000). Oryol's governor, Yegor Stroyev, has had ties both with the Yeltsin camp and with the opposition: on the one hand, he is close to Gennady Zyuganov; on the other, he is a member of the council of Chernomyrdin's *Nash Dom Rossiia* and is regarded by radical communists as "a pillar of the existing regime" (Sokolov 1998). Stroyev is also an important figure in national politics: he has chaired the Federation Council (the upper house of the Russian parliament) and the CIS Inter-Parliamentary Assembly.

The RNU in Oryol Province

The RNU organization in Oryol Province was founded at the end of 1993 as a result of the defection to the RNU of the local branch of the Russian Party, whose leader, Igor Semyonov, became the provincial RNU leader. Semyonov, formerly an attendant at a psychiatric hospital, brought with him into the RNU a militarized organization with detachments of storm troopers and its own intelligence and counterintelligence (Zhdakaev 2000).

In the fall of 1994, Semyonov was approached by a man who asked him to arrange the murder of his daughter-in-law and her eleven-year-old son, whom he no longer wanted in his apartment. The commission was accepted, and the victims were duly stabbed to death by three of Semyonov's RNU comrades. This was the first of four "wet affairs" involving the RNU in Oryol.

The contract killings did not undermine the RNU's position in Oryol. Quite the contrary. In early 1995 Semyonov reached an informal understanding with Governor Yegor Stroyev (who had been elected in April 1993) and the provincial administration, permitting him to act openly without fear of arrest. As a result, from this time onward the RNU Oryol organization was able to hold demonstrations, complete with chants of "Death to the Jews!," and to conduct large-scale public propaganda, with prominent and sympathetic coverage of its activity in *Orlovskaya pravda*, the official newspaper of the provincial administration (Mendelevich 1997; Zhdakaev 2000). In a letter to a comrade, Semyonov boasted:

> Now we are beating the Yids real good. They have shut up here in Oryol. Thanks to our work, Oryol has become red-brown. . . . Our headquarters is in the building of the provincial administration. The authorities respect and fear us. (Quoted in Zhdakaev 2000)

By 1997, according to one estimate, the RNU had between seventy and one hundred members in Oryol (Likhachev and Pribylovskii 1997, p. 51). It had good relations with the local communists, especially with the artist and former Duma deputy Vladimir Frolov, who was an "honored guest" at RNU gatherings.

Nevertheless, a prosecution was finally mounted against Semyonov. Despite opposition on the part of the provincial administration and its press, he was put on trial charged with inciting ethnic hatred (calling for "real terror" against the Jews), for running an illegal organization (neither the Russian Party nor the RNU had official registration in the province), and for inciting citizens to commit illegal acts. Although the judge is alleged to have shown bias in favor of the accused (Mendelevich 1998), in the fall of 1998 Semyonov was found guilty and sentenced to two years in prison. He was released early and has returned to the Russian Party, having been disowned by Barkashov (Zhdakaev 2000).

The RNU in Voronezh Province

A small RNU organization existed in Voronezh in 1993–94, but it came into conflict with the central leadership and was dissolved by a decree of Barkashov. In 1995, a group of comrades-in-arms led by Yevgeny Lalochkin was sent to Voronezh to set up a new organization, which was registered in December of that year at the provincial department of justice. In 1996, RNU activities in Voronezh were reactivated. Members of the RNU began to make their appearance at communist meetings, armed with rubber truncheons (Likhachev and Pribylovskii 1997, pp. 43–45). In the spring of 1997, the RNU contested elections to the provincial Duma and the city municipal council. In June 1997, joint RNU–militia patrols started to appear on the streets, and in August 1997 RNU guards were posted at the hostel of the agricultural university (Blinov 1997). Protests at these developments, sent to Governor Shabanov by democratic organizations and published in some local newspapers, went unanswered (Osokin 1997). In May 1998, the street kiosks of the official distribution agency *Rospechat* began selling *Russkii poriadok*.

According to one eyewitness, RNU patrolmen on the streets of Voronezh were armed with guns. The central park was taken over by the RNU, and many people became afraid to enter it.[66] The marketplace raids that the RNU carried out, jointly with the OMON special police squads, were evidently rather frightening affairs—unless one was lucky enough to be (or be taken for) an ethnic Russian.[67]

There is ample evidence of the semiofficial links that the RNU established with the provincial power structures. In 1997, the local press published a letter from Lalochkin to Governor Shabanov requesting accommodation, transportation, and money "for the patriotic upbringing of youth." The request was approved by one of Shabanov's assistants. The RNU also got state funding for its police patrols—apparently 250,000 rubles per month. The RNU was allowed to hold press conferences at the provincial parliamentary center. Among the guests at RNU meetings were Alexander Kosyrev, chairman of a permanent commission of the provincial Duma and an organizer of the governor's electoral campaign, and Sergei Shishlakov, a candidate for mayor and one of the city's biggest entrepreneurs. The RNU's claims that it had active secret supporters in the executive and legislative branches of provincial government, as well as in commercial structures, were therefore plausible enough (Blinov 1997).

No less impressive were the RNU's links with educational institutions in Voronezh. The RNU's city center headquarters was housed in a building belonging to one of the city's technical colleges, and one of Lalochkin's deputies was the director of a technical training school (PTU). The RNU recruits were trained in school sports halls, with permission of the school principals (Borodenkov 1997). In summer the recruits were taken to camps in the surrounding countryside. Schoolboys who were RNU members wore the RNU uniform to school, and RNU security guards "educated" the pupils during recess (Lychev 1998).

Among the elderly, too, the RNU had many admirers. When the RNU held a conference in Voronezh in June 1999, the chairwoman of the provincial council of labor veterans mounted the tribune to praise the blackshirts and call on them to join a meeting in Lenin Square in support of old-age pensioners. About 150 RNU men accordingly marched to the square, where a similar number of pensioners had gathered. The Barkashovites then formed a chain around the old people, took over the meeting, and denied the pensioners access to the microphone (Sedov 1999).

Voronezh was regarded by the RNU as one of its greatest success stories, a model worthy of emulation by blackshirts elsewhere. "Nazis visit us from other cities to gain experience," noted one local journalist with regret (Tarasova 1999).

The RNU claimed that by the spring of 1997 it had about 50,000 supporters in the province, including a core of about a hundred comrades-in-arms, organized in twenty-four district and county branches (Blinov 1997). In 1998, RNU branches were said to number several dozen (Shatrov 1998a). Up to a thousand youngsters were reported to be enrolled in the RNU's free courses in face-to-face combat (Blinov 1997). Deputy leader of the Voronezh RNU, Yevgeny Yenshin, claimed that the RNU had 19,000 supporters in the city, including army and police officers (Borodenkov 1997). According to the television station ORT, there were about 200 RNU members in Voronezh in early 1999.

Independent observers suspect that many of these figures, especially those for numbers of supporters, are gross exaggerations, but there can be no doubt that the RNU did possess a powerful public presence in Voronezh. One of my students, who happened to be in the city in the summer of 1999 on an exchange program, told me that he saw hundreds of uniformed RNU men standing along the main street over a distance of about half a kilometer. A Jewish fellow-student of his was beaten up by RNU men.

Most of the RNU's support in Voronezh was concentrated on the east, working-class bank of the River Don, where almost all the city's industrial enterprises and technical schools are located and crime and drug addiction are rampant. On the west bank of the river, where the city's higher educational institutions are to be found, young people tend to be less politicized, and those who are politically active tend to be "democratic" or leftist rather than fascist in orientation (Borodenkov 1997).

The electronic media and some of the print media of Voronezh Province gave the RNU favorable coverage. Programs about its activities were shown on television (Bal′burov 1997). Any critical article that appeared in the press was answered with verbal threats to the publisher and physical assault on the journalist concerned (Borodenkov 1997). One case in which the RNU was portrayed negatively is particularly instructive. On April 6, 1998, a cable television company in the town of New Voronezh (Novovoronezh, situated south of Voronezh) screened a feature showing a local RNU march interspersed with clips of marching Nazis from the Third Reich era. Sergei Nechayev, leader of the town's RNU organization, immediately demanded that the company show a half-hour film "correctly" portraying the RNU, and on being refused took the company to court "in defense of honor, dignity, and business reputation," demanding financial damages, air time, and a formal apology. On May 20, the town court rejected Nechayev's petition, upon which his comrade-in-arms, Yevgeny Yenshin, who had come from Voronezh to support him, declared to the journalists and others present in the courtroom: "We'll simply shoot you all!" This led to

Yenshin's prosecution for threatening murder, but the case was later dropped (Subbotich 1998).

In general, the persistent vigor of resistance to the RNU, at both the official level and the grassroots, distinguished the situation in Voronezh from that in, for instance, the Stavropol and Krasnodar Territories. While Governor Shabanov supported the RNU, Voronezh's mayor, Alexander Tsapin, did what he could to oppose RNU activity, such as suing the organization for defacing the facades of buildings with swastikas (Blinov 1997). The newspaper *Voronezhskii kur'er* was hostile to the RNU. In the summer of 1997, anti-fascist activists created a center for research and information, and in September 1997 they came to an agreement with three of the city's "free" trade unions to form a Workers' Antifascist Front. They contrasted their own approach to the "liberal" antifascism of the Moscow Antifascist Center:

> We do not praise General Pinochet, we do not consider communism a variety of fascism, and we are willing to cooperate tactically with leftists against the Nazi threat. We are not socialists, but neither are we right-wing liberals: we are just ordinary kids who want to fight the brown plague. (Lychev 1998)

The antifascists of Voronezh face an uphill struggle. The general climate of opinion in the province is favorable to extreme Russian nationalist ideas. One incident will serve as illustration. In July 1998, the provincial Duma banned the use in schools of a ninth-grade history textbook on the grounds that the author, A. Kreder, was "a Zionist and Russophobe." At the same time, the deputies asked the local office of the Federal Security Service to investigate the harmful activities of the Soros Foundation, which had sponsored the textbook.[68]

The RNU Rebuffed: Borovichi and Zlatoust

Borovichi

Borovichi is an industrial town of 80,000 people in Novgorod Province in northwestern Russia. There are several small ethnic minority communities, including about 300 Jews. Interethnic relations have traditionally been good.

The RNU did not establish a presence in Borovichi until late 1998, but there had been a local fascist group called *Miortvaia voda* [Dead Water], which had sponsored TV advertisements calling on citizens to take up arms and kill at least one Jew a day. The RNU sent its people to Borovichi initially to back up *Miortvaia voda*. At first they recruited unemployed middle-aged men, and later adolescents aged twelve to fifteen. RNU literature was placed in the newspaper kiosks, and RNU representatives made contact with local Cossacks and military recruiters to discuss future collaboration. Anti-Semitic leaflets, posters, and graffiti appeared all over town; Jewish graves were desecrated; Jewish families received hate mail promising that the streets would be "washed with Jewish blood," and one Jewish family had its doorway set on fire. The RNU, it would seem, was off to a good start.

The Jewish community in Borovichi, however, was well organized and well armed. Most important of all, it had extensive contacts with other Jewish communities and organizations in Russia and abroad. It was therefore able to ignite an international campaign to pressure the authorities both in Borovichi and in Novgorod, the provincial center, to take action against the RNU. Leading roles in this campaign were played by two American organizations, the Bay Area Council for Jewish Rescue and Renewal, and the Union of Councils for Soviet Jews. Borovichi's mayor, Vladimir Ogonkov, and Novgorod's governor, Mikhail Prusak, were astonished to find their offices flooded by faxes of protest from the West.

Although the town authorities at first reacted angrily to the campaign, they subsequently agreed to hold talks with the Jewish community. On December 24, 1999, the Borovichi Duma passed Resolution 180, which condemned the RNU for inciting ethnic hatred, and made a series of recommendations: namely, that law enforcement agencies take measures to prevent the RNU from inciting ethnic hatred, that local organizations and institutions not work with the RNU or allow the RNU to distribute its literature, and that educational institutions and the Committee on Youth Affairs act to combat the spread of nationalistic ideas among young people (Union of Councils 1999, pp. 41–42). As a result, the situation in Borovichi greatly improved.

The positive outcome in this case may be attributed to two main factors. One is the relatively liberal outlook of the provincial authorities: of all of Russia's regional governors, Governor Prusak is one of those most concerned to promote a favorable image for his province in the West and to attract Western investment. But arguably no less important was the good climate of interethnic relations that preceded the activation of fascist organizations.

Zlatoust

Zlatoust is another industrial town, also of about 80,000 population, situated in Chelyabinsk Province in the Urals. According to the 1989 census, the population is about 65 percent ethnic Russian and 25 percent Tatar and Bashkir, with the remainder made up of Ukrainians, Belarusians, Mordva, Chuvash, Germans, Jews, Kazakhs, and other ethnic groups. Established on Bashkir lands by Tula entrepreneurs in the mid-eighteenth century, Zlatoust has always had a multiethnic population: German settlers arrived early on, and Ukrainians and Jews came as evacuees from Kiev in 1941 together with the sewing factory in which they worked.

The RNU arrived in Zlatoust in April 1997 in the person of one Butenko, who had just returned to his native town from the Stavropol Territory, where he had joined the movement. Butenko stood in the marketplace by the sewing factory, offering *Russkii poriadok* to passersby. He found a few sympathizers. One of them, by the name of Panarin, ran a hockey club, which became the local RNU headquarters. Then, at the end of 1997 or the beginning of 1998, a businessman named Yuri Nikitin took the Barkashovites under his wing. He gave them space in two of the town's marketplaces that he owned, and he helped them in other ways. This was not the first time that Nikitin had sponsored nationalist causes: he had paid for the building of a local church, "where the priest's sermons resemble RNU political instruction" (Aizenburg 1999).

Over the next few months, the RNU seemed to be establishing itself in Zlatoust. The number of comrades-in-arms grew to about twenty-five; combat training and political instruction sessions were organized; and the more prominent Barkashovites were interviewed on local television.

The fortunes of the RNU in the town began to change in October 1998, when RNU demonstrators tried to storm the building of the town administration. The local prosecutor issued a warning, and the mayor put pressure on Nikitin to cease his support of the RNU:

> I told [Nikitin] that if he doesn't put an end to this business he'll go in the investigative isolator. Like it or not, life forces you to define your position.

By February 1999, the RNU stands at the marketplaces under Nikitin's control had duly disappeared.

Protest from below, however, also played a part in turning the local authorities against the RNU. The protests were initiated by parents of children who attended Panarin's hockey club, who were disturbed by the RNU presence at the club. They were supported by teachers who said that blackshirts had entered their schools without their consent to talk to their pupils. War veterans joined the protests, including even the Cossacks among them. The police department and other local government offices were inundated by telephone calls from outraged citizens demanding that action be taken to suppress the RNU. And it was.

The Size and Strength of the RNU

How Many Members?

There is no shortage of available estimates of the size of the RNU's membership. The trouble is that the estimates vary over such a wide range, as will readily be seen from the selection of them presented in Table 6.2.

Part of this variation can be attributed to differences in the way RNU membership is defined.

First, some writers use the term "members" to refer to all participants in the movement, whether comrades-in-arms, fellow-builders, or supporters, while others, following the usual practice of the RNU itself, restrict "members" to comrades-in-arms, or to comrades-in-arms and fellow-builders. The largest figures, going as high as Dmitry Borodenkov's astonishing estimate of "almost four million," always refer to membership defined broadly to include all categories of participant. However, the RNU leadership, concerned primarily with keeping track of the number of fighters, did not maintain records of the number of supporters. Nor were outside observers in a position to estimate numbers of supporters, because the latter, unlike fighters, did not wear uniforms. One cannot therefore place any credence in claims concerning the number of RNU members in the broad sense.

Second, it is often unclear whether membership estimates refer to the whole of the former Soviet Union or to the Russian Federation alone. It will be recalled that the RNU recruited members in all the post-Soviet states, regarding them as rightful parts of Russia. In certain parts of the "near abroad"—Latvia, Estonia, Belarus, eastern Ukraine—the RNU presence appeared to be quite substantial. According to one commentator, for example, the RNU in Latvia had about a thousand activists, being larger and better organized than the Latvian nationalist organizations ("Neizbyvnaia" 1998).[69]

Nevertheless, even after taking these issues of definition into account a great deal of the variation in membership estimates remains to be explained. How reliable are the different kinds of sources that are shown in Table 6.2?

The most obvious source of estimates of RNU membership is the data officially made public by the RNU itself. These data refer to comrades-in-arms and fellow-builders. Of greatest value are the figures contained in reports delivered by RNU leaders at RNU conferences and posted on the RNU website. The most recent figure for total membership appears to be that given in September 1998 by Central Council member Oleg Kassin at the conference of RNU organizations of the South of Russia—namely 100,000. It should be noted that Barkashov often gave the press off-the-cuff estimates that diverged sharply from such official RNU data. Thus, at a press conference on

December 23, 1998, he claimed that the RNU had 300,000 members, undoubtedly a gross exaggeration.

But are not even official RNU data bound to be highly exaggerated? There is good reason to think so. By fostering an overblown impression of its size and rate of growth, the RNU gained more publicity, intimidated opponents, and attracted people anxious to swim with the tide. Deliberate deception of the public by the top leadership was not necessarily the only factor at work. It is also likely that in the reports sent up by the hierarchy by lower-level leaders, the latter inserted exaggerated figures for recruitment and membership—"forgetting," for instance, to keep proper track of dropouts—with a view to impressing the top leaders with their performance and thereby increasing their own weight within the movement. We may, in other words, be dealing here with the classical Soviet practice of statistical over-reporting (Shenfield 1983).

How might we correct official RNU data? Let us note that a high-level defector gave a membership estimate of 10,000 at a time (August-September 1994) when the official RNU figure was 20,000 (Khudokormov 1994). This suggests that we should, as a rule of thumb, deflate the RNU data by 50 percent. Thus, the figure of 100,000 fighters, given in September 1998 by Oleg Kassin, one of Barkashov's most important colleagues, would be deflated to 50,000. This roughly corresponds to the estimate offered in December 1998 by a Russian journalist who has made a serious independent study of the RNU: 50,000–70,000 fighters plus a similar number of supporters (Belykh 1998).

However, much lower estimates have been provided by equally reputable and conscientious observers. One such estimate was that of 20,000 members, given on television on December 18, 1998, by Andrei Loginov, a representative of the Directorate of Domestic Policy of the presidential administration. Loginov also stated that the RNU had active branches only in Moscow, Moscow Province, St. Petersburg, Stavropol, Perm, and Voronezh. However, reports in the central and regional press bore witness to RNU activity in Kaliningrad ("Russkii" 1998), Oryol, Krasnodar, Rostov, Volgograd, Saratov, Yekaterinburg, Arkhangelsk, Kostroma, Khabarovsk, Vladivostok, and other places not listed by Loginov. His inaccuracy in this regard also casts doubt upon his membership estimate.

Less credible still are the even lower estimates on occasion given by government sources, such as the figure of 7,000 cited in April 1999 (Babich 1999). Let us consider the plausibility of this figure in light of the account given by one young man who made contact with the RNU. "Maxim" was taken in a closed van to a camp outside Moscow where he watched about 1,500 people undergoing weekend military training (Womack 1998). The

Table 6.2

Estimates of RNU Membership

Date	Membership	Source
According to RNU leaders		
1994[a]	15,000	Likhachev and Pribylovskii (1997, p. 42)
September 1994	20,000	*Izvestiia* 9/24/94
January 1995	15,000 fighters	*Moskovskie novosti* 1995 no. 3
August 1995	20,000 comrades-in-arms	*Kommersant Daily* 8/25/95
April 1996	25,000 comrades-in-arms	Website[b]
April 1997	70,000	Likhachev and Pribylovski (1997, p. 41)
July 1997	Over 25,000	Gritchin and Urigashvili (1997)[c]
September 1997	Almost 4 million	Borodenkov (1997)
September 1998	100,000 fighters	RNU Website[d]
December 1998	Over 300,000	Barkashov press conference, 12/23/98
According to a defector from one of the RNU intelligence agencies		
August 1994	Over 10,000 comrades-in-arms	Khudokormov (1994)
According to official Russian government sources		
May 1995	2,000	Federal Security Service estimate (*Moskovskii komsomolets*, 5/11/95)
December 1998	20,000 members	Andrei Loginov of the Presidential Administration Directorate of Domestic Policy (NTV, 12/18/98)
April 1999	7,000	Babich (1999)

According to the Panorama Expert Group		
Late 1995	5,000 to 6,000	Verkhovskii, Papp, and Pribylovskii (1996, p. 176)
April 1997	6,000 to 12,000	Likhachev and Pribylovskii (1997, p. 41)
March 2000	10,000 to 15,000	E-mail message from A. Verkhovskii
According to an independent journalist		
December 1998	50,000 to 70,000 fighters plus a similar number of sympathizers	Belykh (1998)

[a]Exact date not given.
[b]At http://www.cs.uit.no/~paalde/NazismExposed/scripts/orgs.html.
[c]Citing Sergei Galkin, leader of RNU Mineralnye Vody organization.
[d]Speech by Oleg Kassin, leader of RNU Moscow organization, at http://www.rne.org.

name of the club that ran the camp is not given, but it should be noted that there were at least two RNU military-sports clubs in the Moscow area (*Viking* and *Viktoriya*), and that a new camp near Moscow was under construction that would be even bigger than the giant Stavropol camp *Russian Knights* (Shatrov 1998c).[70]

An important source of information and expertise on fascist and other extremist organizations in Russia is the "Information-Expert Group" Panorama. The Panorama report on the RNU dated April 1997 states that RNU membership for the whole of Russia is "possibly" between 6,000 and 12,000 (Likhachev and Pribylovskii 1997, p. 41). The figure cited by Panorama in March 2000 was 15,000. As Panorama estimates do not apparently include the near abroad, this estimate needs to be corrected upward, perhaps to about 18,000. Panorama relies upon a network of local observers, whose estimates are compared with the official RNU figures for the corresponding localities in order to obtain a coefficient that can be used to correct the RNU figure for the country as a whole.[71]

It was also the view of Panorama experts in early 2000 that the size of the RNU was not sharply growing or declining, but was fairly stable, although shifts did occur in the strength of the street presence that the movement maintained.

Relying on the sources available and not having conducted a field survey of my own, I am reluctant to make any estimate of RNU membership. In mid-2000, on the eve of the split in the RNU, the number of fighters (comrades-in-arms and fellow-builders) was very unlikely to exceed 50,000, or be much smaller than 15,000. If forced to be more precise, I would venture that the figure was quite likely to lie within the range of 20,000 to 25,000.

Geographical Distribution of RNU Members

RNU members were highly concentrated in certain regions of Russia. The greatest strongholds of the movement appear to have been the following:

1. the Russian northern Caucasus—above all, the Stavropol Territory, the only area in which the RNU approached the status of a mass movement, and also the Krasnodar Territory and Rostov Province;
2. Voronezh city and province in western Russia; and
3. Moscow Province (as distinct from Moscow City), especially the eastern and southeastern parts of the province.

The RNU was less strong, but nonetheless active and visible, in perhaps another score or so of cities and provinces scattered across the country. There seems to have been considerable RNU activity in the Far East, where the movement derived advantage from tensions in cross-border relations with China (Alexseev 2000). The RNU flag has even been triumphantly raised over the summit of one of the volcanoes of the Kamchatka peninsula.[72]

In contrast, there are quite a few regions of Russia in which the RNU does not appear to have established itself—including, notably, the ethnic minority republics, where Russian nationalism is in general weak.

Public Support for the RNU

As already mentioned, whenever and wherever RNU candidates have stood for election they have performed very poorly, usually winning well under 5 percent of the vote. Comparable results are given by the few public opinion polls in which respondents have been asked whether or not they support the RNU. Thus, in a poll conducted in October 1997 by the Public Opinion Foundation, 2 percent of respondents expressed unequivocal support for the RNU, with another 4 percent expressing equivocal support.[73] Polls conducted in seven regions in May 1998 on behalf of the LDPR showed 3 percent of the total sample of respondents willing to vote for the RNU in Duma or presidential elections, rising to 5 percent in Rostov and Arkhangelsk Provinces and the Republic of Marii-El.[74]And in February 1999, the newspaper *Novye izvestiia* published a poll in which 3 percent of respondents described themselves as sympathizers of the RNU, and 1 percent said that they were active supporters of the movement.[75]

A couple of caveats are in order. First, it should be noted that the 6 percent of respondents who took a more or less positive attitude toward the RNU in the October 1997 poll were concentrated disproportionately in certain demographic groups. RNU sympathizers were more likely to be men (by a ratio of 2 to 1), to be inhabitants of cities and large towns (by a ratio of over 2 to 1), and to be in the 19–35 age group (49 percent as compared with 35 percent for the sample as a whole).[76] From this we can deduce that the proportion of urban men between nineteen and thirty-five who had a positive attitude toward the RNU must have been well in excess of 10 percent—a figure that no longer seems quite so negligible. Second, none of these polls covered the population group that was the most attracted to the RNU—that is, even younger urban males, those between twelve and eighteen years old. Opinion pollsters, oriented as they are to elections, ignore adolescents, overlooking the unpleasant fact that, while these young people may be too young to vote, they are not too young to fight.

Moreover, public support for the RNU was not only a matter of the small minority who are ideologically conscious fascists. There was a much more broadly based and diffuse kind of public support that was predicated on approval of some or all of the RNU's public activities. Thus, although many people were perturbed or intimidated by RNU patrols, many others appreciated their contribution to maintaining public order, or at least accepted them as a normal feature of the urban landscape. At a session of a district council in Tver, one deputy, the chief physician at the local hospital, is on record as suggesting that "it would take only a hundred RNU members to impose order" in the city—a proposal that evoked applause from the audience and the agreement of other speakers (*Veche Tveri*, June 3, 1998). Most of those who felt this way about the RNU did not agree with, or know much about, the ideology that guided the movement, and it was not an issue that they cared about. It was sufficient for them that "homeless drunks no longer urinate in the children's playgrounds" (Babich 1999).

A large proportion of Russians did nevertheless entertain strong negative feelings about the RNU ("RNE" 1999). According to the polls already cited, about 35 percent wanted the organization banned. Three journalists who dressed up in RNU uniform and stood in the street to test public reaction reported that "it is hard to stand in the crossfire of heavy glances, full of confusion, contempt, and squeamishness," though they added that people seemed afraid to express their hostility openly (Glikin, Remneva, and Sokolov 1999). When fifty or so blackshirts gathered for a rally in front of a cinema in the city of Vladimir, young people passed by without stopping, but older people were openly angry, and one war veteran asked a police officer for a pistol so that he could shoot them (Maiorov 1999).

Not many people were prepared to stick their necks out and oppose the RNU actively and openly. Besides the widespread apathy and disillusionment concerning politics in general, people sensed that such opposition entailed risks to their present and future safety and to the safety of their families. In an atmosphere of insecurity and foreboding about the country's future, the fear that the RNU might come to power and exact revenge on its enemies was no small deterrent. Moreover, many of Russia's citizens have yet to lose the deeply internalized habits of caution that protected them in the totalitarian order of the past. And yet, as the cases of Borovichi and Zlatoust demonstrate, protest against the RNU did occur and could succeed. Protest was most effective right at the beginning, when the RNU made its first appearance in a town, before it had had time to establish close ties with the local establishment or to create a powerful climate of intimidation.

Notwithstanding the various qualifications that I have made, the limited extent of public support for the RNU was an important weakness. Also a weakness was the fact that the support the RNU did enjoy was mainly restricted to particular sections of the population: male urban working-class youth, and also military men, police officers, and other security personnel. A rather sensitive point for the RNU leadership was the underrepresentation among RNU members and supporters of the more highly educated sections of the population.[77] The RNU was not completely absent from Russia's universities, as its "department for the training of national cadres" at Volgograd State University indicates, but even those students who are inclined toward fascism prefer to join organizations that have more to offer from an intellectual and cultural point of view, such as the National-Bolshevik Party (see chapter 7).

One milieu in which the RNU may have appealed to a broader public is the Russian communities of those post-Soviet states in which local Russians have genuine ethnic grievances that the RNU was able to exploit. This applies especially to Latvia, Estonia, and Kazakhstan. I would like to share with the reader a memory of a personal encounter that brought home to me this point.

In June 1996, my colleague Dominique Arel and I interviewed a Cossack ataman who, until forced to take refuge in Moscow, had represented the Russian community of Kokchetav (in northern Kazakhstan) on the Kokchetav city council. He and the young man who assisted him, another Russian from Kokchetav, spoke about the plight of Russians in their native city, the abuse and discrimination they suffered, and their helplessness in the face of criminal attacks, the Kazakh perpetrators of which the police would always refuse to prosecute. I could not help but feel moved. Then the young man offered us a selection of literature. I was startled to see, alongside the periodicals of Kazakhstani human rights groups, copies of the RNU's *Russkii poriadok* and of *Shturmovik* [Stormtrooper], a glossy magazine put out by another fascist organization, Kasimovsky's Russian National Union (see chapter 8).

"But why do you get mixed up with such people?" I blurted out.

"Russians are a divided nation," replied the young man earnestly. "We are prepared to cooperate with anyone who stands for reunification."

Material Assets

"The RNU has quite a powerful material base," Khudokormov (1994) tells us. "To be exact: tent camps, guest houses, leased plots of land, sports stadiums, buildings, inventory, offices, cars[78] and trucks, secret dispersed stores with weapons, gasoline, and uniforms, precious gems (kept mainly in the dachas of 'sympathizers'), sewing workshops [to make uniforms], print workshops, several motor boats and yachts, multi-million bank accounts in the names of trustees, special underground bunkers, and special isolators (for future political prisoners)." To this list might be added the RNU's commercial shareholdings. It has been claimed, for example, that over 20 percent of the shares of the international technology corporation SIRENA belonged to the RNU (Peresvet 1995).

Military Potential

Little information is publicly available that would enable us to assess the military potential of the RNU. Fragmentary data on the numbers of weapons of different types discovered in police searches of the homes and cars of local RNU leaders suggest that the movement's arsenal must have been quite large, but was not technically very sophisticated.[79] We know that the RNU had "mobile units," presumably kept ready at the disposal of the top leadership. According to one source, the Russian capital was surrounded by two rings of such mobile units: an inner ring in Moscow Province and an outer ring in the neighboring provinces of Vladimir, Ryazan, Tula, Kaluga, and Tver (Shatrov 1998c). There were also RNU "partisan camps" in the provinces: one such camp, built in the forest outside Volgograd, is reported to have been equipped with trenches, a shooting range, a perimeter wall three meters high, and a wooden toilet (Kulakova 1999).

Naturally, RNU fighters would not have stood a chance against properly trained and led army units equipped with armor, artillery, and air support. Barkashov and his colleagues surely had no intention of putting their fighters up against combat-capable army units. The RNU might, however, have had the means necessary to initiate guerrilla warfare against a weak regime. It seems, for instance, to have had plenty of explosives for sabotage operations. Also suggestive of an orientation toward guerrilla warfare is the testimony of a counterintelligence officer in the army to the effect that conscripts who before call-up were active in the RNU try to get trained as snipers or saboteurs (Kalinina 1998). Alternatively, the RNU might have tried to intervene militarily in a political crisis, at a moment when the authorities were paralyzed and there was a power vacuum. The outcome, however, would have depended more on the extent to which the RNU had by that time penetrated the armed forces of the state than on its own combat strength.

The RNU's Penetration of State Structures

"When I started to arrest *Barkashovtsy*," we are told by Lieutenant-Colonel Nikolai Gamula, head of the Moscow police district on the territory of which lies Terletsky Ponds, "I had several very unpleasant conversations. Their strength lies in highly placed protectors" (Bal′burov 1999). The penetration of state structures at both federal and regional levels by RNU sympathizers was indeed an essential component of the organization's strength, and helps to explain why many state officials connived at its activity ("Vse vetvi" 1998).

The Armed Forces

We have already examined some of the methods used by the RNU to forge ties with members of the officer corps. Given the large measure of secrecy involved, it is difficult to judge how successful these methods were. The RNU leaders boasted that they had "their people" in the army at the level of battalion and division commander (*Nuzhen* 1996, p. 38)—that is, at the middle levels, but presumably not right at the top, of the military hierarchy. In 1999, two officers at the military university in Smolensk were discovered to be working actively for the RNU, as were two lecturers at the Ground Anti-Air Defense University in Moscow (Kislitsyn 1999; "Razgromleno" 1999). Besides individual sympathizers, there were also RNU "cells" in some military units (Belykh 1998). Certain military units, such as the 101st Brigade and the 21st Airborne Brigade, were reputed to be especially deeply infiltrated by the RNU.[80]

Arguably more significant was a growing tendency among military strategists, and officers in general, to see the RNU as an integral and valuable element of Russia's military system. Hence, at a conference on "National Security: Humanitarian and Social Aspects" hosted in December 1997 by the Institute of Philosophy of the Russian Academy of Sciences, it was argued in a lecture by Professor of the Academy of Military Sciences Colonel (Res.) V. Matyushev that the new kind of military force Russia would need in the twenty-first century could not be created by reforming the existing armed forces, but that use might be made of militarized movements like the RNU (Shatrov 1998c).

The Ministry of Internal Affairs

We have described the extensive cooperation that the RNU developed in the area of policing with the Ministry of Internal Affairs (MIA), and especially with certain city and provincial branch offices of the MIA (Administrations of Internal Affairs). The RNU was also allowed by the MIA to make use, for appropriate payment, of its shooting ranges (Deich 1998b). As in the army, the RNU had "cells" as well as individual sympathizers in the MIA structures. However, some local militia chiefs resisted the policy of cooperation with the RNU, refusing to make use of RNU patrols offered to them (Maksimov 1998; "Igrali" 1999). Also worth noting in this context is the readiness expressed in December 1998 by the head of the Moscow City Administration of Internal Affairs, Nikolai Kulikov, to use force if need be to prevent the RNU from holding its banned Moscow congress (Babichenko 1998b). Nevertheless, there can be little doubt that the MIA was one of the state bodies most deeply penetrated by the RNU.

As might be expected in light of the generally close relations between the RNU and the police authorities, the police usually manifested a clear bias in favor of the RNU in the course of their daily work. They tended to take the

RNU's side in fights between the blackshirts and their opponents, or at best to stand aside, and they were much more permissive in dealing with fascist than with antifascist demonstrations. Thus, chairman of the Moscow Antifascist Center Yevgeny Proshechkin remarks that the police were quick to disperse the demonstration that his center organized in 1995 on the street outside the RNU's headquarters, but seem to have no objection to fascist marches. One reason why the police tend not to take fascist organizations seriously as threats to public order is that most police officers themselves have strong prejudices against the ethnic minorities and others whom the fascists select as their victims (Rstaki 1998a).

The Ministry of Justice

Of particular importance is the stance taken by the Ministry of Justice, both because this ministry oversees the court system and because it is responsible for deciding whether or not a political organization is granted official registration. The attitude of the *federal* Ministry of Justice toward the RNU was consistently negative. It twice turned down applications by the RNU for registration, as it has denied registration to other organizations that it considers unconstitutional, such as the National-Bolshevik Party (Koptev 1998). However, the attitudes of departments of justice in the regions vary from one place to another, apparently depending on the political sympathies of the local elites. In November 1998, the RNU was registered in thirty-four provincial and city departments of justice.[81] The federal Ministry of Justice had not given its regional branches any definite instructions on the matter.

A similar pattern of regional variation is observable in the way that the procuracy (the agency responsible for initiating criminal prosecution and for general oversight of the judicial system) and the courts have handled cases involving the RNU. In areas where the RNU had strong ties with the local establishment, judges tended to manifest a clear bias in its favor (Graev 1998; Mendelevich 1998). Even in Moscow, procuracy officials were reluctant to initiate prosecutions against the RNU (Karamian 1999a). It was rumored that there were among them RNU sympathizers or even comrades-in-arms (RNU Forum).

The State Security Agencies

It is hard to judge the extent to which the RNU may have penetrated Russia's central agencies of state security. Mention has been made of the defector who during his service as an intelligence operative for the RNU maintained contact with secret RNU sympathizers within the Federal Counter-Intelligence Service (Khudokormov 1994). Barkashov also referred in one of his interviews to an unnamed RNU comrade-in-arms who was an officer in one of the security agencies with the rank of lieutenant-general (Barkashov 1995).

Of special importance to the RNU was the Federal Security Service (FSS), which is entrusted with the task of "countering threats to the constitutional order." The head of a new FSS department created in late 1998 for the protection of constitutional security stated in an interview that he did view the RNU as a danger to constitutional security, but was somewhat evasive concerning measures that should be taken to combat it. He denied that there were any RNU supporters in his own agency, but he agreed that such people were to be found in other state agencies (Zotov 1998). A similar cautiously anti-RNU line was taken by the current Russian president, Vladimir Putin, when he headed the FSS (Koptev 1998). In any case, it is widely recognized that "a large proportion of the officials in the security agencies openly or secretly sympathize [with the fascists] and quietly sabotage any steps their directors may take to counteract political extremism" (Mikhailov 1998).

Regional Government

There seems little doubt that the RNU was more successful in penetrating the state bureaucracy at the regional than at the federal level. Thus, among known supporters of the RNU one found the governors of a number of provinces and the mayors of small and large towns,[82] but apparently no ministers of the central government. As a result, the stance taken by a given official with regard to the RNU usually depended much more heavily on regional than on departmental affiliation. With the exception of the most centralized state bodies, such as the security agencies, local offices of governmental ministries, including the ministries of justice and internal affairs, have been more responsive to leading local officials than to their own central headquarters.[83] The position that the RNU established for itself at the regional level may therefore be regarded as one of the consequences of the regionalization of state power in Russia.

The RNU: Strengths and Weaknesses

The RNU possessed a remarkable combination of strengths and weaknesses. We may summarize them in the form of the following balance sheet:

RNU STRENGTHS

1. A relatively large, disciplined, and centralized organization.
2. The support of a sizable portion of Russia's male urban youth.
3. The penetration of various government structures, especially the army, the Ministry of Internal Affairs, and certain regional administrations.
4. Substantial material assets.
5. A significant military potential.

RNU WEAKNESSES

1. Latent internal divisions.
2. An uneven geographical distribution of support.
3. A continuing absence of broad support within the trade union movement, among the intelligentsia, and in the adult public in general.

"The RNU really is a dynamic and dangerous force," conclude the Panorama experts, immediately qualifying this bold assertion by adding that the RNU was oriented exclusively toward violent action in the contingency of a crisis of power in the country, and was badly handicapped as a political force in all other situations by its intellectual and propagandistic weakness (Verkhovskii, Papp, and Pribylovskii 1996, p. 67).

One implication seems fairly clear. *If* the RNU were to have come to power, it would much less likely have done so by legal and peaceful electoral means than by some kind of more or less violent state coup, whether carried out on its own or—arguably a more realistic variant—in collaboration with other forces.

The RNU's Role in Russian Politics

Until 1999 the public face of politics in post-Soviet Russia was dominated by the dramatic confrontation, which in October 1993 briefly exploded into civil war, between the forces supporting the presidential administration of Boris Yeltsin and the main anti-Yeltsin parliamentary opposition, based at first in the Supreme Soviet and later in the State Duma. In much Russian and most Western journalism, and even in a great deal of what purports to be scholarship, the Yeltsin camp was identified with liberalism, democracy, and "reform," whereas the anti-Yeltsin opposition was portrayed as a "red-brown" alliance of communists and more or less fascist Russian nationalists. This interpretation was by no means devoid of truth, but it did caricature a complex reality, ignoring the genuine democrats (such as the constitutional specialist Oleg Rumyantsev) in the ranks of the opposition and the authoritarians and nationalists among Yeltsin's supporters, unjustly painting all Russian nationalists "brown," and leaving out of account important forces like the trade union movement that did not belong to either camp (Buketov 1993; Shenfield 1993).

What role, if any, did the RNU play in the confrontation between Yeltsin and his parliamentary opposition? The Russian sources offer us a choice of answers, each consistent with part of the evidence but in its own way misleading.

One answer, characteristic of Yeltsin supporters, identified the RNU as the "brownest" component of the "red-brown opposition."[84] The most striking piece of evidence adduced in support of this interpretation was the RNU's military participation on the side of the Supreme Soviet in the civil war of October 1993, an episode that for the first time brought the RNU to broad public attention.[85] Emphasis was placed on the close links that existed between the RNU and communist provincial governors such as Nikolai Kondratenko of the Krasnodar Territory, Alexander Chernogorov of the Stavropol Territory, and Ivan Shabanov of Voronezh Province. It was claimed that communist rallies were sometimes controlled jointly by RNU units and Komsomol Operations Squads (Babich 1996),[86] and that Communist Party leader Gennady Zyuganov was protected by RNU men when he visited certain cities (Krasnoyarsk, for example). It was also pointed out that the communist fraction in the Duma had repeatedly blocked the passage of new and more effective legislation directed against the RNU and other fascist organizations.[87]

The point of view that located the RNU within the opposition coalition was contested from a variety of ideological standpoints. It is interesting to contrast the stance of the famous cinematographer and politician Stanislav Govorukhin, a representative of the more democratic and moderately nationalist wing of the opposition, with that of a more extreme opposition figure, Alexander Prokhanov, editor of the flagship periodical of Russian nationalism *Zavtra* (formerly *Den*). There is no reason to doubt the enlightened nature of Govorukhin's patriotism, which was demonstrated in his cosponsorship in December 1998 of the Duma motion of censure against the anti-Semitic speeches of CPRF deputy Albert Makashov. Govorukhin nonetheless belonged to the parliamentary opposition that also included the likes of Makashov. It is natural that a person in this uncomfortable position should wish to evade the question of the opposition's fascist ties, at the same time drawing parallels between "fascism" and the repressive measures of the

Yeltsin administration in October 1993 (Govorukhin 1994, p. 340). Prokhanov, in contrast, felt no embarrassment in recognizing Barkashov as a fellow fighter for the "patriotic" cause, but chided him for his sectarian aloofness from the wider patriotic movement, which objectively strengthened the position of the Yeltsin camp (Prokhanov 1998).

There were some, however, who went further to posit an implicit understanding, or even an explicit agreement, between Yeltsin and the RNU. Before the presidential election of 1996, the CPRF Duma deputy Viktor Ilyukhin claimed that the authorities were counting on the RNU in the event of Yeltsin's defeat and had given it weapons (Bal'burov 1997). This view of the RNU as a reserve force of the Yeltsin administration was shared by Ivanov-Sukharevsky's National People's Party, a bitter fascist rival of the RNU (see chapter 8). In Ivanov's eyes, Barkashov was a "gray TV star" and phony nationalist, and the good relations of which he boasted with the existing power structures proved that he was in the service of the "Yid regime" ("Seren'kaia" 1998).

Some independent liberal critics of Yeltsin likewise accused him of being in cahoots with the RNU. Their most common argument was that Yeltsin, and the oligarchs standing behind him, needed a fascist threat as a frightening but—or so they mistakenly thought—controllable "pocket scarecrow" or "devil in a sack" that would scare a reluctant electorate into voting for Yeltsin as the only viable alternative ("Chert" 1998). Oleg Vakulovsky, who created a TV series on Russian fascism, put it as follows:

> To have strong fascists in the country is today very convenient for our rulers: there is something and someone to frighten people with, there is someone to struggle against, and most importantly there is someone to vanquish. I am very much afraid that those bankers who are perhaps now prepared to invest money in these organizations, thinking only of their loud public victory over them in the year 2000, and confident as always that they are in control of everything, are without realizing it leading the country toward catastrophe. Our fascists are far from being operetta characters. They must not be given the opportunity to grow and gain strength. It can end badly, including for those same very self-confident bankers. (Rstaki 1998a)

Hence the cynical collaboration between the pro-Yeltsin media and the RNU, both interested in cultivating an image of the RNU as a powerful and steadily advancing force—an image that was initially false, but that functioned as a self-fulfilling prophecy.[88] In the most paranoid version of this reading, the RNU's apparent ties with the opposition were not denied, but were interpreted as a ruse on the part of the Yeltsin administration, aimed at dividing and discrediting a gullible opposition. Even the RNU's participation in the civil war of October 1993, according to some, was a provocation originating in the Yeltsin camp (Peresvet 1995).

The final answer on offer was that given by the RNU itself. The RNU claimed to be an independent "third force" in Russian politics, aligned neither with the Yeltsin administration nor with the opposition.

It is not easy to make sense of this morass of competing claims and apparently contradictory evidence. There may be a measure of truth in all of the answers. Neither the Yeltsin administration nor the opposition consistently abjured all ties with the RNU. On both sides there were people willing to strike deals with the RNU for one purpose or another. According to a participant in the RNU Forum, there have been a number of personal meetings between Barkashov and Yeltsin. But this does not mean that either Yeltsin or the opposition had a continuing relationship with the RNU that could reasonably be called an "alliance." Indeed, both camps could hardly be allied with the RNU simultaneously! And the RNU did not regard the links it forged with various political forces as fatally compromising its ultimate independence.

On the plausible assumption that the official registration of the RNU in a given region indicated that it had come to some kind of understanding with the political elite of that region,[89] we can test the relative strength of the RNU's ties with the different political camps at the regional level by comparing the political orientations of the governors of provinces in which the RNU is known to have acquired registration with those of the whole population of Russian provincial governors.[90] The results of this comparison are set out in Table 6.3. It will be observed that the RNU was somewhat more likely to have acquired registration in a province with a communist governor than in a province with a pro-Yeltsin governor, but that the margin of difference between the two frequency distributions is not very great. The RNU established links with regional leaders aligned with the Yeltsin administration, with regional leaders aligned with the CPRF, and with regional leaders whose alignment was unclear or unstable, such as Oryol governor Yegor Stroyev (see the Oryol case study above).

This pattern becomes more comprehensible when it is realized that RNU leaders sought to build ties with regional politicians not so much on the basis of shared ideological sympathies (although these may have played some role) as on that of mutual personal obligation. We can gain some idea of how the RNU went about the task from the example of Chuvashia. When the RNU first appeared in the Chuvash Republic in 1994, it had to operate half-underground in the face of official hostility. In 1995 the RNU center sent the

Table 6.3

Relationship Between RNU Registration at Regional Level and Political Party Affiliation of Governor or Mayor

Political party affiliation of governor or mayor	The 25 ethnically Russian regions in which RNU was registered at the Department of Justice[b]		The 68 ethnically Russian regions[a]	
Party connected to the Yeltsin regime[c]	11	44%	35	51%
Party of the communist opposition	7	28%	12	18%
Other party or no party	7	28%	21	31%

Notes:

[a]All the subjects of the Russian Federation are included in the analysis except the republics bearing the names of non-Russian ethnic minorities—that is, the 6 territories, the 49 provinces, the cities of Moscow and St. Petersburg, and the 11 Autonomous Provinces (which are not in practice controlled by their titular ethnic groups).

[b]As of December 1998, the RNU was registered in 31 to 34 regions (sources vary). From the information at my disposal I have been able to identify 25 of them.

[c]"Parties connected to the Yeltsin regime" are Chernomyrdin's "Our Home Russia" (*Nash Dom Rossiya*) and Shumeiko's "Reforms—New Course" (*Reformy—Novyi Kurs*). "Parties of the communist opposition" are the Communist Party of the Russian Federation and the Agrarian Party of Russia. "Other parties" include the Liberal-Democratic Party of Russia in Pskov Province, Rutskoi's "Great Power" (*Derzhava*) in Kursk Province, and Rossel's regional party "Transformation of the Fatherland" (*Preobrazhenie Otechestva*) in Sverdlovsk Province.

Chuvash organization a more experienced leader from St. Petersburg named Imendayev, who cultivated close relations with local CPRF politicians, especially Shurchanov, chairman of the State Council of the Chuvash Republic, and became an aide to the local CPRF deputy Malinov. Now he "no longer needed to fear prosecutors and courts" (Nikolaev 2000). Documents were drawn up with a view to getting the RNU officially registered, but the affair was leaked to the press, with the result that the minister of justice of the Chuvash Republic refused to approve the registration. The RNU continued to support the CPRF in Chuvashia, although it was unclear when, if ever, the payoff would be forthcoming.

While neither the Yeltsin camp nor the opposition was internally united on the issue of fascism, it is true that active opponents of fascism did have more influence on Yeltsin than they had on Zyuganov. The presence of a more effective antifascist lobby in the Yeltsin camp accounts for the fact that Yeltsin, unlike Zyuganov, did at least have a clear declaratory policy against fascism that found expression in his public speeches and in occasional presidential decrees. The limited practical impact of such decrees may be explained sufficiently well by bureaucratic sabotage and the counteraction of other lobbies. Thus, in early 1999 an official of the Moscow procuracy explained the reluctance of his agency to prosecute Barkashov for incitement of ethnic hatred by reference to the strength of the communist opposition at that time:

> It isn't 1991 now. Our agency does not especially want to quarrel with the opposition. It isn't clear who will be the next president. (quoted in Karamian 1999a)

We should also bear in mind Yeltsin's own impulsive character, which did not allow him patiently to sustain any effort in the face of resistance. These same factors suffice to account for the alternation of contradictory measures. For example, in March 1995 Yeltsin signed a decree to coordinate state action against fascism,[91] while in May 1996 he signed another decree that served to legalize the RNU's cooperation with the army in the sphere of predraft training. While the Machiavellian motives posited by the "devil in a sack" theory may not have been altogether absent, I find it more convincing to put the main emphasis on more mundane sources of Yeltsin's inconsistencies.

Account should, moreover, be taken of definite shifts over time in the relations between the RNU and the two blocs. In its early years, the RNU was more willing to recognize itself as part of a broader "patriotic camp," albeit with some reluctance, given the ideological gap that always divided the national-fundamentalists from the "patriotic" mainstream. Until March 1993, the RNU took part in the "patriotic" umbrella forum headed by General Alexander Sterligov, the Russian National Assembly, and only in mid-1994 was a definite decision taken no longer to be involved in attempts to create broad alliances of "patriotic" forces (which did not, however, rule out the possibility of concluding agreements with other organizations for specific purposes, such as trade union work). Barkashov now began to speak dismissively of the "patriotic" alliances as futile talking-shops (Likhachev and Pribylovskii 1997, p. 27; Prokhanov 1998). The RNU went its own way as a "third force," concentrating on building up its own organization with a view to future struggles.

From the end of 1994, Barkashov's public statements concerning the Yeltsin regime started to become less hostile, as he approvingly acknowledged the drift of the regime in a "national" direction (Shatrov 1998a). A crucial turning point was the military intervention in Chechnya in December 1994, which the RNU ardently welcomed, offering to send its own fighters to the war. This moment of convergence between Yeltsin and the RNU was but one element in the deep realignment of Russian politics triggered by the war in Chechnya, which alienated many of Yeltsin's former supporters from the "democratic" movement while winning him the plaudits of many Russian nationalists, including Zhirinovsky's LDPR and Rogozin's Congress of Russian Communities as well as the RNU. Besides the impact of the Chechen war, Barkashov was aware of the presence at that time within Yeltsin's entourage of two men who advocated that the regime rely more heavily on Russian nationalism—namely, the head of the Presidential Security Service, Alexander Korzhakov, and the Commandant of the Kremlin, Mikhail Barsukov—and established tentative contact with them (Prokhanov 1998).[92] Barkashov even entertained the possibility that in some future political crisis a more nationalist Yeltsin might invite him to take over the government, as President Marshal Paul Hindenburg had invited Hitler in 1933 (*Nezavisimaia gazeta*, April 4, 1998).

Barkashov was able to justify in doctrinal terms his willingness to come to Yeltsin's aid because, unlike the simpler-minded People's National Party, the RNU made a distinction between the ruling "democratic" regime and the state machine nominally under its command. While still condemning the political philosophy and many specific policies of the regime, it believed that the state machine nonetheless continued to embody much that was of value from the "national" point of view. It therefore sought to protect the state from possible "destabilizing" or "anti-state" action, even if such a threat were to come from the "patriotic" anti-regime opposition—in the event, for instance, of a refusal by the CPRF to accept electoral defeat (Simonsen 1996a, p. 45; Shatrov 1998a).

In the late 1990s, there was a reverse shift in the RNU's position in Russia's political system. On the one hand, there was a gradual activation of Yeltsin's declaratory antifascist policy, beginning with the formation in October 1997 of a special presidential commission on political extremism. On the other hand, Barkashov moved to distance himself from Yeltsin. In an interview published in *Zavtra* in November 1998, Barkashov signaled a desire to mend his fences with the mainstream "patriotic" opposition. He admitted that he abstained from confrontation with the Yeltsin regime for a certain period of time, explaining that he considered it necessary to allow socioeconomic conditions to deteriorate further in order that social and ethnic discontent among Russians might increase to a level that would make the victory of the RNU possible—a task that had now been accomplished (Prokhanov 1998).

The stances that the RNU adopted toward the dominant political forces of Russian society can be understood primarily as a reaction to the stances that those forces adopted toward the RNU. The RNU was an organization oriented to the long term. It did not aspire to exert a serious influence upon immediate political developments, such as changes in the composition of the government.[93] At the same time, the legitimacy of the RNU's activity was widely questioned, so that it could not take its own continued existence for granted. Under these circumstances, the aspect of state policy of most urgent concern to the RNU must have been state policy regarding itself. The RNU would, in general, extend its support to those politicians and officials who proved themselves willing to foster its growth; it would adopt a neutral position toward those who would passively tolerate it; and it would treat as its mortal enemies those who sought to suppress it. Unless it had a very strong motive for behaving otherwise, the RNU would accordingly do whatever it could to make itself useful to anyone who possessed effective power in a given region or in the country as a whole, keeping "order" on his behalf, and not worrying unduly about his ideological orientation or political alignment, provided only that he allowed the RNU to survive and develop freely in his domain. Thus, there can be no doubt that Barkashov preferred Boris Yeltsin to Yuri Luzhkov, notwithstanding that the "liberal Westernizer" Yeltsin was further removed from him ideologically than the "Russian patriot" Luzhkov, because Yeltsin, unlike Luzhkov, "[did] not impede our work" (Bal′burov 1997).

Of course, any but the most short-sighted of Russian politicians would surely have understood that the "support" so generously extended to him by the RNU was, to borrow Lenin's felicitous expression, "the support that the rope gives to the hanged man." This "devil" had no intention of waiting obediently in his "sack" at his master's beck and call. For the RNU, the tactical alliances into which it entered were mere stepping-stones on the road to its own undivided power.

The RNU's Political Strategy

Undivided power was not necessarily the clearly envisaged goal of the RNU from the very beginning. There are indications that in the early 1990s the RNU did not aim to take power directly, but rather hoped to catalyze a military coup that would lead to "the establishment of a national dictatorship by patriotically inclined military men" (Pribylovskii 1994, p. 20). "Russia's liberation is approaching," proclaimed one RNU flier from that period. "Every officer and soldier, policeman and security man will have to choose sides" (Union of Councils 1997, p. 117).

As the RNU grew stronger, however, and distanced itself from the mainstream of the "patriotic" movement, it came to see itself as the core and precursor of the future "national" regime to be established upon the seizure of state power. At the same time, it was resolved "not to risk adventures, but to come to power slowly and carefully" (Khudokormov 1994). A strategy was worked out that might be characterized as a gradual or creeping coup, accomplished by means of the steady penetration of state and social structures and the accumulation of military and economic potential. This process of penetration also had an ideological dimension: Barkashov expressed satisfaction at the fact that "aspects of the national ideology formulated by us . . . are echoed in the speeches of state figures at various levels" ("I Vserossiiskii" 1997). Maximum possible use would be made of legal means, without ruling out the use of illegal methods. "We shall reach as many people as possible, but quietly," a regional RNU leader in Stavropol explained. "When the time comes, power will flow to us" (Gritchin and Urigashvili 1997).

The creeping coup was not necessarily envisaged as proceeding all the way to its culmination in a smooth and peaceful manner. It has been suggested that the RNU may have intended its gradual seizure of power to culminate in a "controlled explosion" (Perova 1996). In his 1998 *Zavtra* interview, Barkashov agreed that the work of the RNU to date had been no more than preparation for a more active phase that might be entered in the near future:

> *Question*: To create a political organization is to create a social weapon. And when will your weapon begin to fire?
> *Answer*: I shall not reveal my designer's secrets, but I say: we are constantly at work, and the time for the launch is near, although much depends on circumstances, on how rapidly they develop in the needed direction. (Prokhanov 1998)

It is hard to avoid the conclusion that the "launch" was to entail considerable violence. Otherwise what would all the combat training of RNU members have been for? "Our movement values clever people, but it is no bad thing to be at the same time a strong, bold lad who knows how to fight," one comrade-in-arms replied to a critic who had questioned the RNU's emphasis on raw physical strength, "because it seems that soon that will be needed here in Russia" (RNU Forum). Also suggestive of violence to come was an order issued by Barkashov that each RNU member and sympathizer was to equip himself, allegedly for the purpose of planting trees to beautify the urban landscape, with a small sapper's shovel of army make—the same kind of shovel that acquired notoriety when soldiers used it against demonstrators in Tbilisi on April 9, 1989 ("Barkashovtsy" 1998; Iur′ev 1999; Sokovnin 1999).

What kind of violent events did the leaders of the RNU expect, and what part did they intend their movement to play in them? Did they have in mind a struggle for power between other forces, in which the RNU would intervene as a third and ultimately victorious force? Or a direct showdown between the RNU and its enemies? Or a popular uprising that the RNU would try to channel in a "nationally conscious" direction—or help to put down?

Here we are forced to resort to speculation. We do, however, have a clue in Barkashov's statement that the RNU takes into account both the way that the Nazis came to power in Germany in the early 1930s and the way that the Bolsheviks came to power in Russia in 1917, but that it does not commit itself to any single historical model (Prokhanov 1998). It is therefore likely that various strategies were under consideration, corresponding to different ways in which events might unfold, and that these included a "Nazi" and a quasi-bolshevik strategy, adapted to the situation of contemporary Russia. It may be supposed that had the RNU (and others) succeeded in channelling rising popular discontent primarily against the ethnic minorities and "traitors" whom the RNU regarded as its own enemies, then the RNU would have attempted to enact a quasi-bolshevik strategy for the conquest of power, placing itself at the head of the rebellion of "the [Russian] people." A former RNU member puts it in classically bolshevik fashion: "If the authorities rot and the masses come on to the streets, then the main task of the RNU will be to direct [the masses] into the right channel" (interviewed in Subbotin 1999). Should the RNU, however, have found itself faced with a popular uprising in forms not susceptible to its control and directed against its tactical allies in the political and economic elites, then it might have offered the latter—at the price of a share of state power for itself—its services as a special reserve force of mass repression.

In this eventuality, the only issue remaining unresolved would have been that of the relations between the RNU and its allies in the ruling coalition that emerged. Would the RNU, as the best organized and most ruthless part of the coalition, have repeated the "Nazi" endgame and concentrated a monopoly of power in its own hands? Or would the allies have created a "national dictatorship" of their own, and suppressed the RNU as a henceforth unneeded nuisance? Who, in other words, would have double-crossed whom?

The Anti-RNU Campaign of 1998–1999

In the second half of 1998 and the first half of 1999, there was finally a determined effort, on the part first of Yeltsin's presidential administration and then of Moscow Mayor Yuri Luzhkov, to take effective practical action against the RNU.

Expedition to the South

The first target was the RNU stronghold in the Russian south. At the end of July 1998, then deputy head of the presidential administration, Yevgeny Savostyanov, traveled to the Stavropol Territory, and at a closed meeting of regional government officials devoted to "the situation concerning political extremism and measures of counteraction" set the territory's law enforcement agencies the task of revoking the RNU's registration and bringing its activity in the territory to a halt by November 1, 1998. Soon thereafter there appeared on the RNU website a statement about this meeting, denying Savostyanov's right to decide such matters and warning that "Savostyanov and those who implement his illegal instructions (if any such individuals can be found) will not be able to escape responsibility now, and all the more so later."

Some local officials were nevertheless prepared to defy the RNU's threats, for in December 1998 it was reported in the Moscow press that thanks to "operational measures" by the MIA in the Stavropol Territory about 800 youths had been "removed from the influence of the RNU." In addition, the bank accounts of eighteen RNU branches had been frozen, and the publication of fascist literature in the territory had been almost completely curtailed. However, the goal of bringing RNU activity to a complete halt had evidently not been met, and the head of the territorial department of justice had refused to revoke the RNU's registration (Babichenko 1998a; 1999).

Later in the same month, the chief of the presidential administration, General Nikolai Bordyuzha, sent military inspectors to the Stavropol and Krasnodar Territories to analyze the situation there as it pertained to the RNU (*INTERFAX*, December 21, 1998). The inspections apparently led to the disbanding of army and internal troops units in which RNU influence had been particularly strong (RNU Forum).

Moscow Takes on the RNU

Meanwhile, the RNU leaders were making preparations for the second national congress of the organization, which was scheduled for December 19, 1998. The first congress had been held in February 1997 in Reutov, a small town to the east of Moscow, with 1,075 delegates in attendance ("I Vserossiiskii" 1997). This time the proclaimed intention was to gather 4,500 delegates[94] and 500 guests, and to hold the event in Moscow itself, at the "Izmailovo" sports complex.

The Moscow congress was to serve several important purposes for the RNU. First, a congress in the capital and on such an impressive scale was to bring unprecedented publicity, turning the RNU into "a real movement with a claim to power in the country."[95] Second, the congress was to ratify amendments to RNU documents—drafted, I suspect, on the advice of sympathetic insiders—that were to clear the way for registration at the federal level, enormously strengthening the RNU's legal position and permitting its direct participation in forthcoming Duma and presidential elections. And third, the congress was to provide Barkashov with a welcome opportunity to reaffirm his leadership of the movement (Zverev et al. 1999).

Just a few days before the congress was scheduled to convene, with many delegates already on their way to Moscow from all over Russia, Moscow's mayor, Yuri Luzhkov, suddenly announced that "such a gathering will not be permitted, now or in the future." On December 15, his decision was formally confirmed in a resolution of the Moscow city government (Babichenko 1998b). Luzhkov's aides linked the ban to a European antifascist congress due to be held shortly in Moscow (Deich 1998a); Barkashov attributed it to Luzhkov's desire to suppress a political rival, pointing out that the RNU congress would have taken place on the same day as the founding congress of his own new party "Fatherland" [*Otechestvo*] (Barkashov press conference, December 23, 1998).

Mayor Luzhkov took prompt and firm action to enforce the decision. The management of the "Izmailovo" complex was prevailed upon to cancel the RNU's booking "for technical reasons"—that is, on the grounds that the seating was in such poor condition that accidents were possible (Likhachev 1999). Delegates arriving at the airport were stopped by Moscow police and made to fly back home.

How to react to the ban proved a contentious issue within the RNU leadership. Barkashov's initial response was to threaten an invasion of Moscow by his followers. On December 16, he declared on television that unless "Luzhkov and his Jewish band" withdrew the ban, 150,000 strong young men would gather in Moscow from all over Russia to defend their civil rights. "They won't be in uniform, but they will know what to do" (Karamian 1999a). He announced that the RNU would postpone the congress, as he wanted to avoid a violent confrontation with ethnic Russian policemen, but that it was a matter of principle that the congress should eventually be held in Moscow. The RNU would appeal against Moscow's decision to the procuracy and, if necessary, to the Constitutional Court.

Some of Barkashov's followers were said to be furious at his "retreat in the face of the enemy." The RNU press secretary, Alexander Rashitsky, warned of the likely consequences: much as RNU commanders might wish to restrain their fighters, he explained with a nice touch of hypocrisy, some comrades-in-arms were bound to avenge the "insane policy" of the Moscow government by beating up Muscovites of non-Russian nationality (Komarova and Karamian 1998)—as if they did not do so in any case! Other RNU leaders urged Barkashov to transfer the congress to one of the provincial cities where the RNU was more strongly entrenched, such as Stavropol, Krasnodar, or Voronezh. In Stavropol or Krasnodar, they promised him, he would be received virtually as a state dignitary, welcomed by the governor in person, and provided with excellent facilities and hotels (Zverev et al. 1999). But Barkashov insisted on holding out for Moscow.

Press commentators questioned the legal validity of the ban on the RNU congress (Amelina 1998b; Punanov 1998). The ban also proved counterproductive in one respect: the publicity attendant upon the controversy attracted more public attention to the RNU and won widespread sympathy for it as a "persecuted" movement. A flood of new recruits flowed into the organization, increasing membership in Moscow by one-third in the week following the ban (Politkovskaia 1998). An RNU spokesman ironically thanked Luzhkov for the service he had unintentionally rendered the RNU (Khristinin 1999).

Luzhkov, however, did not allow the RNU to consolidate its position in Moscow. On the contrary, he followed up the ban on the congress with further measures to suppress RNU activity in the capital. The first sign of the new policy that observers noticed was that the Metro police began to disperse RNU gatherings that had traditionally been held inside certain Metro stations (Zverev et al. 1999). Then in early January 1999 the RNU was expelled from Terletsky Ponds. Its headquarters buildings there were locked up and fenced off—after failing to pass a fire inspection! The mayor's office "recommended" Moscow entrepreneurs not to lease any other premises to the RNU, and also to stop hiring guards from RNU protection agencies. Most entrepreneurs proved receptive to the "recommendations." The city itself stopped using RNU men to patrol suburban trains and other public facilities. The Moscow police were instructed to arrest any uniformed Barkashovites who tried to hold marches or conduct agitation on the streets.[96] Finally, in April 1999, the Moscow registrations both of *Russkii poriadok* and of the RNU itself were revoked by court decision (Bronzova 1999; Karamian 1999b; Sterkin 1999; Strogin 1999b; "Vodit′sia" 1999). Luzhkov was thwarted only on one point: the Moscow procuracy did not accede to his request that Barkashov be prosecuted for inciting ethnic hatred (Koptev 1998; Ofitova 1998).

There is no doubt that Luzhkov succeeded in greatly weakening the Moscow City Organization of the RNU in all respects—legal, financial, and political. The RNU in Moscow was not completely eliminated, but it was forced underground—in a literal and a metaphorical sense. Ownerless basements were taken over and converted for use as makeshift RNU headquarters, barracks, and literature stores (Karamian 1999b).[97] The national headquarters of the movement was transferred to a newly constructed building in Podolsk, a town to the south of the capital in Moscow Province, the governor of which, Anatoly Tyazhlov, was not willing to follow Luzhkov's lead in regard to the RNU (Bal′burov 1999; Pravosudov 1999a).

Some commentators in the Russian press predicted that Luzhkov's measures against the RNU would be imitated by many mayors and governors in other parts of the country, especially by those who aspired to prominent roles in *Otechestvo*, the electoral bloc headed by Luzhkov. There appears to have been some tendency of this kind, but it was a rather weak one. For example, the mayor of Yekaterinburg, Arkady Chernetsky, did nothing to obstruct an unauthorized march and picket that the RNU held in his city to protest against Luzhkov's policy, even though he sought the leading position in the regional branch of *Otechestvo* (Ivanenko 1999).[98] With a view to assessing the impact that Luzhkov's campaign had outside of Moscow, the newspaper *Kommersant-Daily* conducted in April 1999 a survey of regional mayors and governors, each of whom was asked whether he intended to follow the example set by Moscow in dealing with the RNU ("Priamaia rech′" 1999). Of the seventeen respondents whose answers were published, seven expressed themselves in favor of a ban on the RNU and nine against.[99] However, most of those favoring a ban had already adopted such a stance before Luzhkov suppressed the RNU in Moscow. The only respondent who stated specifically that he was "following Luzhkov's example" was the governor of Perm Province, Gennady Igumnov.

Prospects of the RNU

The anti-RNU campaign of 1998–99 broke the momentum of the RNU as a movement and prevented it from establishing itself as a serious political force at the national level. At the same time, the RNU was far from broken, especially in regional strongholds like Stavropol and Voronezh, where it had entrenched itself as a widely accepted part of the public scene with strong ties to the local elite. It is also likely that the RNU has influenced to some extent the general atmosphere of Russian society and politics. For these and other reasons, I believe that it is misleading to dismiss the RNU, as some observers are inclined to do, as a small and marginal organization, "not fascists but hooligans" (Paniushkin 2000).

In light of the many weaknesses of the RNU, ranging from the restricted nature of its social base to Barkashov's personal inadequacies and lack of charisma, it is in fact remarkable that the organization achieved even the limited success that it did. Where did the ultimate source of its strength lie? Certainly not in its ideology, the real origins of which it went to such lengths to camouflage. Our study of the mode of operation of the RNU suggests that its crucial asset was the ability of many of its leaders to establish mutually advantageous relationships with members of Russia's political and economic elite, especially at the regional level. In those places where the RNU succeeded in establishing such relationships, it enjoyed the political patronage that protected it from police and legal counteraction, and was guaranteed access to the material and financial resources that it needed for its activities.

But if this was the ultimate source of the RNU's strength, it was also arguably the ultimate source of its weakness. The movement was abjectly dependent on the local elites, who clearly had it in their power—irrespective of legal niceties—to decide what they would do with the RNU: actively sponsor it, passively tolerate it, or decisively suppress it. It is the extent of its dependence on other political actors that, perhaps more than anything else, distinguished the RNU from Hitler's NSDAP (Shevelev 1999). I see no way in which the RNU could have escaped from this dependence, at least under "normal" conditions of basic sociopolitical stability. It is conceivable that, in the event of a really deep crisis that threw Russia's entire political system into chaos, the RNU might have made some impact, but even then it would have been much more likely to find itself the instrument of some other political force than to take and hold power in its own hands.

In September 2000, Barkashov was ousted from his position as RNU leader in an internal coup. As a result, the movement underwent a split. Since none of the successor organizations continue to identify themselves as the Russian National Unity, it may be concluded that the RNU no longer exists. The successor organizations may, however, be expected to bear many similarities to their parent movement. These developments are discussed further in the Afterword.

Appendix
The RNU Oath and Code of Honor

The RNU Oath

I, [name], a son of the Russian Nation, entering the ranks of Comrades-in-Arms of the Russian National Unity, swear loyalty to the Russian Nation, and swear:

with dignity and honor to bear the lofty title of Comrade-in-Arms;

to be honest, brave, manly, and an active fighter for the freedom of Russia and of the Russian Nation;

to be a firm, consistent, and principled defender of the interests of the Russian Nation, of its culture, and of the territory of Russia;

in all ways to further the ingathering and strengthening of the Russian land;

to strengthen the military might of Russia;

constantly to raise the level of my combat and political training;

to treat with vigilance all of alien faith and alien stock[a];

strictly to preserve military, national, and state secrets;

to be merciless to external and internal enemies of Russia and of the Russian Nation;

always to be ready on the order of the Chief Comrade-in-Arms to defend the interests of Russia and of the Russian Nation, and to my last breath to struggle against the external and internal enemies of the Russian Nation inside Russia and beyond its boundaries.

If I should break this Oath, then let my Comrades-in-Arms deal with me as the Code of Honor of the Comrade-in-Arms requires.

---

[a] The words used here—*inovertsy* [people of alien faith] and *inorodtsy* [those of alien stock]—are those that were used in tsarist Russia.

The RNU Code of Honor

1. The honor and dignity of the Comrade-in-Arms of the Russian National Unity are inseparable from the honor and dignity of the Russian Nation.
2. Any infringement of the honor and dignity of the Russian Nation is a most serious crime, and is regarded by the Comrade-in-Arms as an infringement of his own honor and dignity.
3. Any infringement of the honor and dignity of the Comrade-in-Arms is a crime against the Russian Nation.
4. The Comrade-in-Arms is obliged to defend his honor and dignity by all available means.
5. The Comrade-in-Arms, being a plenipotentiary representative of the Russian Nation, is obliged to restore justice for Russian people by means of his own power and his own arms, without appeal to courts or other authorities.
6. The Comrade-in-Arms decides all questions guided only by national law-consciousness in accordance with the prerogatives given him by the Chief Comrade-in-Arms, and does not subordinate himself to any other laws.
7. In his relations with Russian people the Comrade-in-Arms is guided by the teachings of Jesus Christ.[b]
8. The Comrade-in-Arms is obliged to be a model Russian National-Patriot, and by his conduct to give an example to all Russian people.
9. The Comrade-in-Arms bears full responsibility for the conduct and moral character of the members of his family.
10. The Comrade-in-Arms is obliged to be honest, brave, manly, and an active fighter for the freedom of Russia and the flourishing of the Russian Nation.
11. The Comrade-in-Arms is obliged to share with the Nation all its woes and misfortunes.
12. The Comrade-in-Arms grows rich only together with the Nation.
13. The Comrade-in-Arms is obliged to know the history of Russia and of the Russian Nation, to preserve its culture and independent identity [*samobytnost'*], and to cut short at the roots any attempts made by those of alien faith or stock to change them.

[b] Note that this rule applied only to relations with Russian people. The RNU recruit was taught that in his relations with non-Russians he was not to be guided by the teachings of Jesus Christ.

14. The Comrade-in-Arms is obliged always to remember that Russia has no friends. He who forgets this becomes a traitor.
15. The pursuit of the external and internal enemies of the Russian Nation, however far from Russia's borders they may be, is a matter of honor for the Comrade-in-Arms.
16. Only with blood can the Comrade-in-Arms wash away shame.
17. Only death may serve as a justification for the failure of the Comrade-in-Arms to observe this Code of Honor.
18. For the Comrade-in-Arms to break the Oath of loyalty he has sworn to the Russian Nation is treason.
19. Treason for the Comrade-in-Arms is the most serious crime, and is punished by death.
20. The basic principle of life for the Comrade-in-Arms is the motto: "Everything for the Nation, nothing against the Nation, the Nation above all."

Source: Russkii poriadok 1993, no. 12, pp. 28–29, 31.

7
Dugin, Limonov, and the National-Bolshevik Party

The National-Bolshevik Party (NBP) of Eduard Limonov was formed in 1993. It has demonstrated a pattern of steady growth, with the result that it is now one of the largest political organization of fascist orientation in Russia, with a membership estimated to be in the range of 6,000 to 7,000.[1] The NBP has about 500 members in Moscow alone, several hundred more in St. Petersburg, functioning groups in more than half of Russia's regions (Verkhovskii 2000), and some kind of presence in almost all parts of the Russian Federation.[2] (It also has branches in some cities of other post-Soviet states; for instance, NBP activities in Riga, Latvia, have drawn considerable attention.) Moreover, "members" can in principle be equated with "activists," for the NBP, like the RNU but unlike some other fascist groups, requires of its members a high level of activism.

The NBP is significant also on account of the social characteristics of its members. The *natsboly*, as they call themselves, are overwhelmingly young. They include not only unemployed and working-class youth, and some politicized skinheads, but also many students, a significant number of engineers, and other highly educated youngsters. Many young recruits are attracted by the artistic, literary, and intellectual creativity that makes the party's journal *Limonka* by far the most interesting and (in "patriotic" circles) popular of Russian fascist periodicals. The close links between the NBP and youth subcultures, and also a relatively non-dogmatic approach to doctrinal matters, contribute to its appeal to young people.

Therefore, while the NBP is not and may never become a mass organization, there is good reason to believe that it has the potential for further growth, and that it may leave a palpable mark on Russian political, intellectual, and cultural life.

The NBP is the creation of two men: the prominent writer and poet Eduard

Limonov, and the mystical philosopher and political theorist Alexander Dugin (who amicably departed from the NBP in 1998). The cultural and intellectual influence in Russian society that Limonov and Dugin possess as prominent creative figures in their own right is much broader than any influence that the NBP may have as an organization. Accordingly, I focus in the first half of the chapter on Dugin and on Limonov as individuals—their personal backgrounds, the formation of their political views, the style and content of their published works, and the nature and extent of their social influence. In the case of Dugin, I present an analysis of his overall worldview, which is in some ways distinct from the official worldview of the NBP. (No distinction can be drawn between Limonov's worldview and that of the party that he dominates.)

In the second half of the chapter, I proceed to analyze the National-Bolshevik Party as a political organization. I start with the question of the puzzling relationship between style and ideology in the NBP, and then consider the party's program and its other policy documents, its symbols, its structure, the nature of its activities, its strategy, and its prospects. Finally, I discuss the significance of the NBP as a social phenomenon.

Dugin

Alexander Gelevich Dugin was born in 1962 into a military family: his father was a colonel, and his grandfather and great-grandfather had also been army officers (Verkhovskii et al. 1996, p. 262).[3] At the end of the 1970s, he became a student at the Moscow Aviation Institute. It is not, however, to any formal schooling that he owes his vast erudition—he is said to know no fewer than nine foreign languages—or the historical and theological learning that was to shape the meaning of his life. These he acquired in an informal setting of a very special kind.

Depressed and alienated from the Soviet reality around him, he encountered by chance, through a neighbor of his parents, a secretive group of intellectuals who gave him the existential home he sought. The three most important members of this circle, who first came together in the 1960s, were all scholars steeped in the mystical traditions of Europe or the Orient: Yevgeny Golovin, a specialist in European mystical literature and poetry; Yuri Mamleyev, a Christian philosopher; and Geidar Jemal, a Muscovite of Azeri origin who specialized in the metaphysics of Islam.[4] Dugin deeply revered these men; later he was to speak of them as "the true masters of the Moscow esoteric elite" (Limonov 1993a). Keeping their distance both from official Soviet culture, which they looked down upon as "a zoo," and from the Western-oriented and Slavophile dissident milieus, the "masters" and their pupils read and translated the works of foreign writers who shared their preoccupation with mysticism, including the French devotee of Sufism René Guénon, the Italian pagan-fascist philosopher Julius Evola, and the German war novelist Ernst Jünger—figures in whom the West European New Right were also finding their inspiration.[5]

Dugin rapidly made himself a valued member of the Golovin circle. His first major contribution to their work was to make the first translation into Russian of the book *Pagan Imperialism*, by Julius Evola, an author who clearly exerted a crucial influence on the young man. It is doubtless from Evola that Dugin took the central strand of his emerging worldview—allegiance to the "Tradition" that supposedly has its origin in a primordial heroic age.

Dugin's unofficial activities did not long remain unnoticed by the authorities. It was learned that he had sung "mystical anticommunist songs" at a party. He was detained by the KGB, and forbidden literature was discovered in his apartment. Expelled from his institute, he resorted—like many other nonconformists of the Soviet period—to a menial occupation that would allow him to continue pursuing his philosophical interests, in his case that of street sweeper. It was at this time that he met and married his first wife, whom he describes as a hippie.

The advent of perestroika presented Dugin with new opportunities. In 1987, he joined *Pamyat*—not really backward-looking enough for Dugin's taste, but "the most reactionary organization available." For a few months in late 1988 and early 1989, he sat on *Pamyat*'s Central Council. Dugin did not, however, derive a great deal of satisfaction from his collaboration with *Pamyat*. He found his new comrades prone to hysteria and schizophrenia, and he was disappointed by their lack of interest in Traditionalism. Clearly the low cultural and intellectual level of the majority of *Pamyat* activists did not equip them to appreciate what Dugin had to offer. He dropped out of *Pamyat* and resumed the quest for his own path.[6]

Dugin spent much of 1989 on visits to West European countries, where he strengthened his links with such New Right figures as the Frenchman Alain de Benoist, the Belgian Jean-François Thiriart, and the Italian Claudio Mutti. His first direct encounter with Western life had the effect of moderating his hostility to the Soviet system, which he now regarded as being less incompatible with traditional values than the social order in the West. This belated reconciliation with Soviet reality, at a time when it already faced collapse, led him at the beginning of the 1990s to associate with the "statist patriots" of the communist camp. He was at this time close to Gennady Zyuganov, and probably played a significant part in formulating the nationalist-communist ideology that was to be Zyuganov's hallmark. From 1991 onward, Dugin wrote extensively for the flagship periodical of the "red-brown" opposition *Den* [Day] (later renamed *Zavtra* [Tomorrow]), edited by Alexander Prokhanov. He also joined its editorial board.

Throughout the 1990s, Dugin was very active in elaborating and propagating his ideology. Early in the decade, he set up his own publishing house, *Arktogeya*, with a bookstore and a Center for Special Metastrategic Research attached. *Arktogeya* has put out a long series of books by Dugin himself—eleven titles in all, not counting reprints—and by various authors of the West European New Right, as well as a number of journals that Dugin has launched. The first journal, appearing in 1991, was called *Giperboreyets* [Hyperborean]. It was followed by an almanac under the name *Milyi angel* [Dear Angel], devoted to Christian mysticism. However, the principal vehicle for the propagation of Dugin's ideas has been a lavishly illustrated magazine titled *Elementy: evraziiskoe obozrenie* [Elements: A Eurasian Review], published twice and later once a year from July 1992 with a print run averaging 5,000 to 10,000.[7] In 1999, Dugin revived *Milyi angel* and created a new monthly titled *Evraziiskoe vtorzhenie* [Eurasian Invasion].

Occasionally, Dugin has gained access to a much wider audience through television and radio. In September 1993, his series "Mysteries of the Century" (made together with Yuri Vorobyev) was broadcast on the first and fourth *Ostankino* channels (Verkhovskii et al. 1996, p. 262). In 1997 Dugin had a weekly hour-long radio program called *Finis Mundi* [End of the World] on the popular music station FM 101. This series, which attracted a cult following of university students, was suspended after sixteen weeks. Dugin later established a second program on a less well-known station, *Free Russia*. Mention should finally be made of the large collection of texts available on Dugin's website (www.arctogaia.ru).

A general idea of the content of Dugin's prolific output will be conveyed by a review of the titles of his works. Three books—*The Conservative Revolution* (1995), *Goals and Tasks of Our Revolution* (1995), and *Knights Templar of the Proletariat: National-Bolshevism and Initiation* (1997)—explain the character and goals of the social revolution that he seeks. *Paths of the Absolute* (1990) is devoted to mysticism, as is *Mysteries of Eurasia* (1996), an exposition of the lost medieval discipline of sacral geography. *Conspirology: The Science of Conspiracies, Secret Societies, and Occult War* (1993) speaks for itself. The mystical racist doctrine of Ariosophy is the subject of two books, *The Hyperborean Theory: An Ariosophical Investigation* (1993) and *Crusade of the Sun* (1996). In *Metaphysics of the Gospel: Orthodox Esotericism* (1996) and *The End of the World: The Eschatological Tradition* (1997), Dugin expounds the Christian Orthodox theology of apocalyptic eschatology. Finally, Dugin sets out his view of global geopolitics in *Foundations of Geopolitics: Russia's Geopolitical Future* (1997).

Dugin and Limonov seem to have made one another's acquaintance in late 1992 or early 1993, either shortly before or shortly after Limonov broke with Zhirinovsky. In fact, by offering Limonov new theoretical moorings and practical prospects, Dugin may have catalyzed Limonov's decision to leave the LDPR. On May 1, 1993, Limonov and Dugin circulated a jointly signed leaflet calling upon like-minded groups to unite in a National-Bolshevik Front. No such front came into being. Dugin, Limonov, and their supporters had to content themselves with creating instead a National Bolshevik Party. In the NBP, Dugin occupied the position of second in command and chief theoretician.

Dugin stood as a candidate in the Duma elections of 1995 in a suburban district of St. Petersburg—apparently his sole excursion into the electoral fray. His campaign received wide publicity thanks to the support of the popular jazz and rock musician Sergei Kuryokhin, who promoted the NBP line in press interviews and organized a free concert under the motto "Kuryokhin for Dugin." Nevertheless, Dugin won a mere 0.85 percent of the vote.

The partnership between Dugin and Limonov lasted five years, and it worked fairly well. There was a mutually acceptable division of roles between the two men: Dugin had no ambition to supplant Limonov as supreme leader, while Limonov was prepared to defer to Dugin in matters of theory. To the extent that the NBP may be said to possess a coherent ideology, that ideology is primarily Dugin's creation. At the same time, there is much in Dugin's elaborate ideological system—for example, his religious mysticism—that was never absorbed by the NBP. Ultimately, the attempt to combine Limonov's populism with Dugin's esoteric elitism did not succeed: Dugin found it difficult to accept the simplification of his ideas that was required for mass propaganda, while many NBP members simply could not understand Dugin's writings. In May 1998, Dugin left the NBP, taking with him a small group of followers from the Moscow organization.

Dugin's Worldview

Dugin's worldview is highly syncretic in character, evolving over time as new elements are incorporated. The name of his magazine, *Elements*, borrowed from the theoretical journal of the French New Rightist Alain de Benoist, says as much. Dugin's syncretism permits him to tackle a strikingly wide range of topics, from "the mysteries of the Judaic Kabbala" and "the metaphysics of sex" to the geopolitical decomposition of Ukraine and the "sacral geography" of Eurasia (Ianov 1999). At the same time, his commitment to the "Tradition" lends his thought a certain, albeit imperfect, coherence and stability.

The number of elements that can be identified in Dugin's massive intellectual output is quite large. I would emphasize five of them: the conservative revolution; Dugin's geopolitical model; national-bolshevism; Ariosophy; and Christian eschatology.

The Conservative Revolution

Crucial to Dugin's politics is the classical concept of the "conservative revolution" that overturns the post-Enlightenment world and installs a new order in which the heroic values of the almost forgotten "Tradition" are renewed. It is this concept that identifies Dugin unequivocally as a fascist. For Dugin, the conservative revolution is "the Last Revolution," "the greatest Revolution in history, continental and universal, . . . the return of the angels, the resurrection of the heroes, and the uprising of the heart against the dictatorship of reason" (Dugin 1997b, p. 26).

Most of Dugin's writings serve the purpose of creating an intellectual climate that will make this revolution possible. This, for example, is why he devotes a whole issue of *Elementy* (No. 7, 1996) to the task of relegitimizing aggressive violence, unnaturally rejected by the humanistic civilization of modern times, which views violence only from the perspective of the victim (Dugin 1996b). And this is why he makes such enormous efforts to revive medieval belief systems such as alchemy, astrology, magic, and sacral geography (in *Mysteries of Eurasia*), for he believes that traces of the "Tradition," completely expunged in contemporary rationalist and empiricist thought, were still preserved in these old "sciences."

Dugin's Geopolitical Model

Dugin's geopolitics may appear at first glance far removed from his mysticism. In the introduction to his treatise on *The Foundations of Geopolitics*, he defines his subject as a branch of practical knowledge needed by those who wish to rule the state (Dugin 1997b, p. 7).

The geopolitical model on which Dugin relies takes the basic form first proposed in 1904 by the British geographer Sir Halford Mackinder—that of a perennial confrontation between the land power of the central continental states of the Eurasian "heartland," above all Russia and Germany, and the sea power of the "oceanic" states situated on the fringes of Eurasia (Britain) or in the Americas (the United States).[8] Dugin is especially attracted to the figure of Karl Haushofer, who further developed Mackinder's conception in Germany both during the Weimar period and under the Nazi regime. Haushofer stressed, as does Dugin, the imperative of Russo-German solidarity against the Anglo-American adversary.

Moreover, for all the members of this geopolitical school, the opposition of sea to land assumes the moral dimensions of a Manichean struggle between good and evil. Which side represents good and which evil depends, of course, on the nationality of the writer concerned. In Dugin's vision, the "Atlanticist" powers are animated by a mercantile, individualistic, materialist, and cosmopolitan outlook, whereas "Eurasia" stands for spirituality, ideocracy, collectivism, authority, hierarchy, and tradition.

When, however, we look more deeply into Dugin's geopolitical ideas, we discover an essential difference marking Dugin off from the mainstream of the Mackinder school. For the other geopoliticians, the confrontation between sea power and land power is a historical generalization open to sociological explanation and empirical criticism. Dugin traces the roots of the confrontation to other realms lying well beyond the reach of empirical investigation—to a conspiratorial contest between ancient secret orders of Eurasianists and Atlanticists, and ultimately to a clash of forces emanating from two of the four elements of alchemy—namely, water and fire. In Dugin's worldview, even geopolitics is built on mystical foundations.

National-Bolshevism

Dugin draws inspiration both from the national-bolsheviks of the Russian emigration, who interpreted the Russian Revolution of 1917 in terms of Russian nationalism (chapter 2), and from German leftists of the same period, such as Ernst Niekisch, who similarly combined bolshevik revolutionism with German nationalism. He also takes a sympathetic attitude toward the left-wing tendency within the German Nazi movement represented by the Strasser brothers (Dugin 1997c, pp. 5–6). In Dugin's reading of history, the Orthodox tsars of Holy Russia, the bolshevik revolutionaries of Russia and Germany, and the German Nazis embodied, each after their own fashion, the true and ancient values of Eurasia, and faced in the Atlanticist West a common enemy. He strives accordingly to merge them all into a higher unity by means of such magical spells as "the dialectical triad 'The Third Rome—The Third Reich—The Third International' " and "the cause of Atsefal, headless bearer of the cross, the hammer and sickle, and the sun crowned by the eternal swastika" (Dugin 1997c, p. 26).

Ariosophy

Dugin counterposes not only an "Eastern" (Eurasian) to a "Western" (Atlantic) civilizational heritage, but also a "Northern" to a "Southern" tradition. He believes that in the distant past there was an island paradise in the Arctic north called Hyperborea that was home to a pure Aryan or Hyperborean race, the ancestors of today's Russians. The Hyperboreans were in touch with a transcendent spiritual reality. Later they migrated south through Eurasia, where they established great civilizations but also lost their original racial purity and spiritual powers. The Aryans are set against the more primitive and earthbound dark-skinned people of the tropical south (Dugin 1996a). These ideas are taken from the mystical racist doctrine of Ariosophy that appeared in Germany and Austria at the end of the nineteenth century and was one of the precursors of Nazism (Goodrick-Clarke 1992).[9]

Christian Eschatology

Although Dugin's beloved Tradition has pagan roots that are much older than Christianity, he does believe that remnants of the Tradition are preserved in Christian Orthodoxy, and especially in the Old Belief, to which he formally committed himself in 1999.[10] He has an abiding fascination with Christian apocalyptic eschatology. Here Dugin's Manicheanism points in a new direction. If in his geopolitical model (for instance) the contemporary world is the arena for a more or less equal struggle between the forces of good and the forces of evil, in his eschatology the contemporary world is the world of the Antichrist. Salvation, fortunately, is at hand—in the comforting form of the end of the world:

> The meaning of Russia is that through the Russian people will be realized the last thought of God, the thought of the End of the World. . . . Death is the way to immortality. Love will begin when the world ends. We must long for it, like true Christians. . . . We are uprooting the accursed Tree of Knowledge. With it will perish the Universe. (Cited in Ianov 1999)

Alexander Yanov, quoting these lines, concludes that Dugin's "real dream is of death, first of all the death of Russia." In his reply, Dugin avoids dealing directly with the substance of Yanov's critique, but observes that he fails to appreciate the positive significance of death (Dugin 1999).

The Question of Coherence

In any syncretic worldview, that of Dugin included, it is difficult to maintain logical coherence. Not that incoherence is necessarily perceived as a problem by Dugin himself: fascists, after all, are opposed to rationality as a matter of principle. "Dugin," observes Limonov, "is a paradoxical man who can support ten points of view or more at the same time" (Lee 1997, p. 320)

—and Limonov is here expressing his admiration of Dugin, not criticizing him. In any case, it is easy enough to find contradictions among the various elements of Dugin's unwieldy construction. The way in which he handles such contradictions tells us a great deal about the relative importance of the elements.

For example, Japan's position as an island nation on the fringes of Eurasia and its history as a big naval power should logically place it alongside Britain and the United States on the evil oceanic side of Dugin's model of geopolitics. And yet Dugin never mentions Japan as an enemy of Eurasia: on the contrary, he regards Japan—unlike China—as a potential ally of the Eurasian powers. The crucial point here is that Dugin is a great admirer of Japanese traditionalism, especially of the ethos of the samurai. He also believes that Japan is "a country in which there still exist traditions and sacred values" (Limonov 1993a). Thus, seagirt Japan is treated as a kind of honorary continental power.

What has always mattered the most to Dugin is undoubtedly mysticism. It is, after all, with mysticism that Dugin began his intellectual journey as a young initiate of "the Moscow esoteric elite," and the mystic remains for him the ultimate reality and the sole source of value.

Dugin's Influence on Russian Society

There is no evidence that Dugin's ideas have had any palpable influence on the general public. Indeed, his language is too esoteric even to be understood by most ordinary people, nor is his work easy to popularize. However, it is Russia's present and future intellectual and political elite that Dugin has always regarded as his priority target audience. His collaboration with Limonov in the NBP represents in this respect a detour from the main path. And the influence that Dugin has achieved over at least some parts of the elite is by no means insignificant.

First, Dugin has consolidated his early ties with the leadership of the CPRF. He has established especially close relations with Gennady Seleznev, Speaker of the last Duma, who enjoys a reputation as an enlightened communist of social-democratic inclinations. In a March 1999 radio interview, Seleznev revealed that Dugin was one of his advisers, and he urged that Dugin's geopolitical doctrine be made a compulsory part of the school curriculum (Nosik 1999).

Admirers of Dugin's geopolitics are also to be found within the military, especially among circles of military intellectuals close to the Academy of the General Staff (AGS). Thus, a roundtable discussion at the AGS was featured in the very first issue of *Elementy*, while various periodicals of the Ministry of Defense have for a number of years now been publishing advertisements for Dugin's books and articles in which he provides a geopolitical interpretation of current events, such as the conflict in the former Yugoslavia. There is considerable circumstantial evidence suggesting that General Igor Rodionov was particularly well-disposed toward Dugin during his tenure as head of the AGS and then (briefly) as defense minister in 1996–1997.[11]

Civilian as well as military analysts of state affairs were impressed by Dugin's treatise on geopolitics when it appeared in 1997. Jacob Kipp, Adjunct Professor of Russian History at the University of Kansas and U.S. editor of *European Security*, reports that:

> When I was in Moscow in June [1997], the Dugin book was a topic of hot discussion among military and civilian analysts at a wide range of institutes, including the Academy of State Management, and in the [presidential] offices at *Staraia ploshchad'* [Old Square]. My impression was that there was more discussion than actual reading.

In the most recent period, since he left the NBP, Dugin has devoted his principal efforts toward increasing his influence on young people whom he expects to enter Russia's future ruling elite. To this end, he has created the New Ideological Movement, also known as the New University, through which he aims to influence circles of sympathetic students at elite institutions. About fifty students in Moscow currently consider themselves his followers.

Dugin's influence on the Russian elite remains limited and highly uneven. He appears to have few connections with key economic elites: one important exception is his relationship with Alexander Tarantsev, head of the company Russian Gold [*Russkoe zoloto*], who has helped to finance some of his activities. Moreover, Dugin's geopolitical ideas are clearly much more influential than are the other, more openly mystical and esoteric, sides of his philosophy. Nevertheless, Dugin's position in Russian society is such that he cannot be dismissed out of hand as a figure of the "lunatic fringe."

Limonov

Limonov is a *nom de plume.* The original surname of the person known as Eduard (alias Edik, Edward, or Eddie) Limonov was Savenko. He was born on February 22, 1943, in the town of Dzerzhinsk, Gorky Province. His father was a Ukrainian from near Voronezh, his mother a local Russian. He grew up, however, in postwar Kharkov in eastern Ukraine, where his father was serving as an officer.[12] In *We Had a Great Epoch*, the first of Limonov's three novels about his early years in Kharkov, he reveals the powerful hold that the military world exerted on his childish imagination:

> On Cold Hill were the divisional barracks for soldiers and unmarried officers. Edik imagined the world . . . as a series of divisional headquarters, oases lost in a sea of valleys. (Limonov 1998a, p. 110)

But Edik's father was not a military man in the strict sense. He was an NKVD (secret police) officer, who in the 1950s was in charge of a military convoy unit that accompanied train transports of convicted prisoners to and from Siberian labor camps. Limonov reverently describes him as "a dangerous, good, honest, almost ascetic type of officer, who did not drink or smoke, . . . without weakness, a metallic, harsh, disciplined man." The writer recalls how, at the age of thirteen, he went to the railroad station to welcome his father home from one of his trips, and eventually found him

> on the outskirts of the station with a semicircle of soldiers, their bayonets pointed at prisoners descending from a [cattle] wagon into a Black Maria. My father was reading out names. . . . His holster was open, the body of his naked pistol shining in the spring sun. (Limonov 1998h)

In his teens, Edik got mixed up with a gang of young thieves, from whom he learned how to pick pockets and carry out burglaries. At the age of fifteen, he got into serious trouble with the police—he had been arrested before, but only for hooliganism—by robbing his first store (Akopov 1999b). It was also about this time that Edik found himself drawn into the world of literature when he accidentally came across a collection of the verse of the early Soviet poet Alexander Blok (Pribylovskii 1995, p. 66). He felt moved to start writing poems of his own. At sixteen he left school and found employment as a welder.

A picture of the world of Edik's adolescence is drawn in the second of the Kharkov novels, *The Youth Savenko.* The story revolves around the disillusionment that the growing boy feels in women when he discovers that his first love, Svetka, is no longer a virgin, but has already had sexual relations with several men. Svetka tries to explain how she was raped two years before by a drunken friend of her father's, but Edik is unsympathetic: he rapes her, and then wants nothing more to do with her (Limonov 1983, pp. 248–51). Meanwhile, Edik's gang has committed a murder: his friends end up in jail or before the firing squad, and he is spared only thanks to the coincidence that he was not with them on the fateful night. He does contemplate committing a murder of his own—knifing Svetka. His friends, he is sure, will think the more highly of him for it, but he lacks the willpower to go ahead and kill his "unfaithful" girlfriend. At the end of the novel, Edik and a friend board a train bound for Rostov, whence they intend to roam the northern Caucasus, living by their wits.

In the last novel of Limonov's Kharkov trilogy, *The Young Ruffian*, Edik is back in Kharkov, working at a variety of occupations, from tailor to stonebreaker. In 1965 his life took a new direction when he became friends with some of Kharkov's bohemian writers and artists. These people encouraged him to pursue a literary career, and one of them, the artist Vagrich Nakhchanyan, thought up for him the *nom de plume* Limonov. But Kharkov was too provincial to satisfy Edik's new-found ambitions. He longed for the capital.

Limonov (as we might as well now call him) made his first attempt to settle in Moscow in 1966. He had no residence permit, and he earned money by sewing pants. He returned temporarily to Kharkov. On September 30, 1967, he came to Moscow again, and managed this time to stay. He was now twenty-four. Later he was to reminisce how he had got off the train, dressed in black and carrying a wooden trunk containing his notebooks and other belongings, had gone to stay with friends from Kharkov, and had then embarked upon "the stormy, creative, very poor life of an underground writer, composing poetry ten hours a day, . . . constantly hungry." Evenings he mostly spent at impromptu parties in the studios of artist friends, "drinking, reciting poetry, discussing art, looking at new paintings, gossiping, and flirting with girls" (Limonov 1999a). He smoked hashish when he could get hold of it. With the help of his friends and occasional paid work, he somehow evaded the Soviet laws against "parasitism," wrote avant-garde stories and samizdat poetry, and kept body and soul together.

Nevertheless, Limonov's irregular lifestyle was not to the liking of the Soviet authorities. In 1973, after rejecting a request from the KGB that he become an informer, he was given the choice of leaving Moscow or emigrating. And so, on September 30, 1974, seven years to the day since arriving in Moscow from Kharkov, he departed by plane for Vienna. He was to stay in the West for eighteen years. For several years he lived in New York, making his living as before at a variety of occupations. At the beginning of the 1980s, he took up residence in Paris, and in 1987 acquired French citizenship.

Limonov did not think highly of Western, and especially of American, society. "Disillusionment" is the self-explanatory title of an article by him that appeared in September 1974 in the Russian émigré newspaper *Novoe russkoe slovo*.[13] He wrote at greater length about how he experienced life in the United States in his American trilogy. *It's Me, Eddie*, a bestseller that eventually came out in sixteen languages, drew public attention mainly through its graphic portrayal of homosexual sex (Limonov is bisexual), but the work is above all an expression of nostalgia for Russia and a philippic against the coldness, materialism, and philistinism of American life, as observed by a Russian émigré recently arrived in New York (Ryan-Hayes 1993). The eloquently titled *Diary of a Loser, Or the Secret Notebook* is pervaded by the same gloomy atmosphere; the narrative culminates in an ecstatic account of how good it would be to shoot a "good hot avenging bullet" into the belly of the president of the United States (Limonov 1998a, vol. 2, p. 406). *Story of His Servant* is set in the town house of a millionaire who hires Limonov as his "mad Russian housekeeper": Limonov is in love with his employer for the first two months, but then starts to hate him when he is berated for mistakenly sending a pair of pants to the dry cleaners. The millionaire later apologizes, but Limonov still feels humiliated.

In 1989, Limonov's novels began to be published in the USSR. In 1990, he became a participant in Soviet public life as a regular contributor to the national-communist newspaper *Sovetskaia Rossiia*. In 1991, his Soviet citizenship was restored, and in early 1992 he returned at long last to Russia. In February 1992, he made the acquaintance of Vladimir Zhirinovsky, and by June was a member of the leadership of the LDPR, holding the post of head of its "All-Russian Bureau of Investigation." He quickly grew disillusioned with Zhirinovsky and left the LDPR in November 1992 (chapter 5). It was in this period also that Limonov undertook an international tour of battle zones in Yugoslavia—it was his third visit to the war there—and the former Soviet Union. In November 1991 he was in Vukovar (Slavonia), in July 1992 in Transdniestria, in October 1992 in Pale (Bosnia), and in November 1992 in Abkhazia. He boasts that he took part in the fighting himself: "I was not just an observer, but a direct participant in History with a capital letter" (Limonov 1993b, p. 5).

At the end of 1992 or the beginning of 1993, as we know, Limonov met Dugin, leading to their collaboration in creating the NBP.

The Formation of Limonov's Worldview

How and when did Limonov become a fascist and a national-bolshevik?

Limonov himself claims that when he arrived in Moscow in 1967 his worldview had already "taken shape, although it was not yet fully formulated intellectually" (Limonov 1993a). He points out that as an underground Moscow poet he adopted a clearly militarist and nationalist stance: in 1971 he composed an *Ode to the Army*, and his first collection of verse, *Russkoe*, explored the nature of Russian identity (Limonov 1979). It is indeed clear that Limonov's basic values were deeply inculcated in him as a youth in

Kharkov. In addition to nationalism and militarism, he was already obsessed with the harsh "heroic" ideal inspired by the image of his Chekist father and with an ideal of female sexual purity, expressed in his hatred of real women who "betrayed" that ideal. Violence may also be regarded as one of the ideals that Limonov brought with him to Moscow. And let us recall the deep impression made on the young Limonov by the verse of Alexander Blok, whose pro-Bolshevik nationalism and mystical Asiatic vision of Russia must surely have had a great influence on the formation of his outlook (Agursky 1987, pp. 171–75).

Whether these elements yet constituted a coherent political or philosophical worldview is another matter. For many years, in Moscow and the West, Limonov's primary concerns remained cultural rather than specifically political, although politics did gradually become more important for him. His friends were mostly artists and musicians rather than political theorists or philosophers. In a conversation with Dugin, he says that he knew Golovin and Mamleyev back in the 1970s, but was not especially close to them (Limonov 1993a). Limonov was certainly not, as was Dugin, a member of the "esoteric elite." Nevertheless, he did have some contact with mysticism; in 1972 he was engaged in translating poems by George Trakl, a mystical expressionist Austrian poet of the World War I period (Limonov 1999a). It was in the United States that he happened to come across a book by Julius Evola, his first encounter with the thought of the West European New Right. Later, in Paris, he met Alain de Benoist: he and Limonov worked together for a time on the editorial board of *Idiot International*, a journal of left and right extremism founded by Jean-Paul Sartre. Thus, it was only after many years of living in the West that Limonov found a political home and a way to "formulate intellectually" his values and ideals.

Limonov also developed a strong interest in left-wing ideas and movements. In 1972–1973, he was friendly with an Austrian woman living in Moscow by the name of Liza Yvary. Yvary, an employee of the Austrian Embassy, was a member of the Socialist Party, and Limonov writes that he learned from her "the language of socialist ideas" (Limonov 1999a). In the United States, Limonov established contact with anarchist and Trotskyist organizations, and appeared to sympathize with them. We may assume that his interest was genuine, and that he was to some extent open to the influence of socialist ideas. At the same time, we must take account of the fact that in certain important areas—in particular, attitudes toward nationalism and internationalism, peace, war, and violence—the socialist ideas that Limonov was now exploring must have been sharply at odds with the "heroic" nationalist and militarist values of his youth.

Limonov's exposure to the left led him not to abandon his old values, but rather to seek to combine them with those left-wing ideas that he found compatible with them. And it was Dugin, with his national-bolshevism and "left-wing fascism," who finally supplied Limonov with the conceptual formulas that enabled him to achieve the desired synthesis.

Limonov's Other Published Works

Further light will be cast upon Limonov's character and worldview by a brief survey of his other books, apart from the autobiographical novels and articles already discussed.[14]

Although the Kharkov and American trilogies comprise the most important of Limonov's autobiographical novels, two other novels appear to be more or less autobiographical in character. Both are set in the dissolute bohemian milieu of West European cities, mainly in France and Italy. *Taming of the Tiger in Paris* is, strictly speaking, about two "tigers" who try to tame one another, one being a Russian émigré singer named Natalya and the other Limonov himself. At the end of the book, poor Eddie is yet again "betrayed" by his lover, although a close reading reveals that in fact he "betrays" her first. I shall spare the reader an account of the similar but murkier plot of *Death of Contemporary Heroes*.

Also autobiographical, although probably not a novel, is Limonov's account of his relations with Zhirinovsky, *Limonov Against Zhirinovsky* (Limonov 1994a). And Limonov promises his fans yet another exposé of his sex life, to be entitled *Anatomy of Love* (Voznesenskii 1998).

In Limonov's collected works we find two less autobiographical novels. (Perhaps nothing that Limonov writes should ever be unequivocally described as wholly non-autobiographical.) *Tormentor* is set in New York; its hero is a man who makes his living as a professional sadist, willingly paid and looked after by his female victims. The book *316, point B* is Limonov's only known attempt at a futuristic novel. The action takes place in New York between July and September 2015, four years after a nuclear war, in a world ruled jointly by the United States and the Russian Union (with a new capital named Sovetsk). The principal hero is Sol Jenkins, Secretary of the U.S. Department of Demography, who introduces Law 316, point B, to kill old people at a certain age as a measure against overpopulation. In the introduction, Limonov explains that he justifies the action of his hero and is "psychologically ready to turn into Jenkins" (Limonov 1998a, vol. 1, pp. 11–12).[15]

Finally, a number of volumes of Limonov's political and journalistic writing have appeared, mostly collections of short pieces already published elsewhere. *Murder of a Sentry* was intended by Limonov as an obituary to Marshal Sergei Akhromeyev, the former Soviet chief of General Staff who died under suspicious circumstances in 1991. Akhromeyev is indeed the "sentry" of the title, the "watchman of the Eurasian spaces, removed by enemies" (Limonov 1993b, p. 5). The essay contains, *inter alia*, reflections on the phenomenon of war and Limonov's reportage of his 1992 international tour of battle zones. The same volume includes *The Disciplinary Sanatorium*, Limonov's analysis of Western society as a form of totalitarianism like its Soviet counterpart, only more pragmatic and selective in its operation and therefore more effective. Limonov's new book, *Gospels from War*, is to consist of more war reminiscences and reflections on war (Voznesenskii 1998).[16]

The Meaning of Limonov's Work

To understand the overall meaning and purpose of all these novels, stories, essays, and articles, we might start by considering how Limonov explains himself in the introduction to his collected works. He first quotes some unsympathetic literary critics who have called him "an alien writer . . . for whom there is no place within the humanist myth"—and wholeheartedly agrees with this assessment. He then describes his work as follows:

> These are disturbing, unavoidably vulgar, revolutionary, explosive books about the tragedy of man on Earth. Above all, they are books about the total impossibility of love for women. About how man is malicious by his very nature. And about the sole alternative possible for a man . . . whose professional disease is death, about the heroic attitude to life. (Limonov 1998a, pp. 11–12)

Several of Limonov's most frequently recurring themes are packed into this short passage: the denial of humanism, the urge to disturb and shock respectable society, revolution, tragic fate, misogyny, the obsession with death ("Yes, death!" is the NBP greeting), and the heroic ideal. Limonov is driven endlessly to affirm, assert, and prove himself as the heroic manly rebel against an ill-defined "system." The specific doctrine of national-bolshevism, as one commentator observes, is above all the means chosen for such virile self-affirmation (Voznesenskii 1998). At the same time, Limonov is surely keenly aware of the flattering attention and publicity that he can gain by such assiduous cultivation of his image as the "leather-clad bad lad" with the "charming hoodlum air" (Lee 1997, pp. 311–12).

Nor do the contradictions inherent in this stance lie far from the surface. For example, it is not easy for Limonov to combine the spontaneous and disorderly "revolutionary" spirit of rebellion with the strict order and discipline embodied in his father's "heroic" ideal. That, however, is an old problem. Another problem is even more glaring. One cannot help but notice that playing the hero does not come at all naturally to Limonov. He must strain himself constantly in order to suppress an inner self that is by no means heroic. This was the self that held him back in his youth when he conceived of the plan to knife Svetka—what many would regard as a decent self, but one that Limonov despises. The struggle against this inner enemy manifests itself in diatribes against the weak and useless sentimentality of the Russian psyche or "soul," and against Russians in general, whom he excoriates as masochistic arse-lickers:

> I feel deep shame to be a Russian, to drag my Slavic face across the world. . . . That fucking Russian soul! (Limonov 1998e)

Can the most strident Russian nationalism ever serve as sufficient compensation for such passionate feelings of inferiority and self-hatred?

The contrast with Dugin's calm pride in the greatness of Russian civilization could hardly be more striking. Dugin's erudition gives him a strong sense of continuity with Russia's great past and greater future, thereby protecting him against the humiliation and insecurities of the present. Limonov, blind to the "interconnection of ages" upon which Dugin relies, is locked inside the prison of his personal experience. Dugin and Limonov do nevertheless share the same basic worldview, but it springs from different psychological sources in the two cases.

Limonov's Violence

One aspect of Limonov's work merits separate discussion: his treatment of violence. For Limonov as for Dugin, both true to the fascist tradition, violence—even in the form of unprovoked terror or aggression—is not a necessary evil, justified by the end it serves, but a positive value in itself. A large proportion of what Limonov has written is, in fact, devoted to the existential analysis, esthetic celebration, and philosophical defense of aggressive violence. Moreover, Limonov—in this respect perhaps unlike the theorist Dugin—does not merely preach violence, but as the opportunity arises practices it too. A few examples will demonstrate the point. At a writers' conference Limonov reacted to an "anti-Russian" remark by smashing a champagne bottle over the head of the British culprit (Lee 1997, p. 313). (Konstantin Leontiev, whom Limonov admires as "the Russian Nietzsche," had in his time caused a diplomatic incident by responding to an insult against Russia in similarly violent fashion.) And Limonov writes about his own violence without a trace of embarrassment or apology. In his account of what he had done in 1997, Limonov records: "On November 11, I met Liza. We went to a nightclub. . . . Afterwards we quarreled. I beat her up and we made love" (Limonov 1998b). On May 1, 1998, Limonov was followed in the street by a man who shouted: "Limonov, I want to talk to you!" For his impertinence, he was beaten up by Limonov's bodyguards (Limonov 1998d).

The most concentrated form of violence is war, and Limonov is all for it. For Limonov, war is life at its peak (Lee 1997, p. 311). "The fresh air of war" attracts him (Voznesenskii 1998). "War," he proclaims, "freshens the blood of a nation."[17] Nor is he squeamish about the methods to be employed in war, urging that Russia put to use in Russian-populated areas of the former Soviet Union the "Serbian tactics" he had observed in Bosnia.

Violent crime also has Limonov's approval. *Limonka* has carried laudatory pen-portraits not only of politicians like Stalin and Beria, but also of the famous non-political murderer Charlie Manson and other "independent geniuses."[18] Limonov, it is true, did eventually suspend the series on famous murderers, explaining that it had reinforced the passivity of readers, who were invited to write in about their own exploits.

A great deal of Limonov's violence is directed against women, although this does not scare off the numerous female admirers who are said to surround him. His views on relations between the sexes are conveniently summarized in a list of twenty-eight rules intended to regulate the relations of NBP members with women (*Limonka* no. 55, p. 4). Rule 6 states that a party member is required to beat any woman he meets more than twice, the ideal ratio being "one beating for every ten fuckings," while Rule 7 grants a party member "the right to kill any woman who does not understand him and constantly wants something from him." At war, the party member has the right to rape captured enemy women (Rule 25). Limonov should not, however, be accused of failing to respect the sanctity of human life. Rule 21 obliges the party member "to prevent abortions, the murder of his own children."[19]

Besides its direct significance, Limonov's violence toward women functions as a central metaphor for the violence that he hopes to inflict upon Russian society as a whole, and especially upon the liberal Russian intelligentsia. Just as women really long to be raped, so do all Russians, whether they know it yet or not, really long to be "raped" and subjugated by their fascist saviors. Limonov makes this most evident in his essay *Who Needs Fascism in Russia?*

> Insensitive, reacting only to supershocks, to especially bloody and cruel events, Russia's citizens really want the FASCISTS to come—terrible, tensed, young—and solve all problems. Yes, the philistine fears them, and

still votes against them, but he sees and desires them in his dreams. He wants the fascists to come at last and impose order. . . . The lazy philistine will greet with pleasure the kick up his backside that will straighten him out and liven him up. . . .

Life will suddenly become easy for the kept intelligentsia. . . . A boss will come, take her by the hair, pull her to him, and use her in accordance with her purpose. The masochist Novodvorskaya [leader of the Democratic Union] wants young broad-shouldered rapists at last to throw themselves on her carcass and roughly rape her, together with her ma, grandma, and cat. . . .

The young women of Russia dream of real men who will kick out the bandits, drunk traders, and pot-bellied pervert businessmen. At last it will be possible to take pride in one's man, and holding his firm hand stroll with him, the armed fascist, along the night streets of Russia's towns. And by morning to be happily pregnant by him. (NBP 1997, pp. 16–17)

Limonov's Social Influence

Limonov occupies a fairly prominent place among those who claim the status of serious writers in post-Soviet Russia. The print runs of his novels, while rather shorter than those of the most popular writers of detective fiction, are quite respectable by contemporary standards: typically 50,000, occasionally rising to 100,000.[20] Limonov's status and prestige as a man of letters afford him the opportunity to propagate his political ideas to an audience much wider than those who habitually read the tracts of extremist organizations. Of no less importance, they provide him with an entrée into "respectable" circles that would otherwise be closed to him. For example, for several years Limonov has had a regular column of his own in the weekly magazine *The eXile*, published in English by and for expatriate Westerners living in Moscow.[21]

As in the case of Dugin, one should take care not to exaggerate the extent of Limonov's influence in Russian society. There are quite a few writers in Russia today whose popularity equals or exceeds that of Limonov, and the ideas expressed by most of them are far removed from fascism. But, again like Dugin, Limonov cannot be dismissed as a negligible or peripheral figure.

The National-Bolshevik Party

The NBP: Style and Ideology

The first point of the program of the NBP defines the essence of national-bolshevism as "an incinerating hatred of the anti-human system of the triad:

liberalism/democracy/capitalism" (NBP 1997). The same point goes on to state that this system is to be replaced by "a traditionalist hierarchical society, based on the ideals of spiritual manliness, and social and ethnic justice." Point 17, in contrast, declares support for "modernization, the up-to-date, and the avant-garde"—a contradiction characteristic of fascism. The economic basis of the new-old order is specified in point 10 as "Russian Socialism, an economic system oriented toward the welfare of the majority of the population." Other party documents explain that the NBP stands for a double revolution, at once national (ethnic) and social, that will both bring ethnic Russians to power and establish social justice within the nation (Verkhovskii and Pribylovskii 1996, p. 133).

Judging from such programmatic statements, the NBP might seem to possess a clear and straightforward ideology of a left-fascist character. When, however, we take into account the contents of *Limonka*, the picture becomes cloudier, and we realize that the left fascism has been mixed with several other hues. While some of the additional elements, such as Dugin's Eurasianist geopolitics, do not clash with left fascism, others certainly do. In particular, we find in the pages of *Limonka* a great deal of straightforward Stalinism, and also of anarchism, both of which are logically inconsistent with left fascism and with one another. And yet Limonov clearly does strive to combine fascism, Leninism, Stalinism, and anarchism. Among those historical figures for whom he has expressed his admiration are the leaders of fascist Italy and Germany (Mussolini, Ciano, Hitler, Goering, and Goebbels), selected Soviet leaders of the Lenin and Stalin periods (Lenin and Stalin themselves, Dzerzhinsky, Beria, Molotov, Voroshilov, and Zhukov), and the anarchists Bakunin and Nestor Makhno.[22] In other words, he equally lionizes the secret police chiefs who uphold the power of the totalitarian state and the rebels who seek to overthrow all state power.

The "Panorama" analyst Vyacheslav Likhachev has suggested a rather neat solution to this puzzle. He proposes that we view the NBP as "a party of general extremism."[23] This means that one has to be an extremist to join, but that it does not matter what kind of extremist one is. Anarchists, fascists, Stalinists, Christian and Islamic religious extremists are all welcome. What is valued is extremism as such. Thus, the NBP does not promote an ideology in the usual sense, but a "heroic" style or ethos, the display of which by its members *is* obligatory. It is at this level, and not at the level of mundane logic, that coherence is attained.

This interpretation has much to be said for it. It accords quite well with Limonov's personal character. However, it goes a bit too far. Limonov is not completely indifferent to ideology: there are some varieties of extremist whom he surely is not prepared to welcome into his party with open arms—extreme feminists, let us say, or extreme Ukrainian (or other anti-Russian) nationalists.

It is of interest to note what Limonov himself has to say about logical contradictions in the NBP's ideology. *Limonka* no. 67 (June 1997) contains a letter by a Comrade Akimenko, pointing out a few of the contradictions and professing total confusion. In his reply, Limonov congratulates Akimenko on his mental acuity, acknowledges that others also find the NBP confusing, and explains:

> Banal ideas are always untrue. Only paradox is true. The very name of our party is paradoxical from the point of view of customary logic. Our ideology is paradoxical, combining within itself conservatism and revolution, nationalism and Eurasianism, hierarchy and equality. The way we see the situation is paradoxical; so are the remedies we propose. But the merit of man as a species is his ability to overcome banality, to stretch his thought and will, to grasp what is hard to grasp, and to accomplish what is hard to accomplish.

Love of paradox may perhaps be considered part of the NBP's provocative style, one of the means used, alongside obscene language and striking artwork, to shock and confuse the "philistine" sensibility. This in turn is no doubt linked to Limonov's long sojourn in the underground bohemian counterculture of Moscow and the West. This culture is one to which mainstream fascism has always been highly inimical, but Limonov evidently still identifies with it and tries to attract those associated with it into the NBP. To the extent to which he succeeds in this endeavor, *Limonka* tends to become itself a vehicle of the counterculture, as exemplified by the leading role played in its production since 1996 by Alexei Tsvetkov, leader of the Violet International (Tarasov et al. 1997, pp. 56–57). The NBP's superficial flirtation with anarchism is also explicable in this context. There is simply no way in which an orientation toward the counterculture can be combined with fascism without resort to logical incoherence.

The inconsistencies within the ideology of the NBP may, finally, be less serious than they might appear by virtue of the fact that they pertain to what the NBP is *for*, and not to what it is *against*. The NBP's appeal is based mainly on what it is against, and what that is is clear enough: liberal capitalism. Unless and until the NBP comes much closer to taking power, it is not under any great pressure to make clear what it is for.

The NBP Symbols

As our study of Dugin and Limonov might lead us to expect, the symbolism of the NBP combines fascist with leftist motifs. Thus, in the greeting the arm is thrown neither directly forward, as in the Nazi *Heil*, nor straight up over the head, as in the leftist clenched-fist salute, but out to the side at an elevation of forty-five degrees above the horizontal. The fist, it is true, is clenched—but the accompanying cry of *Da, smert'*! ["Yes, death!"] comes straight out of the fascist tradition, reminding us as it does of the battle cry of General Francisco Franco's Spanish Legion: "Long live death!" (Daly 2000).

The NBP flag, in contrast, is distinctly bolshevik in design: a red background, a white circle in the middle, and inside the circle a black hammer and sickle. The red is said to represent the blood spilled by Russian martyrs, white is the color of skin, and the hammer and sickle stand for Russian Socialism. And "we dress in black as a sign of mourning for brothers who have perished, because a war is going on in Russia" (Kolganov 1999).

The party symbol is a picture of a hand-grenade—the "little lemon" [*limonka*]. For the *natsboly*, the word *limonka* therefore has four meanings. It is a play on Limonov's name, the name of the party periodical, a little lemon, and a hand-grenade.

Standard dress for NBP members is a black leather jacket, a black beret, and army boots. Shaving the head is optional (Krasnovskii 2000).

The Program of the NBP

Let us proceed to examine the NBP program in greater detail.

Political System

The NBP sets itself the goal of building a "total state" based on the rights of the nation (as opposed to the rights of the individual). It is to be a strictly unitary state: Russia will be divided into forty-five "strategic districts" governed from the Center.[24] It is also conceived of as a one-party state of the NBP, which promises to "prevent the degeneration of the ruling elite, as happened in the case of the Communist Party of the Soviet Union," by conducting "permanent purges in its ranks, and not only there." Limonov intends to appoint young party members as commissars in the central government and also as leaders in "every provincial town and village" (point 24; Limonov 1998c). The new "iron Russian order" will be suffused by an atmosphere of discipline, bellicosity, and love of labor (points 1, 4, 6, and 25).

Nevertheless, the political system of the total state includes elements of parliamentarism, and even of electoral democracy. The parliament is envisaged as consisting of a legislative and elective Chamber of Deputies and a consultative and non-elective Chamber of Representatives, the members of which are to be appointed "in accordance with popular proposals" as representatives of different occupations, age groups, and religious communities. It is from this latter Chamber of Representatives that the government is to seek recommendations to guide its work (point 5). Thus, most citizens are to have the right to engage in political activity within the limits of the one-party state, although this right (as well as the right to engage in commercial activity) is explicitly denied to former officials of the CPSU (point 22).[25] The corporatist conceptions of Italian fascism are clearly in evidence here.

In its program, the NBP makes clear that the Russian nation in whose name it struggles for power is defined in terms not of blood or of religious faith, but in accordance with the national consciousness of the individual:

> He is a Russian who considers the Russian language and Russian culture his own, Russia's history his own history, who has spilled and is ready to spill his own and others' blood for Russia's sake and only for her sake, and thinks of no other homeland or nation. (point 23)[26]

In principle, therefore, a person who is loyal to Russia, whatever his religion or ethnic origin, may join the NBP and the new national elite. The party even boasts a few Jewish members. In general, racial categories as such are not of great concern to Limonov; unlike Dugin, he does not seem to have been influenced by Ariosophy.

Economic Policy

The economic system of the total state is to be "Russian Socialism," serving the well-being of the majority of the population. All large enterprises, military industry, and land will belong to the state. Small enterprises may be privately or collectively owned, whereas medium-sized enterprises are to belong to regional government.[27] Land will be leased by the state to collective, state, and private farms, with the income from leaseholders going into the state budget (points 10, 12, 13, and 14).

Decisive measures are to be taken to reverse foreign penetration of Russia's economy, the strategic goal being full autarky. Consumer imports will be banned; the state will reacquire a monopoly on the export of oil, gas, electricity, armaments, raw materials, and gold and other precious metals; and banks with branches abroad will be closed to impede capital flight. Russia will break off its relations with international financial institutions:

> We shall send the IMF to hell. . . . We shall confiscate all foreign investments, and ban use of the dollar. To halt the aggressive invasion of foreign goods and trashy mass culture, we shall lower a protective iron curtain

along our borders. Entry into the world market has killed Russia's economy. It is harmful to us. In Russia there is everything. (point 9)

A series of immediate economic benefits are promised to the population: wages not lower than the subsistence level, a freeze on rents and charges for municipal services, and firmly fixed prices for basic food products: bread, potatoes, grains, milk, butter, and beef. Housing is to be transferred without charge to the ownership of those living in it, while empty apartments are to be given to veterans of the Afghan and Chechen wars and to large and young families. Servicemen, state employees, old-age pensioners, and the lowly paid are to be relieved of all taxes. The NBP will impose an "economic dictatorship" in the transition period (points 10 and 11).

Culture and Science

The section of the program devoted to culture and science is distinctly libertarian in tone, and seems out of place in such an otherwise draconian document. "The NBP is firmly convinced that culture must grow like a wild tree. We do not intend to cut it down. Complete freedom. 'Do what you want' will be your sole law," Limonov assures his fellow artists (point 15). Scientists, researchers, and inventors are promised "heavenly conditions" and priority funding from the state budget (point 16). A neat syllogism resolves any apparent inconsistency between the generous bestowal of unlimited cultural freedom and the earlier rejection of the principle of human rights: "The freedom of the nation from the aggression of mondialism is the guarantee of the freedom of the individual" (point 17). Nevertheless, a tension remains between the libertarian approach to culture and the listing in point 2 of the "cosmopolitan intelligentsia," alongside bureaucrats and New Russians, as the "internal enemies" of national-bolshevism.

Penal Policy

A special section of the program deals with "punishments" (points 18 through 21). Those to be tried and duly punished include high officials who have committed state crimes since 1986, and persons who have caused economic damage to Russia or cheated and robbed their fellow citizens. "The managers of fraudulent funds, banks, and companies will be put at the mercy of their investors." However, a certain ambivalence toward ordinary criminals is reflected in point 21: "We shall crush the criminal world. Its best representatives will enter the service of nation and state. The rest will be annihilated by military means."

Foreign Policy

The "external enemy" of national-bolshevism is identified as "the 'Great Satan'—that is, the USA and the mondialists of Europe, united in NATO and the UN" (point 2). The NBP accordingly advocates that Russia turn its back on the United States and abrogate all agreements with the West. Possible friends of Russia on the Eurasian continent are Germany (under an anti-mondialist regime), Iran, India, and Japan (point 8).

The global goal of national-bolshevism is stated to be "the creation of an Empire from Vladivostok to Gibraltar on the basis of Russian civilization." This goal is to be attained in four successive stages: first, a Russian revolution to transform the present-day Russian Federation into a "unitary Russian national state"; then the annexation to Russia of territories of the former Soviet republics populated by Russians; next, the "unification around the Russians of the Eurasian peoples of the former USSR"; and finally, the creation of a "gigantic continental Empire" (point 3). More details about the second stage, the uniting of all Russians in one state, are provided in point 7. Local referenda will be held to justify the annexation of areas of the former Soviet republics with majority Russian populations, such as Crimea, northern Kazakhstan, and the Narva district in northeastern Estonia. (The possibility that any of these populations might vote against being annexed by Russia is not considered.) At the same time, any separatist strivings on the part of ethnic minorities within Russia are to be "mercilessly suppressed."

Other Policy Proposals

The NBP has put forward a variety of specific policy and legislative proposals. Some of these proposals merely repeated or elaborated upon points in the party program relating to the annexation of Russian-populated territories, the exclusion of former CPSU officials from public life, and the elimination of foreign economic influence. Other proposals offered ideas concerning how Russia might deal more effectively with crime and terrorism, improve military discipline, combat demographic decline, or revise its constitution (Verkhovskii and Pribylovskii 1996, pp. 131–32; NBP 1997, pp. 9–16).

A few of the NBP's ideas pertaining to law and order will serve to indicate the general flavor of all its policy proposals. Thus, the authorities are urged to respond to hostage-taking on the part of terrorists by themselves taking hostages, who would preferably be the terrorists' relatives. Russia should learn how to avenge attacks on its civilians from the way Israel acts in Lebanon. (Limonov must by now admit that Russia is indeed learning.)

Russia should also follow China's example in televising the execution of condemned criminals. Finally, it is suggested that Russia introduce the institution of the local sheriff, who would be entrusted with full police powers in a given vicinity, including the right to shoot first without warning. Precedents in Russian tradition for such an institution are cited, presumably to avert any accusation that the NBP may have borrowed the idea as well as the word "sheriff" from England or America.

Abortion is to be prohibited by law as "a crime against the Russian nation." Exceptions are to be allowed only for women with mental illness or incurable hereditary disease and for rape victims. Other women who have abortions are to be sentenced to prison terms: "You, bitch, have killed your baby, a Russian citizen. So go to jail. It is fair" (Limonov 1999b). Pending the passage of such an abortion law, citizens are encouraged to exert psychological pressure on women who have had abortions, whose names physicians are urged to make public.

In September 1994, the NBP made its contribution to constitutional reform when Limonov sent an open letter to the Duma proposing that a new article be added to the constitution. The new article would stipulate that the president of Russia must be of ethnic Russian origin. A proviso allowed the possibility of a president with only one Russian parent, provided that the other parent were Ukrainian or Belarusian. The main purpose of the proposal was evidently that of blocking Zhirinovsky's path to the presidency without disqualifying Limonov himself. Both, it will be recalled, have Russian mothers; Zhirinovsky's father was Jewish, Limonov's Ukrainian.

Structure of the NBP

According to the programmatic documents of the NBP, a local branch is to consist of ten to fifteen members. Local branches are to be grouped into regional "columns," each ideally made up of nine branches. Regional or column commanders are to be appointed by the NBP Center; leaders of branches may presumably be elected by their members. All branches are required to take part in current party campaigns—for example, the boycott of foreign products. Thus, members are required to implement directives issued by the party leadership; at the same time they are urged to take initiatives of their own (NBP 1997, pp. 29–30).

As for the NBP Center, it is unclear whether it has any formal structure. In any case, "the Center" in practice generally means Limonov, whose authority is rarely disputed. The only evidence I have found of internal divisions is a statement purportedly written by "a group of activists of the right wing" within the NBP that appeared in 1998 in the newspaper of the People's National Party (see chapter 8). The right-wing dissidents took objection to the leftist orientation and allies of the NBP, to the friendly attitude toward "Eurasian" Jews shown by Limonov and Dugin, and to the "degeneracy" of the latter, meaning their allegedly homosexual inclinations (Riutin, Sarbuchev, and Razukov 1998).

The NBP's Activities

The NBP conducts activities of a kind that one normally expects of a political organization, such as public meetings, demonstrations, picketing, and leafleting. Until recently, NBP meetings and demonstrations rarely drew more than a hundred or so people, and often considerably fewer.[28] Reports of somewhat larger demonstrations have now begun to appear. On April 8, 2000, for example, 150 young *natsboly* marched through the center of Smolensk to celebrate the anniversary of a local uprising against the Lithuanian overlords that had taken place when the city was under Polish–Lithuanian rule (Krasnovskii 2000).

A campaign was launched in 1993 calling upon young people to boycott foreign products ("Your child's hand reaches out for 'sneakers' and 'Twix'? Smack his hand!"), to refuse to work for foreign firms, and to demonstrate against foreign economic and cultural penetration.

There has been a certain amount of electoral campaigning. The NBP is unable to take direct part in elections because its repeated applications for registration, even when backed up by petitions, picketing, and threats, have been rejected by the Ministry of Justice, and these decisions have been upheld by the courts (Likhachev 1999; "Sud" 1999).[29] Limonov, Dugin, and other NBP members have occasionally stood as candidates in their individual capacities, never with great success. Thus, in 1996, an NBP member, the officer Yevgeny Yakovlev, stood for deputy to the council of a town in Moscow Province (*Limonka* no. 55, December 1996). On the initiative of local *natsboly*, Limonov went for two weeks in the fall of 1997 to the town of Georgievsk in the Stavropol Territory to contest an election to fill a vacant Duma seat. He came in eighth of seventeen candidates with 2.7 percent of the vote.[30]

Other NBP activities are less conventional. Party members in Irkutsk, fulfilling instructions received from Limonov, painted and sprayed slogans—"Eat the Rich!" and "Stalin—Beria—GULAG" being two of the more appealing—on walls in the busiest districts of the city, as well as on the fence that surrounded the theater. The slogans could not be erased and the fence had to be removed (Kolganov 1999). In Moscow, a group of *natsboly*, shouting the same slogans, broke their way into a conference of Yegor Gaidar's Russia's Democratic Choice in January 1999, setting off a mêlée (Timakova

1999). The NBP made a special effort to disrupt a Russian tour of the famous businessman and philanthropist George Soros in October 1997: "At Kazan University students made Soros' speech inaudible by coughing, hissing, sneezing, and cursing. Later an effigy of Soros was thrown under the wheels of a tram" (Limonov 1997b).

There is, in fact, a whole genre of NBP literature providing detailed advice on how to wreak maximum havoc as suddenly and quickly as possible—and then get away before the police have a chance to intervene. Guidance is given, for example, about how to loot stores in the event of mass disorder (NBP 1997, pp. 24–26). A *Limonka* article tells readers "how to behave in a cinema." A gang of at least fifteen visit a cinema where a Western film is being shown. One group secures the exit, while the others seat themselves strategically in the auditorium. At a signal, slogans are chanted, ink is thrown at the screen, and dirt is poured over the projector window. Taking care not to leave fingerprints, the militants are out and away before the alarm is even called. A similar technique, it is noted, can be employed at a theater, concert, exhibition, talk show, or McDonald's restaurant (Khorkhe 1997). From the point of view of the NBP, this sort of thing counts as heroism, although the despised "philistine" might regard it as mere hooliganism.

The value of combat training for party members is recognized, but not much attention is devoted to it. The first priority for Limonov is not, as it was for Barkashov, to train fighters, but to build up a disciplined corps of political agitators or "commissars" (Akopov 1999b). By no means, however, does the NBP renounce military action. A case in point was the party's "Asian expedition" of April–June 1997. Accompanied by a "commando" of nine comrades, Limonov set off by train to the city of Kokchetav in northern Kazakhstan to assist the local Cossacks, who planned to declare Kokchetav Province a Cossack republic and resist by force of arms any attempt to suppress them. Unfortunately, the Kazakhstani authorities foiled the plot and detained the *natsboly* on arrival. After their release, they waited around in Kokchetav for a few days, but when it became clear that there was not going to be an insurrection after all, they proceeded to Dushanbe in Tajikistan. There they managed to get themselves invited, as guests of the 201st Division of the Russian army, on a trip to the Afghan border, before finally returning home, well satisfied with their combat holiday ("Aziatskii" 1997; Limonov 1998b).

Limonov and his comrades tried to establish ties with the coal miners who came from Vorkuta to Moscow in June 1998 to protest against wage delays. Some of the protesters seemed friendly, but on the whole they kept their distance from the NBP, as from other political radicals who sought to attach themselves to the miners' cause (Limonov 1998g).

The NBP does seem to have had some success among students at higher educational institutions. In 1995, with the help of the Violet International, the NBP established links with an organization named Student Defense that was active in the student protest movement (Tarasov et al. 1997, pp. 44–45, 57). As a result, the NBP succeeded in becoming involved in student affairs at various universities. Thus, at the Urals State University in Yekaterinburg there is a large cell of mostly student *natsboly*, who produce a wall newspaper, distribute leaflets, sell Dugin's books, and hold exhibitions and concerts (Dobrynina 1998). Limonov claims that a significant number of young engineers have also been attracted into the NBP.

The greatest asset the NBP has at its disposal in appealing to young people is probably Limonov's connections with several well-known rock, jazz, and folk musicians. Among those willing to associate themselves with the NBP are such performers as Yegor Letov of the rock group *Civil Defense*, Sergei Troitsky (nicknamed "The Spider") of *Metal Corrosion*, Sergei Kuryokhin, Dmitry Revyakin, and Oleg Medvedev (Limonov 1998d; Kolganov 1999). Curiously enough, Limonov, in one of his earlier books, condemned rock music, together with jazz, the Beatles, and pop music in general, as "means of stultification," punk music alone winning his approval for its "youthful aggression" (Limonov 1993b, pp. 326–33). Only later did he and other "patriots" gradually come to realize that rock too could serve as a vehicle for nationalist sentiment.

Strategy of the NBP

In an August 1999 interview, Limonov set out his expectations for the future. The Russian state would not collapse in the near future. Instead, the CPRF would come to power and run the country for three or four years in accordance with "bureaucratic habit," making no more than minor changes to the existing system. Only when experience had dissipated popular illusions in the CPRF would revolutionary movements like the NBP have a chance to seize power (Akopov 1999b). In the meantime, Limonov concentrates his efforts on building up his organization, the social base of which is defined as "socially dissatisfied youth, those lads and girls with national pride, heroic ambitions, and the desire to rise from the depths of society to its summit" (Verkhovskii and Pribylovskii 1996, p. 134). The dual nature of the NBP's radicalism, at once social and national, would enable it to win young people over from both extreme nationalist and extreme leftist movements, such as the RNU on the one side and the Russian Communist Workers' Party on the other, as well as from the counterculture and the rank and file of the CPRF. The NBP would initiate insurrectionary action only when "several million active young Russians" had been mobilized and it was sure that conditions were ripe: "We want to rise up for victory, and not for defeat." Use of terrorism would be avoided unless other channels of political struggle were closed off (NBP 1997, pp. 35–40).

Some ambiguity remains concerning how exactly the NBP envisages its victory. On the one hand, as a bolshevik party (albeit of a special kind) it anticipates coming to power on the crest of a spontaneous popular rising against a weakened state. On the other hand, Limonov in his essay *Who Needs Fascism in Russia?* (a passage from which has already been quoted) revives the memory of disciplined phalanxes of blackshirted young men conquering the city streets as the prelude to fascist takeover of the state. Limonov, like Barkashov, finds it hard to choose between the model of Russia in 1917 and that of Germany in 1933 (or Italy in 1922).

Prospects of the NBP

As argued at the beginning of this chapter, the NBP is a political force of more than negligible strength. It now has some thousands of young activists, and a palpable presence in several provincial cities, such as Yekaterinburg and Orenburg,[31] as well as Moscow and St. Petersburg (not to mention Riga). It has exhibited sustained growth over a period of several years, and it is possible that its growth will continue.

The NBP does, however, have a very long way yet to go. There are still many cities where it has not yet established a presence, and it has not penetrated into the countryside at all. The great majority of the Russian public remains unaware of the very existence of the NBP—in contrast to the RNU, which attracted more extensive media attention. Without federal registration, the NBP is unable to participate directly in the electoral process. It is incapable of formulating a clear and positive program.

The NBP evidently has a real appeal for the most discontented and rebellious strata of Russian youth. It is here that its potential for further growth lies. Sooner or later, however, the NBP will have to face the problem that it has virtually no appeal outside this particular milieu. Indeed, the aggressive and outré style that attracts rebellious youth is just what frightens and repels the conventional ("philistine" in Limonov's terminology) majority of the Russian people. As one elderly woman who had the misfortune to live next door to a group of *natsboly* complained: "They beat people up, they steal, they display strange flags. They are evildoers."[32] In particular, Limonov's reputation as an active bisexual does considerable harm to the public image of his party and keeps away many potential recruits whose leftist nationalism is bound up with a more conventional morality.[33]

The Significance of the NBP

The possibility that the National-Bolshevik Party will ever come to power is extremely remote. That, however, does not deprive the NBP of significance as a social phenomenon. As already noted, the ideas of Dugin and Limonov have been quite widely propagated in Russian society through their writings as individual cultural figures, and it is likely that this has had some effect on the general moral and intellectual atmosphere in the country. But above all, the NBP should be regarded as a warning sign of the destructive potential inherent in the anger and frustration of all those young people of the new post-Soviet generation who feel themselves to be "losers" in the pseudo-market economy.

8
Other Fascist Organizations

To supplement the fuller studies of the LDPR, the RNU, and the NBP, this chapter offers briefer accounts of six other fascist (or, in one case, proto-fascist) organizations that have been active in Russia during the 1990s. All of these organizations are small by comparison with those discussed in the preceding three chapters: it is doubtful whether any of them currently has a membership in excess of a thousand, and some may have only a hundred members or even fewer. Our examination of them will still leave us a long way from a comprehensive overview of contemporary Russian fascism. It is possible that within a few years an organization will rise to prominence that I have neglected to mention, or that does not yet exist. Nevertheless, the reader will gain some idea both of the variety that exists among extreme nationalist movements and of the characteristics that they share in common.

I consider first the People's National Party (PNP),[1] created and led by Alexander Ivanov-Sukharevsky. The PNP may have between 500 and 1,000 members, mostly young people, in various parts of Russia. Then I turn to Nikolai Lysenko's National-Republican Party of Russia (NRPR), which at its height may have had a membership of between 2,000 and 3,000, but later fell apart and ceased to exist. I also touch upon the rival National-Republican Party of Russia of Yuri Belyaev, which probably has a few hundred members, concentrated mainly in St. Petersburg and its environs. Next I discuss the Russian National Union (RNS), founded by Alexei Vdovin and Konstantin Kasimovsky, now renamed the Russian National-Socialist Party. This organization may have had some hundreds of members in the past, but has undergone a sharp decline and may now have only a hundred members, if not fewer.[2] The fifth organization to be considered is the Union "Christian Rebirth" (UCR) of Vladimir Osipov, which exemplifies those organizations that work in circles close to the Russian Orthodox Church. It is thought to have a few hundred members, mostly elderly people and middle-aged women. Finally, I describe Ilya Lazarenko's Society of Nav, a small Moscow-based organization of young men that represents a religious tendency of a rather different kind, one that combines fascism with pagan beliefs.

For each of these six organizations, I begin with a biographical sketch of the leader (in the case of the RNS, two leaders), and then—to the extent that is possible on the basis of the sources available to me—analyze the ideology, program, and symbolism of the organization, describe its activities, and assess its strength, strategy, and future prospects.

Alexander Ivanov-Sukharevsky and the People's National Party

Alexander Ivanov-Sukharevsky

Alexander Kuzmich Ivanov-Sukharevsky was born on July 26, 1950 in Rostov. His father, an army officer, hails from a village in Belarus. His mother, a pharmacist, is the offspring of an illustrious line of Don Cossacks: the Sukharev Tower in the Kremlin is named after an ancestor of hers, Colonel Sukharev of the palace guards [*strel'tsy*]. Alexander's use of a double-barreled name bears witness to the pride he feels in his maternal line (Ivanov 1997, pp. 2, 64). Moreover, his ancestry—the fact that his paternal grandmother was a Belarusian and one of his maternal great-grandmothers a Ukrainian—symbolizes for him the unity of the broadly conceived Russian nation of *russy*, which he holds to consist of eight branches, including not only the usual trio of Ukrainians, Belarusians, and Great Russians, but also the Ruthenians of Carpathia, the New Russians [*novorossy*] of southern Ukraine, the Siberians, the Cossacks, and the *pomory* of Russia's Far North.[3]

Alexander spent most of his childhood (from the age of five) in East Germany, where his father was serving as commandant of the town of Fürstenburg. On graduating from school, he returned with his family to Rostov. At first he intended to follow in his father's footsteps, and in 1967 entered a local military college. Dissatisfied, however, by "the complete absence of warlike spirit in the Soviet Army," he abandoned the idea of a military career, and in 1970 transferred to Rostov State University to study economics. This subject also failed to hold his interest: driven by "boundless creative energy," in 1974 he transferred to the All-Union State Institute of Cinematography. At last he had found his true métier. In 1979, he qualified as a film director, and started work at the Mosfilm studio.

Initially, Ivanov-Sukharevsky had reason for satisfaction: a number of his documentaries on historical themes were well received. In the mid-1980s, however, he came into conflict with "a gang of Yids"[4] who suppressed much of his work on the grounds that it conveyed Russian chauvinism and anti-

Semitism. He was particularly upset by the decision of a vetting commission not to show the film *Ship*, which he shot in 1987. The Jewish head of the commission, the writer and former Duma deputy Alla Gerber, remains a bête noire of his to this day. Although Ivanov-Sukharevsky continued to write film scenarios until 1993, this episode seems to have triggered his drift toward professional politics.

According to the biographical account approved by Ivanov-Sukharevsky himself, he never joined any other political organization—unless one counts as such the Moscow Cossack Guard, which admitted him as a captain[5] in 1992—before setting up his own party in 1994, limiting himself to frequenting "patriotic" gatherings. He still hoped, he explains, to influence his fellow-countrymen through his films (Ivanov 1997, p. 2). In reality, he was at various times a member of several nationalist organizations, including the Russian National Assembly, the All-Russian National Right-Wing Center, the RNU, and the Union "Christian Rebirth" (see below), although he may not have been very active in any of them (Pribylovskii 1995, p. 56). It is very likely that by the early 1990s he was contemplating a political career. In any case, he no longer had the financial resources at his disposal for making films.

It was also during the early 1990s that Ivanov-Sukharevsky completed his ideological formation by reading the works of fascist leaders of the past, including Hitler's *Mein Kampf*. He was especially influenced by Mussolini's *The Doctrine of Fascism*. From this time onward, he may reasonably be regarded as a full-blown fascist, although he himself prefers not to use the word on account of its non-Russian origin.

Ivanov-Sukharevsky made the decision to create a new nationalist party in January 1994. At first he hoped that he might be able to use Sergei Baburin's Russian All-People's Union (ROS) as the base for his party, but he met resistance there, an attempt to elect him to the ROS Coordinating Council being narrowly defeated. Many members of the ROS presumably felt that he was too extreme. In May he tried again, this time with more success. Together with Vyacheslav Demin, editor of the magazine *Zemshchina* and one of the leaders of the Union "Christian Rebirth," he set up an initiative group to create an "Orthodox Party" in consultation with the Moscow Patriarchate of the Russian Orthodox Church. The representatives of the patriarchate, however, were reluctant to play the part assigned to them: they asked Demin and Ivanov-Sukharevsky to choose a name that would not identify the ROC so closely with them, and—just to make sure—brought their influence to bear on the Ministry of Justice not to grant registration to any organization calling itself an "Orthodox Party." In October 1994, Ivanov-Sukharevsky and Demin established their new organization, duly renamed "The Movement of Popular Nationalists." Ivanov-Sukharevsky was elected its head. A merger was then negotiated with the group around the journal *Era Rossii* [Era of Russia], edited by Vladimir Popov; this group called itself the "National-Socialist Movement," and was more openly Nazi, and also monarchist, in orientation. Popov became head of the Press Department of the new party, which in December 1994 adopted as its definitive name the "People's National Party."

Twice Ivanov-Sukharevsky has faced criminal charges. In 1997, he was prosecuted for "inciting ethnic hatred" and "calling for mass disorders" following a meeting at which he demanded the deportation from Moscow of Caucasians, Asians, and Negroes (Vorozhishchev 1998). In the fall of 1998, a criminal prosecution was again brought against him for inciting ethnic hatred (Gerasimov 1999; Lukaitis 1999a). The case was heard on February 15, 1999 in Tver. In the course of the proceedings, Ivanov-Sukharevsky became hysterical, and by order of the judge was arrested in the courtroom and sent for psychiatric evaluation. He was, however, found sane. In October 1999, the Duma deputies Albert Makashov and Yevgeny Loginov and the churchman Father Nikon (Sergei Belavenets) offering themselves as guarantors of his good behavior, he was released and resumed political activity.

A few words on Ivanov-Sukharevsky's personal style. He takes great pride in his "artistic" temperament and creative talent as a thinker, writer, orator, and leader, qualities that he contrasts with Barkashov's mediocrity and bureaucratic grayness ("Seren'kaia" 1998). In the importance that Ivanov-Sukharevsky attaches to the aesthetic dimension, in his desire constantly to challenge and provoke, he bears a certain resemblance to Limonov, although he himself would no doubt deny that he has anything in common with such a "degenerate." The language in which he writes and speaks is highly idiosyncratic, intensely emotional and dramatic, abusive and poetic in turns, at once high-flown and colloquial. The reader or listener has to contend with sudden discontinuities, neologisms, strange expressions, and unusual modes of argumentation. For example, in an interview with party journalist Fyodor Lishny posted on the PNP website, Ivanov-Sukharevsky is asked why he entered politics. He replies:

> I want to lay the foundations for the ideal state. . . . But our readers will not understand me, and probably not trust me, unless you first ask me a different question: Which animal would you most like to be?

Ivanov-Sukharevsky's followers must also now and then find him a bit difficult to understand, but perhaps this merely enhances their awe at his insight and wisdom. Evidently he does not lack a certain charm and charisma. His biographer claims he is "friendly with party comrades, an excellent family man, and merciless toward Russia's enemies" (Ivanov 1997, p. 2).

The People's National Party: Ideology and Program

The ideology of the PNP is called "Rusism." Rusism was, not surprisingly, invented by Ivanov-Sukharevsky. It comprises such components as "popular nationalism," "national-ecologism," "voice of the blood" racial mysticism, Orthodoxy, and the Russian imperial idea. One finds also a clear effort to combine the Black Hundreds tradition of Orthodox monarchism with the ideas of classical fascism—although action is promised "by comparison with which the Union of the Russian People or the pitiful Nazis of the Third Reich will seem mere empty chatterboxes." The most prominent theme, however, is the struggle of the Russian people against the Jewish enemy and their "Yid regime."

One can still detect an ideological as well as stylistic distinction between the literature that serves as a direct mouthpiece for Ivanov-Sukharevsky—that is, the popular newspaper *I Am a Russian* [*Ia—russkii*], the pamphlet on Rusism, and the website—and the more theoretical journals controlled by Popov and his associates from the former National-Socialist Movement, *Era of Russia* [*Era Rossii*] and *Heritage of Our Predecessors* [*Nasledie predkov*]. While Ivanov-Sukharevsky remains by and large loyal to Orthodoxy,[6] the latter journals are implicitly pagan in orientation: although Christianity is not openly attacked in them, they contain an abundance of material on the polytheism of pre-Christian Rus, ancient Greece and Rome, and also ancient India, the supposed cradle of the "Aryan" race and its civilization. There is a great deal too on Ariosophy, "raceology and genetics," and such arcane topics as "Slavic astrology." Diversity of religious orientations within the PNP, however, does not seem to have been a source of internal conflict: Ivanov-Sukharevsky considers religion a matter of secondary importance, and he tolerates the quasi-pagans within his party, in accordance with his motto: "Blood unites; faith divides" (Ivanov 1997, p. 18).

The Future Russian State

How does the PNP envisage the "holy Russian power" or "kingdom of Rusism" to which it aspires?

The party program[7] stipulates, first of all, that Russia is to be a national state uniting all Russians—which, as we recall, includes Belarusians, Ukrainians, and Ruthenians (points 1 and 2). Only those of Russian descent and of

Orthodox faith may be citizens or officials (points 5, 6, and 8). Orthodoxy is to be the state religion, although other religions that "do not contradict the moral conceptions of Russian Orthodoxy" will be tolerated (points 28 and 29). Members of ethnic minorities may live as Russian subjects, but only in their native places; they are to be deprived of the territorial autonomy many of them now possess; and the relations between Russians and the subject peoples are to be "fatherly" in nature (points 1, 6, and 22). All foreigners who have entered Russia since 1991 are to be expelled (point 10).

The structure of the future state is to be unitary, with the central government possessing "unconditional power" over policy (point 30). Parliament is to be replaced by "a system of the personal responsibility of leaders chosen by the people" (point 31). However, the people, organized into a "hierarchy of talents," are to elect a "chamber of representatives of estates (corporations)," as provided for in the classical doctrine of Italian fascism. There will also be a "holy council of elders" and a "holy council of protectors of the Fatherland." Above all these institutions will stand the Supreme Ruler (Ivanov 1997, p. 30). Party members appointed to government positions will be required, as "monk-warriors," to maintain a modest lifestyle (Ivanov 1997, p. 64). Some restrictions on freedom of the press are envisaged: libels against Russian history will be prohibited by law, and non-Russians (as in tsarist times) will need special permission to publish books and newspapers in Russian (point 27).

The economy is to be mixed. The state will own monopolies and participate in the main banks (points 15 and 16). At the same time, private initiative is to be encouraged, with a view to making 70 percent of the population small and medium property owners (point 18), although "private property may not be used to the detriment of the nation" (point 12). Private usufruct of land—that is, possession without the right of sale—will also be allowed. The Cossacks will get back all the lands they used to have before 1914, together with their traditional special form of government and all their other traditional customs (point 20). The elderly will receive decent pensions, women will be released from heavy industrial work, and the youth will enjoy sports, equal opportunity—and universal military service (points 17, 24, 25, and 26). Criminals, speculators, and corrupt officials will be mercilessly suppressed, with ample use of the death penalty (points 13 and 21).

Although the socioeconomic program of the PNP may, by American standards, appear at least moderately left-wing, it must be emphasized that the party firmly rejects the "left-wing" label. Ivanov-Sukharevsky has no truck with national-bolshevism, and identifies himself with the "White" tradition.

The most striking point in the PNP program has to do with Russia's environment, which is to be transformed in accordance with the doctrine of "national-ecologism." Russians are to live in such a way as to facilitate the restoration and maintenance of nature in its "original historical form." This will entail, *inter alia*, dismantling the dams that obstruct the natural flow of the holy river Ra, otherwise known as the Volga (point 23).

What, finally, of the geographical boundaries of the new state? All we are told by the program is that "all the ports of the Russian Baltic" are to be returned to Russia (point 4), and that the Belovezhsk agreements that dissolved the Soviet Union are to be annulled (point 3). However, a statement issued in December 1994 by the Central Council of the PNP, in which Kazakhstan is declared to exist "only in the imagination of television," suggests that much if not all of the near abroad is to be reabsorbed (Verkhovskii and Pribylovskii 1996, pp. 109–10). The ultimate goal is described elsewhere by Ivanov-Sukharevsky in the following terms:

> The mission of the Russian people, given us by the Creator, is to create a great state from Ocean to Ocean. That state will be the bond of the world, the axis of the planet. . . .

Near-Term Policy Proposals

To derive some idea of the kind of nearer-term policy proposals advanced by the PNP, we may consider the program on which Ivanov-Sukharevsky stood as candidate in the 1996 presidential elections. This was a short populist program that concentrated wholly on crime and bread-and-butter issues, giving no indication of the party's long-term goals. Ivanov-Sukharevsky promised to raise living standards by 30 percent by closing down the commercial banks, and by a further 30 percent by confiscating criminally acquired wealth. Education and medicines would be provided free of charge, there would be state support for the family, and pensions and wages would be increased up to "the average subsistence minimum of the city of Moscow." Military field courts would be introduced to suppress crime, and "the fathers of Russian families" would be armed "to protect the honor and dignity of their wives and children from the attacks of Caucasian bands" (Ivanov 1997, back cover). Rather remarkable is the absence of anti-Semitism from the document.

PNP Symbols

The People's National Party appears to be less preoccupied with symbols than are some Russian fascist organizations. Two emblems are used. The first is the *lobarum*, a cross with T-bars across the four end-points inside a circle. This is a monogram of Jesus Christ that was engraved on the crest and shield of the Byzantine Emperor Constantine the Great (RNS Website). The second emblem is the eight-pointed star, also a traditional symbol of Russian Orthodoxy, which appears on the masthead of the party's newspaper over the motto: "Faith, Will, Victory!"

PNP Activities, Strategy, and Prospects

For all his verbal extremism, which on occasion has exposed him to criminal prosecution, Ivanov-Sukharevsky advocates exclusively legal methods of struggle, arguing that this is the only possible way of winning power (Ivanov 1998). The main goal of the PNP's activity is, accordingly, the building of a viable electoral force.

Attempts were made to register the new party at the Ministry of Justice even before its formation was completed. These early applications were rejected, but an appeal to the newly appointed justice minister, Valentin Kovalev, led to the registration of the PNP as an all-Russian party in May 1995. At that point the party claimed about 500 members in forty-seven regional organizations. In September 1995, the PNP registered its list of candidates for the approaching Duma elections, headed by Ivanov-Sukharevsky, Osipov, and Demin. However, the party did not manage to collect the required 200,000 signatures, and so was not allowed to take part in the elections. In the 1996 presidential elections, the PNP supported an independent nationalist candidate, the writer Yuri Vlasov, but were disappointed that Vlasov, who won only 0.2 percent of the vote, did not wage a more militant campaign.[8] In the 1999 Duma elections, the PNP backed the movement "For Faith, Tsar, and Fatherland" of Father Nikon. Nikon's electoral list was headed by Ivanov-Sukharevsky, but it was submitted late, so once again the party was unable to participate. The PNP has not therefore been able to enter politics at the national level, although it has had some success in local elections: eight of its candidates won election to municipal councils in St. Petersburg in 1998 (Ivanov 1998).

The PNP conducts public meetings in Moscow, sometimes in collaboration with other fascist organizations (for instance, the meeting in Theater Square on December 12, 1995, conducted jointly with the Russian National Union). The first PNP public meeting was held on January 22, 1995, in support of the military intervention in Chechnya. In January 1996, the PNP was the main organizer of a "scientific-practical conference" on the topic "The State and National Ideology," attended by guests from several other nationalist organizations, including representatives of the Congress of Russian Communities and Eduard Limonov of the NBP.

The party's publishing activity has been quite extensive. From the National-

Socialist Movement it inherited the journal *Era of Russia*, which has continued to appear on an irregular basis. In late 1995, there appeared the first issue of a new glossy magazine called *Heritage of Our Predecessors: A Journal of Right-Wing Perspective*. This periodical, the arcane content of which has already been described, has come out about twice a year with a print run of 2,000. In 1996, a third magazine, *Russian Perspective* [*Russkaia perspektiva*], began publication as a special supplement to *Heritage of Our Predecessors*, with a print run of 1,000. Produced by the Analytical Center "Polius," *Russian Perspective* focuses on questions of "national ideology," and especially on military affairs, military technology, and geopolitics (without a dogmatic commitment to Eurasianism or any other specific geopolitical school). In 1997, a much more popular four-page party newspaper was launched as a quarterly, with a print run of 10,000, under the name *I Am a Russian*. In December 1998, however, a civil case against the newspaper led to its closure by court order on the grounds that it had instigated ethnic hatred. Another periodical, *Na kazachem postu* [*At the Cossack's Post*], has been produced for the benefit of Cossack readers.[9] The party also distributes a variety of pamphlets, including Ivanov-Sukharevsky's *My Faith Is Rusism*, a collection of his articles, and *Judah on the Wane* by the Russian émigré leader Konstantin Rodzayevsky (Rodzaevskii 1997).[10]

As will already have been noted, the PNP is open to cooperation, and where possible fusion, with other like-minded organizations. This is an essential part of its strategy for creating a viable fascist electoral force. Thus, in the spring of 1995 Vladimir Osipov and other leaders of the Union "Christian Rebirth" joined the PNP and were given senior positions, Osipov being awarded the honorific title of party "elder" [*stareishin*]. This fusion did not prove lasting, and Osipov and most of his comrades left the PNP in 1996. Ivanov-Sukharevsky has also been instrumental in convening a series of Congresses of Russian Nationalists. At the third such congress, held in St. Petersburg on February 11, 1996, he persuaded the leaders or representatives of eight other fascist organizations to set up a Coordinating Council of Radical Nationalist Parties.[11] The following week, on February 17 and 18, there occurred an unprecedented and rather remarkable event—a conference in Kiev of radical Russian *and* Ukrainian nationalists, organized jointly by the Ukrainian National Assembly (UNA–UNSO) and the Party of Slavic Unity. The participants adopted the "Kiev Declaration," proposed by Ivanov-Sukharevsky, in which they pledged to fight together for a united Slavic empire, while letting "Providence . . . decide where its heart will be"—that is, in Moscow or in Kiev. UNA–UNSO and the Transcarpathian Republican Party acceded to the coordinating council.[12]

The alliance that seemed to offer Ivanov-Sukharevsky the greatest prospects, however, was the one he concluded in 1997 with the National-Republican Party of Russia of Yuri Belyaev. Here it needs to be explained that in October 1994 the original NRPR (to be discussed below) split into two separate organizations, led by Nikolai Lysenko and Yuri Belyaev, respectively, both of which retained the previous name, so that from then on there existed two NRPRs, generally referred to as the NRPR (Lysenko) and the NRPR (Belyaev). The rapprochement between the PNP and the NRPR (Belyaev) began in September 1997. In December 1997, a congress of Belyaev's supporters, to which Ivanov-Sukharevsky and his closest comrades had been invited, took the decision to enter the PNP. As part of the deal, Belyaev and his associate V. Kochnov were immediately given senior positions in the PNP: Belyaev was elected chairman of the Central Council, and Kochnov appointed chief editor of the party newspaper. Belyaev subsequently issued an appeal to those of his former comrades who had not attended the unification congress to follow him into the PNP. As a result of the merger, the PNP found itself substantially enlarged, with more than sixty regional organizations. It had a presence not only in many provincial centers, but also in some small towns, industrial settlements, and even villages.[13]

But this alliance was also to prove short-lived. Perhaps discouraged by the prosecution against Ivanov-Sukharevsky, Belyaev and his followers separated from the PNP at the end of 1998 and reconstituted their party. Others also left the PNP at that time.

The willingness of the PNP to work with other organizations, and its ability on occasion to absorb them, are significant assets, enabling it to avoid isolation and bring fresh blood into its ranks. It is, nevertheless, an uphill struggle to try to unite the numerous groups that make up the "patriotic" movement, because the leaders of most such groups much prefer to remain big fish in small ponds. The case of Belyaev is unusual in this respect.

One fascist organization that consistently refused to cooperate with the PNP was the Russian National Unity (RNU). Its leader, Alexander Barkashov, evidently viewed Ivanov-Sukharevsky as a serious rival. In 1995 there were reportedly several physical attacks on Ivanov-Sukharevsky and Popov, as well as burglaries of Ivanov-Sukharevsky's apartment, by persons unknown. The PNP believes that the assailants were RNU fighters acting on Barkashov's orders, and the accusation is plausible enough.

The fact that the PNP is good at attracting those who are already convinced "patriots" does not, of course, guarantee that it will prove capable of recruiting on a large scale from the general population. The forcible closure of *I Am a Russian* was a blow from which the party will find it hard to recover. Ivanov-Sukharevsky urges his supporters to concentrate on winning over active young men who at present work for organized criminal gangs.

These "soldiers of the mafia" could become the basic striking force of the PNP's youth organization, "with the help of which we could conquer the streets of our Russian towns, which in its turn would win us the respect of the passive part of the Russian people" (Ivanov 1997, pp. 58–59). Unfortunately for the PNP, the young criminals will probably find it more profitable to stick to their current occupation.

Nikolai Lysenko and the National-Republican Party of Russia

Nikolai Lysenko and His Party

Nikolai Lysenko was born on May 17, 1961 in the east Siberian town of Kirensk in Irkutsk Province. His father, a civil air pilot, had come from the Kuban in southern Russia; his mother was a teacher of biology and chemistry and a native Siberian. In 1978, Nikolai entered the biology faculty of the pedagogical institute in Ussuriisk, another eastern Siberian town. It was here that he embarked on his career as a Russian nationalist, forming in his first year an underground student circle grandly named "the Union for the Salvation of the Russian Nation." At their gatherings, Nikolai and his friends shared their thoughts about the oppressed position of Russians in the Russian Federation. But there must have been an informer in their midst, for the existence of the circle was exposed. The KGB investigator assigned to the case, however, sympathized with the conspirators, and they escaped with a warning. None of them were expelled from the institute, or even from the Komsomol.

Lysenko graduated from the institute as an epizoologist,[14] in which capacity he went to the remote peninsulas of Taimyr (on the Arctic coast) and Kamchatka (on the Pacific) to take part in biological weapons research. In 1986 he moved to St. Petersburg, where he worked as a veterinarian while attending evening classes at the Leningrad Pedagogical Institute to requalify as a teacher of history and social studies. Somehow he managed at the same time to be active in the Leningrad branch of *Pamyat*. In August 1988, he spoke at a session of the branch council (of which he was a member) against Dmitry Vasilyev, whom he accused of subservience to the Soviet regime, and was duly thrown out of *Pamyat*.

Lysenko now became a full-time politician. He formed his own "White" splinter group, the Russian National-Patriotic Front *Pamyat* (adding "Russian" to the name of Vasilyev's organization, the National-Patriotic Front *Pamyat*). The new organization consisted, according to an interior ministry source, of eight young "fighters." In late 1988 and early 1989, it produced four issues of a typewritten samizdat journal *Holy Russia* [*Sviataia Rus′*]. In

March 1989, Lysenko took part in a conference of local "patriotic" groups held in the Smolny Cathedral, which at that time still housed an anti-religious museum, but again found himself in the minority when he refused to recognize "the leading role of the Communist Party of the Soviet Union in the patriotic movement." He left the conference.

In May 1989, together with Viktor Antonov, Lysenko created the Russian National-Patriotic Center, on the basis of which he organized in April 1990 his own party, initially called the Republican People's Party of Russia (RPPR). The name was changed to National-Republican Party of Russia (NRPR) in November 1991.

In 1990, Lysenko stood in a district of Leningrad as a candidate for the Congress of People's Deputies of the Russian Federation. On this occasion he was not elected, although he made it to the second round, in which he obtained 27 percent of the vote. In the Duma elections of December 1993, however, he won election as an independent candidate in the town of Engels in Saratov Province. (The NRPR was unable to participate as a party because it failed to collect the necessary 100,000 signatures.) In the Duma, Lysenko did not speak a great deal, but he found better ways of attracting attention. Thus, on April 5, 1995, while the question of the Black Sea Fleet was under discussion, he took the tribune and dramatically tore to pieces a Ukrainian flag. He accomplished his most heroic feat on September 9, 1995, when he assaulted his fellow deputy Gleb Yakunin, an Orthodox priest who had been defrocked for his political activity, tore the cross from his breast, and "confiscated" it. Several other deputies joined in the fray, in the course of which Zhirinovsky injured two women deputies who were trying to restore order (White, Rose, and McAllister 1997, p. 187).

Lysenko's career as a parliamentarian and party leader came to a rather ignominious end. On December 5, 1995, there was an explosion in Lysenko's office at the Duma. Who was behind it remains a mystery to this day. Lysenko blamed the Turkish secret services, but it was suggested in the press that Lysenko had arranged the explosion himself as a stunt to attract attention. On May 13, 1996, Lysenko was arrested and placed in detention while the matter was under investigation. Evidently, however, no convincing evidence could be found against him, because when he finally came to trial at the Moscow city court on October 6, 1997, he was found not guilty on the original charge. He *was* found guilty of stealing an office computer, thereby justifying the seventeen months he had already spent in jail, and then set free in the courtroom (Verkhovskii et al. 1998, p. 57).

On release, Lysenko discovered that his party had collapsed in his absence. Most of the members had gone elsewhere. He made some attempt to revive the organization, but gave up in 1998 when it failed to complete successfully the process of re-registration. The NRPR (Lysenko) was never formally dissolved: it just died. Lysenko remained politically active. He stood in the Duma elections of 1999 on the list of Sergei Baburin's Russian All-People's Union (ROS), where he was identified as the political secretary of the ROS for southern Russia.

The NRPR (Lysenko): Ideology and Program

The ideology of Lysenko's party underwent various fluctuations before assuming definitive form. In the fall of 1990, Lysenko declared that the Republican People's Party of Russia (as it still was) would be "the party of the ideas of Solzhenitsyn." The party program composed at that time borrowed extensively from Solzhenitsyn's *How We Should Build Russia*. However, many of Solzhenitsyn's ideas did not really suit Lysenko very well, and he soon began to amend them in important ways. In particular, Solzhenitsyn rejected the imperial aspirations that were so dear to Lysenko: he argued that Russia and Central Asia should go their separate ways, and later even urged Yeltsin to accept Chechen independence (Solzhenitsyn 2000).

In October 1992, Lysenko set aside his previous uncompromising anti-communism to take part in creating the National Salvation Front (NSF), in which Zyuganov and other communists were also closely involved, and was elected to the front's Political Council. His collaboration with the communist "patriots," however, was not to last long. In July 1993, a communist colleague took objection to one of the NRPR's virulently anti-Caucasian leaflets. Lysenko reacted by leaving the NSF. In a statement explaining the move, he criticized the NSF for the "remnants of internationalism" in its outlook and the predominance of communists in its leadership.[15]

The worldview of the NRPR, defined by its political secretary Nikolai Pavlov as "the Russian National Superideology," combined Russian ethnic nationalism with great-power imperialism:

> Russia cannot stand aside from the struggle for world dominion. That is why our state must win back the status of a world superpower. . . . The general idea of the NRPR is the idea of great-power intellectual and technological supremacy over the whole world, the struggle for a great Russian Empire. . . . The acquisition by the Russian state of the messianic status of the world's sole defender of national cultures from cosmopolitan "Americanoidal" expansion, technotronic genocide, and consumer degeneration—that is the main goal of [our] ideology and politics. (Lysenko cited in Verkhovskii and Pribylovskii 1996, p. 45)

Within the former USSR, the NRPR laid claim to Ukraine, Belarus, much of Kazakhstan, and other predominantly Slav territories, and also to territories inhabited by non-Slav peoples with close links to Russia, such as South Ossetia (in Georgia) and northern Azerbaijan (because of its Lezgin population). Like the PNP, the NRPR intended to eliminate the autonomous units of non-Russian ethnic minorities within Russia, although they were—if loyal—to be allowed their own schools and religious associations, while granting full autonomy to the Cossacks (Verkhovskii and Pribylovskii 1996, p. 123).

For Lysenko's NRPR, the main ethnic enemies of the Russians and other Slavs were the "black hordes" of Caucasians and Turks, the latter term referring primarily to Kazakhs, Uzbeks, Azeris, and other Turkic peoples of the former Soviet Union. These peoples were the carriers of crime and filth, and had to be deported from Russia. Lysenko's obsession with the "Turco–Caucasian" threat was so single-minded that he was prepared to ally Russia not only with Germany, Armenia, and Iran, but even with Israel. Lysenko opposed anti-Semitism on the grounds that it discredited the "patriotic" movement and distracted it from struggle against the main enemy. Jews, he argued, were not as influential as many believed, and moreover their influence was declining.[16]

The NRPR proposed to convene an All-Russian National Assembly to establish legitimate state institutions for the future Russia. One of these institutions was to be a consultative Assembly Council [*Sobornaia Duma*], elected on a corporatist basis by social groups and professions.[17] The NRPR, like the PNP and many other nationalist groups, envisaged a mixed economy, with the state playing a strong regulatory role, especially in the banking sector.

The NRPR (Lysenko) stood out among nationalist organizations for its clear commitment to secularism: the special position of Orthodoxy in Russian society would be recognized, but there would be no state religion. Curiously enough in light of the party's name, its commitment to republicanism was a little shaky: Lysenko expressed some sympathy for the idea of restoring the monarchy, though he believed this would not be possible for a long time to come.

Lysenko rejected the label of "fascist," arguing that the term was unacceptable to Russian nationalists for historical reasons. Nevertheless, he admitted to having been influenced by the ideas of Mussolini, as well as by those of Jean-Marie Le Pen, leader of the French Front National, and of contemporary German right-wing radicals (Pribylovskii 1994, p. 10). All things considered, it seems pedantic not to classify Lysenko as a fascist.

Activities and Prospects

Lysenko assigned to the NRPR itself the tasks of propaganda and electoral activity, while creating other closely linked but formally separate organizations to fulfill military and "security" functions. The party's paramilitary auxiliary was called the Russian National Legion (see below). In addition, there was a Russian Security Service, headed by Yuri Belyaev, who at the end of 1992 also created a center in St. Petersburg to recruit volunteers to fight with the Serbs in Bosnia (Verkhovskii et al. 1998, p. 58).

The NRPR appears to have had no difficulty in obtaining its initial registration. In 1993, as noted above, the party did not collect enough signatures to take direct part in the Duma elections, although the election of Lysenko himself to the Duma constituted an unprecedented victory. The next time round, in 1995, the NRPR surmounted the hurdle of signature collection and participated in the elections. The combined vote of its party list candidates was 331,700, not quite one-half of 1 percent of the total. The party did best in three districts of the Krasnodar Territory, where it won 5.7, 4.7, and 3.8 percent, respectively. Similar results were obtained in some of the single-mandate constituencies, notably in a district of Moscow Province (5.3 percent) and in a district of Smolensk Province (3.3 percent). Belyaev stood in a district of St. Petersburg, where he got 5.3 percent (Polivanov 1996). Lysenko was put forward as a candidate in Tver Province, but too few signatures were collected to allow him to stand. His days as a Duma deputy were over. His party again put him forward as a candidate for the 1996 presidential elections, but once more the required number of signatures were not submitted.

Belyaev's Party

In the fall of 1994, Yuri Belyaev and his associate Sergei Rybnikov organized a rebellion in the NRPR against Lysenko's leadership. At an extraordinary plenum of the party's Central Council on October 29, Belyaev announced that Lysenko had been removed from his position. Lysenko, of course, did not accept this claim, and promptly expelled the rebels from the NRPR. On December 3, Belyaev and Rybnikov staged a "Third Congress of the NRPR," at which they brought together their supporters from the NRPR and members of the People's Social Party, an organization that Belyaev had founded back in November 1991, before he entered Lysenko's party in the summer of 1992. Three days later, Belyaev's car was raked by gunfire, badly wounding Belyaev and killing two of his bodyguards.

The split between Lysenko and Belyaev was to a large extent a result of their personal rivalry, but there was also an ideological dimension. In the letter that Belyaev was later to write to his comrades after joining the PNP, he refers to himself as leader of "the militant wing of the NRPR." Clearly he believed that Lysenko had become too soft and respectable since entering the Duma. However, it would be misleading to say that Lysenko was in general less extreme in his views than Belyaev. In some respects, indeed, Belyaev was to prove more moderate than Lysenko. Thus, his party criticized the "imperial romanticism" of Lysenko's NRPR, and expressed itself in favor of "national pragmatism in foreign policy" and "recognition of current geopolitical realities" (Verkhovskii and Pribylovskii 1996, p. 43). To be sure, in one respect Belyaev was the more extreme of the two: he restored the Jews to their rightful place among the enemies of the Russian people (Verkhovskii and Pribylovskii 1996, p. 124). Lysenko's opposition to anti-Semitism may have made good sense in a broader political context, but by alienating many of his existing supporters it had weakened his party.

Belyaev also diverged somewhat from Lysenko in matters of religion. The program of his party, like that of Lysenko's, upheld the principle of secularism, but at the same time expressed opposition to the presence in Russia of Protestantism, Catholicism, Judaism, and Oriental cults. Belyaev's "secularism" means that he maintains a neutral position regarding the choice between Orthodoxy and Zoroastrianism, the original faith of the Aryans (Verkhovskii and Pribylovskii 1996, p. 126).

In 1995, Belyaev aligned his party with the Social-Patriotic Movement *Derzhava* [Great Power] of former vice-president Alexander Rutskoi. In the Duma elections of December 1995, he stood in a St. Petersburg constituency as an independent candidate, winning 5.4 percent of the vote. In February 1996, he was put on trial for the instigation of ethnic and religious hatred, was sentenced to one year's deprivation of freedom deferred by one year, and was then released under an amnesty without having to serve time (Verkhovskii et al. 1998, p. 58). In 1997–1998, as we have seen, Belyaev and his followers formed part of the PNP.

Belyaev's party remains in existence, although it has never acquired registration. Members are concentrated mainly in northwestern Russia. The party is particularly active in the St. Petersburg area, and also in Pskov, where it has enjoyed the patronage of the LDPR provincial governor, Yevgeny Mikhailov.

The Russian National Legion

At the end of 1991, Lysenko created a paramilitary organization called the Russian National Legion (RNL), closely connected to the NRPR but formally separate from it. The group was headed at first by Sergei Maltsev, and from 1994 by the police officer Andrei Sabor, both members of the Central Council of the NRPR. Young men (aged twenty to thirty-five) applying to enter the RNL were selected on a competitive basis and underwent rigorous military and combat training. Some of them were chosen to be Lysenko's personal bodyguards. Others fought—and some died—in the armed conflicts of 1992–1993 in South Ossetia and Transdniestria, as volunteers with the Serbs in Yugoslavia, and in the October 1993 defense of the White House in Moscow. On the night of February 18, 1993, Lysenko led a detachment of RNL members on a march of protest against American and Russian policy in the Balkans; they burned the American flag, and lit up the building of the ministry of foreign affairs with flares.

In October 1994, when the NRPR split, the RNL leaders Maltsev and Sabor took the side of Belyaev, and for the next year the RNL was attached to Belyaev's organization. In October 1995, following a clash between Belyaev and Sabor, the NRPR (Belyaev) and the RNL went their separate ways. As a parting gesture, the legionnaires smashed the windows in Belyaev's office and took the equipment away with them (Verkhovskii et al. 1996, pp. 160–61).

Alexei Vdovin, Konstantin Kasimovsky, and the Russian National Union

Alexei Vdovin and Konstantin Kasimovsky

The Russian National Union (RNS) was the joint creation of two men, Alexei Vdovin and Konstantin Kasimovsky.[18]

Vdovin was born on November 12, 1958 in the town of Bronnitsy, to the south of Moscow. His parents, manual workers, belonged to the underground "catacomb church," from which he received a secret religious education. He trained as a fitter at a technical school, did his army service, and then worked in various local factories. In 1987, he joined *Pamyat* and was appointed commander of the Bronnitsy branch. In 1989 he became a member of Vasilyev's headquarters staff, and in 1991 a deputy chief of staff. He had already chalked up a number of signal achievements as a "patriotic" activist. He had initiated the destruction of the monument to Lenin in Bronnitsy—one of the first such acts to occur in the USSR; he had captured two churches from the authorities; and he had restored a monument to the heroes of World War I.

Kasimovsky is the younger of the two men, and comes from a rather different background. He was born in Moscow on May 26, 1974 in a family of native Muscovites. His father is a hydrologist, his mother a construction engineer. He boasts some famous ancestors—most notably the Tatar khan of Kasimov, Simeon Bekbulatovich, who was baptized a Christian and made Prince of Tver by Ivan the Terrible.[19] (He does not seem to have had any problem in reconciling his ethnic Russian nationalism with his Tatar ancestry.) Kasimovsky joined *Pamyat* in 1989, while still at school. In 1992, he was put in charge of the movement's north Moscow militia. He also helped to produce the journal *Pamyat* and the radio program "The Fatherland, *Pamyat*, and You." Still only eighteen, he undertook a journey to Transdniestria to demonstrate solidarity with the mainly Slavic people of the area in their armed conflict for secession from newly independent Moldova, only to be reprimanded on his return by Vasilyev for going without the latter's permission.

It must have been in 1992 also that Vdovin and Kasimovsky, both now members of *Pamyat*'s core leadership, made one another's acquaintance. Each had his own reason for dissatisfaction with Vasilyev. Kasimovsky was upset at Vasilyev's reaction to his trip to Transdniestria, while Vdovin had fallen out with Vasilyev on a religious issue: Vasilyev had broken off the former ties of the movement with the émigré Russian Orthodox Church Abroad, with which Vdovin wished to maintain relations. The pair left *Pamyat* at the beginning of 1993, together with a group of young followers, to create the Russian National Union (RNS). And so in 1993 Kasimovsky, not yet twenty years of age, became the chairman of a new "patriotic" movement—and a first-year student at the International Institute of Economics and Law.

In May 1993, Kasimovsky ceded the position of chairman to Vdovin, himself becoming first deputy chairman with responsibility for questions of ideology and for teaching the "stormtroopers" hand-to-hand combat. In 1997, Vdovin deserted the RNS to join the RNU, explaining to his former comrades-in-arms that the RNU was a larger and more effective organization and appealing to them to follow his lead (Vdovin 1997).[20] Kasimovsky remained as the sole and undisputed leader of the RNS. Yuri Bekhchanov also came to be referred to in RNS publications as a "leader" [*vozhd'*], but only Kasimovsky has the title of "head" [*glava*].

A criminal prosecution for the instigation of ethnic hatred was lodged against Kasimovsky in 1996. He was not arrested. After repeated delays, the trial began in the Timiryazev municipal court on December 2, 1998. Finally, on October 6, 1999, Kasimovsky was found guilty and sentenced to two years' deprivation of freedom. The sentence, however, was deferred by two years, as a result of which he came under the terms of an amnesty and got off scot-free. Kasimovsky resumed his political activity. In late 1999 he was working in the Duma as a political consultant to its official journal, *Parlamentskaia gazeta* [Parliamentary Journal], thanks possibly to the LDPR, in the apparatus of whose Duma fraction he had worked earlier in the year.

In December 1998, Kasimovsky decided to rename his organization the Russian National-Socialist Party. Nevertheless, to avoid confusion I shall refer only to the Russian National Union (RNS), the name by which the movement is generally known in the literature.

RNS: Worldview, Program, Symbols

The worldview of the RNS is monarcho-fascist in character.[21] The emphasis on Orthodox Christianity, which is the first of four "basic postulates," and on the need to restore the imperial monarchy[22] demonstrates the link to the Black Hundreds tradition. The influence of Codreanu's Romanian fascism, which was also Orthodox and monarchist, is recognized (Verkhovskii et al. 1996, p. 164). At the same time, the contribution to RNS ideology of Hitler's national-socialism is very substantial and overt. It is from German Nazism that the other three of the "basic postulates" are clearly derived—namely, "a strong state as the basis of Aryan order"; "violent Russian nationalism, the defensive reaction of the Russian people"; and "non-Marxist socialism." The anti-Semitism of the RNS is very open and very intense (Verkhovskii and Pribylovskii 1996, p. 150). Unlike the PNP and the NRPR, the RNS does not appear to have been influenced by Italian fascism.

The RNS is a paramilitary organization similar in some ways to the RNU. The most striking contrast between them, reflected in symbolism as well as in explicit ideology, is that the RNS, unlike the RNU, makes no concessions to respectable opinion. What the RNU coyly obfuscated, the RNS proudly proclaims to the world. Thus, for the RNS, Hitler's invasion of the Soviet Union was not—as the RNU preferred to see it—an unfortunate misunderstanding, but a heroic crusade by "Europe" to save its Russian sister, mortally wounded by bolshevism, and Germany's defeat in the war was a defeat for the whole of Europe and the world. The RNU fused its swastika with a star, and explained that it was a Russian, not a German, symbol, while the RNS displays its swastika plain, and does not conceal whence it is taken. (Besides the swastika, the RNS also uses the lobarum and the death's head skull as emblems.) Members of both the RNU and the RNS shout *Glory to Russia*, but only RNS members call themselves "stormtroopers" and cry *Sieg Heil* and *Heil Hitler*.[23]

The RNS worldview reflects the influence of other, more esoteric sources: in particular, that of Julius Evola and other thinkers of the West European New Right, whether absorbed directly or—more likely—via the medium of Alexander Dugin's journal *Elementy* (Verkhovskii and Pribylovskii 1996, p. 63). Evola's view that the entire known history of humanity has been a process of decline and decay toward chaos and darkness is accepted: only "the brilliant movement of Fascism returned us for a time to the Middle Ages"—an accomplishment that the RNS leader regards naturally as being all to fascism's credit. How such a historical philosophy is to be reconciled with adherence to Christianity is not discussed.

The struggle against decline, Kasimovsky explains, has been carried on in recent centuries by special "Orders" such as King Arthur's knightly Order of the Round Table, the Crusaders, Ivan the Terrible's *Oprichnina*, the Catholic Inquisition, and the Nazi SS. It is as an Order of spiritually inspired and self-sacrificing crusaders, not as a political party, that he intends to build his movement, for "ours is a Revolution of the Spirit against the Flesh."

A reference to humanity's "era of Hyperborean youth" suggests that Kasimovsky may be influenced also to some extent by the mystical doctrine of Ariosophy, which as propagated by the Thule Society was one of the sources of early German national-socialism (Goodrick-Clarke 1992). The immediate source is doubtless the neo-paganist Society of Nav, with which the RNS closely cooperates (see below).

The RNS Program

The program of the RNS describes a future Russian Empire that will include "all territories in defense of which Great Russian soldiers have shed their blood." In this empire, the full plenitude of power is to lie in the hands of the Great Russian people. Thus, citizenship is to be restricted to Great Russians. The RNS is in this respect more exclusive than most fascist organizations, which count Belarusians (White Russians) and Ukrainians (Little Russians) as Russians. Moreover, to qualify as a citizen a Great Russian will have to pass a test of intellect and swear an oath of loyalty to the imperial government. A Great Russian living outside the Empire may become a citizen, and his rights will then be defended by the Empire, if necessary by invading militarily his country of residence.

Non-Russians will be allowed to continue living in the Russian Empire as subjects, provided that "their way of life is not a threat to the Empire and the Great-Russian people." They will, however, be segregated under the control of the imperial authorities in "national colonies," outside of which they will not (except in case of imperial necessity) be allowed to spend more than one month a year.[24]

The Party, we learn, "decisively rejects 'human rights' in favor of the rights of the Nation. All political chimeras of the contemporary age, including democracy, communism, anarchy, and parliamentarism, are declared harmful anti-Russian ideologies." Therefore "in the coming historical period the Empire must be run by an authoritarian party system that will prepare the Great Russian people for the adoption of the traditional Aryan system of state power." Except at the lowest level of administration, the election of officials is to be replaced by appointment. All political organizations will be banned as anti-national, and participation in political activity will be forbidden to subjects of the Empire, traders, women, and citizens over the age of sixty. Every male citizen must serve time in the army, and return to duty for one month a year thereafter.

The RNS looks to the eventual restoration of autocracy, based on the unity of monarchical and Orthodox Church power, but in the transitional period before the Assembly of the Lands can be convened there is to be a "strong national authority." Satanism, paganism, and Judaism are to be banned, as also the propaganda of atheism; presumably other non-Orthodox religions, such as Islam, are to be tolerated (Verkhovskii and Pribylovskii 1996, pp. 148–49).

In the economy of the Russian Empire, the state sector will occupy the predominant position. Heavy and extractive industry, transportation companies, banks, information media, and detective and protection agencies are to be nationalized, together with joint and foreign-owned ventures. In other branches, private enterprises are to be permitted, provided that they do not employ more than twenty people and do not engage in the resale trade, which as "speculation" will be illegal. Commercial activity will, however, be prohibited to representatives of the imperial administration and members of their families. Another stipulation implies that private commerce may even be confined to noncitizens: "Every male citizen will be required to work at a state enterprise or in individual labor activity useful to the Empire." In exchange, the citizen will enjoy the right to work befitting his education, to forty days' paid annual leave, to a separate family apartment, and to state benefits "directly proportional to the number of [his] healthy children." The rights of the subject are not so clearly specified.

The penal policy of the Russian Empire will afford broad scope to the death penalty. Thus, all acts aimed at undermining the might or prestige of the Empire or the authority of the armed forces will be punished by death, as will all infringements of military discipline and all economic crimes against the state or against citizens of the Empire. Marriages between citizens and noncitizens will be "racial crimes punished in accordance with the law." It will also be a crime for citizens in good health not to produce a child within three years of their wedding day. "The imperial authorities reserve the right to effect the euthanasia of the incurably sick, of the psychically inferior, and of children with birth defects that shame the human form."

RNS Activities

The RNS held its first public meeting on May 6, 1993, in the square by the Grenadiers' Monument in Moscow. On May 6, 1998, an RNS meeting and demonstration in central Moscow attracted about 200 people; in the evening, a big concert starred such "monsters of the Russian Musical Resistance" as the bands Metal Corrosion, Band of Four, Div, TomSAT, and Terror. On December 5, 1998, about a hundred RNS supporters marched along the Old Arbat from McDonald's to the Lenin Library, beating drums, shouting *Sieg Heil!* and "sowing terror among the monkeys, pederasts, and guests from the South." Although the demonstration was unsanctioned, the police did not interfere, having received no instructions to that effect (Amelina 1998a; Likhachev 1999). As for the "blacks" and other objects of Nazi scorn, they had good reason to be afraid, for it is a hallowed custom of the RNS to arrange after each of its events "a little holocaust" (Karamian 1997).[25]

The RNS conducts its propaganda exclusively among young people—in factories, in higher educational institutions, and on the streets (Filimonov 1998). In 1994, the journal *Shturmovik* [Stormtrooper] was launched, with Kasimovsky as chief editor. At some periods *Shturmovik* has come out as a weekly, at others less frequently. The RNS has also issued a journal called *Natsiia* [Nation] (Pribylovskii 1995, pp. 36, 58). The organization had its own printing press. The content of RNS publications is extremely violent and abusive, even by comparison with the literature of the RNU or PNP.[26] No attempt appears to have been made to engage in electoral activity.

Work with skinheads is a top priority of the RNS. *Shturmovik* regularly carries material aimed especially at skinheads, and the RNS has assisted skinheads in producing their own journal *Pod nol'*, which features mainly triumphant accounts of their exploits. Kasimovsky's strategy is to turn the skinheads into a more organized and consciously political force linked to his own party or—to use his own words—to make them "more Nazis than skins" (Rstaki 1998a).

The RNS does not deny that its activities include a military component. Its website declares that the organization engages in "the necessary minimum of conspiracy and militarization," though it does not have "enormous stocks of weapons." "We have troops to defend our meetings and for other actions." Many comrades-in-arms, it is pointed out, have personal experience in "hot-spots." Some RNS members took part in the armed clashes in Moscow in October 1993 on the side of the Supreme Soviet, Vdovin himself commanding a Cossack unit.

The RNS organizes its "stormtroopers" in a special detachment, which is divided into squads and sections, with eight men in each. The organization has a training camp outside Moscow. Kasimovsky leads in person both the lessons in ideology and the sessions for training in hand-to-hand combat. It is said that he uses as his guide a handbook published in 1938 for the Hitler Youth. In the fall of 1996, a separate detachment was set up consisting solely of skinhead recruits. Every Sunday, a group of between fifteen and thirty of the organization's skinheads carries out a violent "raid" on the streets of Moscow and in the city Metro, beating up nonwhites and anyone else to whom they take a dislike (Filimonov 1998; Rstaki 1998a).

The extent of RNS activity outside Moscow is difficult to assess. One observer mentions branches in Lubertsy (outside Moscow), Nizhny Novgorod, St. Petersburg, Rostov, and Odessa in Ukraine (Filimonov 1998). There is evidence that an explosion at a synagogue in Yaroslavl at the end of 1996 was the work of local RNS skinheads (Rstaki 1998a), and a Nazi skinhead in Voronezh reports that he and his comrades get support from the RNS and from the Russian People's Party[27] (Fishkin 1999). My general impression, nevertheless, is that the RNS is mainly a Moscow-based organization, and lacks a strong presence in the provinces.

Kasimovsky has tried to establish a loose umbrella structure with a view to coordinating the activity of various small fascist organizations under his leadership. Thus, on October 25, 1998, the founding conference took place in Moscow of the Movement "National Front," with the participation of about thirty "patriotic, national-socialist, and skinhead organizations." The organizers were the RNS and the Society of Nav, a pagan sect that has close ties with the RNS (see below). After the conference, participants cemented their new unity in blood by going out together to assault "subhumans."

The RNS in Decline

The RNS has been in decline at least since the departure of Vdovin from the organization in 1997. The Arbat march of December 5, 1998 brought the RNS considerable publicity, but it may have been its swan song. In October 1998, the RNS journal *Shturmovik* was deprived of its official registration by court decision, making its production and distribution illegal. Some of its distributors were arrested. Moreover, to ensure that *Shturmovik* really did cease publication, the Federal Security Service forcibly confiscated the group's printing press. At the same time, as we have seen, Kasimovsky faced prosecution for inciting ethnic hatred, although he was never arrested. In early 1999 the RNS displayed on its website a revived electronic version of *Shturmovik*, but it was unable to sustain the project. It was announced that the organization had decided to go "underground," where its members would live and fight as guerrillas. It was also decided to change the name of the organization to "the Russian National-Socialist Party," and to create a new journal to be called *Armageddon* (Likhachev 1999). It does not, however, appear that much of an underground party or fighting force has in fact been established: from the rudimentary new website (rnsp.wpww.com) we learn that preparations to release the new journal are still underway. Whether Kasimovsky will be able to reconstitute his organization, and on what basis, remains to be seen.

The RNS (RNSP) may or may not qualify as ideologically the most extreme of the fascist organizations that we have so far considered. It is, however, certainly the most violent. As such, it possesses an undoubted appeal for the most violent section of discontented Russian youth, although by the same token it alienates large parts of the broader society. The RNS is, in this respect, in a position similar to that of the NBP. Of course, the two organizations appeal to somewhat different types of youngster. The typical *natsbol*, while by no means averse to violence in principle, prefers a more imaginative kind of hooliganism: he does, after all, have some cultural and intellectual pretensions. The RNS skinhead or stormtrooper, in contrast, is likely to be a less sophisticated character who seeks an outlet for his frustrations in pure and simple aggression.

The open and uninhibited violence of the RNS brought in a stream of recruits, but may also have proven the organization's undoing. Has the RNS been too violent for its own good, provoking even the weak, corrupt, and indolent post-Soviet state for once to effective counteraction? Or was Kasimovsky's mistake not that he was excessively violent, but that he used violence prematurely?

Vladimir Osipov and the Union "Christian Rebirth"

Vladimir Osipov

Vladimir Osipov was born on August 9, 1938 in the town of Slantsy in Leningrad Province.[28] His mother was from a local village, and his father an army officer from Pskov Province. During the war Vladimir lived in evacuation in Saratov Province. In 1955 he entered the history faculty of Moscow State University, but was expelled in 1959 after speaking out in defense of a fellow student who had been arrested, and had to complete his studies at the Moscow Pedagogical Institute on an extramural basis. In 1960 he started work as a schoolteacher.

Osipov's career as a teacher, however, was soon to be cut short. In 1958, young people began to gather by the monument to Mayakovsky[29] in Moscow for literary readings that were not sanctioned or controlled by the authorities. Osipov was a frequent participant in these gatherings. At one such gathering in April 1961, he tried to protect a poet whom the KGB was trying to arrest, and as a result got arrested himself and spent five days in jail. With a view to suppressing the seditious gatherings, the KGB arrested four of the individuals associated with them in October 1961. Osipov was one of the four. The charge was absurd—conspiracy to assassinate Soviet leader Nikita Khrushchev. In February 1962, Osipov was tried and sentenced to seven years, which he served in a labor camp for political prisoners in Mordovia.

In camp, Osipov happened to meet and come under the influence of members of an underground organization of liberal Slavophile orientation: the All-Russian Social-Christian Union for the Liberation of the People. Over time he came to share their outlook. Osipov was probably not a self-conscious political dissident at the beginning of his sentence, but he certainly was on his release. He was allowed to settle in the town of Alexandrov in Vladimir Province, where he worked as a loader and a fireman.

In 1971, with the help of some other nationalist dissidents, Osipov began producing a substantial samizdat journal called *Veche*.[30] Nine issues, totalling about 2,000 pages, appeared in the course of the next three years. The first samizdat publication of Slavophile orientation, *Veche* contained articles of a high professional standard on historical, literary, economic, ecological, and architectural as well as political issues (Yanov 1978, p. 63). However, there emerged ideological differences between Osipov, still at this point a liberal nationalist, and his more chauvinistic collaborators. These differences led to a split in the editorial group: Osipov abandoned *Veche* to his opponents and launched a new journal *Zemlia* [Land], but managed to produce only two issues before being arrested again in November 1974. In court he did not admit guilt, and was sentenced for anti-Soviet propaganda to eight years in a strict regime camp. He served the entire sentence.

In 1982 Osipov went to live in the town of Tarus in Kaluga Province, where he worked as a supply expediter. In 1987, with the advent of perestroika, he resumed publication of *Zemlia*. He also took advantage of the new opportunity that had arisen to form a legal organization, becoming in July 1988 chairman of an initiative group "for the spiritual and biological salvation of the people." In December 1988, the initiative group was reconstituted as the Christian-Patriotic Union (CPU). But Osipov's new associates in the CPU leadership, like his old collaborators on the editorial board of *Veche*, regarded him as too liberal, and in June 1989 his rival, Yevgeny Pashnin, another former political prisoner who held the post of Secretary of the CPU, declared that he had been expelled from the organization for "pro-Zionist activity."

At this period Osipov found himself in the remarkable position of belonging simultaneously to both of the mutually hostile "democratic" and "patriotic" camps.[31] There were many in each camp who held him in high respect, but there were also many in each camp who regarded him with suspicion on account of his ties with the other camp. He took a brief interest in the West European Christian Democrats, establishing tentative contact in October 1989 with the Christian Democratic International.

At the Second Congress of the CPU in January 1990, Osipov's supporters won the upper hand. Osipov was again acknowledged as leader, and the organization received what remains its name today—the Union "Christian Rebirth" (UCR). Nevertheless, there remained ideological differences within the organization: it appears, in particular, that Osipov's deputies, Nikolai Lyzlov and Vyacheslav Demin, held views more extreme than those of Osipov himself. Any such differences as there might have been, however, did not this time give rise to a split. Instead, Osipov adapted his attitudes to those of his comrades. He took part in the defense of the parliament during the attempted hard-line coup against Gorbachev in August 1991, but thereafter increasingly distanced himself from the "democrats," losing his special dual identity as a "patriot-democrat." From October 1992 until April 1994, he even sat alongside leading communists on the Political Council of the National Salvation Front, though at the same time he criticized them in the pages of the "patriotic" press.

In late 1994, the UCR in effect committed organizational suicide when Osipov and its other leaders joined Ivanov-Sukharevsky's People's National Party. This move might be regarded as the culmination of Osipov's sad drift from liberal nationalism to fascism.[32] In 1995, Osipov extricated himself from the PNP and set about rebuilding his own organization. The UCR still makes its presence known. On March 23, 2000, Osipov led a demonstration of about fifty UCR members and supporters outside the Ukrainian Embassy in Moscow in protest against the "anti-Russian" policies of the Ukrainian government, and demanding that Russia impose strict economic sanctions against Ukraine (Nedumov 2000).[33]

Ideology of the Union "Christian Rebirth"

Many Russian nationalist organizations profess, with varying degrees of sincerity, their allegiance to Christian Orthodoxy, but in most cases religion is subordinated to the interests of politics. There is, however, a category of Orthodox Church–oriented organizations for which religion is the primary concern, and politics is placed in the service of religious goals. It is to this category that the Union "Christian Rebirth" (UCR) belongs.[34] Only with reluctance, in fact, does the UCR recognize itself as a political rather than a religious organization: "Russia needs not ideology but faith, not politics but spirituality."

A truly Orthodox society requires a corresponding change in the political order—namely, the reinauguration of a truly Orthodox autocracy. The UCR proclaims its loyalty to the pledge that the Assembly of the Lands [*zemskii sobor*] made in 1613 to enthrone Mikhail Romanov and his heirs. "Relying on God's mercy to forgive the sin of regicide," the UCR calls for the convening of a new all-Russian Assembly of the Lands to restore the legitimate form of Russian statehood, an Orthodox autocratic monarchy headed by the Romanov dynasty. This program is less backward-looking than it may seem, for Osipov proposes that the legal basis of the revived tsarist order be the "Manifesto" that Tsar Nicholas II promulgated on October 17, 1905. Autocracy, in other words, is to be tempered by a small dose of constitutionality and parliamentarism.

The UCR acknowledges its debt to the Black Hundreds tradition, and considers itself the successor to the prerevolutionary Union of the Russian People (URP). One of its two journals, *Zemshchina*, founded in 1990, was accordingly given the same name as the journal published by the URP between 1905 and 1917.

The UCR devotes a large part of its attention to issues concerning the Russian Orthodox Church, invariably taking the side of the most conservative or reactionary forces within the Orthodox Church.[35] It opposes all attempts to form independent national Orthodox churches in Ukraine and the other post-Soviet states, pronounces anathemas against Lenin and other enemies of God, and denounces ecumenism, renewalism, modernism, Tolstoyanism, and—above all—the "Judaizing heresy." It exposes the "truth" about Jewish ritual murder, satanic cults, and the Jewish world conspiracy revealed in *The Protocols of the Elders of Zion*. And it works "to prepare the Christian world for the struggle against the coming Antichrist," whose kingdom is identified with the "united world state that the anti-God forces are striving to create" (Verkhovskii and Pribylovskii 1966, p. 168).

During most of its existence, the UCR has been reactionary rather than truly fascist, seeking not a new order but merely to return to the late tsarist period. However, for a brief period in 1994 and 1995, when the UCR was closely involved with the PNP, its ideology did temporarily acquire racialist features more typical of classical fascism. The attempt was made to combine Orthodoxy and racialism in a "racial theory of Orthodoxy."

The symbols used by the UCR are the black and golden banner of tsarist Russia and a cross bearing the inscription: "God, Russia, Tsar."

The UCR's Activities

Activities of the UCR are rather conventional in character. It "takes an active part in Church and public life, distributes Orthodox literature, holds lectures, forms local communities, and organizes summer camps for children" (Verkhovskii and Pribylovskii 1996, p. 167). Occasional public meetings and demonstrations do not attract large numbers of people. Two journals are published: *Zemlia* for external propaganda and *Zemshchina* for internal use. The UCR is prepared to cooperate only with other Orthodox organizations.

In 1990, several UCR members stood as candidates for election to the Congress of People's Deputies of the Russian Federation. None were elected as people's deputies, but four other members did succeed at the local level: two were elected to district councils and two to the Moscow Soviet. The UCR has not directly contested elections in recent years, being unable to collect the required signatures. In the Duma elections of December 1999, the organization supported the Movement of Patriotic Forces—Russian Cause of Alexander Bazhenov, which won 0.17 percent of the vote (Mikhailovskaia 2000).

The UCR and the Union of Orthodox Brotherhoods

The UCR tries to function both as a political party and as an "Orthodox brotherhood" exerting influence within the Russian Orthodox Church. As such, it formerly played a very active role as a constituent member of the Union of Orthodox Brotherhoods (UOB), the most important of the organizations that represent fundamentalist opinion inside the Orthodox Church.[36] The UCR was instrumental in politicizing the UOB, which was non-political at the time of its foundation in 1990, by providing a link between the religious fundamentalism of the UOB and "patriotic" politics. This process was interrupted in June 1994 when the UOB, under pressure from a patriarchate that sought to constrain the politicization of Church life, expelled twenty brotherhoods, the UCR among them, that were considered too "political." The UOB was not, however, fully or permanently depoliticized, and it continues to occupy a significant place in Church life (Verkhovskii and Pribylovskii 1997, pp. 19–20).

Pagan Organizations

I have already noted the strong interest in pre-Christian pagan beliefs that one finds among members of some fascist organizations, the People's National Party providing perhaps the clearest example. But in those organizations that we have examined so far, paganism is not acknowledged as part of the official ideology, which either—most commonly—pays obeisance to Christian Orthodoxy or (in a few cases, such as the NRPR) is neutral on the question of religion. There do, however, exist a number of fascist organizations that proudly proclaim ideologies drawing on old pagan ideas, while denouncing Christianity as an alien and harmful creed imposed on Russia by the Jews. These organizations in many ways resemble non-pagan fascist organizations, but they have specific features—rituals and activities as well as ideas—of their own. For example, there is a form of combat training known as Slav-Gorets wrestling, invented by Alexander Belov, that is characteristic of pagan fascists; in 1994 there were reported to be fifty Slav-Gorets wrestling clubs in various cities (Shnirelman 1998b, p. 3).

The largest of the pagan fascist organizations is the Union of Veneds, which was founded by Viktor Bezverkhy. (The ancient Veneds were supposedly the true ancestors of the Russians.) It has about 300 members in various parts of Russia, and publishes a monthly periodical with a print run of 1,000 to 2,000. Another pagan fascist group is the Russian National Liberation Movement of Alexander Aratov. In this section I examine a Moscow-based pagan fascist organization created by Ilya Lazarenko, the Society of Nav.[37]

Ilya Lazarenko and the Society of Nav

Ilya Lazarenko was born on June 28, 1973 in Moscow.[38] In 1990, while still at school, he joined a small *Pamyat* splinter group, the Russian Gathering *Pamyat* of the taxi-driver Igor Shcheglov. In 1991, he entered the Moscow State Juridical Academy, from which he was later expelled. At this time he belonged to Osipov's organization, but left the UCR toward the end of 1991 after deciding that he was a fascist rather than a monarchist.

In November 1991, together with Alexei Shiropayev, Lazarenko founded the Union of Russian Youth. In October 1992, there appeared the journal of this organization, *Nash marsh* [Our March], the contents of which reflected the strong influence of Italian fascism.[39] The name of the group was changed in 1993 to the Front for National-Revolutionary Action, and in October 1994 changed again to the Party "National Front" (PNF). The activities of the organization included a demonstration held on March 22, 1994 at the South African Embassy in support of that country's white population. In the spring of 1995, the PNF merged with Alexander Fyodorov's Party of Russian Nationalists, becoming the latter's Moscow branch, but in August 1995 reestablished its separate existence.

The ideology of the PNF was fascist in the classical sense. It looked forward to a "Great National-Socialist Russian Empire" with a corporatist political system headed by a national dictatorship. The faith of the Empire would be Orthodoxy, but an agnostic position was taken regarding when and whether the monarchy would be restored (Verkhovskii and Pribylovskii 1996, pp. 48–49).

The PNF, however, soon went into rapid decline. Many members were lost to Fyodorov's party, while others joined the PNP or the RNS. Lazarenko therefore resolved to consolidate what remained of his political organization by founding "a military-spiritual occult brotherhood" to be called the Society of Nav. Several other names are also used to refer to the sect: the Church of Nav, the Sacred Church of the White Race, and the Russian Ku Klux Klan. The Society of Nav was inaugurated in 1996. The date chosen for this event was April 21, with a view to commemorating Hitler's birthday. The new religious organization, however, was intended to supplement rather than replace the existing political party, although both have the same leader and the same members. On February 14, 1998, for example, the PNF staged a rally at the United States Embassy under the stirring slogan: "Freedom for Texas!"[40]

The Society of Nav: Ideology and Symbolism

Many Russian pagans, such as the members of the Union of Veneds, profess to believe in the gods that the Slavic tribes worshipped before they adopted Christianity, especially Perun, god of storms, thunder, and lightning, and Svarog, god of fire and the sun (Verkhovskii and Pribylovskii 1996, p. 172; Voloshina and Astapov 1996, ch. 4). The members of the Society of Nav despise such "primitive peasant cults" for having "no serious occult-magical content or coherent theology."[41] They regard themselves not as "pagans" but as Ariosophists, and pay homage to the supreme deity Nav, the "father-of-all" [*vse-otets*]. They also revere the "Shining Gods" and the avatars—earthly incarnations of deities in Hindu mythology—who constitute a divine hierarchy under Nav.

In the cosmology accepted by Jews, Christians, and Moslems, the material universe was created out of the primeval void by a god known as Jehovah, which is an anglicized variant of the Hebrew Yahveh ["I Am Who I Am"]. Later, a subordinate being, an angel of Jehovah's called Satan or Lucifer, rebelled against him and was cast out, henceforth becoming the lord of hell and the master of the evil forces of the universe. The Ariosophist cosmology possesses a similar Manichean structure, but an intriguing twist has been added. Jehovah, also called Yav, is identified with the Demiurge, the creator of the material universe in Platonic and Gnostic philosophy, but is subordinate to a greater deity, Nav. Prior to the creation of the material universe, there existed not just a void, but a perfect, self-sufficient, and purely spiritual universe ruled over by Nav. But the "criminal" Jehovah somehow captured the energies of Nav's universe, and used them to create the material universe which was imperfect and therefore subject to the disease of progressive corruption and degradation. Thus, the role of the good and rightful supreme god is taken by Nav, while Jehovah takes on the role of the rebellious and malicious angel that Jews, Christians, and Moslems associate with Satan.

To combat the disease unleashed by Jehovah's crime, Nav created a race of people, the Aryans or Whites, who would carry his spirit into the material universe. For their earthly homeland he gave the Aryans a big island near the North Pole called Hyperborea. Later the Aryans migrated south to Eurasia, "taking with them their high culture, and founded there all known civilizations, but racial mixing and spiritual decline have brought them to their present condition, their native Gods forgotten and their race dying." A crucial role in the Aryans' downfall was played by the plague of Judeo-Christianity, cunningly invented to break their magical tie with the Aryan gods, to silence "the voice of spirit, blood, and soil," to bring about their moral degeneration, and to enslave them spiritually to Jehovah.[42]

What then are the White or Aryan peoples to do? They must recognize themselves as part of the divine hierarchy and return to the faith of their ancestors, the Hyperborean Nordic cult of Ariosophy. They must set themselves "morally higher than the Adamite, slave of Jehovah" by means of "mutual aid and self-sacrifice, love for order and hierarchy, mutual respect, pride, love of honor, lack of pity or fear, irreconcilability to enemies, and loyalty to brothers." They must mend the broken magical ties that once united them with the gods, thereby arousing the gods from their slumber. In this mission they may avail themselves of the help of avatars such as Vodan (alias Veles), "bringer of the runes and runic magic, a mighty weapon in the hands of the Aryans." For while they may be captive to Jehovah, the Aryans have "a spirit that belongs to another universe," giving them "the ability to transform the material and spiritual worlds and throw down a challenge to the demiurgic forces." And when the epoch of the restoration of the ancient cult dawns, the Shining Gods, awakened, will prepare themselves for the Final Battle against Jehovah, thereby concluding the current cycle of existence.

The political aspect of the ideology of the Society of Nav, as one might expect, coincides in most respects with the ideology of its political parent and sister organization, the PNF. One notices, however, that specifically Russian nationalism is now overshadowed by a generic White or Aryan racism. The Russian Empire of the future is, of course, no longer envisaged as an Orthodox realm.

The Society of Nav has two official symbols. One is the Novgorod cross, which is at the same time the symbol of the PNF. The Novgorod cross, we are told, is "a variant of the Celtic cross, used by the Slavo-Russians since ancient times. [It] has a multidimensional mystical meaning, symbolizing at the political level the unity of the Russian Nation and White Humanity." The cross is evidently not considered a Christian symbol. The other symbol is for internal use only, and is presumably kept secret from outsiders. Other symbols are also displayed on the group's website—an encircled swastika and a twin-headed eagle capped by a red orb. The mottoes of the Society of Nav are "Will, Blood, Order" and *Igne Natura Renovatur Integra* [By the Fire of Nature Is the Universe Renewed].

The Society of Nav: Activities

Recruits to the Society of Nav must "belong to the White Race, observe Aryan moral norms, and have a good self-image." Participation both in political actions and in religious rituals is compulsory. "Excessive" consumption of alcohol is forbidden, as are any use of narcotics and cultural entertainments of a non-Aryan nature. Instead, members read the Book of Nav, entitled *The White Stone.* Within the group there also exist inner brotherhoods called "Clans of Nav," recruits to which have to satisfy even stricter requirements. What these requirements are exactly is not made clear, except for the stipulation that clansmen must regularly attend clan seminars.

Rituals and "holy day mysteries" are conducted in accordance with a regular schedule with a view to restoring ties with the Aryan gods. There is an annual cycle consisting of four solar and four lunar festivals. In addition, magical rituals are used for specific purposes. Rituals usually take place in private, but occasionally the Society of Nav organizes public rituals. The first such public ritual was staged at Dyakov on September 29, 1996; the celebrants, we are told, were attacked by police.

Some further insight into Society of Nav rituals may be acquired by studying the seven photographs that are displayed on its website. All but one of the photographs show rituals in progress in a wintry forest setting. The celebrants are mostly attired in the sinister white robes and tall black conical hoods of the Ku Klux Klan, holding aloft poles topped by lighted torches. (One cannot help but wonder whether the ceremonies have been responsible for any forest fires.) In one of the scenes, twenty or so figures in military camouflage gear are gathered in a forest clearing; five of them are holding flags adorned with various abstract patterns in black and white. In another photograph we see two men, naked from the waist up, presumably about to engage in Slav-Gorets wrestling. One scene is set indoors in a chamber prepared for ritual use. A fighter is being blessed by a priest clad in black robe and headdress, orange flaps hanging from his arms.

9

Comparative Overview of Fascist Organizations

This chapter offers a comparative overview of the fascist, semi-fascist, and near-fascist organizations that have been described in the preceding four chapters, focusing on the most significant features of their structure, activity, and ideology.[1] The overview will help us to clarify the crucial choices, dilemmas, and constraints facing those who seek to create and build up fascist movements in post-Soviet Russia.

Organizational Structure

In Russia as elsewhere, fascist movements, to a much greater extent than political movements of other kinds, revolve around a single leader, and they are widely associated with his person. (More rarely, there may for a time be two important leaders, but one of them can be expected to emerge as the supreme leader.) The success of the movement is in large degree determined by the charisma and practical judgment of that leader, and on his abilities as an organizer, writer, orator, and fund-raiser. Barkashov's bureaucratic grayness was a liability to the RNU, as Ivanov-Sukharevsky's tendency to hysteria is to the PNP. Moreover, the leader must be able to remain active continuously over a long period: his movement is likely to fall to pieces should he be removed from the scene for any length of time, as Lysenko for one discovered. And if he is to avoid debilitating splits, he must prevent significant challenges to his authority on the part of rivals within the organization. This personal factor inevitably condemns the great majority of fascist movements to failure sooner or later, although it is always possible that a new leader will prove exceptionally capable and charismatic.

A related structural problem is exacerbated by Russia's huge size: the role to be assigned to regional leaders. Ideally, the supreme leader wants to have regional leaders who are both strong and loyal—that is, men who accept his own supremacy without question, but who are also capable of taking the initiative on their own in response to local circumstances. Limonov, for instance, sets these requirements explicitly. In practice, of course, reliable loyalists tend to lack initiative, while strong subordinates are difficult to control.

Activities and Strategy

The most salient distinction in terms of activities and strategy is that between organizations that are wholly or predominantly military in character, like the RNU and the RNS, and those that are wholly or predominantly political, like the LDPR, the NBP, the PNP, and the two NRPRs. The former place their main emphasis on combat training, the latter on propaganda and (to varying degrees) electoral campaigning. The distinction is not watertight, because a number of political organizations have paramilitary auxiliaries, such as Zhirinovsky's Falcons and Lysenko's (later Belyaev's) Russian National Legion.

It would be mistaken to assume that predominantly military organizations are necessarily committed to coming to power by military means, or predominantly political organizations by political means. For example, the NBP devotes little if any attention to combat training despite the fact that Limonov envisages coming to power as a result of insurrection. It is simply that his first priority is to train "commissars" rather than fighters. The choice of activities by the leaders of fascist organizations is more a matter of immediate tactics and opportunities than of long-term strategy. Their view generally seems to be that the conquest of power is likely to require the use of both political and military means. Many of them would emphasize as well the need for psychic, occult, or religious means (returning to God, mobilizing magical energies, awakening the gods, and so on).

Ideological Dilemmas

Those who elaborate the ideologies of fascist organizations face several difficult and interrelated dilemmas. The most important of these dilemmas are the following:

1. How are the ethnic and the imperial components of Russian nationalism to be balanced and reconciled?
2. Who are to be named the most dangerous internal and external enemies of Russia and the Russians?

3. What attitude is to be taken toward each of the three major periods of Russia's past: the pre-Christian period, the period of Christian tsarism, and the Soviet period?
4. What attitude is to be taken toward classical European (primarily Italian and German) fascism?

Ethnic and Imperial Nationalism

There is an ineradicable tension between the ethnic and the imperial components of Russian nationalism. The imperatives of maintaining or restoring Russia as a vast multiethnic empire cannot but endanger the coherence of ethnic Russian identity, which is best cultivated in a relatively small but purely Russian Russia. Among Russian nationalists one finds some who are prepared to jeopardize ethnic Russian identity for the sake of empire (Soviet loyalists, for example), and others who are prepared to give up empire for the sake of ethnic Russian identity (in principle, Solzhenitsyn's position).[2] These alternative forms of moderation are by definition unacceptable to extreme nationalists, who are reluctant to reconcile themselves either to the dilution of Russian ethnic identity or to the permanent loss of empire.

Nevertheless, some extreme nationalists do clearly come closer than others to making a definitive choice between ethnic and imperial identity. On the one hand, we have Belyaev's repudiation of "imperial romanticism." On the other, we have the Eurasianism of the NBP, a new (or newly revived) post-Soviet ideology of empire. Dugin and Limonov very much wish to combine Eurasianism with ethnic Russian nationalism, but the result of their efforts is not very convincing. Zhirinovsky also gives ultimate priority to imperial over ethnic nationalism. There is, however, one very radical solution to this dilemma, at least in theory: the creation of a vast Eurasian empire in which the ethnic Russians are segregated from other peoples, and all political, economic, and cultural power is firmly held in ethnic Russian hands. This is the program of such fascist organizations as the RNU, the PNP, and (most rigorously) the RNS.[3]

Choosing Enemies

Just as extreme Russian nationalists find it difficult to make the choice between ethnic and imperial nationalism, so they find it difficult to decide whether Russia's most dangerous enemy is the West or the peoples and states to Russia's south (the Caucasian, Turkic, and/or Moslem worlds) and southeast (China). Most commonly, as in the ideologies of the LDPR, the RNU, and the RNS, enemies are found in the West, in the South, *and* in the East. A global perspective is more likely to lead to the identification of the West as Russia's main enemy, the Eurasianism of the NBP again providing an ideal illustration. An orientation toward Russia's immediate geographical surroundings naturally leads to a predominant focus on the South and East: here Lysenko is the most clear-cut case.

Most of the organizations that we have examined number the Jews among the enemies of Russia and the Russians. The Jews serve conveniently as both an internal and an external enemy (through their supposed control over the West), although it is difficult to make of them a truly universal enemy, as this would require a convincing demonstration of links between the Jews and the enemies to the south and east (the Moslems and the Chinese). Only two organizations have dropped the Jews from their lists of enemies: the NRPR (Lysenko), which gave overriding priority to the threat from the south, and the NBP, which decided that Jews straddle the Eurasian/Atlantic divide. Taking this step remains highly controversial in the "patriotic" milieu.

Attitude Toward Different Periods of Russia's Past

The national past is of vital importance to fascists as a source of inspiration. At the same time, as we saw in chapter 1, their approach to the past is flexible and selective, for they do not aim to restore the past in its original form, as do reactionaries, but to re-embody its values in a revolutionary new order.

But in which past does one seek inspiration? Russia has several pasts. Its recorded history consists of two major epochs, that of Soviet rule and that of Christian Orthodox tsarism.[4] Further back in time there was pre-Christian Rus, about which little is reliably known, but the pagan "patriots" think they know a lot about it, and it is the past as it lives in the contemporary "patriotic" imagination that is our concern.[5] And for some, beyond the semi-mythical epoch of pagan Rus, there lies the wholly mythical epoch of the ancestral Arctic homeland of Hyperborea.

The problem with what might appear to be an *embarras de richesses* is that there are quite sharp discontinuities in terms of social and spiritual ethos separating each epoch from the next. In orienting one's discourse toward any one epoch, it is hard to avoid alienating those who feel an attachment to the others. Many Russian fascists try to solve the problem by stressing the undoubted continuities that exist between one epoch and the next, such as the incorporation of certain pagan beliefs and attitudes into Orthodoxy and the traditionally Russian aspects of bolshevism. The most ambitious integrator of Russian history is Alexander Dugin, who draws inspiration from all four sources—Soviet Russia, the Russia of Orthodoxy and tsarism, pagan

Rus, and Hyperborea. But it is very difficult to orient oneself toward four such diverse worlds in equal measure, let alone to create a cogent and organic synthesis of them all.

For this reason, the Russian fascist movement finds itself incapable of overcoming internal divisions arising from divergent choices among the national pasts. These divisions manifest themselves in different forms. One is the division according to religious affiliation, which is a matter of especially great significance for fascists on account of its intrinsic connection with the issue of historical orientation. The "left-right" division among Russian fascist organizations is also important only because it pertains to the choice between "Red" (Soviet) and "White" (tsarist) historical loyalties: the question of the appropriate role of the state in the economy is not in itself of great interest to fascists.

The most typical stance of Russian fascist organizations on the issue of national history is a somewhat ambivalent orientation toward the epoch of Orthodox autocracy. It is in these terms that one might best characterize the attitude taken by the RNU, the PNP, and the RNS. Around this middling position it is possible to identify several "deviations" pointing in very different directions. One of these deviations is a wholehearted and consistent orientation toward Orthodoxy and tsarism, as exemplified by the religious monarchists of the UCR. A second deviation is in the direction of modern secularism, although the tie to Orthodoxy is unlikely to be completely broken. The LDPR and the NRPR may serve as examples of such semi-secular organizations. The pagan organizations represent a third deviation. A fourth is embodied in the eclectic "bolshevism" of the NBP, the only fascist organization to express openly a loyalty to the Soviet epoch of Russia's history.

How are we to explain on the one hand the orientation of most Russian fascists toward Orthodoxy and tsarism, and on the other the ambivalence of this orientation?

On the plane of political tactics, Orthodox Christian believers now constitute once again a substantial, and on the whole a traditionally minded, part of Russian society. The fascists naturally count on this part of society for much of their support. At the same time, they know that substantial parts of society remain indifferent or even hostile to Orthodoxy (or to religion in general), while many contemporary Russians are fascinated by the occult. In particular, the fascists cannot disregard the limited appeal that Orthodox piety has for many of the young people whose recruitment is their top priority. The reader may recall that one of the grievances that moved Barkashov and his followers to break away from *Pamyat* and make the transition from monarchism to fascism was Vasilyev's insistence that they memorize Christian prayers.

On the ideological plane, the Orthodox–tsarist epoch of Russia's history is the clearest and most reliable of the available sources of traditional values. The Soviet epoch is both too recent and too modern, scientific, and "anti-national" in spirit (even if far from completely so) to provide the kind of inspiration that the fascists are looking for. The pre-Christian epoch is too hazy and far off, barely visible through the mists of time. It must seem to most fascists that there is no really practical alternative to an orientation toward the Orthodox–tsarist epoch. Nevertheless, Orthodoxy is not ideal for their purposes. The patient and long-suffering submission to God's will that Orthodoxy preaches can hardly imbue Russians with the heroic and "revolutionary" spirit that is also essential to fascism. As Konstantin Leontiev discovered long ago, reconciling Christianity with the heroic ethos is a matter of extreme difficulty.

Moreover, the closeness of the historical association between Orthodoxy and autocracy threatens to deprive fascists of the flexibility they need to design and construct their new order. As we have seen from the case of the UCR, a single-minded orientation toward Orthodoxy impels people toward straightforward reactionary monarchism rather than fascism.

Given the deficiencies of the Orthodox–tsarist heritage from the fascist point of view and the difficulties entailed in trying to orient oneself to any other period of Russia's history, Russian fascists are strongly tempted to look beyond the borders of Russia for ideas and inspiration—above all, to the example of classical European fascism.

Attitude Toward Classical European Fascism

Since 1945, one of the dilemmas facing all fascists has been that of defining their relationship to the classical European fascism that arose in the interwar period. Should they take classical fascism as their model or try to start anew? This is an especially difficult problem for fascists living outside the countries in which classical fascism flourished—that is, in countries where fascism is perceived as a foreign phenomenon. It is most difficult of all for fascists living in countries that, like Russia, were occupied and devastated by the classical fascist regimes.

The basic distinction here is that between "mimetic" or imitative fascism, which strives to imitate classical fascism and re-enact its experience, and "native" fascism, which strives to produce a self-sufficient fascist practice and ideology fully rooted in the history of its own nation. Mimetic and native fascism are ideal types: contemporary fascists typically combine the two approaches, but in varying proportions.

Classifying the Russian fascist organizations that we have examined according to this criterion, we obtain an incomplete spectrum. At one end, we have in Kasimovsky's RNS an organization whose fascism is openly and wholeheartedly mimetic. The RNU represents a more typical position, also fairly close to the mimetic end of the spectrum, although an effort was made to camouflage the fact and display an appearance that was ostensibly Russian. The fascism of the NBP is likewise to a great extent mimetic. At the other end of our spectrum, we may place the PNP of Ivanov-Sukharevsky, who has worked hard to create a fascism ("Rusism") that can be perceived as authentically Russian. Inasmuch as even Ivanov-Sukharevsky has borrowed from Hitler and Mussolini, however, his "Russianness" is to some extent deceptive. Only the UCR has an ideology that may be regarded as wholly native, but it is a reactionary ideology, not a fascist one.

In short, the crucial handicap and guilty secret of Russian fascism is that it is not really very Russian. For the Russian nationalists whom fascist organizations seek to attract, that is the worst of all sins.

Conclusion
Weimar Russia?

The time has come to summarize the main results of our investigation. How strong are fascist traditions, tendencies, and movements in Russia today?

Fascist Traditions

Russia may be said to inherit fascist traditions, but they are very weak ones by comparison with those of Germany, Italy, or France. Of the numerous political philosophers of nineteenth-century Russia, only Konstantin Leontiev can reasonably be regarded as a precursor of fascism. The Black Hundreds were a proto-fascist movement, but their further development was interrupted by the revolutionary upheaval of 1917. Fascist parties appeared in the Russian emigration, but had no impact on the homeland. A certain fascist potential can be discerned in the last phase of Stalinism. All in all, fascism does not belong to the mainstream of Russian political or cultural tradition.

Fascist Tendencies

Significant fascist tendencies exist within two of the most important institutions of contemporary Russia—namely, the Communist Party of the Russian Federation (CPRF) and the Russian Orthodox Church (ROC).

One of the two top leaders of the CPRF, Gennady Zyuganov, propagates an ideology that while not outright fascist does possess some fascist features. Prospects for the elimination of fascist tendencies in the CPRF are poor, although they may be moderated under the influence of Valentin Kuptsov and his intraparty grouping.

The ROC has a strong fundamentalist and reactionary wing that, like the

Zyuganovite grouping in the CPRF, is not fascist but does share common ground with fascism. The open politicization of this wing of the Orthodox Church is held in check by the current patriarch, but there is no guarantee that this will continue to be the case in the future.

A certain fascist potential exists in Russia's neo-pagan movement, in the Cossack revival movement, and in some of the many subcultures to be found among Russian youth.

Fascist Movements

Vladimir Zhirinovsky's Liberal-Democratic Party of Russia (LDPR) is now in rapid decline, but for the time being it remains the second largest mass party in the country (after the CPRF). The ideological position of Zhirinovsky is ambiguous, veering between fascism and national liberalism, while his party contains both a fascist and a national liberal wing. The possible collapse of the LDPR would release a large number of fascists, many of whom might be expected to strengthen the ranks of existing fascist organizations or to create new ones.

The largest organization with an unambiguously fascist ideology was, until its recent split, the Russian National Unity of Alexander Barkashov. The RNU posed a significant threat by virtue of its relatively large size (20,000 "fighters" by conservative estimate), its highly militarized character, its success in usurping state functions in the areas of policing and predraft military training, and its possession of regional strongholds, such as the Stavropol Territory and Voronezh Province, where it forged close ties with local elites. However, the RNU was plagued by poor leadership, lacked broad public support in the country as a whole, and was vulnerable to changes in the attitude toward it of the local elites upon which it was totally dependent.

Besides the successor organizations to the RNU, the largest fascist organization is now Eduard Limonov's National-Bolshevik Party (NBP). The NBP has between 6,000 and 7,000 members and is growing at a fairly rapid rate. It is much less militarized than the RNU, and it has a more intelligent and imaginative leadership capable of attracting not only "marginals," but also more educated sections of Russian youth, such as students and young engineers. The left-fascist ideology of the NBP enables it to take advantage of both social and ethnic discontent.

Fascist skinheads are also quite numerous in Russia. There are by now perhaps 15,000 of them. They are also extremely violent. The skinheads are not an effectively organized force, but they provide a pool of potential recruits for more political fascist organizations.

Overall Assessment

Our investigation does not permit us to assess the threat posed by Russian fascism with any great degree of precision. Too much remains unclear. As we saw in chapter 6, much uncertainty has surrounded even such an apparently simple question as the true membership of the RNU. Very little is reliably known about the crucial issue of who funds fascist organizations—and why. The public reaction (or lack of it) to fascist activity needs to be better understood. Further research, and research of different kinds, is clearly needed.

Nevertheless, the evidence that has been presented in this book should suffice for the rejection of two extreme, though quite widely held, points of view. On the one hand, fascism in Russia should not be dismissed out of hand as a marginal current with negligible political prospects.[1] On the other hand, no sign is yet visible of that "fairly large, united, and powerful fascist movement on the march" that, as I argued in the introduction, the analogy with Weimar Germany might have led us to expect in Russia by this time. The situation is not remotely comparable with that in Germany in the late 1920s. There is no significant near-term danger of a fascist conquest of power.

A similar conclusion can be drawn concerning the degree to which contemporary Russian society is susceptible to fascism. The time is long past when it could reasonably be assumed that bitter historical experience had provided Russia with a permanent and reliable immunity against fascism. This does not, however, mean that historical experience has proven to be of no value at all. It is an important factor underlying the considerable capacity of Russian society, both at the level of high politics and at the grassroots, to resist and counteract the rise of fascism. Some examples of this capacity for resistance and counteraction have been mentioned in this book.

The possibility of a fascist conquest of power in Russia in the longer term is not completely excluded. But to weigh up this possibility, one needs to do much more than assess the current strength of fascist traditions, tendencies, and movements, which was the task undertaken in this investigation. One needs to tackle more difficult tasks, above all those of comprehending the complex social, economic, and political reality that is contemporary Russia and of projecting how that reality is likely to develop further in the years and decades ahead.

Afterword

This afterword serves two purposes.

First, I offer some remarks concerning the implications that the advent of Vladimir Putin to the presidency may have for the prospects of Russian fascism. The investigation in this book has drawn almost exclusively on evidence pertaining to the period of Boris Yeltsin's presidency, and further research will be needed to ascertain to what extent the book's conclusions continue to hold in the Putin era. However, some indications of what the future may bring are already apparent.

Second, I discuss a late development of the utmost importance—a split that took place in September 2000 within Russia's largest fascist organization, the Russian National Unity. I suggest also a possible connection between the split in the RNU and the coming to power of Vladimir Putin.

Putin and Russian Fascism

In April 2000, President Putin visited Krasnodar and had a private meeting with Nikolai Kondratenko, governor of the Krasnodar Territory (see chapter 6). Asked after the meeting what he had thought of Kondratenko, Putin is reported to have replied: "The views of Nikolai Ignatovich [Kondratenko] are a little unusual. But everyone has the right to his own opinion." Subsequently Putin awarded Kondratenko a medal for service to the Motherland. One press commentator, inferring plausibly enough that Kondratenko had lectured Putin on his pet subject, the Jewish world conspiracy, counterposed Putin's amused tolerance with Moscow mayor Yuri Luzhkov's description of the Krasnodar governor as a "Neanderthal" (Deich 2000).

This has not been the only incident to arouse the concern of observers. It has been pointed out, for example, that Alexander Prokhanov, editor of the Russian nationalist newspaper *Zavtra*, was among those invited to a meeting in August 2000 between Putin and the editors of major national newspapers (Butkevich 2000).

There does not seem to be sufficient evidence to suspect Putin of any special ties with extreme nationalists, but it is reasonable to conclude that he does not regard them as beyond the pale and that he sees no necessity for firm action against fascist organizations of the kind undertaken by Luzhkov in Moscow. We may therefore expect fascists to remain part of the Russian political scene. It appears that Putin aims to include extreme nationalists (though not necessarily all of them) within the broad patriotic national consensus that he is trying to build.

If this is indeed Putin's intention, then he will find plenty of extreme nationalists willing to lend him their support. In the run-up to the presidential elections of March 26, 2000, several leading members of nationalist organizations, including Sergei Baburin (ROS), Yuri Belyaev (NRPR), Nikolai Lysenko (ex-NRPR), and Vladimir Popov (editor of the PNP periodical *Era Rossii*), backed Putin with various degrees of enthusiasm. They were moved to do so by admiration of Putin's uncompromising stand on Chechnya, by the expectation or hope that he would "free Russia from Jewish domination" and pursue the goals of Russian nationalism, or simply—in Lysenko's words—"because there is no alternative now in Russia" (Pribylovskii 2000).[1] At the same time, other extreme nationalist leaders, including Alexander Barkashov (RNU), Eduard Limonov (NBP), and Alexander Ivanov-Sukharevsky (PNP), refused to put their trust in Putin and called upon their supporters either to boycott the elections or to vote against all candidates (Akopov 2000).

The Split in the RNU

On September 12, 2000, Alexander Barkashov issued a communiqué in the name of the Central Council of the RNU in which he accused the RNU's regional coordinator, Oleg Kassin, of conducting a campaign to discredit him; denounced Kassin as a traitor; and excluded him from the ranks of the RNU forever.[2] In order to preclude the future occurrence of such treason, Barkashov called upon his comrades-in-arms to take a personal oath of loyalty to himself and proposed that the organization be renamed "Barkashov's Guard."

The attempt to dispose of a rival in this way had the contrary effect of triggering an internal coup against Barkashov himself. The very next day, September 13, there appeared a "Declaration of Regional Organizations of the Movement 'Russian National Unity.'" Although all but one of the twelve signatories of this document were leaders of regional RNU organizations, the lead signatory was a member of the central leadership—namely, Kassin.

The signatories declared their lack of confidence in the ability of Barkashov to provide adequate leadership of the movement, and stated their intention to establish as quickly as possible a new sociopolitical movement based on the RNU's active regional organizations.

On September 21–22, a plenary meeting of the Central Council, convened by Kassin, excluded Barkashov from the RNU. Kassin explained that Barkashov's removal was necessitated by his passivity and by his "complete moral and physical degeneration." The RNU newspaper had stopped appearing; no Congress had been convened for three years; Barkashov was continually drunk; and in a fit of rage he had shot up and burned an icon of the Virgin Mother. Barkashov had been leading the RNU to its destruction, thereby playing into the hands of Russia's enemies. On October 13, Kassin and several of the regional RNU leaders announced the creation of a new organization, to be called "Russian Rebirth" [*Russkoe vozrozhdenie*].

It was soon to become clear, however, that at least one important regional RNU organization was unwilling to follow the lead of either Barkashov or Kassin. On September 26, the Council of the Voronezh organization issued a declaration critical of both men. It was accompanied by a communiqué over the name of the leader of the Voronezh organization, Mikhail Lalochkin, in which he called for a new central leadership to be established by an All-Russian Council of Commanders that he proposed to convene on October 15.[3] Given the great prestige that the Voronezh organization has long enjoyed within the RNU and the horizontal ties that its tutelage of weaker regional organizations (such as the St. Petersburg RNU) has fostered, we can be sure that at least a few regional RNU leaders will respond to Lalochkin's initiative, although others will recognize Kassin's authority. The Stavropol organization, the RNU's stronghold in the south, is apparently with Kassin.

Thus, the RNU is currently in the process of breaking up into three—or possibly more than three—fragments. There will be "Russian Rebirth," controlled from Moscow by Kassin and his supporters from the old Central Council, Lalochkin's interregional network with its hub in Voronezh, and possibly a rump group of Barkashov loyalists. Considering the widespread disillusionment with Barkashov among RNU members, "Barkashov's Guard" will doubtless be the weakest of these three successor organizations. The regional organizations may end up about equally divided between Kassin and Lalochkin. It is also conceivable that neither Kassin nor Lalochkin will succeed in restoring effective centralized control of the movement. In that case, the stronger regional organizations will continue to operate on an autonomous basis, while the weaker ones will collapse or be absorbed by other fascist organizations.

Ideological differences among the successor organizations are at this stage rather difficult to discern, and may not be very substantial. The declaration of the Voronezh organization appeals to "other viable regional branches of the RNU that conduct their work exclusively in the interests of the Russian nation and on the basis of an Orthodox worldview"—a reaction perhaps against Barkashov's inclination toward the occult. A striking feature of the declaration issued by Kassin's group is an opening reference to "a number of positive changes that have recently occurred in the political life and leadership of the country." In this connection we may note that Barkashov's communiqué accuses Kassin of seeking to pander to unnamed "political and financial forces that are ready to give big money if the RNU removes Barkashov, the emblem, and the greeting." This is admittedly very little to go on, but it does lead me to suspect that the goal of Kassin's maneuvers may be a mutually supportive and advantageous modus vivendi between a revamped and less blatantly fascist RNU and the Putin administration.

Notes

Notes to the Introduction

1. I discuss the demographic decline in Russia and the fear of national extinction, and also the problem of the oligarchs and anti-Semitism, in Shenfield (2000). The role of Jewish bankers in Weimar Germany is discussed in Feldman (1995).

2. This argument has been developed by Stephen E. Hanson and Jeffrey S. Kopstein in debate with myself (Hanson and Kopstein 1997; Shenfield 1998; Kopstein and Hanson 1998).

3. This is not meant to be a full list even of the most important points of comparison. I hope to return to a more thorough examination of the strengths and weaknesses of the analogy between post-Soviet Russia and Weimar Germany in a future work.

4. The Soviet order began to fall apart at the end of the 1980s. Its final dissolution occurred in three stages: the disorganization and demoralization of the central Soviet bureaucracy as a result of the collapse of the attempted hardline putsch in August 1991, the formal abolition of the Soviet Union in December 1991, and the launching in January 1992 by the newly appointed government of Yegor Gaidar of the radical economic reform that irreversibly dismantled the central institutions of the Soviet economic system.

5. For a survey of other pertinent sources, see the Bibliographical Note at the end of the book.

6. I provide biographical sketches of the organizations' leaders, with the exception of Zhirinovsky, about whom a number of English-language books are readily available—for instance, Kartsev (1995) and Solovyov and Klepikova (1995).

Notes to Chapter 1

1. Some political scientists, such as Juan J. Linz (Laqueur 1976, pp. 9–10), do insist on the fundamental nature of the difference between Italian fascism and German national-socialism. Some ultranationalist organizations in contemporary Russia, in particular the Russian National Unity, similarly insist that they are "national-socialist and not fascist."

2. Strictly speaking, twenty-nine writers. I count the two co-authors of one analysis as a single author.

3. I have not included any authors who are themselves fascist in orientation. Although the views of such writers are of great interest, assessing them presents special problems.

4. In a speech to foreign diplomats and journalists delivered on April 18, 1934 (Prussakov 1994, p. 13). For an excellent discussion of the antimodern and anti-Enlightenment thrust of fascist ideology, see Neocleous (1997), chapters 1 and 5.

5. Both Evola and Dugin refer to "Tradition" (with a capital T) to refer to what they believe was a unique and integral tradition common to all cultures before the dawn of historical time but later lost and fragmented, as distinct from the diverse imperfect "traditions" (with a small t) that succeeded it. For an analysis of "the world of Odysseus," see Finley (1956).

6. For Neocleous (1997), war is "the entelechy of fascism" (ch. 1).

7. "The new nationalism wants Germany's future, not the restoration of a past whose continuity is now shattered," stated Joseph Goebbels in 1931 (Griffin 1995, p. 121).

8. For a vivid example of such literature, see the pamphlet by Alexander Ivanov-Sukharevsky, leader of the People's National Party (Ivanov 1997). The reader is advised by the author of the pamphlet to take note that it was written only for Russians and only for men.

9. For two analyses of the left-wing tendency within German Nazism between 1925 and 1934, see Broszat (1966) and Nyomarkay (1972). Nyomarkay attributes less significance to the tendency than does Broszat.

10. Addressing a meeting of the SS in occupied Paris, Degrelle said: "Europe fights in Russia because it is socialist. . . . When we have put paid to communist barbarism, we shall aim at the plutocrats, for whom we are saving our last shots. . . . The war cannot end without the triumph of socialist revolution." The speech was published by the SS (Weber 1964, pp. 41–47).

11. This movement became better known as the Iron Guard, but the original name reveals its religious inspiration (Griffin 1995, p. 219). For an account of the movement, see Weber (1964, pp. 96–105).

12. The Russian People's League (Union) named after the Archangel Michael. See chapter 2.

13. Griffin has given several versions of his definition, but there are no substantive contradictions between them. The first of the versions cited here is taken from the Introduction to Griffin (1998); the second is from Cronin (1996, p. 143).

14. It may be noted in this context that when Zhirinovsky sued the former Russian foreign minister Andrei Kozyrev for calling him a fascist on television, Kozyrev defended himself in court by arguing that the views expressed in *Final Spurt to the South* were "consonant with the ideology and practice of fascism" (FBIS-SOV-95–076 Daily Report, April 19, 1995).

15. However, as Norman Finkelstein has demonstrated, close parallels can be drawn between the ideologies of European conquest and colonization, including Zionism, and the ideology of German Nazi conquest and colonization in Eastern Europe (Finkelstein 1995, pp. 88–120).

Notes to Chapter 2

1. The book contains an introduction, the text of a respectfully critical letter written to General Fadiev by Samarin, and an essay by Dmitriev.

2. At his interview with the tsar, Samarin was contrite, and the tsar, taking into account his friendship with Samarin's parents, ordered his release.

3. The mainstream Slavophile view was that universal human values did exist, and that it was Russia that best embodied them. The westernizers recognized Western Europe as the source of universal values.

4. For studies of the philosophies of history of Ranke and Fichte, see Krieger (1977) and Stine (1945). It might be added that Karl Marx followed in Hegel's footsteps, but diverged from the tradition on some points. For Marx, it is social classes rather than nations that are the main bearers of historical missions. Marx also substitutes an abstract "History" for God.

5. For a recent study of Leontiev's relation to pan-Slavism, see Kosik (1997).

6. Leontiev's attitude to Christianity was in fact a complicated and ambiguous one: he was aware of the tension between Christian morality and his aristocratic esthetics.

7. There were also various local groups of similar orientation, such as the Religious Banner-Carriers in Moscow and the Fatherland Union in St. Petersburg (Rogger 1986, p. 215).

8. For more on the political background to the emergence of the Black Hundreds, see Rogger (1986).

9. The Union of the Archangel Michael, the second largest Black Hundreds organization, had at its height about 60,000 members.

10. Johnston (1988) provides a general survey of political life among the Russian exiles in Paris between 1920 and 1945.

11. Apart from the White émigrés, there were émigrés who opposed the Bolsheviks from other standpoints, such as the followers of Kerensky, the Mensheviks, and the anarchists. These groups are not relevant to our topic.

12. An account of the Russian fascist movement in exile, focusing primarily on Manchuria, is given by Stephan (1978). Unfortunately, this book, while of interest in many ways, fails to deal adequately with the evolving ideology of the Russian fascists. The fullest available analysis of this subject, though a tendentious one, seems to be that of Prussakov and Shiropaev (1993).

13. Taken by Prussakov and Shiropaev from *Natsiia* no. 5, 1937—the periodical of the All-Russian Fascist Party. Another useful primary source is the *ABC of Fascism* edited by Rodzayevsky and reproduced in *Zvezda* (1994, pp. 191–270). Other discussions of Russian émigré fascism are those of S.V. Kuleshov in his afterword to *Zvezda* (1994, pp. 271–312) and of Anatoly Akhutin in Krakhmal'nikova (1994, pp. 87–90).

14. "We need to find here our own egotistically Russian point of view. . . . The Hitlerite point of view regarding the Jews, it seems to me, is very good for Germany. In defending his country from the approaching revolution, Hitler was obliged to constrain Jewry in iron bonds. We should have done this before the revolution. But we were able neither to constrain nor to defend" (Solonevich 1997, p. 187).

15. While a contemporary non-fascist Russian nationalist like Mikhail Nazarov tries to remove the stigma of fascism from the White movement, the

fascist publicist Alexei Shiropayev tries equally hard to claim the White movement, at least to some degree, for fascist: "The White movement did not become fascist. But there is no doubt that it bore within itself a powerful fascist impulse, deep inner proto-fascist features" (cited in Verkhovskii and Pribylovskii 1996, p. 129).

16. Savitsky himself credits the idea that "Russia by its nature represents a special world" to G.I. Tanfilev, "the patriarch of Russian geography" (Savitskii 1931, p. 51). The geopolitical and cultural concepts of the Eurasianists are discussed by Hauner (1990, pp. 60–61, 158), and by Bassin (1991, pp. 13–17). An all-sided analysis of the Eurasianist ideology does not seem to be available in English; the best account of the movement seems to be that of Shlapentokh (1997b). A stimulating critical discussion of Eurasianist ideas is that of Omel′chenko (1992).

17. "Russian culture is not only not in decline, but is on an upward line of energetic expansion. . . . Russian culture in 1932 is not weaker but stronger than ever before. The task of every Russian is to value the past of his culture, to participate creatively in its present, and to prepare for it an even greater future" (Savitskii 1997, p. 139).

18. Eurasianism had apparently had an influence on KGB officials independently of Gumilyov's mediation, as a result of the KGB surveillance of the Eurasianists in exile (Yasmann 1993, p. 25).

19. Anti-Soviet Russian émigrés have generally taken this view. See, for example, Kurganov (1961), who denies any connection between the USSR and "Russia."

20. Mikhail Agursky was a Soviet émigré who had worked in the military-industrial complex. For a full exposition of his analysis of the evolution of intraregime national-bolshevism, see Agursky (1987).

21. In its later phase, émigré national-bolshevism continued to differ from intraregime national-bolshevism, but for the opposite reason, as it now glorified the Soviet internationalism that intraregime national-bolshevism merely tolerated as a necessary evil.

22. For example, the linguist Nikolai Marr came under attack in 1950 precisely on the grounds that he had counterposed Soviet to Russian culture (Barghoorn 1956, p. 245).

23. Gennady Zyuganov, leader of today's Communist Party of the Russian Federation, has argued that if Stalin had lived a few years longer the "russianization" of Soviet state ideology would have been completed and made irreversible (Yanov 1996). See chapter 3.

24. From an interview with Yakovlev in *Izvestiia* (Iakovlev 1998). Extracts from the interview were published in English in *Transitions: Changes in Post-Communist Societies* 5, no. 8 (August 1998), p. 18.

25. The distinction between Orthodox and non-Orthodox tendencies is not in practice very clear-cut, but will do as an approximation. For studies of the main ideological tendencies within Russian nationalism in the Brezhnev period, see Yanov (1978, 1987).

26. See Yanov (1978, pp. 167, 182–83). Yanov translates this material from a book by Grigory Svirsky, another Soviet émigré (Svirskii 1974, pp. 449–50). Similar unpublished research was carried out inside the USSR by Ruth Okunova.

27. Also associated with the pamphlet, which formed part of the Library of the Club of Lovers of the History of the Fatherland, was the Military-Patriotic Literary Union *Otechestvo* [Fatherland].

28. In the summer of 1992, a group called "Black Hundred" formed around the samizdat journal of the same name produced by *Pamyat* activist Alexander Shtilmark. Attempts to "reestablish" the Union of the Russian People were undertaken in Moscow in 1991 and, more successfully, in Volgograd in 1994 (Verkhovskii and Pribylovskii 1996, pp. 73–74, 78–79).

29. The best account of the anti-Semitic campaign in the late Soviet period is that of Reznik (1996). The book by Korey (1995) contains useful information, but is very weak from the analytical point of view.

30. For a short account of Gumilyov's thought in English, see Yasmann (1993). A full book-length study is sorely needed. His central theoretical work is *Ethnogenesis and the Biosphere* (Gumilyov 1990); for an example of the way in which he applies his concepts to Russian history, see *Ancient Rus and the Great Steppe* (Gumilev 1989). Also useful is the dialogue between Gumilyov and Alexander Panchenko (Gumilev and Panchenko 1990).

31. Konstantin Dolgov's study of Leontiev's life and work, for instance, was published with a print run of 3,000. The author remarks that Leontiev is almost forgotten in Russia. Selected extracts from the writings of Leontiev, Danilevsky, and other Russian thinkers can also be found in edited collections such as Gulyga (1995) and *In Search of Its Path: Russia Between Europe and Asia* (*V poiskakh* 1997), with print runs of 25,000 and 10,000 copies, respectively.

32. The reference to Speransky, who was an adviser to Tsar Alexander I, comes in a declaration of the All-Russian Party of the Monarchist Center (Verkhovskii and Pribylovskii 1996, p. 106). The other prerevolutionary writers are mentioned in a *Pamyat* document as "great minds of Russia [that] warned us of the creeping danger of rotten liberalism" (Verkhovskii and Pribylovskii 1996, p. 118). Berdyaev and Ilyin are cited in an article by Alexei Shiropayev published in *Narodnyi stroi*, journal of the National Front (Verkhovskii and Pribylovskii 1996, p. 129).

33. It may be objected that the authors of some documents might have been influenced by writers without citing them. This is true, but it is also true that Russian nationalists may cite classical writers without being significantly influenced by them, as a mere formality—in the same way that communist writers often cite their classics. If Russian nationalists were seriously concerned with reviving an old intellectual tradition, then one would expect to find more frequent references to that tradition in their documents.

34. For accounts of the Union for the Rebirth of Russia, see Slater (1993) and Ingram (1999, ch. 5).

35. For an example of Solovyov's criticism of Russian imperialism in relation to Poland, see Solov'ev (1911, pp. 34–38).

36. Berdyaev wrote a book condemning anti-Semitism as anti-Christian (Berdiaev 1952). Solovyov also took a strong position against anti-Semitism.

37. The manual of the "Spiritual Heritage" Foundation on "the contemporary Russian idea and the State" makes reference to Danilevsky on pages 15–16, to Leontiev on page 16, to the Eurasianist Trubetskoi on pages 29 and 31, and to Gumilyov on page 30 (*Sovremennaia* 1995).

38. See also the analysis of Limonov's thinking offered by Voznesenskii (1998).

39. For further discussion of Dostoevsky's influence on contemporary Russian nationalism in general and on Gennady Zyuganov's national-communism in particular, see Scanlan (1996).

40. It was the Front for National-Revolutionary Action that published the essays on émigré fascism referred to earlier in this chapter (Prussakov and Shiropaev 1993).

Notes to Chapter 3

1. Public opinion surveys in recent years have estimated the proportion of the population that is attached to great-power values [*derzhavnost'*] variously as 21 percent, 35 percent, and 52 percent (Kutkovets and Kliamkin 1997; Popov 1998). The proportion of the population that is attracted to stronger forms of Russian nationalism is difficult to assess: it depends on the exact criteria used, but does not exceed 10 percent to 15 percent.

2. The title that Lebed chose for his memoirs is the Russian saying "[I am] offended for the great power" [*za derzhavu obidno*].

3. Sevastopol is the main base of the Black Sea Fleet in Crimea. The "glory" was won in the Crimean War (1853 to 1856).

4. The term *erefiia* is used in the literature of the People's National Party (see chapter 8). Simonsen (1996c) divides Russian nationalism into four types in accordance with two criteria: whether or not the Russian Federation is accepted as the legitimate form of Russian statehood, and whether the conception of Russian identity is primarily civic or ethnic.

5. Ingram mentions the Congress of Russian Communities as an organization that takes such a self-critical approach. He notes that the existence of an enemy conspiracy against Russia is not denied, but that its importance as a causative factor is downplayed.

6. See the discussion of Osipov and *Veche* in chapters 2 and 8. Moderate "patriots" are occasionally referred to as "demopatriots."

7. "Ideology of state patriotism" is the subtitle of the book in which Gennady Zyuganov most clearly sets out his ideology (Ziuganov 1996).

8. A favorite archfiend for Zyuganov, as he was for Stalin, is Trotsky.

9. "Democratic centralism" was likewise proclaimed to be the principle according to which the internal life of the Communist Party of the Soviet Union was organized. The CPRF leaders acknowledge that before the late 1980s only the "centralist" part of the formula was put into practice. The CPRF is supposedly run in accordance with genuine democratic centralism.

10. Left-communists call this position "capitulationism." In the context of the broader spectrum of Russian politics, it may be termed "centrist." The classification of positions given here is a simplified version of that given by Kurashvili (1994, pp. 36–39). In particular, I have glossed over Kurashvili's distinction between those leftists who wish to replace private enterprise by Soviet-style state ownership and planning and those who want ownership by self-managing work collectives to be the predominant form. To take this properly into account, we would need a fuller specification of the ideological field. For instance, a third dimension might be added corresponding to a "democracy–authoritarianism" axis.

11. The schema originates with Urban and Solovei (1997, pp. 55–59), and is retained in later Western sources (Sakwa 1998; Flikke 1999). Some Russian political scientists use this schema as well—for instance, Buzgalin (1997), although his terminology differs somewhat from that of Urban and Solovei ("social-statist" instead of "Marxist reformer," "social-imperialist" [*sotsial-derzhavnyi*] instead of "nationalist"). Kholmskaia (1998) also makes approving reference to the schema of Urban and Solovei (p. 40), but this is not the schema upon which her analysis primarily relies.

12. For a portrait of Kuptsov, see Simonsen (1997).

13. One obvious source of discrepancies among different schemas is the fact that their authors are analyzing the intraparty situation at different points in time. However, close analysis reveals that this is not the main source. The judgments of different observers diverge in important respects.

14. It was these deputies who initiated the proceedings to impeach President Boris Yeltsin. Key members of the grouping are given as Anatoly Lukyanov, Vladimir Shevelukha, Viktor Ilyukhin, Oleg Mironov, and Viktor Zorkaltsev.

15. The authors note that one important party figure, former Duma Speaker Gennady Seleznev, does not belong fully to any of these groupings, although he is inclined toward the "pragmatists."

16. Kuptsov had previously been an internationalist opponent of Zyuganovism, and even at the founding congress of the CPRF he at first spoke against "clogging up" the communist movement with nationalists. In the course of the proceedings he came to an understanding with Zyuganov, whose position he then adopted, at least verbally. Subsequently, he established a firm partnership with Zyuganov, turning against former fellow internationalists such as Krasnitsky and Semago (Tarasov, Cherkasov, and Shavshukova 1997, pp. 167–68). Kuptsov has, however, always distanced himself somewhat from Zyuganov's ideology, without openly criticizing it.

17. The course of the CPRF during the 1990s can be viewed as a zigzag between two alternating strategies: left-centrist intraregime parliamentary reformism and antiregime mobilization on a "patriotic" basis (Flikke 1999).

18. The current version of the program states that the CPRF "sees its task as that of uniting the social-class and the national-liberation movements into a single mass movement of resistance. . . . The Party struggles for the unity, integrity, and independence of the country, the welfare and security of its citizens, the physical and moral health of the people, and a socialist path of development for Russia." The CPRF's main goals are declared to include "justice, equality, patriotism, the equal rights of nations, the friendship of peoples, the unity of patriotic and international principles, responsibility, renewed socialism, and communism as the historical future of humanity" (http://www.kprf.ru/program.htm). The controversial word "internationalism" is still avoided.

For examples of communist critiques of Zyuganovism, see the collection of articles by Kurashvili (1994) and Slavin (1997). Also of interest in this respect is the "Red Crossroads" [*Krasnyi perekrestok*] website of the International Center for the Formation of Communist Doctrine at http://www.aha.ru/~intcentr.

19. To some extent this has been happening all along. For example, Boris Slavin, who prior to leaving the CPRF in early 1995 was one of the most prominent advocates of an internationalist line, is now one of the leaders of the Party of Labor Self-Management.

The analyst cited goes on to speculate that a large-scale outflow of orthodox communists from the CPRF might significantly strengthen the left-communist parties, perhaps making it possible for a left-communist electoral bloc to surmount the 5 percent barrier and enter the Duma (Kholmskaia 1998, p. 73).

20. The political commentator Boris Kagarlitsky expressed such hopes at that time in conversation with me.

21. In the preceding Duma elections, another bloc led by Tyulkin, Communists for the Soviet Union, had won 4.5 percent.

22. Tyulkin and Anpilov were popularly known as "the two Viktors." Tyulkin was First Secretary of the RCWP; Anpilov headed the RCWP Moscow organization and also the "Laboring Russia" movement that was closely associated with the RCWP. Between 1994 and 1996, each of the Viktors controlled one of the RCWP's main periodicals: Tyulkin was editor of *Trudovaia Rossiia* [Laboring Russia], Anpilov of *Molniia* [Lightning]. The discrepancy between Tyulkin's internationalism and Anpilov's nationalism was only one of the factors in the growing conflict between the two men, and not necessarily the most important.

A wide selection of RCWP literature can be read on the Internet at www.marketsite.ru/rkrp/smi.html. For a biography of Tyulkin, see Tarasov, Cherkasov, and Shavshukova (1997, pp. 215–17).

23. Andreyeva was one of the leading opponents of Gorbachev's perestroika in the late 1980s. For more information on her party, see Tarasov, Cherkasov, and Shavshukova (1997, pp. 187–90).

24. For more information on the Russian Party of Communists, see Tarasov, Cherkasov, and Shavshukova (1997, pp. 201–4). The "democracy" in question is primarily the "genuine Soviet" democracy of self-managing socialism, although the virtues of "bourgeois democracy" may also to some extent be acknowledged.

25. A general history of the ROC is Pospielovsky (1998); Fireside (1971) deals with the ROC in the Soviet period and under the Nazi occupation. For more contemporary accounts, see Ellis (1986, 1996). The role of the ROC in the politics of post-Soviet Russia is also discussed by Bacon (1997), Verkhovskii, Pribylovskii, and Mikhailovskaia (1998, pp. 168–89), and Kornblatt (1999). Another valuable source on the affairs of the ROC is the site maintained by Paul Steeves: www.stetson.edu/~psteeves/relnews. The official site of the Moscow Patriarchate of the ROC is www.russian-orthodox-church.org.ru. In addition, resources of various kinds relating to the ROC are available from the Institute for East-West Christian Studies (Wheaton College, Illinois) and from the Centre for the Study of Religion and Communism (Keston College, Oxford, UK).

26. For a sociological study of this problem, see Vorontsova, Filatov, and Furman (1997). A liberal Orthodox journalist estimates that about 20 percent of nominal believers—that is, about 10 percent of the population—are "real" believers. However, only about a million go to church regularly—a large number in absolute terms though less than 1 percent of the total population (Krotov 1994).

27. In a poll conducted in early 2000 by the Russian Independent Public Opinion Research Center, 57 percent of respondents said that they trusted the ROC; 32 percent said that they mistrusted the ROC (N = 1,500 in 40 regions). The ROC was more widely trusted than central and local government, the Duma, the police and judiciary, the media, and the banks; only the Federal Security Service and the armed forces had better ratings.

28. Patriarch Alexy II was a high-profile presence at the inauguration of

Vladimir Putin as Russian president on May 7, 2000. Following the ceremony, the patriarch conducted a service in honor of Putin and presented him with the icon of St. Prince Alexander of Neva (Nevsky) to serve as his protector (ITAR-TASS, 1315 GMT, 7 May 2000; FBIS-SOV-2000–0507, via World News Connection).

29. For a critique of the belief in a Satanist threat as it exists in the United States, see Victor (1993).

30. For a report of such a case in Tula Province, see *Komsomolskaia pravda* no. 124(21858), July 8, 1999.

31. Berdyaev, Bulgakov, and Frank were severe critics both of the tsarist regime and the church hierarchs and of Russia's atheist revolutionary intelligentsia. All three were contributors to the famous collection of articles criticizing the latter that was published in 1909 under the title "Landmarks" [*Vekhi*] (Shatz and Zimmerman 1994).

32. The majority (80 percent) of priests have no theological education whatsoever (Krotov 1994).

33. For a more detailed account of the organizational structure of the ROC and its relations with the state, see Ellis (1996, chs. 5 and 6.) The old Russian term *pomestnyi sobor* is rendered by Ellis as "Local Council," but I think that "Church Council" is less confusing.

34. Not all of the Orthodox Brotherhoods are fundamentalist or Russian nationalist in orientation, but most are.

35. For the sake of clarity, I have made some minor changes to the terminology used by Kyrlezhev and Troitsky. In particular, they do not use the term "centrist."

36. Although Yoann has been the most influential figure on the fundamentalist wing of the church, some attention also needs to be devoted to the views of other influential fundamentalists—for instance, the well-known church journalist Valentin Lebedev, editor of the journal *Pravoslavnaia beseda* and secretary-coordinator of the Union of Orthodox Citizens. Lebedev was one of the top ten names on the federal list of the *Spas* [Salvation] bloc—a front for the Russian National Unity of Alexander Barkashov—in the Duma elections of December 1999 (Sevast'ianov 2000).

37. Yoann's writings on political themes are collected in Ioann (1995a, 1995b).

38. All the fundamentalists are passionately opposed to the ecumenical movement and to the participation in it of the ROC. This is connected to the fact that the more liberal of the hierarchs, such as Metropolitan Kirill, tend to be those who have taken part in ecumenical gatherings and whose outlook has been broadened by extensive interaction with Christians of other denominations (Komarov 1998).

39. It is sometimes argued that the symphonic ideal acted as a significant constraint on the pre-Petrine autocracy (Petro 1995, ch. 3). In any open conflict between church and state, however, it was invariably the state that won. For example, several church hierarchs did chastise Ivan the Terrible in private for spilling innocent blood in the *oprichnina* of 1565 to 1582, but when Metropolitan Filip did so publicly he was deposed, put on trial, and later strangled (Warhola 1993).

40. There is one passage in Yoann's address to the All-Russian Monarchist Convention that might be read as casting doubt on this assessment,

where he speaks of being selective in borrowing from the past, of "creatively developing the mechanisms of Russian statehood," and of avoiding a "literal return to the pre-1917 reality" (Ioann 1995a, pp. 343–44). However, these remarks have to be taken in the context of Yoann's work as a whole, which is overwhelmingly permeated by a backward-looking spirit. Moreover, Yoann's critique of the pre-1917 reality is made not from the vantage-point of the contemporary world, but (as I have shown) from that of the pre-1700 reality of his pre-Petrine golden age.

41. For further discussion of cooperation between Orthodox priests and the RNU, see chapter 6.

42. The report comes from the information bulletin of the Anti-Fascist Congress of the South of Russia, *Anti-Fa Info* No. 8 (May 2000), which took it from the Samotlor-Express press agency. The report does not specify at whose initiative the book-burning took place.

43. Most popular are books by the late Father Alexander Men, who was murdered under suspicious circumstances. Although Father Alexander was a priest of the ROC, his books have been published only by non-Orthodox publishing houses (Krotov 1994).

44. Professor Pospielovsky also expressed his alarm at the persecution by fundamentalists of Father Georgy Kochetkov and other priests and believers. When he received no reply from the patriarch, he decided to publish the letter.

45. Newcomers, complains Innokenty, get upset by the fundamentalist broadcasts of Radio Radonezh, not realizing that this radio station does not represent the official position of the ROC.

46. Alexy publicly criticized the fundamentalists for the first time in April 1994 (Dunlop 1995).

47. The commission, which sat in 1998 under the chairmanship of then First Deputy Prime Minister Boris Nemtsov, came to the conclusion that the shooting of the tsar's family was not a ritual murder (*Pokaianie* 1998, pp. 241–64).

48. The term used by churchmen in referring to past splits in the history of the ROC—*raskol*—has extremely negative emotional connotations.

49. The Russian Orthodox Church Abroad (ROCA) was founded by Russian émigrés who refused to accept the decision of the ROC to submit to the Soviet regime. Since 1991 the ROCA has reestablished itself in Russia. The official website of the ROCA is at www.synod.com. See also the interview with the patriarch of the ROCA, Metropolitan Vitaly (Vitalii 1992).

50. Alexy is reported as saying the following: "The West used to support Russian political dissidents, promoting the collapse of the communist regime, but also that of a mighty state. Now, well aware that Russia will stand as long as Christian Orthodoxy stands, the West is encouraging religious dissent in order to undermine the Eastern Christian cause" (Shevchenko 1997). In other words, those who dissent against the ROC are agents of the West.

51. In his *Slovo protiv iudeev* [Word Against the Jews] Yoann Zlatoust wrote: "In the synagogue there live demons, and not only there, but in the very souls of the Jews" (Levinskaia 1996, p. 234).

52. Here I would like to interject into my report of Krotov's remarks that the new hierarchs will willingly collaborate with the Federal Security Service, the KGB's successor.

53. In 1997, a Center for Temporal Problems was created in the Presidential Administration, specializing in astrological and clairvoyant forecasts of the political situation. Similar centers exist in the Ministry of Defense and the Ministry for Emergency Situations (Ustiuzhanin 1998).

54. Thus, it is not immediately obvious whether the contents of the popular magazine *Golos vselennoi* [Voice of the Universe] are Christian or pagan in character. For a very useful survey of neo-pagan movements in Russia and in Eastern Europe as a whole, see Shnirel'man (1998a).

Notes to Chapter 4

1. Scholars who wish to stress the lack of continuity and similarity between the original Cossacks and those who now claim to be Cossacks prefer to speak of the "neo-Cossack revival" (Derluguian and Cipko 1997).

2. The origin of the Cossacks is well described in Kliuchevsky (1994, pp. 109–35). For a general history of the Cossacks before 1917, see Longworth (1969). McNeal (1987) provides an in-depth study of the Cossacks in the period between 1855 and 1914.

3. My account of the Cossack revival in the Kuban draws mainly on Derluguian and Cipko (1997). For an alternative sociological account of the stages of development of the movement in the Kuban, see Skorik (1994). Other useful sources of information on the contemporary Cossack movement in Russia are Mukhin and Pribylovskii (1994), Mukhin (1995), and Laba (1996).

4. Although he remained in office as president of the USSR until December 1991, Gorbachev was in a greatly weakened position after the failed putsch. Within the Russian Federation, Yeltsin was already in effective control.

5. There are close connections between autonomism and anarchism: the periodical of the Federation of Anarchists of the Kuban is called *Avtonom*.

6. In some places, ataman administration has been introduced with the consent of regional authorities. It has not been very successful, as the atamans lack the necessary administrative skills (Mukhin 1995, p. 36).

7. A survey conducted in August 1992 found non-Cossacks in the Kuban evenly divided in their attitude toward the Cossack revival (Ter-Sarkisiants 1994, pp. 9–10). In another survey, conducted in Rostov Province, 65 percent of non-Cossacks and 46 percent of Cossacks answered yes to the question: "May the Cossack revival lead to the infringement of the rights of other people living on the Don?" (Gradnitsyn 1991).

8. There have been cases of Cossacks refusing to assume police functions on the grounds that they did not wish to be "gendarmes of Russia" (Mukhin and Pribylovskii 1994, p. 117).

9. However, the technical level of the Cossacks' weaponry is not very high. Most of it is written-off equipment from Russian army units (Mukhin 1995, p. 34).

10. The Cossacks being overwhelmingly Orthodox, there is a considerable overlap between the two.

11. I have been assured by a Kiev colleague with close family ties to the Kuban Cossacks that despite their abstract belief in a world Jewish conspiracy the Cossacks do not in fact feel any hostility to local Jews. The role of trader that was once played by Jews is now occupied by Armenians, whom the Cossacks

truly hate. The few Jews who remain in the Kuban are for the most part medical people, whom the Cossacks respect. Lacking the personal experience to form my own judgment, I simply repeat what my colleague told me without comment.

12. The subject of Russian youth subcultures is badly neglected by both Western and Russian researchers. What little I know about the subject I owe to Hilary Pilkington of the Centre for Russian and East European Studies, University of Birmingham, England.

13. E-mail communication from Hilary Pilkington. It is not only in Russia that many skinheads come from quite well-off backgrounds. The same is true, for instance, of Germany (Staunton 2000). For further discussion of "aggressive subcultures" among Russian youth, see Pilkington (1996, pp. 202–3, 249–53).

14. Even now the RNU suspects that heavy rock contains satanic themes (Subbotin 1999), and prefers to stick to traditional folk music (Maiorov 1999). The late Igor Talkov, a popular "patriotic" singer and poet who was also obsessed with the Devil, called himself a "bard" (*Igor´* 1993). Indeed, some bands, such as the heavy metal group *Alisa*, exploit the widespread obsession with Satan by incorporating "satanic" elements into their performance.

15. Among the founders of "national rock" are Andrei Arkhipov and Sergei Zharikov, also known as the "rock Nazis," who have been active in the LDPR and the NBP (see chapters 5 and 7). Other prominent fascist rock musicians are Yegor Letov and Sergei Troitsky, nicknamed "The Spider" [*Pauk*], leader of the band *Metal Corrosion*. Troitsky's fan club functions as a loose fascist youth movement (Shapovalov 2000). An example of a band that is nationalist and militarist, but not in my view fascist, is *Liube*. (I make this judgment on the basis of sound tapes of their songs kindly lent to me by Marina Aptekman.)

16. In the West there do exist groups of non-fascist or even anti-fascist skinheads, who cultivate the same appearance as fascist skinheads (except that they do not sport Nazi insignia) and share the same taste for "oi" music, beer, and violence (*The Skinhead International* 1995, p. 5). I have come across no evidence of the existence of non-fascist skinheads in Russia.

17. The number "18" is code for "AH"—that is, Adolf Hitler.

18. The website of Blood and Honor is www.whitepower.com/skinheads/bloodhonourskinz.html.

19. This estimate was made by Alexander Verkhovsky of the Panorama group in E-mail correspondence with me. There appears to be no serious published research on skinheads in Russia. The best general journalistic account is that of Rstaki (1998a, 1998b).

20. Almost certainly this list is far from complete.

21. In an incident in May 1997, ten skinheads attacked a camp in Moscow for Uzbek refugees. One child died of his injuries.

22. The main assailant in the case, Semyon Tokmakov, was charged, but only with hooliganism. It appears to be the standard practice of the police and courts to treat cases of bodily assault by skinheads as hooliganism, or even as petty hooliganism (Ageichev 2000).

23. Some skinheads have been attracted to Eduard Limonov's National-Bolshevik Party (see chapter 7). The Russian National Unity (RNU) seems to keep its distance from the skinheads.

24. The leader of Russian Goal is Semyon Tokmakov, who assaulted the

American marine. On June 29, 2000, there was a large-scale clash between police and fascist youths in Moscow's Savelovsky Park. Many of the over 100 youths detained were found to be members of Russian Goal (*Anti-Fa Info* no. 10).

25. One of the skinheads charged was a student at the medical academy who had initiated attacks on Indian fellow students. This again demonstrates that some skinheads come from quite high-status families.

26. This is the estimate provided by the press service of the city police department. Journalists at the local newspaper *Oblastnye vesti* believed that the organization had more than two hundred members.

27. Whether any adults had been involved in the creation of the Volga National Front remained unclear. No evidence was found of any links between the organization and the Volgograd organization of the Russian National Unity.

28. Torpedo is also sponsored by ZiL [*Zavod imeni Likhacheva*], an old Moscow enterprise that manufactures trucks and limousines.

29. In Russian: *Tsentral'nyi sportivnyi klub Armii* (TsSKA). I am grateful to Sergei Khrushchev for explaining to me the historical background of the various Moscow soccer teams.

30. As the families of most CASC fans have close ties with the armed forces, their culture is no doubt more heavily militarized than that of the fans of other teams. The material in this paragraph comes from the website www.bwd.soccer.ru.

Notes to Chapter 5

1. An initiative group for forming the LDPSU had been set up in the spring of 1989. There are strong grounds to suspect that Zhirinovsky's venture had support from within the Soviet power structures, which appreciated his emphasis on preserving the Soviet Union and hoped to keep the emerging multiparty system under their own control. The next new party to appear after the LDPSU was the more authentically independent Democratic Party of Russia, founded by Nikolai Travkin in May 1990.

2. The "Bloc of Vladimir Zhirinovsky" contested the Duma elections in place of the LDPR, which had difficulty in registering.

3. In the Duma elections of December 1993, the LDPR won over 40 percent of the vote in Pskov province (Vaguine 1997, p. 2).

4. In 1998, the LDPR claimed for itself over half a million members (Ushakova 1998, p. 0; Zhirinovskii 1998b). Plekhanov (1994), however, states that the LDPR had 100,000 members in 1994, as against 500,000 members in the CPRF. The LDPR has lost much of the public support it enjoyed in 1994, and presumably now has fewer members than it had then.

5. In March 1995, LDPR deputy Vyacheslav Marychev raised doubts in the Duma concerning Zhirinovsky's sanity, recounting how on a visit to Iraq Zhirinovsky had "put on Saddam Hussein's gown and run around the palace thinking he was the president of Iraq." Zhirinovsky responded by revealing that Marychev was "uncontrollable and only wanted to go on stage and try on various hats, knickers, and cufflinks)" (FBIS-SOV-95–048, March 10, 1995).

6. This literature, issued on a very large scale, appears in part under Zhirinovsky's name and in part without indication of authorship. It may be assumed that the latter, and probably much of the former, embodies the

contributions of individuals besides Zhirinovsky himself. It may also be assumed, however, that none of this literature appears without Zhirinovsky's approval of its contents.

7. Zhirinovsky has been inconsistent in his attitude toward sexual minorities. He made a publicized visit to a gay club in Moscow.

8. For a collection of such views, see the book *Neizbezhnost' imperii* [The Inevitability of Empire] (1996), produced under the aegis of the Union for the Rebirth of Russia. Also eloquent is the title of the book by LDPR politician Yevgeny Mikhailov: *Bremia imperskoi natsii* [The Burden of an Imperial Nation] (1995).

9. Plekhanov took part in Zhirinovsky's electoral campaign in summer 1991.

10. Laqueur (1993, pp. 254–59) also gives some credence to Zhirinovsky's liberalism by locating him as a figure of the "radical center" rather than of the right.

11. Zhirinovsky does attack "democrats," but this term has acquired a special meaning in contemporary Russia, referring not to all who support democracy in principle, but to the particular group of politicians brought to power under the Yeltsin regime. Unlike fascist leaders such as Alexander Barkashov, Zhirinovsky does not attack "democracy" as a system.

12. The movement for the development of local self-government in the late nineteenth century.

13. See, for instance, the LDPR pamphlet exposing, from a "Christian" perspective, the activity of "pseudo-Christian religious organizations in Russia" (Zhirinovskii and Krivel'skaia 1997). The frontispiece displays a rare photograph of Zhirinovsky standing in the presence of the Patriarch, looking distinctly uncomfortable.

14. The position of the LDPR on this issue coincides with the "new state doctrine" advocated by Valery Tishkov, director of the Institute of Ethnology and Anthropology of the Russian Academy of Sciences and former head of the State Committee on Nationalities, whose liberal credentials few would dispute. The main difference is that Tishkov, unlike Zhirinovsky, urges that "de-ethnicization of the state and de-etatization of ethnicity" be carried out gradually (Tishkov 1997, pp. 259–60).

15. In Russian, the word *rossiiskii* refers to Russian in the sense of pertaining to Russia as a state, as opposed to *russkii*, which means Russian in the ethnic sense.

16. However, Zhirinovsky does sometimes identify "mondialism" as Russia's main enemy (*Programma* 1998, p. 11). This term usually, though not always, implies a belief in the Jewish world conspiracy.

17. The same idea receives less coherent expression in Zhirinovsky's *Final Spurt to the South*: "Let us concern ourselves with problems connected with the neighboring region. For America that will be the Southern States, Mexico, adjacent areas, the region of the Caribbean Sea. For France that is Northern Africa. And for Russia it is Afghanistan, Iran, and Turkey. On this there must be agreement, not to interfere. The same for China. It has interests in Mongolia, in Southern Asia. But it must not look askance at the Russians' actions in Afghanistan, and all the more so in Iran and Turkey. The same goes for Japan. It is ready to agree to Russia's outlet to the shores of the Indian Ocean, but it needs some islands in the Kuriles chain" (Zhirinovskii 1993, p. 73). For further source material on Zhironovsky's geopolitics, see Zhironovskii (1998a).

18. Haushofer associated each zone with a distinct "pan-idea." See chapter 5 in Parker (1985), and especially the map on p. 74.

19. See, for example, Dugin (1997b, pp. 68–73), or the material in Dugin's magazine *Elementy: Evraziiskoe obozrenie* [Elements: Eurasian Review], no. 7, 1996, pp. 32–36.

20. The evidence was found in archives in the city of Almaty, Kazakhstan, where Zhirinovsky was born. Zhirinovsky has claimed that the documents were forged (Solovyov and Klepikova 1995, pp. 26–29). Zhirinovsky's patronymic Volfovich also suggests that his father was not a Russian, though not necessarily that he was a Jew.

21. However, when asked on a visit to Germany whether relatives of his had died during the war, Zhirinovsky acknowledged only an uncle who had been killed fighting in the battle for Moscow.

22. According to the results of sociological surveys, about 30 percent of the Russian public are influenced by anti-Semitic stereotypes, but of these only about 5 percent are strongly anti-Semitic.

23. This term is used in Russia to refer to those entrepreneurs who are oriented toward autonomous development of the Russian economy, rather than cooperation with Western governments, institutions, and corporations.

24. The view expressed here is close to that of Allensworth (1998, p. 200), who writes of the LDPR's "eclectic liberal-democratic/national socialist socioeconomic and political program." The point about eclecticism is well taken; nonetheless, it seems to me that the basic structure of the ideology is taken from liberalism.

25. A musician, Bogachev had been a dissident since 1967. He was elected chief coordinator at the founding congress of the LDPR in March 1990. After failing to oust Zhirinovsky as leader, he left the LDPR and founded his own Russian Liberal-Democratic Party in October 1990.

26. Six departments of the central apparatus were created, each headed by one of the party's deputy chairmen: the Department of Ideological Work, the Department of Organizational-Party Work, the Central Control Commission, the Department of Party Affairs, the Security Department, and the Information-Economic Department.

27. In practice, a popular regional leader in the LDPR may not be completely dependent on Zhirinovsky. This is illustrated by the case of Valery Zlobin, the head of the Komi party organization. When in January 1998 Zhirinovsky replaced Zlobin by the writer Alexander Nekrasov, Zlobin took many followers with him out of the LDPR. He became head of the Komi branch of the Union of Popular Power and Labor. The split severely weakened the local position of the LDPR, and in April 1998 Zhirinovsky invited Zlobin to meet with him and restored him to his previous post.

28. While many studies have been published of Zhirinovsky, there do not seem to be any devoted to other LDPR figures. For works by other LDPR politicians, see: Mikhailov (1995), which contains an autobiography of the Pskov governor Yevgeny Mikhailov and a collection of articles co-authored by Mikhailov and his associate I. Sebezhev; Mitrofanov (1997), a treatise on "the new geopolitics" by the LDPR "foreign minister"; and Kas′ianov and Cherednik (1997), a book presenting the "Economic Program for the Revival Of Russia" proposed by the regional leader of the LDPR in Rostov-on-Don.

29. This interpretation of the internal LDPR regime basically coincides with that given by Allensworth (1998, pp. 200–202).

30. Most of the information in this section is taken from Solovyov and Klepikova (1995) and Umland (1997).

31. Limonov first met with Zhirinovsky in the winter of 1991–92. He tells the story of his relationship with Zhirinovsky in Limonov (1994a).

32. For a time he remained the member of the LDPR Central Committee for Moscow Province.

33. This committee was created in December 1993 especially to cater to the concerns of the LDPR fraction.

34. Mitrofanov, whose geopolitical and other views differ in some significant respects from those of Zhirinovsky, is particularly concerned with the destabilizing consequences for world order of the approaching transition from the age of the Fish (Pisces) to the age of Aquarius (Mitrofanov 1997, p. 269).

35. It is true that the most fascist issue of *Liberal* appeared at the beginning of 1993, about two months after the departure of the "trio." One must take account, however, of the time lag between the preparation of an issue and its publication.

36. Moscow has agreed to make territorial concessions to China along the Amur River and around Lake Khanka, but Nazdratenko, governor of the Maritime (Primor′e) Province, opposes any border adjustments.

37. See Kashin's speech at the LDPR's Eighth Congress in April 1998, in which he offers his own explanation of how he was able to win in a region with a majority non-Russian population (Zhirinovskii 1998b, pp. 57–59).

38. Top of the pre-election poll came the liberal (not "national-liberal"!) politician Grigory Yavlinsky with 23 percent. Next, in descending order, came Zyuganov, Luzhkov, and Primakov, all scoring better than Zhirinovsky. At the time of the poll, Vladimir Putin had not yet risen to prominence. He won the presidential elections in Pskov Province hands down with 63 percent of the vote (*Nezavisimaia gazeta—regiony*, April 25, 2000). The poll data, and also other information in the second half of this paragraph, come from the Radio Liberty's Correspondent's Hour of Anna Lipina (http://www.svoboda.org/programs/CH/1999/CH.041799.shtml).

39. I am indebted to Zoya Anaiban of the Institute of Ethnology and Anthropology of the Russian Academy of Sciences for briefing me on the ethnopolitical situation in Tuva.

40. *Russian Regional Report* Vol. 5, No. 17, May 5, 2000, citing *Kommersant-Daily*, April 26, 2000.

41. This information is based on statements made by Zhirinovsky on the radio station *Ekho Moskvy*, as reported in the information bulletin of the Anti-Fascist Congress of the South of Russia, *Anti-Fa Info* No. 8 (May 2000).

42. I am indebted to Vyacheslav Likhachev of the "Panorama" Research Group in Moscow for a very helpful discussion of this point.

Notes to Chapter 6

1. This is the form that the announcement took in January 1999, with eleven recruitment meetings a week. The accelerating growth of the organization was

demonstrated by the increase over time in the number of weekly recruitment meetings. A few months previously there were only four meetings a week. Alan Ingram has informed me that in spring 1995 there was only one such meeting a week.

The internal passport remains, as in Soviet times, the essential document by which a citizen of Russia establishes his or her identity.

2. Besides these categories, full membership of the RNU (as "comrades-in-arms") is also denied to individuals "inclined toward excessive mysticism" or "incapable of prolonged efforts of the will" (Barkashov 1994, p. 50).

3. If Barkashov's grandfather had really been an important official in the Central Committee, would he not have ensured a better education and job for his grandson? It may also be noted that Barkashov married a woman from his ancestral village. One commentator finds this symptomatic of his parochial mentality (Zherebyatev 1999).

4. Rumors that Barkashov had links with the KGB are mentioned by a number of authors (e.g., Peresvet 1995). Dunlop (1996) suspects that both Vasilyev and Barkashov had such links.

5. In Russian, "Free Strong Just Russia" has the same acronym as the USSR.

6. For a fuller account of the emergence of the RNU, see Likhachev (1997, pp. 5–9). Also of interest is the account on the RNU Website.

7. The first issue of *Pamyat*'s weekly newspaper includes an article in which Archbishop Averky (1991) denounces the new orthography introduced by the Bolsheviks in December 1918, declaring that only the old orthography is "true writing" [*pravo-pisanie*]. The *Pamyat* website, which unlike the RNU website contains an English-language section, is at http://www.ruspatriot.com/pamyat.

8. An army instructor at an RNU military training club, asked what attitude he, as a Russian officer, had toward the swastika on the sleeves of his companions, replied: "They explained everything to me. This is our Russian swastika" (Gritchin and Urigashvili 1997). For further discussion of the origin and meaning of the RNU swastika, see Zolotarevich (1998).

9. In one interview, he reveals that his enemies are using occult methods against him, and threatens to respond in like measure (Prokhanov 1998).

10. The information on symbols is taken from Barkashov (1994, pp. 51–55, 64–67). It was also on the RNU website.

11. For more information in English on the RNU's ideology, see the accounts by Dunlop (1996, pp. 523–27); Simonsen (1996a, pp. 33–48; 1996b); and Allensworth (1998, pp. 215–40). For succinct analyses in Russian, see Verkhovskii and Pribylovskii (1996, pp. 68–70), and *Na semi vetrakh(*1998, pp. 110–18). A useful collection of ideological documents disseminated by the RNU is that of Likhachev and Pribylovskii (1997, pp. 69–159).

12. This is not to deny that "spiritual Russianness" was also taken into account in vetting recruitment applications. Even individuals of wholly non-Russian descent might be accepted provided that they were recognized as being "spiritually Russian." It might be required of such recruits that they should have undergone Orthodox Christian baptism.

13. This distinction was not drawn so sharply at the beginning. Thus, the first edition of what became Barkashov's handbook, *The ABC of a Russian Nationalist*, was entitled *The ABC of a Russian Patriot.*

14. For a popular account of the Khazars, see Koestler (1976). In fact, as th research of the Soviet historian M. I. Artamonov has shown, relations betwee the Khazars and ancient Rus' included important elements of mutual influenc and respect as well as of rivalry and enmity.

15. For a report of such activity in Tver', see *Nezavisimaia gazeta*, July 7 1998, p. 7.

16. Novgorod, of course, did not exist at the time of Christ. The Slavic tribes did not yet live in towns.

17. The RNU program has appeared in a number of versions, but the differences among them are minor. This section draws on the most recent version, as given in Likhachev and Pribylovskii (1997, pp. 106–13), and on the RNU website.

18. *Sobor* is a rather archaic word, no doubt intended to recall to mind the *zemskii sobor* [Assembly of the Lands] of Tsarist times. The Russian Orthodox Church uses the word to refer to its councils.

19. The Ossets are sometimes mentioned approvingly as a non-Slavic people who have a tradition of loyalty to Russia.

20. The following passage from Barkashov (1994, p. 99) may be read as implying that genocide of the Jews is justified by the alleged "Jewish genocide of the Russian people": "Inasmuch as the genocide [of the Russians] was on a scale unprecedented in the history of humanity, and the planning of anti-Russian activity has been global in character, the responding measures of the Russian State must be on a corresponding scale and of a corresponding character."

21. The most recent version of the program is less harsh on this point than earlier versions, which demanded that mixed marriages and interethnic sexual relations be prohibited by law (as they were by the Nuremberg laws). Nevertheless, the RNU's visceral hostility to mixed marriages was evident in numerous statements of its leaders. Yevgeny Yenshin, deputy leader in Voronezh, refers to the offspring of mixed marriages as "degraded" and "stray dogs" (Bakinskii 1997). For a similar example from Samara, see Kilina (1999).

22. This was not stated explicitly, but can be inferred from a variety of sources, which show that the RNU regarded all parts of the former Soviet Union as rightfully belonging to Russia. For example, the Tajik-Afghan border was considered part of "the southern border of the Russian Empire" ("Neizbyvnaia" 1998). Also pertinent is the fact that the RNU recruited members in all the post-Soviet states.

23. As already noted, the religious component of the ideology can be traced much further back—to the medieval, and even to the ancient, age.

24. A useful comparative analysis of the programs of the RNU and of the NSDAP is provided by the Russian research group NAMAKON (*Na semi vetrakh* 1998, pp. 113–18).

25. The overwhelming majority of RNU leaders, as of RNU members, were men. I have come across a reference to only one woman in a leadership position—Lyudmila Bileva, formerly leader of the Moscow Province Organization (Likhachev and Pribylovskii 1997, p. 51). Different sources contradict one another on the question of whether the RNU admitted women: RNU practice may have been inconsistent in this respect.

26. A few issues of *Russkii stiag* appeared in 1991, but the periodical was dormant thereafter until it was revived in October 1995. Apart from the central RNU periodicals, several periodicals were produced on a regional basis.

27. The Russian word used [*kuratory*] is the same word that was used in the Soviet period for the officials of the Communist Party central apparatus responsible for "supervising" the work of various government ministries or public organizations. The corresponding verb [*kurirovat'*] is likewise used by the RNU.

28. See the report of the conference of RNU organizations of the South of Russia held in Stavropol on September 5, 1998 (http://www.rne.org/presslug2.htm).

29. A well-funded "mobile unit" led by Yevgeny Lalochkin, until then leader of the Voronezh organization, went to St. Petersburg, rented a headquarters, and set to work (Shatrov 1998a).

30. The RNU was officially registered in Crimea, and had unregistered organizations in eight other provinces of Ukraine: Kharkov, Poltava, Zaporozhye, Dnepropetrovsk, Donetsk, Odessa, Sumy, and Voroshilovgrad.

31. See report of the conference of RNU organizations of the South of Russia, September 1998.

32. Considerable confusion surrounds this subject and many journalistic accounts contain serious errors, although it is clearly explained in RNU literature—for example, Barkashov (1994, pp. 47–48), or the RNU website.

33. Barkashov later tried to placate the misgivings of his comrades-in-arms concerning this episode by arguing that the RNU had acted not in support of the Supreme Soviet, but in accordance with the dictates of "Russian honor" (Barkashov 1994, p. 88). A contributor to the RNU Forum makes the point clearer: the RNU "was not defending the parliament, that talking-shop of Khasbulatov and the communists, [but] came to fight evil in its concentrated form—the pro-Zionist government and president." For further examples of intra-RNU dissent on this issue, see Likhachev and Pribylovskii (1997, pp. 41, 59–61).

34. The St. Petersburg sociologist Zinaida Sikevich remarks that this was "perhaps the most alarming fact discovered in the course of my research" (Sikevich 1996, p. 126).

35. A number of commentators have drawn attention to the virtual absence of organized activities for young people in Russia today as one reason for the appeal of movements like the RNU ("Oni uzhe zdes'" 1998; Farutin 1999). There are indications that Vladimir Putin will take steps to restore such activities in the framework of a new official youth organization to be called "Soyuzmol" (Averbukh, Vladimirov, and Punanov 2000).

36. A journalist who asked a squad of ten RNU youths what jobs they had was told by eight of them that they worked as private security guards. The ninth refused to reveal his employment, while the tenth "muttered under his breath that he was a hospital orderly" (Babich 1996). Sadly, it is prestigious for a young man to be a security guard, but not for him to care for the sick.

37. There is an intriguing parallel here with the youth organizations of fascist Italy and Nazi Germany, the appeal of which was similarly based on companionship and "sports"—that is, physical and military training—rather than on ideology (De Grand 1995, pp. 65–67).

38. According to *Argumenty i fakty* no. 7, 1998, more than 800,000 young people in Moscow alone are addicted to some drug.

39. In 1999 a displaced army officer could earn 400 to 500 rubles per month working for the RNU (Buldakov and Selezneva 1999).

40. SAMBO is the Russian acronym for "self-defense without weapons" [*samooborona bez oruzhiia*]. It is a special fighting technique developed during the Soviet period. Another special technique on offer at some clubs is the Kodochnikov method.

41. In early 1998, predraft training was reintroduced into school programs in Moscow (*RFE/RL Daily Report*, March 16, 1998). Under Vladimir Putin it is being reintroduced throughout the country.

42. "Persons of Caucasian nationality" is the term ignorantly used by the police for dark-skinned people from the Caucasus, who really belong not to one but to many different ethnic groups.

43. Interview with Vyacheslav Likhachev of the "Panorama" Information-Expert Group.

44. In this case, the MIA, in the person of its local representative, the head of the Saltykovka police station, eventually had enough of the RNU "people's patrolmen" and sent them packing.

45. This emerges clearly from Karamian (1997), who describes several horrific examples of violent assaults perpetrated by RNU men on passersby.

46. Thus, at the conference of RNU organizations of the South of Russia held in Stavropol on September 5, 1998, Central Council member Oleg Kassin named acting minister of justice Krasheninnikov, then deputy head of the presidential administration Savostyanov, and acting minister of internal affairs Stepashin as "enemies and traitors to the Nation" (RNU Website). Enemies were also named at the local level. For instance, at a conference of RNU organizations in the Far East held in Khabarovsk on October 4, 1998, the deputy governor of the Khabarovsk Territory, Mrs. Strelkova, was named an enemy, as was Mr. Galiant, head of the youth department of the territorial administration ("Far Eastern Nazis" 1998).

47. A democratic wing of the CFTUR, having failed to prevent the shift, broke away and joined the Association of Free Trade Unions of Russia (Marakasov 1996).

48. At the same time, the CFTUR confirmed its new nationalist orientation by renaming itself the National Association of Russian Trade Unions.

49. For a vivid account of the Cherepovetsk experience in the context of the general problems of the contemporary Russian trade union movement, see Buketov (1994). See also the article by Aleksandr Burtin in *Novaia ezhednevnaia gazeta*, September 9, 1994.

50. Article 152 of the Civil Code of the Russian Federation allows an individual to petition a court "in defense of his honor, dignity, and business reputation"; an organization is allowed to petition in defense of its business reputation. The landmark case of the court action taken by the RNU against Galina Tuz in the Stavropol Territory is described below.

51. The fabrication of such "exposés" ostensibly originating from Jewish sources is a century-old tradition going back to *The Protocols of the Elders of Zion*. In the late Soviet period, there circulated a similar document entitled *Catechism of the Jew in the USSR* (*Nuzhen* 1996, pp. 323–27).

52. In some cases, in particular in places where the RNU lacked official registration with the local authorities, RNU members stood as "independent" candidates, without denying their membership in the RNU.

53. Barkashov at a press conference, December 23, 1998. See also Barinov (1998).

54. The RNU claimed to receive numerous letters from grateful parents to this effect.

55. Thus the RNU protected the country summer residences of wealthy people in the vicinity of certain cities (for example, Omsk).

56. The mayor of Krasnodar, Valery Samoilenko, distances himself from Kondratenko's anti-Semitism, albeit in terms that are not wholly reassuring: "I don't know why the Jews bother him. They don't bother me. I have long told Nikolai Ignatovich—well, let's get stuck in, let's move from words to deeds. Let's hoist one Zionist up on a pitchfork and see what we get from it, how people's lives will improve. It's all chatter" (Khokhlov 1998).

57. *Otechestvo* has ten out of thirteen seats in the Duma and thirty-eight out of fifty seats in the assembly (*Russian Regional Report*, December 3 and 17, 1998). Kondratenko's *Otechestvo* is not to be confused with the party of the same name later formed by Moscow's mayor, Yuri Luzhkov.

58. "Cossack leaders believe that an argument in a café or at a dance could trigger mass ethnic mobilization" (*Izvestiia*, April 25, 1998).

59. The Meskhetian Turks are denied all official documents (residence permits, internal passports, drivers' licenses, etc.), are unable to register their marriages, are ineligible for welfare or pension payments, and are not admitted to educational institutions.

60. Data given by speakers at the conference of RNU organizations of the South of Russia held in Stavropol on September 5, 1998 (RNU Press-Service, September 8, 1998, RNU Website). The general picture is confirmed by Bal'burov (1997), who refers to RNU cells "in practically every population point."

61. Gritchin and Urigashvili (1997) mention one kindergarten in which a group of six- to eight-year-olds were being taught by two RNU instructors.

62. For more on the failure of the state to provide funds, food, or fuel to troops deployed in the Stavropol Territory, see Nikolai Gritchin in *Izvestiia* no. 209(15309), November 5, 1998.

63. "On [RNU's] initiative, part of the [205th] Brigade was quartered in the empty barracks at the military airfield near Stavropol, which happens to be next to one of the bases of *Russkie Vitiazi*'" (Gritchin and Urigashvili 1997).

64. The RNU originally petitioned the court in defense of its "honor, dignity, and business reputation." However, as Article 152 of the Civil Code of the Russian Federation permits only an individual to petition in defense of "honor and dignity," while an organization can petition only in defense of its "business reputation," the petition was later amended accordingly.

65. *Stavropolskaia pravda* had to pay the RNU 6,000 rubles, equivalent to $1,000 (*Izvestiia*, May 30, 1998).

66. These two points were mentioned in an interview with a former resident of Voronezh, conducted in October 1998 following a return visit by her to the city. This informant has also contributed other information used in this section.

67. In one such raid, described by Borodenkov (1997), about ninety persons were arrested, all of them without exception non-Russians. Yevgeny Yenshin, deputy leader of the Voronezh RNU, boasts that in the space of a few months RNU patrolmen arrested about 600 non-Russian lawbreakers on the streets, in the marketplaces, and at the railroad station (Bakinskii 1997).

68. See Iurii Mukhin in *Zavtra* no. 30(243), July 31, 1998; and *Kommersant-*

Daily, July 23, 1998. The local FSS replied that it did not consider the activities of the Soros Foundation to be suspicious.

69. The organization of the RNU in Latvia claimed to have branches in the towns of Riga, Daugavpils, Rezekne, Liepaja, Yelgava, Balvi, and Ventspils (Shcherbakov 1999). In Belarus, the RNU had branches in Minsk and Vitebsk. It had good relations with the local police and military. The activity of the RNU in Belarus included physical attacks against members of the Belarusian-nationalist opposition (Anis'ko 1999; Anis'ko and Koretskii 1999; Diupin and Neverovskii 1999; Feduta 1999).

70. Especially low figures for RNU membership are given by government officials who are seeking to justify the reluctance of their agencies to act against the RNU. "The RNU is not a dangerous organization; the press blows everything up," an investigator of the Moscow procuracy is quoted as complaining. "In St. Petersburg, for instance, they have twelve members. What is there to react to?" (Karamian 1999a). However, a British correspondent who observed an RNU weekend meeting in St. Petersburg's Victory Park on September 19, 1998, reports seeing a group of about fifty RNU men in black leather jackets or camouflage gear.

71. This description of Panorama's methodology is taken from my E-mail correspondence with Alexander Verkhovsky. Unfortunately, Panorama has not published an account of its methodology. Nor do other Russian writers explain how they derive their estimates.

One approach to estimating RNU membership that I tried but decided to abandon makes use of information on the rate of recruitment (the size and frequency of recruitment meetings, etc.). This method is misleading because it leaves out of account the high turnover rate. There does not seem to be information available on the proportion of recruits who stay on in the RNU rather than quickly dropping out.

72. *Russkii poriadok* no. 4(45), 1997, p. 60. A poster celebrating the triumph bears the slogan: "RNE mozhet vse!" [The RNU Can Do Anything!].

73. The poll by the Public Opinion Foundation was conducted on October 25, 1997, with an all-Russian urban and rural sample of 1,500. See *FOM-INFO Bulletin* no. 45(189), November 13, 1997, at http://www.fom.ru/fominfo/info189.htm#5.

74. The LDPR poll had a sample size of 926. The question asked: "For which of the following parties would you vote if an election were held today? CPRF, LDPR, Yabloko, NDR, KRO, RNU, against all, don't know." The data are displayed on the LDPR website at http:/www.ldpr.org/region/default.htm.

75. See *Novye izvestiia*, February 25, 1999.

76. It is suggestive of the RNU's peculiar social base that both the unemployed and those with relatively high incomes were overrepresented in the subsample that expressed a positive attitude toward the RNU.

77. In his press conference of December 23, 1998, Barkashov claimed that 40 percent of participants in the RNU either had a higher education or were students. Even if this was true, which is doubtful, the proportion of RNU *members* who fell into either of these categories must have been much lower.

78. Barkashov traveled in a Volga, his middle-level commanders in good foreign cars (Bal'burov 1999). This source is also impressed by the mobile telephones of the RNU men, and by their good winter clothing.

79. For example, the police found the following in a search of the home and car of an air force corporal and RNU district instructor by the name of Kuzmenko: "210 explosive devices, 20 mines, 33 electronic detonators, one AKM machine-gun, various pistols and other firearms, silencers, 7,000 bullets, etc." (Karamian 1999a). For one of many other similar examples, see "Arms Cache" (1997).

80. On the 101st Brigade, see *Izvestiia*, July 12, 1997, and *Obshchaia gazeta*, May 15, 1997. On the 21st Airborne Brigade, see *Komsomolskaia pravda*, March 3, 1998, and *Nezavisimoe voennoe obozrenie*, February 27–March 5, 1998.

81. The exact figure is subject to some uncertainty. Different sources give different estimates, though always in the area of thirty-five.

82. For an account of the close relations between the RNU and the mayor and other authorities of the small town of Balakovo on the Volga River, in Saratov Province, see Radaeva (1998).

83. This is likely to be less true in the future, because Vladimir Putin's reform of center-regional relations in 2000 has strengthened centralized control of the regional branches of state bodies.

84. This, for instance, is the impression one gains from coverage of the RNU in *Izvestiia*, or from the portrayal of the opposition by Alexander Yanov (Ianov 1995), although Yanov does not pay much attention to the RNU.

85. The RNU was one of fourteen organizations incriminated by the procuracy and the Ministry of Justice as directly participating "at the level of organizing structures" in the armed attacks of October 3 and 4, 1993, on the building of the Moscow mayoralty and the Ostankino television tower. Two RNU men were killed in the fighting.

86. However, Jackson (1999, p. 37) reports that the RNU stewards at communist rallies that he observed in 1993 and 1995 were self-appointed, and were greeted with hostile chants of "*Vlasovtsy!*"—that is, followers of the Soviet General Andrei Vlasov, who fought on the side of Hitler.

87. This is not necessarily to be attributed to sympathy for fascism: communist deputies fear that "anti-extremist" legislation may be used against themselves.

88. Suspicions have been voiced that Albert Shatrov, one of the most prolific publicists writing in the Russian press about the RNU, was in fact an RNU infiltrator.

89. Whether or not the RNU was registered in a given region is not a perfect indicator of whether it had any official support there. As the case of Oryol demonstrates, lack of registration did not necessarily indicate the absence of official support.

90. "Provinces" should here be taken to include the cities of Moscow and St. Petersburg, which are federal subjects in their own right, and "governors" to include their mayors.

91. This was Presidential Decree 310 of March 23, 1995, entitled: "Measures Designed to Ensure the Coordinated Action of Bodies of State Power in the Struggle Against Manifestations of Fascism and Other Forms of Political Extremism in the Russian Federation."

92. Korzhakov and Barsukov were ousted from their positions in 1996 at the demand of General Alexander Lebed, then secretary of the Security Council.

93. "While other parties and politicians live from election to election and talk about personnel changes in the government, the RNU works to build up its structure" (Shatrov 1998a).

94. One commentator opines that the number of delegates at the congress might really have been "only" about 3,000 (Belykh 1998).

95. From a reply on the RNU Forum to a contributor who had questioned the necessity of holding the congress in Moscow. The full reply was as follows: "Unfortunately the center of visible political life is Moscow. If today we hold the congress in Moscow, tomorrow the RNU will be a real movement with a claim to power in the country. In view of the RNU's growing popularity, holding the congress outside Moscow would be a step backwards."

96. Police officers who had been accustomed to tolerating—indeed, working with—RNU men found it difficult to adjust to the new policy. One police officer even apologized to some Barkashovites whom he had arrested and taken to the station. Unfortunately for him, a journalist was present, and the apology became the subject of a scandal in the press. The officer concerned was fired (Strogin 1999a). A special police unit was also created to protect the premises of Jewish organizations in Moscow ("Vlast'" 1999).

97. To avert suspicion, the basements were registered as belonging to church communities.

98. This was one of ten public meetings that the RNU held in provincial cities to protest against Luzhkov's anti-RNU policy. The meetings were not very well attended (Kashin and Smirnov 1999; Pankov 1999).

99. The meaning of one response was unclear.

Notes to Chapter 7

1. This estimate was made by Vyacheslav Likhachev, an analyst of the Panorama group who is currently engaged in a detailed study of the NBP. I am greatly indebted to him and to his colleague Alexander Verkhovsky for sharing with me their insights into the NBP. Limonov himself has mentioned a similar figure (Akopov 1999b). In his latest analysis, Verkhovsky placed the NBP alongside the LDPR and the RNU as one of the largest national-patriotic organizations (Verkhovskii 2000).

2. Information from Vyacheslav Likhachev, supported by reports in the NBP journal *Limonka* and in the general press. Current and back issues of *Limonka* are available on-line at www.limonka.com. The articles that Limonov wrote for the English-language magazine *The eXile* are at www.exile.ru.

3. Besides other sources indicated, this section draws upon the work of Mark Sedgwick of the American University in Cairo on the Traditionalist Sufism of the Golovin circle (Sedgwick 1999) and on Russian Traditionalism in general (Sedgwick 2000). I am grateful to Mark Sedgwick for allowing me to make use of his unpublished papers. The information derived from his interview with Dugin was especially valuable. Also of value is Rosenthal (1997), where Dugin is placed in the context of the role that the occult has played in Russian and Soviet culture.

4. In recent years, Jemal has been a leader of the movement for Islamic revival in Russia and the former USSR. Doubts have been expressed regarding the true depth of his knowledge of Islam: apparently he cannot read Arabic (Nekhoroshev 1999).

5. The reader may wonder how the "masters" got hold of books by such authors. The answer is simple: they borrowed them from the Lenin Library.

6. Dugin joined *Pamyat* together with Jemal. They also left the organization

at the same time. Although they did not continue to collaborate closely, they remained on good personal terms.

7. Two issues appeared in 1992, two in 1993, and one in each succeeding year. Most issues have a unifying theme or "dossier," for example: the conservative revolution; Serbia and the New World Order; the elite; socialism; democracy; eroticism; terror, aggression, and violence. The initial print run was an ambitious 50,000; by 1996 it was down to 2,000. The journal is now available in hard copy only as an insert to *Zavtra*, though it still appears on the Internet.

8. For a critical survey of the geopolitical tradition that stems from Mackinder, see the books of Geoffrey Parker. Parker (1985) provides a historical overview of the tradition; Parker (1988) is especially useful for its focus on Russia.

9. For a fuller account of one variant of the Ariosophical doctrine, see the section on the Society of Nav in chapter 8.

10. Dugin was re-baptized into the United Church, a small church that uses the liturgical rites of the Old Believers while recognizing the authority of the Orthodox Patriarch.

11. The hypothesis of a link between Dugin and Rodionov is supported by the fact that the NBP journal *Limonka* published a highly sympathetic article about Rodionov, written by a military officer, on the occasion of Rodionov's dismissal as defense minister by Boris Yeltsin (Savushkin 1997). I do not, however, mean to imply that Dugin's links with the military ended when Rodionov was replaced. Thus, articles by Dugin appeared in military periodicals not only in 1996 and 1997, when Rodionov was occupying senior positions (for example, on April 22 and 25, 1997, in *Krasnaia zvezda*), but also in March and April 1999. I am grateful to Jacob Kipp and Bob Otto for E-mail discussions of the relationship between Dugin and the military.

12. Published autobiographical material on Limonov is unusually rich. Most of Limonov's numerous novels are directly or indirectly autobiographical in nature, and many of his political articles contain personal reminiscences or accounts of his day-to-day experience. His nine most important novels, including the Kharkov trilogy about his childhood and youth and the American trilogy about his years in the United States, are brought together in his collected works, published in three volumes (Limonov 1998a).

13. In 1976, the Soviet magazine *Nedelia* reprinted this article, as a result of which many other Soviet émigrés turned against Limonov. Perhaps Limonov's "disillusionment" should not be taken at face value, as it is doubtful whether he was ever an admirer of the United States or the West.

14. I omit discussion of Limonov's poetry, which I do not consider myself competent to assess. Documents issued in the name of the NBP, most of which are also undoubtedly Limonov's work, are considered in the second half of the chapter.

15. There are two more books of Limonov's fiction that I have not read: a novel titled *Foreigner in a Time of Confusion*, published by the Omsk Book Publishing House in 1992, and a collection of stories called *Cognac "Napoleon,"* published by M. Mikhelson Publishers of Tel Aviv in 1990.

16. A collection of Limonov's articles and essays was issued in 1992 by the Moscow publisher Glagol under the title *Extinction of the Barbarians*. There is also a political book entitled *Anatomy of a Hero*, published in Smolensk in 1998 by Rusich. I have not read either of these.

17. *Moskovskie novosti* no. 25(942), June 30, 1999.

18. For the articles on Stalin and Manson, see *Limonka* no. 55, December 1996. Beria is featured in issue no. 69, July 1997.

19. Among other rights bestowed by the rules on the party member are his right to live off the earnings of the woman with whom he lives (assuming he does live with a woman), not to pay back money he has borrowed from her, not to listen when she is talking, and to eat meals that she has prepared for her children.

The rules imply that only men may become members of the NBP. However, this is nowhere made explicit, and sometimes Limonov does appeal to both sexes to join the party. Among prominent contributors to *Limonka*, there is one woman, the poet Alina Vitukhnovskaya; it is not clear whether she is a member.

Some colleagues question whether material of this kind should be taken seriously. May it not be intended as humor? Indeed it may, but one may choose to take seriously the question of why certain things are regarded as funny.

20. For comparison, the detective pulp fiction of Viktor Dotsenko is published in print runs of 150,000. The print runs of the books of Viktor Pelevin, a serious, well-respected, and popular writer of philosophical fiction, are in the same range as those of Limonov's books. Of course, print runs are in general much lower nowadays than they were in Soviet times.

21. Part of the explanation no doubt lies in the fact that Limonov, unlike the leaders of other Russian fascist organizations, makes an effort to cultivate Westerners living in Moscow. However, even were other fascist leaders to try doing so, it is unlikely that they would have the same success as Limonov.

22. The list of historical figures whom Limonov admires was compiled from various issues of *Limonka*, especially from Limonov's "Answers of the Leader to a Worker's Questions" in issue no. 55 (December 1996), and from the names mentioned in point 24 of the NBP program. The reference to Nestor Makhno is in the poem by "Red Wolf" in issue no. 66, where the intention is expressed to "erect a monument to Makhno on the site of the Cathedral of Christ the Savior"—not, one would have thought, a very "traditionalist" sentiment.

23. Personal conversation.

24. I infer the number forty-five from the NBP text about the need for forty-five strong regional leaders in the struggle for power: "We need 45 Goebbels and Dzerzhinskys" (NBP 1997, pp. 10–11).

25. Former rank-and-file members of the Communist Party, however, are to have the right to engage in political activity.

26. In the original, the whole of this definition is printed in capital letters.

27. This is explained in terms of "the principle of progressive nationalization": "If 5 people work at an enterprise, it can be private. If 55, it must be collective. If 555, it will be in regional ownership. If 5,555, it will belong to the state" (point 10).

28. For instance, the number of participants in an NBP demonstration held in Moscow on May 9, 1997 is reported as "over a hundred" (*Limonka* no. 66, June 1997, p. 1). About seventy people attended a rally in Moscow held on March 14, 1998 together with the Officers' Union. A public meeting held by the NBP in Astrakhan on April 17, 1999 attracted about thirty (Reshetniak 1999).

29. In January 1999, the NBP was maintaining daily pickets outside the building of the Ministry of Justice in Moscow in support of its latest bid for

registration. Limonov has warned that continued refusal to register the party might "force" it to take the path of terrorism (Likhachev 1999).

30. Three other Russian nationalist candidates did better than Limonov: Nikolai Lyashenko, who was backed by the Congress of Russian Communities, obtained 14.1 percent; the LDPR candidate Vladimir Bryukhanov won 6.0 percent; and an RNU member, Mikhail Burlakov, garnered 3.6 percent (FBIS-SOV-97–258). For Limonov's own account of the campaign, see Limonov (1997a).

31. There are reported to be about a hundred NBP activists in Orenburg (Chernykh 1999).

32. Quoted in the Latvian press in connection with the arrest in Riga of seven NBP members on suspicion of taking psychotropic drugs (Chuchkova 1999; Sorokin 1999). The reaction of neighbors would surely not have been much different had the arrests taken place in Russia.

33. How, asks one contributor to the RNU Forum, can "a neurasthenic poet and pederast" like Limonov lead Russia's patriots?

Notes to Chapter 8

1. Sometimes also called the All-Russian National People's Party.

2. Golovanivskaia, Kostikov, and Diupin (1999) offer somewhat higher estimates: 3,000 to 4,000 members for the PNP, 2,000 to 3,000 for the NRPR, and "up to 1,000" members for the RNS. Vyacheslav Likhachev of the "Panorama" Information-Expert Group believes that the PNP has only about 500 members, the majority of whom are not active. My own estimates are compromises between these two sources, with account taken also of information from the press and from the websites of the organizations themselves.

3. Ivanov-Sukharevsky's schema does have some ethnographic basis. For instance, the *novorossy* have a mixed Russian-Ukrainian identity, and the *pomory* have their own distinct Russian dialect.

Except where otherwise indicated, information on Ivanov-Sukharevsky and the People's National Party is taken from: Pribylovskii (1995, pp. 55–56); Verkhovskii, Papp et al. (1996, pp. 117–20); Verkhovskii and Pribylovskii (1996, pp. 36–39); Verkhovskii and Pribylovskii (1997, p. 10); and from the website http://people.weekend.ru/nnp (now no longer in operation). I am grateful to Alexander Verkhovsky for providing me with additional information on the most recent developments.

4. The phrase used by Ivanov-Sukharevsky is *zhidovskii kagal*, a reference to the *kahal*, the traditional form of organization of Jewish communities in tsarist Russia (Ivanov 1997, p. 2).

5. According to Pribylovskii (1995, p. 55), only as an undercaptain.

6. Ivanov-Sukharevsky is not completely consistent in his religious views: it seems that he believes in the mysteries of "secret Tibetan centers" (Ivanov 1997, p. 52).

7. The PNP's program consists of thirty-two points. The party program should not be confused with the seven-point "electoral program of presidential candidate Alexander Kuzmich Ivanov" (Ivanov 1997, back cover).

8. For a collection of Vlasov's historical and political writings, see Vlasov (1995).

9. This publication used to have its own webpage at http://people.weekend.ru/kosaken.

10. Some of this literature is published and distributed by Vladimir Popov through the publishing house "Pallada," without direct reference to the PNP.

11. The agreement to set up the coordinating council was signed by Alexander Ivanov-Sukharevsky, head of the People's National Party; Yuri Belyaev, chairman of one of the rival National-Republican Parties of Russia; Eduard Limonov, chairman of the National-Bolshevik Party; Georgy Shepelev, leader of the New Public Russian Movement (NORD); Oleg Bakhtiyarov, chairman of the Party of Slavic Unity; Andrei Arkhipov, chairman of the Right-Radical Party; and representatives of the Russian Party, and of the editorial board of the journal *For the Russian Cause* [*Za russkoe delo*]. There was one more signatory whom I have not been able to identify. The text of the agreement was published in *Era Rossii* nos. 16–17.

12. For further analysis of relations between Russian and Ukrainian radical nationalists, see Khomchuk (1995).

13. The PNP website lists 104 names and addresses through which inquirers may establish contact with the party. Twenty-seven of the contact persons named—that is, over a quarter—are women. Fifty different locations in all of Russia's major regions are represented, of which thirty-five are cities or large towns, ten small towns, three industrial settlements, and two villages.

14. A specialist in epidemics among animals. Information on Lysenko's background is taken mainly from Pribylovskii (1995, pp. 69–71). For the account of the demise of Lysenko's party, I am indebted to Alexander Verkhovsky.

15. For the text of one of the NRPR's anti-Caucasian leaflets, dated 1993 and with a print run of 250,000, see Verkhovskii and Pribylovskii (1996, pp. 121–22). The communist who objected to the leaflet was Sazha Umalatova, herself of Caucasian origin.

16. Lysenko took a favorable attitude to "nationally conscious" Jews. He did not like semi-assimilated Russian Jews. This, however, was not anti-Semitism as such, but rather the prejudice that is commonly found among nationalists of all ethnic groups against people whose ethnic identity is mixed or unclear.

17. The term *Sobornaia Duma* is difficult to translate. Those who coined it presumably had in mind a parliament that possesses the quality of *sobornost*—that is, the spiritual harmony supposedly inherent in Russian national character and tradition.

18. I cannot use the acronym "RNU" for "Russian National Union" because I have already used it for "Russian National Unity." Instead I use "RNS," taken from the Russian *Russkii natsional'nyi soiuz*. The information on Vdovin and Kasimovsky is taken from Pribylovskii (1995, pp. 36, 58).

19. Kasimov is a city to the west of Kazan. The Tatars of Kasimov, unlike those of Kazan, did not put up armed resistance to their incorporation into the young Muscovite empire.

20. The article in *Russkii poriadok* in which Vdovin appeals to his former comrades-in-arms identifies him as "an associate of the RNU, former chairman of the RNS." Despite his leadership status in his previous organization, he was not allowed to join the RNU as a full comrade-in-arms.

21. The source of my information on the RNS (RNSP) where other sources are not indicated is the former website of the organization at www.ruspatriot.com/rns.

The new website at rnsp.wpww.com is much less informative. An earlier version of the RNS program is given by Verkhovskii and Pribylovskii (1996, pp. 148–50). A collection of RNS texts is provided in Verkhovskii and Pribylovskii (1997, pp. 148–53). I am grateful to Alexander Verkhovsky for providing me with additional information on the most recent developments.

22. The RNS takes no position concerning who should succeed to the throne (Verkhovskii et al. 1996, p. 164).

23. Often represented by the numerical code 88, standing for HH, H being the eighth letter of the Latin—not of the Cyrillic!—alphabet.

24. The sole concession made to the autonomy of non-Russian peoples is a provision that one-third of the representatives of the imperial authorities in the national colonies may be subjects—that is, natives. The other two-thirds must be citizens—that is, (Great) Russians.

25. Among other victims of RNS violence have been members of minority religious sects.

26. For quotations from *Shturmovik*, see Deich (1999). A couple of illustrative samples: "If you're a nigger, a yellow or a Yid, you'll be paid back for your appearance with a series of good blows to various parts of the body." "If to secure world dominion for the Russian race we have to drown two billion aliens in blood, we shall not waver."

27. I have not been able to obtain any more information on this organization.

28. The information on Osipov is taken from Pribylovskii (1995, pp. 77–78); Verkhovskii et al. (1996, pp. 298–99); and Verkhovskii et al. (1998, pp. 35–37).

29. Vladimir Mayakovsky was a famous poet of the early Soviet period.

30. The *veche* was the traditional assembly of citizens in the free cities of Pskov and Novgorod in the times before Ivan the Terrible imposed a centralized autocracy on Russia. The choice of this name therefore expresses Osipov's desire to combine Russian nativism with democracy. For a fuller discussion of the politics of the journal, see Yanov (1978, ch. 4). It was also in 1971 that Osipov made the acquaintance of Alexander Solzhenitsyn, with whose views he was in general sympathy.

31. For a short time in 1989, Osipov was a member of the coordinating council of the Popular Front, the umbrella organization of the democratic movement, and tried to create a faction of "patriotic democrats" or "democratic patriots" within the Front.

32. Yanov (1978) argues that inconsistencies inherent in liberal nationalism make such transformations inevitable. One need not necessarily accept such an absolute formulation to appreciate the difficulties of maintaining a liberal nationalist position.

33. As Osipov explained to the press, the UCR found two Ukrainian policies especially objectionable: the refusal to grant Russian the status of an official language in Ukraine, and "the attempt of the Ukrainian authorities to split the Russian Orthodox Church by imposing independence of the Moscow Patriarchate on the Kiev Metropolitanate." The religious slant of the UCR's ideology was also expressed in the main slogan chanted by the demonstrators: "Anathema to the Russophobes!"

34. Information about the ideology of the UCR is taken mainly from Verkhovskii et al. (1996, pp. 201–204); Verkhovskii and Pribylovskii (1996, pp.

75–77); and Verkhovskii and Pribylovskii (1997, pp. 167–70). Other Church-oriented religio-political organizations of "patriotic" orientation are the Union of Orthodox Citizens, "For Faith and Motherland," and the Russian Orthodox Party of Russia (Verkhovskii 2000).

35. It should be noted that not all members of the UCR adhere to the official Russian Orthodox Church. Some support the émigré Russian Orthodox Church Abroad, others the dissident True Orthodox Church.

36. Other prominent brotherhoods belonging to the UOB are the St. Petersburg brotherhood led by Konstantin Dushenov, editor of the newspaper *Pravoslavnaia Rossiia* [Orthodox Russia], and the brotherhood named in honor of the wonder-workers Sergy of Radonezh and Serafim of Sarov, led by the psychiatrist Nikolai Filimonov, former head of one of the offshoots of *Pamyat* (Verkhovskii 2000).

37. Shnirelman (1998a, b) gives a general survey of the pagan fascist scene.

38. Biographical information on Ilya Lazarenko is given by Pribylovskii (1995, p. 66), and by Verkhovskii et al. (1996, p. 276).

39. The first issue, a copy of which is in my possession, contains a long article in memory of Mussolini, who is also quoted in the editorial. The motto on the journal's masthead reads: "Toward unity, recuperation, and awakening!" According to the website of the Society of Nav, *Nash Marsh* was later banned. In 1994 it was replaced by *Narodnyi stroi* [People's Order].

40. It seems that in 1996 Lazarenko was also involved for a time in the Russian Socialist Party of the wealthy businessman Vladimir Bryntsalov.

41. Information on the Society of Nav, unless otherwise indicated, is taken from the website of the organization at http://www.chat.ru/~navi1.

42. It is granted that Orthodoxy is not quite as bad as other branches of Christianity, having been superficially Russified through the adoption of some forms taken from the Nordic (i.e., Hyperborean) tradition.

Notes to Chapter 9

1. A more detailed classification of Russian "national-patriotic" organizations is given in an essay by Verkhovskii and Pribylovskii (1996, pp. 93–102). A number of the points I make in this section are developed in that essay. I am also grateful to Andreas Umland for my discussions with him on this topic, and in particular for impressing upon me the crucial significance of the distinction between native and mimetic fascism.

2. The big problem in implementing the principle is, of course, that of defining the borders of the "small but purely Russian" Russia in such a way as to include as many Russians as possible while keeping out as many non-Russians as possible.

3. In his typology of Russian nationalisms, Simonsen (1996c) names the three possible variants presented here "empire-saving nationalism," "ethnic core nationalism," and "Russian supremacist nationalism," respectively. Simonsen's fourth category, "Russian Federation nationalism," is not to be found in the part of the political spectrum with which I am concerned.

4. This is the crudest possible periodization. I neglect issues relating to subtler distinctions, such as that between the tsarism of the Kievan, Muscovite, and St. Petersburg periods.

5. There is a *Book of Vles* that is widely read in "patriotic" circles and that

purports to be a chronicle of pagan Rus predating all other known documentary sources. There is general agreement among professional historians that the *Book of Vles* is a forgery (Shnirelman 1998b, pp. 3–11).

Note to Conclusion

1. For one such dismissive view, see Paniushkin (2000), who argues that the RNU should be regarded as "marginals" and hooligans, not as a serious political organization. It is, in any case, arguable whether in the unstable conditions of post-Soviet Russia the distinction between the political mainstream and the political margins is a valid one. I shall not address this theoretical issue here.

Notes to Afterword

1. Among other manifestations of the pro-Putin trend in nationalist circles, we may note the Tenth Congress of the Russian All-People's Union (ROS) on February 5, 2000, which voted 62 to16 with 12 abstentions to break with the custom of putting forward their own leader, Sergei Baburin, as candidate for president and to support Putin instead, and the Fifth Congress of Russian Nationalists in St. Petersburg on February 18, 2000, which passed a resolution expressing conditional support for Putin (Panchenko 2000; Pribylovskii 2000).

2. In describing the split in the RNU, I rely primarily on the account given by Likhachev (2000) and on a series of documents that were posted during September 2000 on the RNU website at www.rne.org/news. I am grateful to Bob Otto for printing these documents and mailing them to me.

3. In the light of Lalochkin's evident hostility toward Kassin, it is puzzling that Lalochkin's name should appear on the list of signatories of the declaration of Kassin's grouping. Perhaps it was put there without his consent.

Bibliographical Note

English-language scholarly sources on fascist tendencies and movements in post-Soviet Russia are meager. There are quite a few scholars who write about Russian nationalist politics, and some of these have written something about fascist movements, usually the RNU, but fascism is not central to their work (Allensworth 1998; Dunlop 1996; Simonsen 1996a, 1996b). An exception is Laqueur (1993), which though outdated remains valuable from a historical point of view. Also worthy of note is the short monograph of Victor Shnirelman on the neo-pagan fascists (Shnirelman 1998b). There are a few younger scholars who are doing excellent research on topics related to Russian fascism, but hardly any of their work has yet appeared in print.

The situation is somewhat better when it comes to Russian-language sources. The Information-Expert Group "PANORAMA" produces a continuing series of excellent general volumes containing analytical as well as reference material about fascist and near-fascist ("national-patriotic") movements and tendencies in Russia (Pribylovskii 1994, 1995; Verkhovskii et al. 1996; Verkhovskii and Pribylovskii 1996, 1997; Verkhovskii et al. 1998, 1999). In addition to these general volumes, there are volumes devoted to particular organizations, such as Verkhovsky (1994) on the Liberal-Democratic Party of Russia and Likhachev and Pribylovsky (1997) on the Russian National Unity. I understand that Vyacheslav Likhachev is currently preparing a volume on the National-Bolshevik Party.

The Russian central and provincial press carries a considerable amount of material, of widely varying quality, about fascist organizations. Of particular interest are the "inside scoops" that appear in *Moskovskii komsomolets*. Relevant articles from newspapers throughout Russia are conveniently brought together in the bulletin "National-Extremism in the Regions of the Russian Federation," distributed by the What the Papers Say (WPS) press service.

Several periodicals are distributed by antifascist activists in Russia. I have made use of four of them: *Diagnoz*, published by the All-Russian

Jewish Congress; the St. Petersburg *Bar'er; Tum-balalaika;* and the especially useful *Anti-Fa Info* (Information Bulletin of the Antifascist Congress of the South of Russia), which is available from the Voronezh Antifascist Center by E-mail <war@horror.vrn.ru>. There are apparently yet other antifascist periodicals, but it is difficult to get hold of them.

A vast quantity of material pertinent to the study of Russian fascism is now accessible on the Internet. Lists of sites of extremist organizations are available at http://www.panorama.ru/works/patr/extr.html and at http://www.geocities.com/averh/extr.html. Also worth consulting is the list of sites of political organizations at http://www.politika.ru.

Another source of some interest is *Nuzhen* 1996. Finally, Alexander Yanov's book is stimulating and provocative, but not scholarly (Ianov 1995).

Bibliography

Ageichev, Igor′. 2000. "Draka u muzeia Lenina" [Fight by the Lenin Museum]. *Nezavisimaia gazeta*, April 22.

Agursky, Mikhail. 1986. "The prospects of National Bolshevism." In*The Last Empire: Nationality and the Soviet Future*, ed. Robert Conquest, pp. 87–108. Stanford, CA: Hooper Institution Press.

———. 1987. *The Third Rome: National Bolshevism in the USSR*. Boulder, CO: Westview Press.

Aizenburg, Olia. 1999. "Vy slyshite, grokhochut sapogi?" [Do You Hear the Rumble of Boots?]. *Cheliabinskii rabochii*, April 21 and 22.

Akopov, Petr. 2000. "Te, kto protiv vsekh" [Those Who Are Against All]. *Izvestiia*, March 24, p. 3.

———. 1999a. "Rossiiskii elektorat medlenno, no verno dreifuet v storonu RNE" [The Russian Electorate Slowly But Surely Drifts Toward RNU]. *Nezavisimaia gazeta*, February 4.

———. 1999b. "Tak my dozhivem do kanibalizma" [So We Shall Live to See Cannibalism], *Nezavisimaia gazeta: Figury i Litsa*, no. 9 (August 5).

Aksenov, Dmitrii. 1999. "RNE: 'spodvizhniki' i 'soratniki' " [The RNU: "Fellow-Builders" and "Comrades-in-Arms"]. *Samarskoe obozrenie*, August 23.

"Aktivistov RNE potianulo na ugolovku" [RNU Activists Pulled Into Crime]. 2000. *Kriminal-ekspress* (Omsk), March 29, p. 1.

Albaut, Tatiana. 1999. "Ne zapadlo" [It Didn't Sink]. *Novaia sibir′* (Novosibirsk), June 14.

Alexseev, Mikhail A. 2000. *Are Chinese Migrants at Risk in Primorskii krai? Monitoring Interethnic Relations with Opinion and Event Data.* Paper presented at the Fifth Annual World Convention of the Association for the Study of Nationalities, Columbia University, New York, April 13–15.

Alexseev, Mikhail A., and Vagin, Vladimir. 1999a. "Fortress Russia or Gateway to Europe? The Pskov Connection." In Mikhail A. Alexseev, ed. *Center-Periphery Conflict in Post-Soviet Russia: A Federation Imperiled*, pp. 167–203. New York: St. Martin's Press.

———. 1999b. "Russian Regions in Expanding Europe: The Pskov Connection." *Europe–Asia Studies* 51, no. 1 (January): pp. 43–64.

Alferov, Sviashchennik Timofei. 1996. "Otkrytaia subtserkov′" [An Open Sub-Church]. *Russkii pastyr,′* no. 26(III).

Allensworth, Wayne. 1998. *The Russian Question: Nationalism, Modernization, and Post-Communist Russia.* Lanham and Oxford: Rowman & Littlefield.

Amelina, Iana. 1998a. "Svoboda slova po-natsistski" [Freedom of Speech á la Nazi]. *Express-Chronicle*, December 14.

———. 1998b. "Zapret s″ezda RNE nezakonen" [The Ban on the RNU Congress Is Illegal]. *Express Chronicle*, December 21.

Andreev, Andrei. 1997. *Politicheskii spektr Rossii* [Russia's Political Spectrum]. Moscow: Editorial URSS.

Anis′ko, Sergei. 1999. "Belorusskii filial RNE prosypaetsia ot spiachki" [The Belarusian Branch of RNU Wakes Up]. *Segodnia*, no. 25 (February 5).

Anis′ko, Sergei; and Koretskii, Aleksandr. 1999. "RNE namereno vziat′ Moskvu sudebnym izmorom" [The RNU Intends to Take Moscow by Courtroom Attrition]. *Segodnia*, no. 31 (February 12).

Anti-Fa Info. 2000. Information Bulletin of the Anti-Fascist Congress of the South of Russia. Available from the Voronezh Antifascist Center at war@horror.vrn.ru.

"Arms Cache Seized from Chief of Air Force Unit Near Moscow." 1997. *Moskovskii komsomolets*, May 6.

Arshanskii, Roman. 1999. "S krikom 'kiia!' i udarom nogi" [With a Cry of "Kiya!" and a Kick]. *Moskovskii komsomolets*, no. 23 (February 6).

Avdeeva, L.P. 1992. *Russkie mysliteli: Ap. A. Grigor′ev, N.Ia. Danilevskii, N.N. Strakhov. Filosofskaia kul′turologiia vtoroi poloviny XIX veka* [The Russian Thinkers Ap.A. Grigorev, N.Ya. Danilevsky, and N.N. Strakhov: Philosophical Culturology of the Second Half of the Nineteenth Century]. Moscow: Izdatel′stvo Moskovskogo universiteta.

Averbukh, Viktor; Vladimirov, Dmitrii; and Punanov, Grigorii. 2000. "Molodezhnaia organizatsiia budet sozdana po obrazu Komsomola" [A Youth Organization Will Be Set Up on the Pattern of the Komsomol]. *Izvestiia*, April 10.

Averbukh, Viktoriia. 2000. "Anti-antifashisty" [Anti-antifascists]. *Izvestiia*, May 4, p. 1.

Averkii, Archbishop. 1991. "K voprosu o staroi i novoi orthografii" [On the Question of the Old and New Orthography]. *Pamyat′*, no. 1 (January).

"Aziatskii pokhod NBP" [The NBP's Asian Expedition]. 1997. *Limonka*, no. 67 (June), p. 1.

Babich, Dmitrii. 1998. "170 Hectares in Downtown Moscow Have Been Seized by Commandos." *Komsomol′skaia pravda*, May 16.

———. 1999. "The National Socialists." *The Moscow Times*, April 24.

Babichenko, Denis. 1998a. "Istoricheskii udar po KPRF" [A Historical Blow Against the CPRF]. *Segodnia*, no. 269 (December 2).

———. 1998b. "Moskva zapretila s″ezd chernorubashechnikov" [Moscow Has Banned the Blackshirts' Congress]. *Segodnia*, no. 279 (December 16).

———. 1999. "Kreml′ vzialsia za RNE" [The Kremlin Takes On RNU]. *Segodnia*, no. 8 (January 16).

Bacon, Edwin. 1997. "The Church and Politics in Russia: A Case Study of the 1996 Presidential Election." *Religion, State & Society*, vol. 25, no. 3, pp. 253–65.

Badkhen, Anna. 1998. "City Police Chief Plans Mounted Cossack Patrols." *St. Petersburg Times*, no. 376 (June 26).

Bakinskii, Aleksandr. 1997. "Belye vorony: kak zhivetsia 'tsvetnym' v Rossii" [White Crows: How "Colored People" Live in Russia]. *Izvestiia*, September 23.

Balburov, Dmitrii. 1997. "Shashka Barkashova posluzhit Prezidentu" [Barkashov's Outfit Will Serve the President]. *Moskovskie novosti*, no. 7 (February 18).

———. 1999. "Novoe russkoe edinstvo" [The New Russian Unity]. *Moskovskie novosti*, no. 2 (January 19).

Banerjee, Neela. 1998. "Hitler's Skinhead Fans on a Racist Rampage." *Sydney Morning Herald*, May 9.

Barghoorn, Frederick C. 1956. *Soviet Russian Nationalism*. New York: Oxford University Press.

———. 1980. "Four Faces of Soviet Russian Ethnocentrism." In *Ethnic Russia in the USSR: The Dilemmas of Dominance*, ed. Edward Allworth, pp. 55–66. New York: Pergamon Press.

Barinov, Dmitrii. 1998. "Moskovskomu meru groziat otomstit′ na vyborakh" [They Threaten to Take Revenge on the Moscow Mayor at the Elections]. *Novye izvestiia*, December 17.

Barkashov, A.P. 1994. *Azbuka russkogo natsionalista* [ABC of a Russian Nationalist]. Moscow: Slovo-1.

______. 1995. Interview. *Moscow News*, no. 3, January 20–26, p. 6.

———. 1997a. "Razoblachennaia doktrina" [The Doctrine Unmasked]. *Russkii poriadok*, no. 4(45), pp. 32–34.

______. 1997b. "Znaki vremen" [Signs of the Times]. *Russkii poriadok*, no. 4(45), pp. 35–37.

"Barkashovtsy nachnut sazhat′ derev′i?" [Are the Barkashovites Going to Start Planting Trees?]. 1998. *Komsomol′skaia pravda*, no. 201 (October 27).

Barkov, Leonid. 2000a. "Studenty v Volgograde postradali za 'ne tot′ tsvet kozhi" [Students in Volgograd Suffer for the Wrong Skin Color]. *Vremia*, April 8, p. 2.

______. 2000b. "Vozmozhen li fashizm v gorode, polveka nazad ego pobedivshem?" [Is Fascism Possible in a City That Defeated It Half a Century Ago?]. *Vremia MN*, May 11, p. 6.

Bassin, Mark. 1991. "Russia Between Europe and Asia: The Ideological Construction of Geographical Space." *Slavic Review* 50, no. 1 (Spring), pp. 1–17.

Belasheva, Irina. 1999. "Tirazhi i mirazhi" [Print Runs and Mirages]. *Vremia-MN*, March 25, p. 3.

Belykh, Vadim. 1998. "RNE obvinilo mera Moskvy v politicheskom ekstremizme" [RNU Has Accused the Mayor of Moscow of Political Extremism]. *Novye izvestiia*, December 17.

Berdiaev, Nikolai. 1952. *Christianity and Anti-Semitism*. Aldington, Kent: Hand and Flower Press.

Berghahn, Volker R. 1994. *Imperial Germany, 1871–1914: Economy, Society, Culture, and Politics*. Providence and Oxford: Berghahn Books.

Blinov, Aleksandr. 1997. "Rossiiskie natsisty patruliruiut ulitsy Voronezha" [Russian Nazis Patrol the Streets of Voronezh]. *Nezavisimaia gazeta*, October 18.

Bondarenko, Mariia. 1998. "Vyvedut li barkashovtsy Rossiiu iz krizisa?" [Will the Barkashovites Lead Russia Out of Crisis?]. *Nezavisimaia gazeta*, August 16.

Borisov, Sergei. 1999. "Parallel′nye miry" [Parallel Worlds]. *Nezavisimaia gazeta—Religii*, February 3.

Borodenkov, Dmitrii. 1997. "Deti smuty" [Children of Confusion]. *Ogonek*, no. 36, September 8.

Borovoi, S.Ia. 1997. "Evrei v Zaporozhskoi Sechi" [Jews in the Zaporozhye Fortress]. In *Evreiskie khroniki XVII stoletiia* [Jewish Chronicles of the Seventeenth Century], pp. 207–50. Moscow and Jerusalem: Gesharim.

Bourdeaux, Michael, ed. 1995. *The Politics of Religion in Russia and the New States of Eurasia.* Armonk, NY, and London: M.E. Sharpe.

Bronzova, Mariia. 1999. "Ataka na RNE usilivaetsia" [Attack on the RNU Grows]. *Nezavisimaia gazeta*, no. 40 (March 5).

Broszat, Martin. 1966. *German National Socialism 1919–1945.* Santa Barbara, CA: Clio Press.

Buketov, Kirill. 1993. "The Russian Trade Unions and Yeltsin's Coup." *Russian Labor Review*, no. 3, pp. 34–38.

———. 1994. "Russian Fascism and Russian Fascists." *Russian Labor Review*, no. 5.

Buldakov, Valerii, and Selezneva, Iva. 1999. "Moskovskii masshtab" [On the Scale of Moscow]. *Argumenty i fakty*, no. 17, April 28.

Butkevich, Nickolai. 2000. "Putin Flirts with Extremists," *Transitions Online* (www.tol.cz), September 25.

Buzgalin, Aleksandr. 1997. "Russia's Communist Party: A Party With a Communist Name, Great-Power Policies, and Nostalgic Members." *Prism*, vol. III, no. 11, part 3.

Chelnokov, Aleksei. 1999. "Gesheft na fashistakh" [The Business With the Fascists]. *Literaturnaia gazeta*, no. 12 (March), p. 4.

Cherkasov, Valerii. 1999. "Britogolovye 'mstiteli'" [Skinhead Avengers]. *Izvestiia*, February 17, p. 8.

Cherniak, Igor'. 1995. "O generale Filatove" [On General Filatov]. *Komsomol'skaia pravda*, February 22.

Chernykh, L. 1999. "Limonov—net. Limonov—est'" [Limonov Is Not There. There He Is]. *Orenburzh'e*, June 23.

"Chert v meshke" [Devil in a Bag]. 1998. *Rossiiskie vesti*, August 12.

Chistiakov, Georgii. 1996. "Otkuda etot gnev?" [Whence This Anger?]. *Russkaia mysl'* (Paris), October 10.

Chuchkova, Diana. 1999. "Natsboly v nokdaune" [National Bolsheviks in Knockdown]. *Chas* (Riga), July 30.

Clark, Victoria. 1997. "Church Leads March Out of Western Path." *The Times* (London), August 31.

Cohn, Norman Rufus Colin. 1957. *The Pursuit of the Millennium: Revolutionary Millenarians and Mystical Anarchists of the Middle Ages.* London: Secker & Warburg.

———. 1967. *Warrant for Genocide: The Myth of the Jewish World Conspiracy and the Protocols of the Elders of Zion.* New York: Harper & Row.

Conquest, Robert, ed. 1986. *The Last Empire: Nationality and the Soviet Future.* Stanford, CA: Hoover Institution Press.

Cronin, Mike, ed. 1996. *The Failure of British Fascism: The Far Right and the Fight for Political Recognition.* New York: St. Martin's Press.

Daly, Emma. 2000. "Women Join Franco's Top Fighting Unit." *The Guardian Weekly*, March 23–29, p. 7.

Danilevskii, N.Ia. 1889. *Rossiia i Evropa: Vzgliad na kul'turnye i politicheskie otnosheniia slavianskogo mira k germano-romanskomu* [Russia and Europe: A View on the Cultural and Political Relations of the Slav to the Germano-Roman World]. St. Petersburg.

Davydova, Nadezhda. 1998. "Regional Specifics of Russian Mentality." *Social Sciences*, no. 1.

De Felice, Renzo. 1977. *Interpretations of Fascism*. Cambridge, MA: Harvard University Press.

De Grand, Alexander J. 1995. *Fascist Italy and Nazi Germany: The "Fascist" Style of Rule*. London and New York: Routledge.

Deich, Mark. 1998a. "Luzhkov v interesnom polozhenii" [Luzhkov in an Interesting Situation]. *Moskovskii komsomolets*, no. 238 (December 15).

———. 1998b. "Yurii Luzhkov: 'Vyzov vsei Moskve' " [Yuri Luzhkov: "A Challenge to the Whole of Moscow"]. *Moskovskii komsomolets*, no. 242 (December 19).

———. 1999. "Nashi uzhe prishli" [Ours Have Already Come]. *Moskovskii komsomolets*, no. 213, November 5.

———. 2000. "Psikho-lingvisticheskie igry" [Psycholinguistic Games]. *Moskovskii komsomolets*, April 24, p. 2.

Deinekin, Petr. 1999. "Kazakov pora vooruzhat'" [It's Time to Arm the Cossacks]. *Nezavisimaia gazeta*, November 27, p. 4.

Dennen, Xenia. 1997. "Persecution of the True Orthodox Church Today: Russian Authorities Use Repressive Methods of Soviet Past." *The Shepherd* (UK), April.

Derluguian, Georgi M., and Cipko, Serge. 1997. "The Politics of Identity in a Russian Borderland Province: The Kuban Neo-Cossack Movement, 1989–1996." *Europe-Asia Studies*, vol. 49, no. 8 (December), pp. 1485–1500.

Diupin, Sergei, and Neverovskii, Al'gerd. 1999. "Barkashovtsy vyshli iz podpol'ia" [Barkashovites Emerge from Underground]. *Kommersant-Daily*, no. 16 (February 9).

Dobrynina, Svetlana. 1998. "Zloveshchaia ten' svastiki" [The Sinister Shadow of the Swastika]. *Nezavisimaia gazeta*, no. 87(1658), May 18.

Dolgov, K.M. 1997. *Voskhozhdenie na Afon: zhizn' i mirosozertsanie Konstantina Leontieva* [Ascent to Mount Athens: Life and Worldview of Konstantin Leontiev]. Moscow: Raritet.

Dostoevskii, F. 1877. *Dnevnik pisatelia* [Diary of a Writer]. Moscow.

Dugin, Aleksandr. 1996a. *Misterii Evrazii* [Mysteries of Eurasia]. Moscow: Arktogeia.

———. 1996b. "Sub"ekt bez granits" [Subject Without Boundaries]. *Elementy*, no. 7, pp. 3–6.

———. 1997a. "Evrei i Evraziia" [The Jews and Eurasia]. *Zavtra* 47(208), November 25.

———. 1997b. *Osnovy geopolitiki: Geopoliticheskoe budushchee Rossii* [Foundations of Geopolitics: Russia's Geopolitical Future]. Moscow: Arktogeia.

———. 1997c. *Tampliery proletariata: Natsional-bol'shevizm i initsiatsiia* [Knights Templar of the Proletariat: National-Bolshevism and Initiation]. Moscow: Arktogeia.

———. 1999. "Ot imeni Evrazii" [In the Name of Eurasia]. *Moskovskie novosti*, no. 7 (February 24).

Dunlop, John B. 1995. "The Russian Orthodox Church as an 'Empire-Saving' Institution." In Bourdeaux, ed., 1995, pp. 15–40.

———. 1996. "Alexander Barkashov and the Rise of National Socialism in Russia." *Demokratizatsiya* IV, no. 4 (Fall), pp. 519–30.

Ebata, Michi. 1997. "The Internationalization of the Extreme Right." In *The Extreme Right: Freedom and Security at Risk*, ed. Aurel Braun and Stephen Scheinberg, pp. 220–49. Boulder, CO: Westview Press.

Eliseev, Ierei Vladimir. 1995. *Pravoslavnyi put' ko spaseniiu i vostochnye i okkul'tnye misticheskie ucheniia* [The Orthodox Path to Salvation and Eastern and Occult Mystical Teachings]. Moscow: *Danilovskii blagovestnik.*

Ellis, Jane. 1986. *The Russian Orthodox Church: A Contemporary History.* Bloomington: Indiana University Press.

———. 1996. *The Russian Orthodox Church: Triumphalism and Defensiveness.* Houndmills, U.K. and New York: Macmillan and St. Martin's Press.

Evola, Julius. 1995. *Revolt Against the Modern World.* Rochester, VT: Inner Traditions International.

"Far Eastern Nazis." 1998. *Hello Russia/Privet Rossiia* (Khabarovsk), no. 7 (October 11).

Farutin, Andrei. 1999. "Barkashovtsy zameniat Komsomol" [Barkashovites Replace the Komsomol]. *Nezavisimaia gazeta—Regiony*, no. 9 (May).

Feduta, Aleksandr. 1999. "Mezhdu Pepsi i kvasom" [Between Pepsi and Russian Beer]. *Moskovskie novosti*, no. 3 (January 26).

Feldman, Gerald D. 1995. *Jewish Bankers and the Crises of the Weimar Republic.* The Leo Baeck Memorial Lecture 39. New York: Leo Baeck Institute.

Filatov, S.B., and Furman, D.E. 1992. "Religiia i politika v massovom soznanii" [Religion and Politics in Mass Consciousness]. *Sotsiologicheskie issledovaniia*, no. 7, pp. 3–12.

Filimonov, Dmitrii. 1998. "Korichnevaia Rossiia" [Brown Russia]. *Izvestiia*, no. 104 (June 9), p. 5.

Filonenko, Valerii. 2000. "Russkii poriadok nagrianul neozhidanno" [Russian Order Arrives Unexpectedly]. *Novye izvestiia*, April 1, p. 5.

Finkelstein, Norman G. 1995. *Image and Reality of the Israel–Palestine Conflict.* London and New York: Verso.

Finley, M.I. 1956. *The World of Odysseus.* London: Chatto & Windus.

Fireside, Harvey. 1971. *Icon and Swastika: The Russian Orthodox Church Under Nazi and Soviet Control.* Cambridge, MA: Harvard University Press.

Fishkin, Vitalii. 1999. "Skinkhedy—znachit britogolovye" [Skinheads Mean Shaven Heads]. *Molodoi kommunar* (Voronezh), May 22.

Flikke, Geir. 1999. "Patriotic Left-Centrism: The Zigzags of the Communist Party of the Russian Federation." *Europe–Asia Studies*, vol. 51, no. 2 (March), pp. 275–98.

Forman, James D. 1974. *Fascism: The Meaning and Experience of Reactionary Revolution.* New York: Franklin Watts.

Furman, Dmitrii. 1997. "Russkie i ukraintsy: trudnye otnosheniia brat'ev" [Russians and Ukrainians: The Difficult Relations of Brothers]. In *Ukraina i Rossiia: obshchestva i gosudarstva.* [Ukraine and Russia: Societies and States], pp. 3–18. Moscow: Prava cheloveka.

———. 1999. "Oni v svoikh koridorakh" [In Their Corridors]. *Obshchaia gazeta*, no. 2 (January 14).

Gamaiunov, Igor'. 1993. "Kazaki-razboiniki" [Cossack-Bandits]. *Literaturnaia gazeta*, no. 4, January 27, p. 12.

Garin, Petr. 1999. "Barkashovtsev sudiat, no poka bezuspeshno" [Barkashovites Prosecuted, But So Far Without Success]. *Nash variant* (Kirov), May 20.

Gellner, Ernest. 1983. *Nations and Nationalism.* London: Blackwell Publishers.
Gerasimov, Aleksei. 1999. "Natsionalista obviniaiut v prizyvakh k besporiadkam" [Nationalist Accused of Appeals for Mass Disorders]. *Kommersant-Daily*, May 13.
Gessen, Masha. 1997. "Fashistskaia pressa" [The Fascist Press]. *Itogi*, no. 12 (March 25), pp. 59–60.
Glikin, Maksim; Remneva, Kira; and Sokolov, Dmitrii. 1999. "Prosto russkii esesovets, po goroskopu 'Vesy'" [Simply a Russian SS Man with Horoscope "Libra"]. *Obshchaia gazeta*, no. 67 (April 21).
Golovanivskaia, Maria; Kostikov, Roman; and Diupin, Sergei. 1999. "Fashizm proshel" [Fascism Has Passed]. *Kommersant-Daily*, no. 11, February 2.
Golts, Aleksandr. 1999. *Itogi*, no. 26(111), July 8, pp. 23–25.
Goodrick-Clarke, Nicholas. 1992. *The Occult Roots of Nazism: Secret Aryan Cults and Their Influence on Nazi Ideology. The Ariosophists of Austria and Germany, 1890–1935.* New York and London: New York University Press.
———. 1998. *Hitler's Priestess: Savitri Devi, the Hindu–Aryan Myth, and Neo-Nazism.* New York and London: New York University Press.
Govorukhin, Stanislav. 1994. *Strana vorov na doroge v svetloe budushchee* [The Country of Thieves on the Road to a Bright Future]. Narva: Shans.
Gradnitsyn, A.A. 1991. "Obshchestvennoe mnenie o vozrozhdenii donskogo kazachestva" [Public Opinion on the Revival of Don Cossackdom]. *SOTSIS: Sotsiologicheskie issledovaniia*, no. 12, pp. 78–84.
Graev, Viktor. 1998. "Natsisty ne khotiat byt' fashistami" [Nazis Do Not Want to Be Fascists]. *Diagnoz: antifashistskoe obozrenie*, no. 3 (June), pp.14–15.
Gregor, A. James. 1997. *Interpretations of Fascism.* New Brunswick, NJ, and London: Transaction Publishers.
Griffin, Roger. 1991. *The Nature of Fascism.* New York: St. Martin's Press.
———, ed. 1995. *Fascism.* New York: Oxford University Press.
———, ed. 1998. *International Fascism: Theories, Causes and the New Consensus.* New York: Oxford University Press.
———. 2000. "Plus ça change! The Fascist Mindset behind the Nouvelle Droite's Struggle for Cultural Renewal." In *The Development of the Radical Right in France 1890–1995*, ed. Edward Arnold. London: Routledge.
Gritchin, Nikolai. 1998. "'Front osvobozhdeniia' priblizilsia k Stavropol'iu" [The "Liberation Front" Has Approached Stavropol]. *Izvestiia*, April 25.
Gritchin, Nikolai, and Urigashvili, Besik. 1997. "Rossiiskie neonatsisty utverzhdaiut, chto ikh liudi pronikli vo vse vlastnye struktury" [Russian Neo-Nazis Claim That Their People Have Penetrated All Power Structures]. *Izvestiia*, July 12.
Gulyga, Arsenii. 1995. *Russkaia ideia i ee tvortsy* [The Russian Idea and Its Creators]. Moscow: Soratnik.
Gumilev, L.N. 1989. *Drevniaia Rus' i Velikaia step'* [Ancient Rus and the Great Steppe]. Moscow: Mysl'.
———. 1990. *Ethnogenesis and the Biosphere.* Moscow: Progress Publishers.
Gumilev, Lev, and Panchenko, Aleksandr. 1990. *Chtoby svecha ne pogasla: dialog* [So That the Candle Does Not Go Out: Dialog]. Leningrad: Sovetskii pisatel'.
Hanson, Stephen E., and Kopstein, Jeffrey S. 1997. "The Weimar/Russia Comparison." *Post-Soviet Affairs*, vol. 13, no. 3 (July–September), pp. 252–83.

Hardeman, Hilde. 1994. *Coming to Terms with the Soviet Regime: The "Changing Signposts" Movement among Russian Emigres in the Early 1920s.* DeKalb: Northern Illinois University Press.

Hauner, Milan. 1990. *What Is Asia to Us? Russia's Asian Heartland Yesterday and Today.* Boston: Unwin Hyman.

Herf, Jeffrey. 1984. *Reactionary Modernism: Technology, Culture, and Politics in Weimar and the Third Reich.* Cambridge: Cambridge University Press.

Hutchinson, John, and Smith, Anthony D., eds. 1994. *Nationalism.* Oxford and New York: Oxford University Press.

"I Vserossiiskii Uchreditel'nyi S"ezd Dvizheniia 'Russkoe Natsional'noe Edinstvo'" [First All-Russian Founding Congress of the Movement "Russian National Unity"]. 1997. *Russkii poriadok*, no. 4 (45), pp. 57–58.

Iakovlev, Aleksandr. 1998. "KGB porodil russkikh fashistov" [The KGB Gave Rise to Russian Fascists]. *Izvestiia*, June 17.

Ianov, Aleksandr. 1995. *Posle El'tsina: "Veimarskaia" Rossiia* [After Yeltsin: "Weimar" Russia]. Moscow: KRUK.

———. 1999. "Krovavaia i oslepitel'naia sud'ba" [A Bloody and Blind Fate]. *Moskovskie novosti*, no. 3 (January 27).

Igor': Pesni, stikhi, proza, publitsistika, interv'iu Igoria Tal'kova, otkliki na gibel' russkogo poeta-patriota [Igor: Songs, Verses, Prose, Journalism, and Interviews of Igor Talkov. Responses to the Death of a Russian Poet and Patriot]. 1993. Moscow: *Molodaia gvardiia.*

"Igrali mal'chiki v fashistov" [Little Boys Play at Fascism]. 1999. *Komsomol'skaia pravda* (Kaliningrad), March 12, pp. 1, 10, 11.

Il'in, Ivan. 1993. *O griadushchei Rossii: izbrannye stat'i* [On the Coming Russia: Selected Articles]. Moscow: Voennoe izdatel'stvo.

———. 1997. *Esse o russkoi kul'ture* [Essay on Russian Culture]. St. Petersburg: Akropol'.

Il'ina, Natal'ia, ed. 1996. *Pochemu Ziuganov dolzhen stat' prezidentom* [Why Zyuganov Must Become President]. Moscow: Voenizdat.

Ingram, Alan. 1999. "'A Nation Split into Fragments': The Congress of Russian Communities and Russian Nationalist Ideology." *Europe–Asia Studies*, vol. 51, no. 4, pp. 687–704.

Innokentii, Egumen. 1996. "Ia vsegda rad zametit' raznitsu" [I Am Always Glad to Note a Difference]. *Segodnia*, October 10.

Ioann, Mitropolit. 1995a. *Odolenie smuty: slovo k russkomu narodu* [The Overcoming of Confusion: A Word to the Russian People]. St. Petersburg: Izdatel'stvo "Tsarskoe Leto."

———. 1995b. *Samoderzhavie dukha: ocherki russkogo samosoznaniia* [Autocracy of the Spirit: Essays on Russian Self-Awareness]. St. Petersburg: Izdatel'stvo "Tsarskoe Leto."

Iur'ev, Evgenii. 1999. "Barkashovtsy zapasaiutsia sapernymi lopatkami" [The Barkashovites Stock Up on Sappers' Shovels]. *Segodnia*, no. 26, February 6.

Ivanenko, Aleksei. 1999. "V Ekaterinburge privechaiut fashistov" [Yekaterinburg Greets Fascists]. *Moskovskii komsomolets*, no. 62 (April 3).

Ivanits, Linda J. 1989. *Russian Folk Belief.* Armonk, NY, and London: M.E. Sharpe.

Ivanov, Aleksandr. 1997. *Moia vera—rusizm!* [My Faith Is Rusism!]. Moscow: Nasledie predkov.

———. 1998. "Nashi raznoglasiia" [Our Disagreements]. *Ia—russkii*, no. 4(7), p. 1.

Jackson, William D. 1999. "Fascism, Vigilantism, and the State: The Russian National Unity Movement." *Problems of Post-Communism* 46, no. 1 (January), pp. 34–42.

Johnston, Robert H. 1988. *"New Mecca, New Babylon": Paris and the Russian Exiles, 1920–1945.* Kingston and Montreal: McGill–Queen's University Press.

Kak otnosit'sia k sviatyne [How to Relate to Holy Things]. 1998. Moscow: Izdatel'stvo Moskovskoi Patriarkhii.

Kalinina, Iuliia. 1998. "Ne nado boiat'sia cheloveka s ruzh'em" [No Need to Fear the Man with a Gun]. *Moskovskii komsomolets*, no. 245 (December 24).

Kaminskii, Stanislav. 1999. "Raskol v riadakh RNE" [Split in the RNU]. *Vechernie vedomosti* (Ekaterinburg), February 26, p. 1.

Karachinskii, Artem. 1999. "Gadiushnik dlia patriotov" [A Vipers' Nest for Patriots]. *Moskovskii komsomolets*, no. 36 (February 25).

Karamian, Evgenii. 1997. "Vypem krov': gde stakan" [Let's Drink Blood: Where's the Glass?]. *Moskovskii komsomolets*, October 21, p. 1.

———. 1999a. "Sledstvie po delu Iuriia Luzhkova" [Investigation of the Case of Yuri Luzhkov]. *Moskovskii komsomolets*, no. 6 (January 14).

———. 1999b. "Podval dlia Barkashova" [A Basement for Barkashov]. *Moskovskii komsomolets*, no. 29 (February 16).

Karatnycky, Adrian. 1996. "The Real Zyuganov." *The New York Times*, March 5.

Karl Marx and Frederick Engels: Selected Works in One Volume. 1968. Moscow and London: Progress Publishers and Lawrence & Wishart.

Kartsev, Vladimir. 1995. *!Zhirinovsky!* New York: Columbia University Press.

Kashcheev, Nikolai. 2000. "Provokator amnistirovan" [Provocateur Amnestied]. *Tomskii vestnik*, April 21, p. 3.

Kashin, Sergei, and Smirnov, Viktor. 1999. "U nas net opredeleniia fashizma" [We Have No Definition of Fascism]. *Kommersant-Daily*, no. 46 (March 23).

Kas'ianov, A.A., and Cherednik, V.B. 1997. *Ekonomicheskaia programma vozrozhdeniia Rossii* [An Economic Program for the Revival of Russia]. Rostov-on-Don: Rostizdat.

Kharatian, Dmitrii. 1999. "V chem delo?" [What Is It About?]. *Kommersant-Vlast,'* no. 5 (February 9).

Khokhlov, Aleksandr. 1998. "Demokratiia na chernozemakh ne rastet" [Democracy Does Not Grow in the Black Earth Zone]. *Novye izvestiia*, December 10.

Kholmskaia, M.R. 1998. *Kommunisty Rossii: Fakty, idei, tendentsii* [The Communists of Russia: Facts, Ideas, Tendencies]. Moscow.

Khomchuk, Oksana. 1995. "The Far Right in Russia and Ukraine." *The Harriman Review* 8, no. 2 (July), pp. 40–44.

Khorkhe, Evgenii. 1997. "Kak vesti sebia v kinoteatre" [How to Behave Oneself in the Cinema]. *Limonka*, no. 67(2), June.

Khristinin, Iurii. 1999. "RNE blagodarit Luzhkova" [The RNU Thanks Luzhkov]. *Severnyi Kavkaz* (Nal'chik), no. 10 (March), p. 2.

Khudokormov, Andrei. 1994. "Budet li Rossiia fashistskim gosudarstvom?" [Will Russia Be a Fascist State?]. *Izvestiia*, August 18.

Kilina, Olga. 1999. "Barkashovtsy uvazhaiut Gitlera i bliudut chistotu porody" [Barkashovites Respect Hitler and Guard Purity of the Race]. *Vedomosti Samarskoi gubernii*, March 5, p. 3.
Kislitsyn, Lieut.-Gen. Mikhail. 1999. Interview in *Segodnia*, no. 97 (May 7).
Klimentovich, Nikolai. 1998. "Sueveriia" [Superstition]. *Russkii telegraf*, no. 92 (May 28).
Kliuchevsky, V.O. 1994. *A Course in Russian History: The Seventeenth Century*. Armonk, NY, and London: M.E. Sharpe.
Koehl, Robert. 1972. "Feudal Aspects of National Socialism." In Turner 1972, pp. 151–74.
Koestler, Arthur. 1976. *The Thirteenth Tribe: The Khazar Empire and Its Heritage*. London: Pan Books.
Kolesnikov, Vladimir. 1997. *Segodnia*, January 22.
Kolganov, Andrei. 1999. "Natsboly v Irkutske raspisali steny" [National Bolsheviks in Irkutsk Writing on the Walls]. *SM-nomer odin*, October 21.
Kolosov, V.A., and Turovskii, R.F. 1997. "The Electoral Map of Contemporary Russia: Genesis, Structure, and Evolution." *Russian Politics and Law* 35, no. 5 (September–October), pp. 6–27.
Komarov, Evgenii. 1998. "Tserkov' stala delit'sia na 'svoikh' i 'chuzhikh'" [The Church Has Begun to Divide Into "Our Own" and "Aliens"]. *Novye izvestiia*, July 22.
Komarova, Alla, and Karamian, Evgenii. 1998. "No pasaran" [They Shall Not Pass]. *Moskovskii komsomolets*, no. 239 (December 16).
Kopstein, Jeffrey S., and Hanson, Stephen E. 1998. "Paths to Uncivil Societies and Anti-Liberal States: A Reply to Shenfield." *Post-Soviet Affairs*, vol. 14, no. 4 (October–December), pp. 369–75.
Koptev, Dmitrii. 1998. "Predvybornaia bitva s natsionalizmom" [Pre-Electoral Battle With Nationalism]. *Izvestiia*, no. 236 (December 18).
Korbut, Andrei. 1999. "Vozrozhdenie DOSAAF" [DOSAAF Reborn]. *Nezavisimoe voennoe obozrenie*, no. 31(154), August 13–19, p. 3.
Korey, William. 1995. *Russian Antisemitism, Pamyat,' and the Demonology of Zionism*. Chur, Switzerland: Harwood Academic Publishers.
Kornblatt, Judith Deutsch. 1999. "'Christianity, Antisemitism, Nationalism': Russian Orthodoxy in a Reborn Orthodox Russia." In *Consuming Russia: Popular Culture, Sex, and Society Since Gorbachev*, ed. Adele Marie Barker. Durham and London: Duke University Press, pp. 414–36.
Korol'kov, Aleksandr. 1991. *Prorochestva Konstantina Leont'eva* [The Prophecies of Konstantin Leontiev]. St. Petersburg: Izdatel'stvo S.-Peterburgskogo universiteta.
Kosik, V.I. 1997. *Konstantin Leont'ev: Razmyshleniia na Slavianskuiu temu* [Konstantin Leontiev: Reflections on the Slavic Theme]. Moscow: Zertsalo.
Kostikov, Viacheslav. 1998. "Chernyi kvadrat na krasnom fone" [Black Square Against a Red Background]. *Moskovskie novosti*, no. 47 (January 12).
Kozlov, Aleksei. 1998. *ROK: istoki i razvitie* [ROCK: Sources and Development]. Moscow: Mega-Servis.
Kozyreva, Anna. 1996. "Short Memory: Is the Black Spider Stalking?" *Rossiiskaia gazeta*, November 23.
Krakhmal'nikova, Z.A., ed. 1994. *Russkaia ideia i evrei. Rokovoi spor. Khristianstvo. Antisemitizm. Natsionalizm. Sbornik statei* [The Russian Idea and the Jews. The Fateful Argument. Christianity. Antisemitism. Nationalism. Collection of Articles]. Moscow: NAUKA—Vostochnaia literatura.

"Krasnodarskie fashisty zovut k genotsidu" [Krasnodar Fascists Call for Genocide]. 1998. *Kommersant*, no. 233 (December 15).

Krasnov, Vladislav. 1986. "Russian National Feeling: An Informal Poll." In Conquest 1986, pp. 109–30.

———. 1993. "Pamiat: Russian right-wing radicalism." In *Encounters with the Contemporary Radical Right*, ed. Peter H. Merkl and Leonard Weinberg, ch. 5. Boulder, CO: Westview Press.

Krasnovskii, Igor'. 2000. "Mal'chiki mechtaiut o revoliutsii" [Little Boys Dream of Revolution]. *Rabochii put'* (Smolensk), April 11, p. 1.

Krieger, Leonard. 1977. *Ranke: The Meaning of History.* Chicago: University of Chicago Press.

Kritskii, Evgenii, and Savva, Mikhail. 1998. *Krasnodarskii krai: model' etnologicheskogo monitoringa* [The Krasnodar Territory: Model of Ethnological Monitoring]. Moscow: Institut etnologii i antropologii RAN.

Krotov, Yakov. 1994. "The Condition and Prospects of the Russian Orthodox Church." Sound tape of talk at the Institute for East–West Christian Studies (Wheaton College), October 25.

Kulakova, Olga. 1999. "Volgogradskie rneshniki stroiat shturmovuiu polosu" [Volgograd RNU Members Build a Combat Outpost]. *Gorodskie vesti*, August 7.

Kurashvili, B. 1994. *Kuda idet Rossiia?* [Whither Goes Russia?]. Moscow: Prometei.

Kurganov, I.A. 1961. *Natsii SSSR i russkii vopros* [The Nations of the USSR and the Russian Question]. Frankfurt-am-Main: Possev-Verlag.

Kurkin, Boris. 2000. "Natsionalisty obid ne proshchaiut" [Nationalists Do Not Forgive Offenses]. *Vremia novostei*, April 3, p. 48.

Kutkovets, T.I., and Kliamkin, I.M. 1997. "Russkie idei" [Russian Ideas]. *POLIS: Politicheskie issledovaniia*, no. 2, pp. 118–40.

Kyrlezhev, Aleksandr. 1995. "Tserkov' ili 'pravoslavnaia ideologiia?'" [Church or "Orthodox Ideology"?]. *Kontinent* (Moscow and Paris), no. 80, pp. 284–303.

Kyrlezhev, Aleksandr, and Troitskii, Konstantin. 1993. "Sovremennoe rossiiskoe pravoslavie" [Contemporary Russian Orthodoxy]. *Kontinent* (Moscow and Paris), no. 75, pp. 241–62.

Laba, Roman. 1996. "The Cossack Movement and the Russian State." *Low Intensity Conflict & Law Enforcement*, vol. 5, no. 3 (Winter), pp. 377–408.

Lanting, Bert. 1996. Interview with Alexander Vengerovsky. *De Volkskrant* (Amsterdam), May 14.

Laqueur, Walter, ed. 1976. *Fascism: A Reader's Guide. Analyses. Interpretations. Bibliography.* Berkeley and Los Angeles: University of California Press.

———. 1993. *Black Hundred: The Rise of the Extreme Right in Russia.* New York: HarperCollins Publishers.

Lee, Martin A. 1997. *The Beast Reawakens.* Boston, New York, Toronto, and London: Little, Brown and Co.

Leont'eva, Liudmila. 1999. "Spisannyi raion chrezvychainogo polozheniia" [Written-off District in State of Emergency]. *Moskovskie novosti*, no. 6 (February 16).

Levinskaia, Irina. 1996. "Dialog: protiv mifov" [Dialogue: Against Myths]. In *Nuzhen* 1996, pp. 234–38.

Likhachev, Viacheslav. 1997. "Istoriia RNE" [History of the RNU]. In Likhachev and Pribylovskii 1997, pp. 5–40.

———. 1999. "Chem zakonchitsia zimnee nastuplenie na natsistov?" [How Will the Winter Offensive Against the Nazis End?] *Russkaia mysl,'* no. 4254 (January 21).

______. 2000. "Raskolotoe edinstvo (RNE: Barkashov bez barkashovtsev)" [Split Unity (The RNU: Barkashov Without Barkashovites)]. *Russkaia mysl,'* no. 4334, September 28.

Likhachev, V., and Pribylovskii, V., eds. 1997. *Russkoe Natsional'noe Edinstvo: Istoriia, politika, ideologiia. Informatsionnyi paket.* [The Russian National Unity: History, Politics, Ideology. Information Packet]. Moscow: Informatsionno-ekspertnaia gruppa "PANORAMA."

Limonov, Eduard. 1979. *Russkoe (Stikhotvoreniia, poemy, teksty)* [Being Russian (Verses, Poems, Texts)]. Ann Arbor, MI: Ardis.

———. 1983. *Podrostok Savenko* [The Youth Savenko]. Paris: Sintaksis.

———. 1993a. "Ia liubliu 'shampanskikh geniev' " [I Love "Champagne Geniuses"]. *Elementy: Evraziiskoe obozrenie*, no. 4, pp. 49–52.

———. 1993b. *Ubiistvo chasovogo* [The Murder of the Sentry]. Moscow: Molodaia gvardiia.

———. 1994a. *Limonov Protiv Zhirinovskogo* [Limonov Against Zhirinovsky]. Moscow: Konets veka.

———. 1994b. *Ukroshchenie tigra v Parizhe* [Taming of the Tiger in Paris]. Moscow: MOKA.

———. 1997a. "Elections in a Hot District." *The eXile*, no. 18 (September 25–October 8).

———. 1997b. "George Soros: Rip-Off Artist Triumphs in Russia." *The eXile*, no. 21 (November 6–19).

———. 1998a. *Sobranie sochinenii v trekh tomakh* [Collected Works in Three Volumes]. Moscow: Vagrius.

———. 1998b. "A Year in Mad Dog's Life of a Radical Politician in Russia." *The eXile*, no. 25 (December 30–January 13).

———. 1998c. "Limonov's Cabinet—Who I'd Put in Charge Instead of That Runt Kiriyenko." *The eXile*, no. 37 (April 23–May 6).

———. 1998d. "Holiday of Men Without Women." *The eXile*, no. 38 (April 23–May 6).

———. 1998e. "Carla Feltman's First Commandment." *The eXile*, no. 39 (May 21–June 4).

———. 1998f. "We Will Eat You, Westerners, Dearest Yankees, and Arrogant Europeans." *The eXile*, no. 40 (May 21–June 4).

———. 1998g. "Bourgeoisie to the Gaz Chambers!" *The eXile*, no. 42 (July 2–15).

———. 1998h. "Doctor Limonov's Advices for Travelling in a Cattle Vagon." *The eXile*, no. 47 (September 10–24).

———. 1999a. "Memory of Underground Moscow's Life." *The eXile*, no. 69 (July 15–29).

———. 1999b. "Dr. Limonov's Abortion Law." *The eXile*, no. 77 (November 18–December 2).

Liubin, V. P. 1998. "Zhurnal 'Politiia': obretenie litsa" [The Journal *Politiya*: Acquiring a Face]. *POLIS: Politicheskie issledovaniia*, no. 5, pp. 169–74.

Liubosh, S. 1925. *Russkii fashist: Vladimir Purishkevich* [A Russian Fascist: Vladimir Purishkevich]. Leningrad.

Liudi pogibeli. Satanizm v Rossii: popytka analiza [People of Perdition. Satanism in Russia: An Attempt At Analysis]. 1994. Moscow: Moskovskoe Podvor'e Sviato-Troitskoi Sergievoi Lavry.

Longworth, Philip. 1969. *The Cossacks.* New York: Holt, Rinehart, & Winston.

Lööw, Heléne. 1998. "Swedish National Socialism and Right-Wing Extremism After 1945." In *Modern Europe After Fascism, 1943–1980s*, ed. Stein Ugelvik Larsen. Vol. II, pp. 1127–83. Boulder, CO: Social Science Monographs.

Lukashevich, Stephen. 1967. *Konstantin Leontev (1831–1891): A Study in Russian "Heroic Vitalism."* New York: Pageant Press.

Lunin, Vsevolod. 1996. "Russkii natsionalizm" [Russian Nationalism]. *Duel'*, no. 3(25).

Lychev, Aleksei. 1998. Untitled report on fascism and antifascism in Voronezh.

MacMaster, Robert E. 1967. *Danilevsky: A Russian Totalitarian Philosopher.* Cambridge, MA: Harvard University Press.

Maiorov, M. 1999. "Barkashovtsy obviniaiut Moskovskogo mera i sami narushaiut zakon" [Barkashovites Accuse Moscow Mayor and Break Law Themselves]. *Molva* (Vladimir), March 11, pp. 1, 2.

Makhno, Nestor. 1991. *Vospominaniia* [Memoirs]. Kiev: "Ukraina." [Reprint of book published in Paris, 1929].

Maksimov, Vladlen. 1998. "Saltykovka." *Novaia gazeta*, nos. 22 and 23 (June 8 and 17).

Manifest vozrozhdeniia Rossii [Manifesto for the Rebirth of Russia]. 1996. St. Petersburg: Glagol.

Marakasov, Vladimir. 1996. "Cherepovetskii poligon" [The Cherepovets Test-Site]. In *Nuzhen* 1996, pp. 60–62.

Martin, Seamus. 1998. "Yeltsin in Message of Support to Neo-Fascist." *The Irish Times*, April 27.

McNeal, Robert H. 1987. *Tsar and Cossack, 1855–1914.* New York: St. Martin's Press.

Medvedev, Roi. 1998. *Kapitalizm v Rossii?* [Capitalism in Russia?]. Moscow: Prava cheloveka.

Meek, James. 1998. "They Wear the Swastika and Hate Jews But No One Dares Call Them Fascists." *The Guardian* (UK), July 5.

Mendelevich, Emmanuel. 1997. "Orel: Extremist Groups Are Active in Local Politics." In Union of Councils 1997, pp. 70–72.

———. 1998. "Sud v Orle: ubivat' evreev nel'zia, oskorbliat'—mozhno" [Court in Orel: It Is Not Allowed to Kill Jews, But It Is Allowed to Insult Them]. *Diagnoz: antifashistskoe obozrenie*, no. 3 (June), p. 3.

Merkacheva, Irina. 1999. "Barkashovtsy" [The Barkashovites]. *Brianskii rabochii*, March 27.

"Meskhetian Turks Facing Threats in Krasnodar." 1998. *The Forced Migration Monitor* (Open Society Institute), no. 22 (March), pp. 6–7.

Mikhailov, Evgenii. 1995. *Bremia imperskoi natsii* [The Burden of an Imperial Nation]. Moscow.

Mikhailov, Iurii. 1998. "Ia vam pokazhu!" [I'll Show You!]. *Kommersant-Daily*, no. 235 (December 17).

Mikhailovskaia, Ekaterina. 2000. *Results of the Parliamentary Election 1999 for National-Patriots.* Paper available at http://www.panorama.ru:8101works/patr/bp/3eng.html.

Miloslavskaia, Ekaterina. 1998. "Luzhkov protiv Barkashova" [Luzhkov Against Barkashov]. *Nezavisimaia gazeta*, no. 235(1806), December 17.

Minasian, Liana. 1992. "Poriadok budet navodit'sia rukami atamanov" [Order Will Be Imposed by the Atamans]. *Nezavisimaia gazeta*, November 20, p. 3.

Mitrofanov, A.V. 1997. *Shagi novoi geopolitiki* [Steps to a New Geopolitics]. Moscow: Russkii vestnik.

———. 199[-]. *AntiNato. Novaia ideia rossiiskoi geopolitiki. Taktika i strategiia na sovremennom etape (doklad)* [Anti-NATO. A New Idea for Russian Geopolitics. Tactics and Strategy at the Contemporary Stage (Report)].

Moiseenko, Yurii, and Iurenkov, Mikhail. 1999. "Etikh chlenov dazhe na tantsakh ne b'iut" [These Members Don't Get Beaten Even at Dances]. *Komsomol'skaia pravda*, August 4.

Mukhin, A.A. 1995. "Sovremennoe kazachestvo na severnom Kavkaze" [Contemporary Cossackdom in the North Caucasus]. In *Mezhnatsional'nye otnosheniia v Rossii i SNG. Seminar Moskovskogo Tsentra Karnegi. Vypusk 2: Doklady 1994–1995 gg.* [Inter-Ethnic Relations in Russia and the CIS. Seminar of the Moscow Carnegie Center. Issue 2: Lectures 1994–95]. Moscow: AIRO-XX.

Mukhin, Aleksei, and Pribylovskii, Vladimir. 1994. *Kazach'e dvizhenie v Rossii i stranakh blizhnego zarubezh'ia (1988–1994 gody)* [The Cossack Movement in Russia and the Countries of the Near Abroad]. 2 volumes. Moscow: Informatsionno-ekspertnaia gruppa "PANORAMA."

Na semi vetrakh. Kuda griadesh,' ochnis,' Rossiia! Ugroza fashizma v Rossii real'naia i mnimaia [On the Seven Winds. Where Are You Going, Wake Up, Russia! The Real and the Illusory Threat of Fascism in Russia]. 1998. Moscow: Al'manakh "Vympel."

Nazarov, Mikhail. 1993. "Russkaia emigratsiia i fashizm: nadezhdy i razocharovaniia" [The Russian Emigration and Fascism: Hopes and Disappointments]." *Nash sovremennik* 3 (May–June), pp. 124–37.

NBP: programmnye dokumenty [The NBP: Programmatic Documents]. 1997 (probable: date not indicated). Moscow.

Nedumov, Oleg. 2000. " 'Khristiane' reshili ne bit' stekla ukraintsam" ["Christians" Decide Not to Break Ukrainians' Glass]. *Nezavisimaia gazeta*, March 24, p. 4.

Neizbezhnost' imperii [The Inevitability of Empire]. 1996. Moscow: INTELLEKT.

"Neizbyvnaia toska po imperii" [An Ineradicable Nostalgia for Empire]. 1998. *Obshchaia gazeta*, no. 37(267), September 17–23.

Nekhoroshev, Grigorii. 1999. "Muedzin pod krasnym flagom" [The Muezzin Under the Red Flag]. *Nezavisimaia gazeta—Figury i litsa*, no. 18 (November 12), pp. 5–13.

Neocleous, Mark. 1997. *Fascism*. Minneapolis: University of Minnesota Press.

Nikolaev, I. 2000. "Kommunisty v ob"iatiiakh RNE" [Communists in the Embraces of the RNU]. *Sovetskaia Chuvashiia* (Cheboksary), March 16, p. 2.

Nol'de, Baron B.E. 1978. *Iurii Samarin i ego vremia* [Yuri Samarin and His Times]. Paris: YMCA-Press.

Nosik, Anton. 1999. "Otvetnyi udar" [Counterstrike]. *Moskovskie novosti*, no. 8 (March 2).

"Novye komsomol'tsy protiv RNE" [New Young Communists Against the RNU]. 1999. *Viatskii nabliudatel'* (Kirov), September 10.

Nuzhen li Gitler Rossii? [Does Russia Need Hitler?]. 1996. Moscow: Nezavisimoe izd-vo PIK.

Nyomarkay, Joseph L. 1972. "Factionalism in the NSGWP, 1925–26: The Myth and Reality of the 'Northern Faction.'" In Turner , ed., 1972, pp. 21–44.

Ofitova, Svetlana. 1998. "Rukovodstvo RNE otkladyvaet provedenie s"ezda" [The RNU Leadership Defers Congress]. *Nezavisimaia gazeta*, no. 237(1808), December 19.

———. 1999. "Anpilov stal liderom novogo bloka" [Anpilov Becomes Leader of a New Bloc]. *Nezavisimaia gazeta*, January 13, p. 3.

Oganian, Stanislav. 1999. "Poka patronov khvatit" [So Far There Are Enough Patrons]. *Moskovskaia pravda*, June 3.

Omel'chenko, N.A. 1992. "Spory o evraziistve: Opyt istoricheskoi rekonstruktsii" [Arguments About Eurasianism: An Attempt at Historical Reconstruction]. *POLIS: Politicheskie issledovaniia*, no. 3 (May–June), pp. 156–63.

"Oni uzhe zdes'" [They Are Already Here]. 1998. *Rossiiskaia gazeta*, July 10.

Osipov, A.G., and Cherepovaia, O.I. 1996. *Narushenie prav vynuzhdennykh migrantov i etnicheskaia diskriminatsiia v Krasnodarskom krae. Polozhenie meskhetinskikh turok* [Infringement of the Rights of Forced Migrants and Ethnic Discrimination in the Krasnodar Territory: Situation of the Meskhetian Turks]. Moscow: Pravozashchitnyi tsentr "Memorial."

Osokin, Dmitrii. 1997. "Mezhpartiinaia bor'ba: 'Demokraty'—RNE" [Interparty Struggle: "Democrats" versus RNU]. *Bulleten' Instituta gumanitarno-politicheskikh issledovanii*, no. 8.

Ostow, Mortimer. 1996. *Myth and Madness: The Psychodynamics of Antisemitism*. New Brunswick, NJ, and London: Transaction Publishers.

Ostretsov, V. 1991. *Chernaia sotnia i krasnaia sotnia* [The Black Hundred and the Red Hundred]. Moscow: Voennoe izdatel'stvo, Voenno-patrioticheskoe literaturnoe ob"edinenie "Otechestvo."

O'Sullivan, Noel. 1983. *Fascism*. London and Melbourne: Dent & Sons.

Panchenko, Mikhail. 2000. "Za fiurera!" [For the Fuhrer!]. *Versiia*, no. 11, March 21–27, p. 11.

Paniushkin, Valerii. 2000. "Eto ne fashisty, eto khuligany" [These Are Not Fascists, These Are Hooligans]. *Kommersant-Vlast,'* no. 5 (February 9).

Pankov, Gennadii. 1999. "Administratsiia Voronezha zapretila aktsiiu RNE" [Voronezh City Administration Bans RNU Action]. *Izvestiia*, no. 36 (March 2).

Parfenov, Victor, and Sergeeva, Marina. 1998. "Sowing Nationalist Grapes of Wrath." *Russia Today*, August 7.

Parker, Geoffrey. 1985. *Western Geopolitical Thought in the Twentieth Century*. London and Sydney: Croom Helm.

———. 1988. *The Geopolitics of Domination*. London and New York: Routledge.

Pashkov, Vladimir. 1999. "Ia veriu. Sokoly Mitropolita Kirilla" [I Believe. The Falcons of Metropolitan Kirill]. *Moskovskii komsomolets*, January 19.

Pavlovskii, Oleg. 1998. "Pogrom sredi iasnogo neba. On eshche ne nachalsia. No zhdite" [Pogrom From Out of the Blue. It Hasn't Started Yet. But Wait]. *Novaia gazeta*, August 3.

Payne, Stanley G. 1980. *Fascism: Comparison and Definition*. Madison: University of Wisconsin Press.

Peresvet, Aleksandr. 1995. "Ad"iutanty 'chernoi kassy'" [Adjutants of the 'Black Box']. *Ogonek*, no. 11, pp. 18–20.

Periwal, Sukumar, ed. 1995. *Notions of Nationalism*. Budapest, London, and New York: Central European University Press.

Perova, Liudmila. 1996. "Russian Rightists Search for Themselves: 'Unity' for Whose Sake?" *Pravda-5*, November 26.

Petro, Nicolai N. 1995. *The Rebirth of Russian Democracy: An Interpretation of Political Culture*. Cambridge, MA: Harvard University Press.

Pilkington, Hilary. 1994. *Russia's Youth and Its Culture: A Nation's Constructors and Constructed*. London and New York: Routledge.

______, ed. 1996. *Gender, Generation and Identity in Contemporary Russia*. London and New York: Routledge.

———. 1999. "Looking West? Youth and Cultural Globalisation in Post-Soviet Russia." Paper presented to panel on "Youth in Contemporary Russia" at conference of the British Association of Soviet and East European Studies, Fitzwilliam College, Cambridge, UK, March 27–29.

Platonov, Andrei. 1998. "O sobytiiakh v Ekaterinburge" [On the Events in Yekaterinburg]. *Nezavisimaia gazeta*, June 12.

Plekhanov, S. 1994. *Zhirinovskii: kto on?* [Zhirinovsky — Who Is He?]. Moscow: Yevraziia-nord and Bimpa.

Pokaianie: Materialy pravitel'stvennoi Komissii po izucheniiu voprosov, sviazannykh s issledovaniem i perezakhoroneniem ostankov Rossiiskogo Imperatora NIKOLAIA II i ichlenov ego sem'i Izbrannye dokumenty [Repentance: Materials of the Government Commission for the Study of Questions Connected with the Investigation and Reburial of the Remains of the Russian Emperor Nicholas II and of Members of His Family. Selected Documents]. 1998. Moscow: Vybor.

Politkovskaia, Anna. 1998. "Ia i sem' minuvshikh dnei—utro v Terletskom lesu" [The Last Seven Days and I—A Morning in the Terletsky Woods]. *Obshchaia gazeta*, no. 51 (December 24).

Polivanov, Sergei. 1996. "Fashizm ne proshel" [Fascism Did Not Pass]. *Moskovskie novosti*, no. 9 (March 3–10).

Popov, Nikolai. 1998. "Po raznye storony" [On Different Sides]. *Nezavisimaia gazeta*, August 6, p. 8.

Popper, Karl R. 1966. *The Open Society and Its Enemies*. Princeton: Princeton University Press.

Pospielovsky, Dmitry V. 1995. "The Russian Orthodox Church in the Postcommunist CIS." In Bourdeaux, ed., 1995, pp. 41–74.

———. 1998. *The Orthodox Church in the History of Russia*. Crestwood, NY: St. Vladimir's Seminary Press.

Pravosudov, Sergei. 1999a. "Tiazhlov ne podderzhal initsiativu Luzhkova" [Tyazhlov Does Not Support Luzhkov's Initiative]. *Nezavisimaia gazeta*, September 2.

Pribylovskii, Vladimir. 1994. *Russkie natsional-patrioticheskie (etnokraticheskie) i pravo-radikal'nye organizatsii (Kratkii slovar'-spravochnik)* [Russian National-Patriotic (Ethnocratic) and Right-Radical Organizations (Short Reference Dictionary)]. Moscow: Informatsionno-ekspertnaia gruppa "PANORAMA."

———. 1995. *Vozhdi. Sbornik biografii rossiiskikh politicheskikh deiatelei natsionalisticheskoi i impersko-patrioticheskoi orientatsii* [Leaders: A Collection

of Biographies of Russian Politicians of Nationalist and Imperial-Patriotic Orientation]. Moscow: Informatsionno-ekspertnaia gruppa "PANORAMA."
———. 2000. " 'Natsional-patrioty i novyi prezident" [The "National-Patriots" and the New President], *Russkaia mysl'*, no. 4315, May 11, pp. 3–4.
Programma Liberal'no-Demokraticheskoi Partii Rossii [Program of the Liberal-Democratic Party of Russia]. 1998. Moscow: LDPR.
Programmy politicheskikh partii Rosii. Konets XIX-nachalo XX vv. [Programs of the Political Parties of Russia: End of 19th and Beginning of 20th Centuries]. 1995. Moscow: ROSSPEN.
Prokhanov, Aleksandr. 1998. "Nas s Makashovym 130 millionov" [We and Makashov Are 130 Million Strong]. *Zavtra*, no. 45(258), November 12.
———. 1999. *Krasno-Korichnevyi: Roman* [Red-Brown: A Novel]. Moscow: ITRK.
Proshechkin, Yevgeni. 1999. "Fascism Gets Boost From Communists." *Perspective*, vol. 9, no. 3 (January–February).
Pruss, I.V. 1997. "Ryvok v budushchee ili dvizhenie po krugu? (Ekonomicheskie vzgliady sovremennykh russkikh natsionalistov)" [Leap into the Future or Movement in a Circle? (The Economic Views of Contemporary Russian Nationalists)]. *POLIS: Politicheskie issledovaniia*, no. 3 (May–June), pp. 53–64.
Prussakov, V. 1994. *Germanskii natsional-sotsializm* [German National-Socialism]. Moscow: Pallada.
Prussakov, V., and Shiropaev, A. 1993. *Slava Rossii!* [Glory to Russia!]. Moscow: Front natsional-revoliutsionnogo deistviia.
Punanov, Grigorii. 1998. "Luzhkov zakon ne narushal" [Luzhkov Has Not Broken the Law]. *Novye izvestiia*, December 17.
Radaeva, Galina. 1998. "RNE v Balakove: 'vospitanie molodezhi' " [The RNU in Balakova: "The Upbringing of Youth"]. *Express-Chronicle*, December 14.
Radzikhovskii, Leonid. 1996. "Antisemitskoe schast'e evreia Zhirinovskogo" [The Antisemitic Joke of the Jew Zhirinovsky]. *Ogonek*, no. 33(4464) (August), p. 16.
———. 2000. "Vokrug 'ostrova Moskva' " [Around the "Moscow Island"]. *Segodnia*, no. 93 (April 27).
Raskin, David. 1996. "Ob odnoi istoricheskoi teorii, unasledovannoi russkim fashizmom" [On One Historical Theory Inherited by Russian Fascism]. In *Nuzhen* 1996, pp. 157–58.
Rawson, Don C. 1995. *Russian Rightists and the Revolution of 1905*. New York: Cambridge University Press.
"Razgromleno gnezdo Barkashovtsev v voennom universitete" [Nest of Barkashovites in Military University Crushed]. 1999. *Moskovskii komsomolets*, no. 62A (April 4).
Razuvaev, Vladimir. 1998. "Ideologiia lidera" [Ideology of the Leader]. *Nezavisimaia gazeta—Knizhnoe obozrenie*, July 9, p. 6.
Reich, Wilhelm. 1970. *The Mass Psychology of Fascism*. New York: Farrar, Straus & Giroux.
Reshetniak, Elena. 1999. "Na glavnuiu ploshchad' goroda vyshli liudi so svastikoi" [People with a Swastika Have Come Out on to the Main Square of the Town]. *Mig* (Astrakhan'), April 29.
Reznik, Semyon. 1996. *The Nazification of Russia: Antisemitism in the Post-Soviet Era*. Washington, DC: Challenge Publications.
———. 1998. "Red-Brown Cloud Over Russia." *Fascism Watch* (Balkan Institute, Washington, DC), vol. 2, no. 3 (February 5).

Riutin, Sergei; Sarbuchev, Mikhail; and Razukov, Mikhail. 1998. "Raskol v natsional-bol'shevistskoi partii" [Split in National-Bolshevik Party]. *Ia—russkii*, no. 4(7), p. 1.
"RNE: dobro ili zlo?" [The RNU: Good Or Evil?]. 1999. *Tverskaia zhizn',* April 27.
RNU Forum, http://www.anmweb.com/rne.
RNU Website, http://www.rne.org.
Rodion, Sviashchennik. 1991. *Liudi i demony. Obrazy iskusheniia sovremennogo cheloveka padshimi dukhami* [People and Demons: Forms of Temptation of Contemporary Man by Fallen Spirits]. St. Petersburg.
Rodzaevskii, K.V. 1997. *Iuda na ushcherbe* [Judah on the Wane]. Moscow: Pallada.
Rogger, Hans. 1986. *Jewish Policies and Right-Wing Politics in Imperial Russia.* London: Macmillan.
Rogozhin, S.V., Captain. 1994. "O natsional'nom proiskhozhdenii Iisusa Khrista" [On the Ethnic Origin of Jesus Christ]. In Barkashov 1994, pp. 68–71.
Rosenthal, Bernice Glatzer, ed. 1997. *The Occult in Russian and Soviet Culture.* Ithaca, NY, and London: Cornell University Press.
Rstaki, Arsen. 1998a. "Diviziia 'Britaia golova.' Rossiiskii fashizm: komu eto vygodno?" [The "Skinhead" Division. Russian Fascism: To Whose Advantage?]. *Novaia gazeta—ponedel'nik*, no. 19 (May 18).
———. 1998b. "Diviziia 'Britaia golova'—2. Oni ne fashisty, oni tol'ko uchatsia" [The "Skinhead" Division—2. They Are Not Fascists, They Are Only Learning]. *Novaia gazeta-ponedel'nik*, no. 20 (May 25).
"Russkii natsionalizm po-Kaliningradski" [Russian Nationalism the Kaliningrad Way]. 1998. *Kaliningrad*, no. 41.
Ryan-Hayes, Karen. 1993. *Limonov's "It's Me, Eddie" and the Autobiographical Mode.* Carl Beck Papers in Russian and East European Studies no. 1004. Center for Russian and East European Studies, University of Pittsburgh.
Sakharov, Andrei. 1999. "Russkii natsionalizm: istoki, osobennosti, etapy" [Russian Nationalism: Sources, Peculiarities, Stages]. *Nezavisimaia gazeta—Stsenarii*, no. 1(35), January 13.
Sakwa, Richard. 1998. "Left or Right? The CPRF and the Problem of Democratic Consolidation in Russia." *The Journal of Communist Studies and Transition Politics*, vol. 14, nos. 1–2 (March/June), pp. 128–58.
Samarin, Iu., and Dmitriev, F. 1875. *Revoliutsionnyi konservatizm* [Revolutionary Conservatism]. Berlin: B. Behr's Buchhandlung (E. Bock).
Samokhin, A.A. 1997. "Rubezhi kazachestva" [The Boundaries of Cossackdom]. *Duel',* no. 3(25), February 11.
"Sataninskie nalogi" [Satanic Taxes]. 2000. *Izvestiia*, March 10.
Savitskii, Petr. 1931. *V bor'be za Evraziistvo* [In Struggle for Eurasianism]. Paris.
———. 1997. *Kontinent Evraziia* [Continent Eurasia]. Moscow: AGRAF.
Savushkin, I., Col. 1997. "Golgofa Igoria Rodionova" [The Golgotha of Igor' Rodionov]. *Limonka*, no. 66, p. 1.
Scanlan, James P. 1996. "The Russian Idea from Dostoevskii to Ziuganov." *Problems of Post-Communism* 43, no. 4 (July), pp. 35–42.
Sedgwick, Mark. 1999. "Traditionalist Sufism." ARIES (Paris), vol. 22, pp. 3–24.
———. 2000. *Russian Traditionalism*. Paper presented at the 14th International Con-

ference of the Centre for Studies on New Religions in Riga, Latvia, August 29–31, 2000.

Sedov, M. 1999. "RNU vykhodit na pensiiu?" [Is the RNU Retiring on Pension?]. *Voronezhskii kur'er*, June 29.

Serdiukov, Vladimir. 1998. "Kuda smotrit partiia" [In Which Direction the Party Is Looking]. *Izvestiia*, March 4.

"Seren'kaia telezvezda Barkashov" [The Gray TV Star Barkashov]. 1998. *Ia—russkii*, no. 19.

Sergeev, V.M., et al. 1999. "Stanovlenie parlamentskikh partii v Rossii: Gosudarstvennaia duma v 1994–1997 godakh" [The Establishment of Parliamentary Parties in Russia: The State Duma in 1994–97]. *POLIS: Politicheskie issledovaniia*, no. 1, pp. 50–71.

Sevast'ianov, Aleksandr. 2000. "Otdel'no ot 'Spasa'" [Apart From "Salvation"]. *Nezavisimaia gazeta—Religii*, no. 2 (January 26).

Shapovalov, Anton. 2000. "Dukhovnye nasledniki" [The Spiritual Inheritors]. *Moskovskie novosti*, no. 12 (March 28–April 3), p. 10.

Shatrov, Al'bert. 1998a. *Nezavisimaia gazeta*, no. 61(1631), April 8.

———. 1998b. "Bednost' plodit patriotov" [Poverty Gives Birth to Patriots]. *Nezavisimaia gazeta*, July 9, p. 4.

———. 1998c. *Novosti razvedki i kontrrazvedki*, no. 6(111).

———. 1998d. "Russkie vitiazi" [Russian Warriors]. *Spetsnaz*, nos. 2–3.

Shatz, Marshall S., and Zimmerman, Judith E., eds. 1994. *Vekhi—Landmarks: A Collection of Articles about the Russian Intelligentsia.* Armonk, NY, and London: M.E. Sharpe.

Shcherbakov, Aleksei. 1999. "Barkashovtsy poshli po Latvii" [Barkashovites Go Around Latvia]. *Kommersant-Daily*, no. 22 (February 17).

Shenfield, Stephen D. 1983. "*Pripiski*: False Statistical Reporting in Soviet-Type Economies." In *Corruption: Causes, Consequences and Control*, ed. Michael Clarke, pp. 239–58. London: Frances Pinter.

———. 1993. "Violence: No Shortcut on the Road to Reform." *The Providence Sunday Journal*, October 10.

———. 1998. "The Weimar/Russia Comparison: Reflections on Hanson and Kopstein." *Post-Soviet Affairs*, vol. 14, no. 4 (October–December), pp. 355–68.

———. Forthcoming 2000 or 2001. "Foreign Assistance as Genocide: The Crisis in Russia, the IMF, and Inter-Ethnic Relations." In Milton Esman and Ronald Herring, eds., *Carrots, Sticks, and Ethnic Conflict: Rethinking Development Assistance.* Ann Arbor: University of Michigan Press.

Shevchenko, Maksim. 1997. "Rozhdestvenskie chteniia v Moskve" [Christmas Readings in Moscow]. *Nezavisimaia gazeta*, no. 12 (January 26).

Shevelev, Mikhail. 1999. "Kogo my boimsia?" [Whom Do We Fear?]. *Moskovskie novosti*, no. 16 (April 27).

Shlapentokh, Dmitry V. 1997a. "Bolshevism, Nationalism, and Statism: Soviet Ideology in Formation." In *The Bolsheviks in Russian Society: The Revolution and the Civil Wars*, ed. Vladimir N. Brovkin, pp. 271–97. New Haven, CT, and London: Yale University Press.

———. 1997b. "Eurasianism: Past and Present." *Communist and Post-Communist Studies* 30, no. 2, pp. 129–51.

Shnirel′man, V.A. 1996. "Evraziitsy i evrei" [The Eurasianists and the Jews]. *Vestnik evreiskogo universiteta v Moskve*, no. 1(11), pp. 4–45.

______. 1998a. *Neoiazychestvo i natsionalizm: Vostochnoevropeiskii areal* [Neopaganism and Nationalism: The East European Area]. Moscow: Institut etnologii i antropologii RAN.

———. 1998b. *Russian Neo-Pagan Myths and Antisemitism.* Analysis of Current Trends in Antisemitism no. 13. Jerusalem: The Vidal Sassoon International Center for the Study of Antisemitism, The Hebrew University of Jerusalem.

Shpak, G.I., Col.-Gen. 1998. "Vozdushno-desantnye voiska v period reformirovaniia Vooruzhennykh Sil" [The Paratroops in the Period of Reform of the Armed Forces]. *Voennaia mysl′,* no. 1 (January–February).

Sikevich, Z.V. 1996. *Russkie: "obraz" naroda. Sotsiologicheskii ocherk* [The Russians: "Image" of a People. A Sociological Essay]. St. Petersburg: Izd-vo S.-Peterburgskogo universiteta.

Simonsen, Sven Gunnar. 1996a. *Politics and Personalities: Key Actors in the Russian Opposition.* PRIO Report 2/96. Oslo: International Peace Research Institute.

———. 1996b. "Aleksandr Barkashov and Russian National Unity: Blackshirt Friends of the Nation." *Nationalities Papers* 24, no. 4, pp. 625–39.

———. 1996c. "Raising the Russian Question: Ethnicity and Statehood, *russkie* and *Rossiya*." *Nationalism and Ethnic Politics*, vol. 2, no. 1 (Spring), pp. 91–110.

———. 1997. "Still Favoring the Power of the Workers." *Transitions*, vol. 4, no. 7 (July), pp. 52–56.

Sinyavsky, Andrei. 1997. *The Russian Intelligentsia.* New York: Columbia University Press.

Sirotin, Vladimir. 1998. "Korichnevyi tuman provintsial′nogo razliva" [Brown Mist of a Provincial Flood]. *Novaia gazeta*, July 6.

Skorik, A.P. 1994. "Kazach′e vozrozhdenie: obrazy, etapy, perspektivy" [The Cossack Revival: Forms, Stages, Prospects]. In *Vozrozhdenie kazachestva: istoriia i sovremennost′* [The Revival of Cossackdom: History and the Present Day], pp. 123–30. Novocherkassk: Novocherkasskii gosudarstvennyi tekhnicheskii universitet, Rostovskii gosudarstvennyi universitet.

Slater, Wendy. 1993. "The Center Right in Russia." *RFE/RL Research Report* 2, no. 34, pp. 7–14.

Slavin, Boris. 1997. *Posle sotsializma. . . Metamorfozy rossiiskoi politiki kontsa XX veka* [After Socialism: Metamorphoses of Russian Politics at the End of the 20th Century]. Moscow: Flinta.

Slivko, Veronika, and Babich, Dmitrii. 1998. "Virtual′nyi Gitler" [Virtual Hitler]. *Novye izvestiia*, June 19.

Smith, Anthony D. 1979. *Nationalism in the Twentieth Century.* Oxford: Martin Robertson.

Sokolov, V. 1998. "Krasnyi Orel s chernymi otmetinami" [Red Oryol with Black Spots]. *Trudovaia Rossiia*, no. 5(64).

Sokovnin, Aleksei. 1999. "Barkashovtsy khotiat zasadit′ Rossiiu" [The Barkashovites Want to Greenify Russia]. *Kommersant-Daily*, no. 19 (February 12).

Solonevich, Ivan. 1997. *Belaia imperiia. Stat′i 1936–1940 gg.* [The White Empire. Articles 1936–1940]. Moscow: Izdatel′stvo zhurnala Moskva.

Solov'ev, Vladimir. 1911. *Russkaia ideia* [The Russian Idea]. Moscow: Tovarishchestvo tipografii A.I. Mamontova.

Solovyov, Vladimir, and Klepikova, Elena. 1995. *Zhirinovsky: Russian Fascism and the Making of a Dictator.* New York and Menlo Park, CA: Addison-Wesley Publishing Company.

Solzhenitsyn, Alexander. 2000. "Russia's Darkest Night of the Soul." *The Guardian* (UK), March 18.

Sorokin, Vladislav. 1999. "Natsional-bol'sheviki zaderzhany po podozreniiu v narkomanii" [National Bolsheviks Held on Suspicion of Drug Addiction]. *Diena* (Riga), July 30.

Sovremennaia russkaia ideia i gosudarstvo [The Contemporary Russian Idea and the State]. 1995. Moscow: RAU-Korporatsiia–Obozrevatel'.

Spechler, Dina Rome. 1990. "Russian Nationalism and Soviet Politics." In *The Nationalities Factor in Soviet Politics and Society*, ed. Lubomyr Hajda and Mark Beissinger, pp. 281–304. Boulder, CO, San Francisco, and Oxford: Westview Press.

"Sponsory RNE lezut v gorodskuiu vlast'?" [Are the RNU's Sponsors Infiltrating the City Authorities?]. 1999. *Moe* (Voronezh), no. 19 (May 11–17).

Staunton, Denis. 2000. "Rise of Neo-Nazism Alarms Germany." *The Guardian Weekly*, August 10–16, p. 4.

Steeves, Paul D. 1994. "Russian Orthodox Fascism After Glasnost." Paper presented to the Conference on Faith and History, Harrisburg, Pennsylvania, October 8.

Stepanov, S.A. 1993. "Chernosotentsy: 'revoliutsionery naiznanku'" [The Black Hundreds: "Upside-Down Revolutionaries"]. *POLIS: Politicheskie issledovaniia*, no. 1 (January), pp. 154–61.

Stephan, John J. 1978. *The Russian Fascists: Tragedy and Farce in Exile, 1925–1945.* New York: Harper & Row Publishers.

Sterkin, Filipp. 1999. "Fashizm bez RNE" [Fascism Without the RNU]. *Vremia-MN*, no. 67 (April 20).

Stine, Russell Warren. 1945. *The Doctrine of God in the Philosophy of Fichte.* Philadelphia: University of Pennsylvania Press.

Strogin, Aleksandr. 1999a. "Pervyi izvinivshiisia militsioner sniat s dolzhnosti" [The First Policeman Who Apologized Fired]. *Kommersant-Daily*, no. 12 (February 3).

———. 1999b. "Natsisty ostalis' bez pressy" [Nazis Left Without a Press]. *Kommersant-Daily*, no. 69 (April 23).

Subbotich, Veronika. 1998. "Natsisty i demokraty: kto kogo?" [Nazis and Democrats: Who Whom?]. *Express-Chronicle*, December 14.

Subbotin, Anton. 1999. "RNE zakhvatit vlast' esli polovina naseleniia budet podderzhivat', a polovina ne budet meshat'" [The RNU Will Take Power If Half the Population Supports It and the Other Half Does Not Interfere]. *Gubernskie vesti* (Perm'), no. 12 (March 19–25).

"Sud priznal zakonnym otkaz miniusta zaregistrirovat' 'limonovtsev'" [Court Recognizes as Legal the Refusal of the Ministry of Justice to Register "Limonovists"]. 1999. *Segodnia*, August 19.

Sukhoverkhov, Vadim. 1999. "Legendy i mify zheleznogo Shurika" [Legends and Myths of Iron Alex]. *Moskovskii komsomolets*, no. 27 (February 12).

Svirskii, Grigorii. 1974. *Zalozhniki* [Hostages]. Paris: Les Éditeurs Réunis.

Tabolina, T.V. 1994. *Panorama sovremennogo kazachestva: istoki, kontury, tipologizatsiia* [Panorama of Contemporary Cossackdom: Sources, Contours, Typology]. Issledovaniia po prikladnoi i neotlozhnoi etnologii, No. 58. Moscow: Rossiiskaia akademiia nauk, Institut etnologii i antropologii.

Tarasov, Aleksandr. 1996. "Est′ li budushchee u molodezhi?" [Does Youth Have a Future?]. *Svobodnaia mysl′*, no. 7, pp. 21–26.

Tarasov, A.N.; Cherkasov, I.U.; and Shavshukova, T.V. 1997. *Levye v Rossii: Ot umerennykh do ekstremistov* [The Left in Russia: From Moderates to Extremists]. Moscow: Izdatel′stvo "Institut eksperimental′noi sotsiologii."

Tarasova, Svetlana. 1999. "Zabor dlia RNE" [Fence for the RNU]. *Voronezhskii kur′er*, April 20.

Tekhnologiia uspekha. Na puti k vyboram-95 [The Technology of Success: On the Way to the 1995 Elections]. 1995. Moscow.

Ter-Sarkisiants, A.E. 1994. *Mezhnatsional′nye otnosheniia v Krasnodarskom krae (1993 g.) (osnovnye tendentsii razvitiia)* [Inter-Ethnic Relations in the Krasnodar Territory (1993) (Basic Tendencies of Development)]. Issledovaniia po prikladnoi i neotlozhnoi etnologii, No. 55. Moscow: Rossiiskaia akademiia nauk, Institut etnologii i antropologii.

The Skinhead International: A Worldwide Survey of Neo-Nazi Skinheads. 1995. New York: Anti-Defamation League.

Theweleit, Klaus. 1987, 1989. *Male Fantasies* (2 vols.). Cambridge: Polity Press.

Timakova, Natalia. 1999. "Fashizmom zaimutsia posle 2000 goda" [Fascism Will Be Dealt With After the Year 2000]. *Kommersant-Daily*, no. 12 (February 3).

Tishkov, Valery. 1997. *Ethnicity, Nationalism and Conflict in and after the Soviet Union: The Mind Aflame*. London, Thousand Oaks, CA, and New Delhi: Sage Publications.

———. 1998. "Taking Responsibility." *War Report: Bulletin of the Institute for War and Peace Reporting*, no. 58 (February–March), pp. 71–72.

———. 1999. "Strategii protivodeistviia ekstremizmu" [Strategies for Counteracting Extremism]. *Nezavisimaia gazeta*, no. 48 (March 18).

Tokareva, Elena. 1999. "Utomlennyi demon ishchet teplyi ugol" [Tired Demon Seeks Warm Corner]. *Obshchaia gazeta*, no. 25 (June 24).

Tokareva, Marina. 2000. "Vziali Shutova" [They've Taken Shutov]. *Obshchaia gazeta*, no. 7 (February 18).

"Tsvety vozlozhili, narod zashchitili" [They Laid Flowers, Defended the People]. 1999. *Vechernyi Stavropol*, March 23, p. 2.

Tsyganov, Andrei. 1999. "Barkashovtsy sobiralis′ vzryvat′ Peterburgskie shkoly" [Barkashovites Planned to Blow Up Petersburg Schools]. *Kommersant*, June 24.

Turner, Henry Ashby, Jr. ed. 1975. *Reappraisals of Fascism*. New York: New Viewpoints.

Tuz, Galina. 1997. *Provintsial′nyi fashizm* [Provincial Fascism]. Moscow: Nezavisimoe izdatel′stvo PIK.

Umland, Andreas. 1997. *Vladimir Zhirinovskii in Russian Politics: Three Approaches to the Emergence of the Liberal-Democratic Party of Russia 1990–1993. Dissertation*. Berlin: Free University of Berlin.

Union of Councils for Soviet Jews. 1997. *Antisemitism in the Former Soviet Union 1995–1997*. Washington, DC.

———. 1999. *Antisemitism, Xenophobia and Religious Persecution in Russia's Regions 1998–1999*. Washington, DC.

Urban, Joan Barth, and Solovei, Valerii D. 1997. *Russia's Communists at the Crossroads*. Boulder, CO: Westview.

Ushakova, I.K. 1998. *Liberal'no-demokraticheskaia partiia Rossii. Letopis' sobytii* [The Liberal-Democratic Party of Russia. Chronicle of Events]. Moscow: LDPR.

Ustiuzhanin, Vasilii. 1998. "Temnaia komnata" [The Dark Room]. *Komsomol'skaia pravda*, no. 142 (August 4).

V poiskakh svoego puti: Rossiia mezhdu Evropoi i Aziei. Khrestomatiia po istorii rossiiskoi obshchestvennoi mysli XIX i XX vekov [In Search of Its Path: Russia Between Europe and Asia. Reader in the History of Russian Social Thought in the Nineteenth and Twentieth Centuries]. 1997. Moscow: Izdatel'skaia korporatsiia "Logos."

Vaguine, Vladimir V. 1997. *Politicheskaia legitimatsiia LDPR v Pskovskoi oblasti* [The Political Legitimization of the LDPR in Pskov Province]. Washington, DC: Kennan Institute for Advanced Russian Studies.

Vaksberg, Arkady. 1995. *Stalin Against the Jews*. New York: Vintage Books.

Vdovin, A.V. 1997. "Pochemu ia vstupil v RNE" [Why I Joined the RNU]. *Russkii poriadok*, no. 3 (44).

Verkhovskii, Aleksandr. 1994. *Vladimir Zhirinovskii i Liberal'no-demokraticheskaia partiia Rossii. Informatsionnyi paket* [Vladimir Zhirinovsky and the Liberal-Democratic Party of Russia. Information Package]. Moscow: Informatsionno-ekspertnaia gruppa "PANORAMA."

______. 2000. *Ultra-Nationalists in Russia at the Beginning of the Year 2000*. Paper presented at the Institute of Governmental Affairs, University of California, Davis, on February 23, 2000.

Verkhovskii, Aleksandr; Papp, Anatolii; and Pribylovskii, Vladimir. 1996. *Politicheskii ekstremizm v Rossii* [Political Extremism in Russia]. Moscow: Izd-vo "Institut eksperimental'noi sotsiologii."

Verkhovskii, Aleksandr, and Pribylovskii, Vladimir. 1996. *Natsional'no-patrioticheskie organizatsii v Rossii: istoriia, ideologiia, ekstremistskie tendentsii* [National-Patriotic Organizations in Russia: History, Ideology, Extremist Tendencies]. Moscow: Izd-vo "Institut eksperimental'noi sotsiologii."

———. 1997. *Natsional'no-patrioticheskie organizatsii: Kratkie spravki. Dokumenty i teksty* [National-Patriotic Organizations: Brief Descriptions. Documents and Texts]. Moscow: Informatsionno-ekspertnaia gruppa "PANORAMA."

Verkhovskii, Aleksandr; Pribylovskii, Vladimir; and Mikhailovskaia, Ekaterina. 1998. *Natsionalizm i ksenofobiia v rossiiskom obshchestve* [Nationalism and Xenophobia in Russian Society]. Moscow: Informatsionno-ekspertnaia gruppa "PANORAMA."

———. 1999. *Politicheskaia Ksenofobiia. Radikal'nye gruppy. Predstavleniia Liderov. Rol' tserkvi* [Political Xenophobia. Radical Groups. Leaders' Conceptions. Role of the Church]. Moscow: Informatsionno-ekspertnaia gruppa "PANORAMA."

Victor, Jeffrey S. 1993. *Satanic Panic: The Creation of a Contemporary Legend*. Chicago and La Salle, IL: Open Court.

Vitalii, Mitropolit. 1992. Interview. *Nezavisimaia gazeta*, November 5, p. 5.

Vlasov, Iurii P. 1995. *Rus' bez vozhdia* [Russia Without a Leader]. Voronezh: Voronezh Provincial Organization of the Union of Journalists of Russia.

"Vlast′ beret pod okhranu ob″ekty 'riska'" [The Authorities Take Objects of "Risk" Under Guard]. 1999. *Vecherniaia Moskva*, January 14.

"Vodit′sia s Barkashovtsami ne dadut dazhe na kommercheskoi osnove" [You Won't Be Allowed to Ride with the Barkashovites Even on a Commercial Basis]. 1999. *Moskovskii komsomolets*, no. 27 (February 12).

Volgin, D. 1997. "Khazary" [The Khazars]. *Russkii poriadok*, no. 4(45), pp. 49–50.

Voloshina, T.A., and Astapov, S.N. 1996. *Iazycheskaia mifologiia slavian* [The Pagan Mythology of the Slavs]. Rostov-on-Don: Feniks.

Vorontsova, L.M.; Filatov, S.B.; and Furman, D.E. 1997. "Religion in the Contemporary Mass Consciousness." *Russian Social Science Review*, January–February, pp. 18–39.

Vorozhishchev, A.V. 1998. "Pochemu my trebovali vyseleniia kavkaztsev, aziatov i negrov na mitinge 12 dekabria 1996 g." [Why We Demanded the Deportation of Caucasians, Asians, and Negroes at the Meeting on December 12, 1996]. *Ia—russkii*, no. 4(7), p. 1.

Voznesenskii, Aleksandr. 1998. "'Limonoff-kokteil,' ili ne tol′ko anatomiia" [The "Limonov Cocktail," Or Not Only Anatomy]. *Nezavisimaia gazeta*, August 13.

"Vse vetvi vlasti potvorstvuiut natsistam" [All Branches of Power Connive at the Nazis]. 1998. *Express-Chronicle*, December 14.

Walicki, Andrzej. 1975. *The Slavophile Controversy: History of a Conservative Utopia in Nineteenth-Century Russian Thought.* Oxford: Clarendon Press.

Warhola, James W. 1993. *Russian Orthodoxy and Political Culture Transformation.* Carl Beck Paper No. 1006. Center for Russian and East European Studies, University of Pittsburgh.

Weber, Eugen. 1964. *Varieties of Fascism: Doctrines of Revolution in the Twentieth Century*. Princeton, NJ: D. Van Nostrand.

White, Stephen; Rose, Richard; and McAllister, Ian. 1997. *How Russia Votes.* Chatham, NJ: Chatham House Publishers.

Wimbush, S. Enders. 1978. "The Great Russians and the Soviet State: The Dilemmas of Ethnic Dominance." In *Soviet Nationality Policies and Practices*, ed. Jeremy R. Azrael, pp. 349–60. New York: Praeger Publishers.

Womack, Helen. 1998. "Voices: Tapping into the Wisdom of the Young." *Moscow Times*, November 28.

Yanov, Alexander. 1978. *The Russian New Right: Right-Wing Ideologies in the Contemporary USSR*. Berkeley: Institute of International Studies, University of California.

———. 1987. *The Russian Challenge.* New York: Basil Blackwell.

———. 1996. "Behind Zyuganov's Smile." *Perspective*, vol. 6, no. 4 (March–April).

Yasmann, Victor. 1993. "Red Religion: An Ideology of Neo-Messianic Russian Fundamentalism." *Demokratizatsiya: The Journal of Post-Soviet Democratization* 1, no. 2, pp. 20–40.

Zaharescu, Vladimir. 1998. *National Communist Ideologues' View on Russian Messianic Role and Confrontation with the West: Intellectual Roots*. Paper presented to Third Congress of the Association for the Study of Nationalities, New York, April.

Zainashev, Iurii. 1998. "Interv″iu s Galinoi Starovoitovoi" [Interview with Galina Starovoitova]. *Moskovskii komsomolets*, November 25.

Zav'ialova, Viktoriia. 2000. "Zachem vy, devochki, natsistov liubite?" [Why, Girls, Do You Love Nazis?]. *Argumenty i fakty—Moskva*, no. 10 (March), p. 3.

Zernov, Nicolas. 1963. *The Russian Religious Renaissance of the Twentieth Century.* New York: Harper & Row.

Zhdakaev, Sergei. 2000. "Patrioty s bol'shoi dorogi" [Highway Patriots]. *Izvestiia*, March 28, p. 9.

Zherebyatev, Mikhail. 1999. "Russian National Unity: A Political Challenge for Provincial Russia." *PRISM: A Biweekly on the Post-Soviet States* (The Jamestown Foundation), vol. 5, no. 6 (March 26).

Zhirinovskii, V.V. 1993. *Poslednii brosok na iug* [Final Spurt to the South]. Moscow: Pisatel'.

———. 1995. *Plevok na zapad* [Spit on the West]. Moscow: LDPR.

———. 1997a. *Dumskaia fraktsiia LDPR za vyvod strany iz krizisa (osenniaia sessiia 1996 g.)* [The LDPR Duma Fraction for Bringing the Country Out of the Crisis (Fall 1996 Session)]. Moscow: LDPR.

———. 1997b. *Ideologiia dlia Rossii* [An Ideology for Russia]. Moscow: LDPR.

———. 1997c. *LDPR kak partiia sostoialas'! (Ot s"ezda—k s"ezdu)* [The LDPR as a Party Has Established Itself! (From Congress to Congress)]. Moscow: LDPR.

———. 1997d. *Russkii vopros: puti resheniia* [The Russian Question: Paths to a Solution]. Moscow: LDPR.

———. 1998a. *Geopolitika i russkii vopros* [Geopolitics and the Russian Question). Moscow: Galeriia.

———. 1998b. *Ob istoricheskoi roli LDPR v sovremennoi Rossii* [On the Historical Role of the LDPR in Contemporary Russia]. Moscow: LDPR.

Zhirinovskii, Vladimir, and Davidenko, Vladimir. 1997. *Genotsid: zapad unichtozhaet russkii narod* [Genocide: The West Annihilates the Russian People]. Moscow: 4–i filial Voenizdata.

Zhirinovskii, V.V., and Krivel'skaia, N.V. 1997. *Psevdokhristianskie religioznye organizatsii Rossii. Informatsionno-analiticheskoe issledovanie* [Pseudo-Christian Religious Organizations in Russia. Information and Analysis]. Moscow: LDPR.

Zhirnov, Oleg. 1997. "Primet li Duma vyzov?" [Will the Duma Take Up the Challenge?]. *Moskovskaia pravda*, March 15.

Ziuganov, G. A. 1995a. *Za gorizontom* [Over the Horizon]. Moscow: Informpechat'.

———. 1995b. *Rossiia i sovremennyi mir* [Russia and the Contemporary World]. Moscow: Obozrevatel'.

———. 1996. *Rossiia—rodina moia. Ideologiia gosudarstvennogo patriotizma* [Russia—My Homeland: The Ideology of State Patriotism]. Moscow: Informpechat'.

———. 1998. "O natsional'noi gordosti patriotov" [On the National Pride of Patriots]. *Sovetskaia Rossiia*, December 24.

Znamenski, Andrei A. 1996. "In Search of the Russian Idea: Igor Shafarevich's Traditional Orthodoxy." *The European Studies Journal* XIII, no. 1, pp. 33–47.

Zolotarevich, Viktor. 1998. "Stanet li znak bedy simvolom griadushchei Rossii?" [Will the Sign of Woe Become the Symbol of the Future Russia?]. *Diagnoz: antifashistskoe obozrenie*, no. 3 (June), pp. 10–11.

Zotov, Gennadii, Maj.-Gen. 1998. "Zashchita lichnosti, obshchestva, gosudarstva" [Protection of the Personality, Society, and the State]. *Nezavisimoe voennoe obozrenie*, no. 44(118), November 20.

Zverev, Aleksei, et al. 1999. "Pauk ugodil v svoiu pautinu" [The Spider Has Fallen into His Own Web]. *Moskovskii komsomolets*, no. 1 (January 4).

Zvezda i svastika. Bol'shevizm i russkii fashizm [Star and Swastika: Bolshevism and Russian Fascism]. 1994. Moscow: TERRA.

Index

Stephen D. Shenfield is an independent researcher specializing in contemporary Russian and post-Soviet politics and society. He has had a long association with Brown University's Watson Institute for International Studies. Previously he was a research associate at the Center for Foreign Policy Development. He is the author of *The Nuclear Predicament: Explorations in Soviet Ideology* (London: Routledge & Kegan Paul, 1987), one of the earliest studies of Gorbachev's "new thinking." He has a Ph.D. in Soviet Studies from the Centre for Russian and East European Studies, University of Birmingham, U.K.